Studies in Item Analysis and Prediction

Stanford Mathematical
Studies in the
Social Sciences, VI

Studies in Item Analysis and Prediction

Edited by HERBERT SOLOMON

With Contributions by

ROSEDITH SITGREAVES
GUSTAV ELFVING
PAUL F. LAZARSFELD
R. R. BAHADUR
HOWARD RAIFFA
MILTON VERNON JOHNS
EDWARD PAULSON
HERBERT SOLOMON
DANIEL TEICHROEW
ALBERT H. BOWKER

STANFORD UNIVERSITY PRESS • STANFORD, CALIFORNIA • 1961

Stanford University Press
Stanford, California

Library of Congress Catalog Card Number: 60-15885
Printed in the United States of America

Dedicated to the memory of

IRVING LORGE

Preface

The chapters in this volume are directed to the study of a number of specific problems in psychology in the areas of item analysis, test design, and classification. However, they should also be viewed in the larger context of the applications of mathematics in social science, a topic which has recently reached a very active state of development. In general these applications may be categorized in two broad classes of subject matter. The first class comprises social and psychological processes that are identified either implicitly or explicitly by the manner in which the behavior of a variable or set of variables changes with time or other-ordered dimensions. Studies in this class have led to the development of the various mathematical learning theories. The second class of subject matter is more static in nature, and the problems in this class are usually identified as measurement problems. For this situation studies have led to the mathematical models of factor analysis and latent-structure analysis, and to various scaling models. Both classes call heavily on probability theory; the first on the mathematics of time-dependent processes, especially Markov processes; the second on more classical probability theory, especially the techniques of statistical multivariate analysis.

This volume is concerned with problems in the second class. It explores and develops some recent work in psychological measurement in a subject of rather old vintage but with appealing new interests. The specific interests of the chapters are (1) the design of measuring instruments, and (2) the resolutions of the prediction problem that arises when classification is attempted from the resulting test scores. By "measuring instruments" we mean mental and achievement tests, attitude scales, personality inventories, projective tests, and biographical inventories. Throughout the volume, the word "test" is used generically to describe any measuring device or instrument employed by psychologists to study behavior. The context of each chapter will suggest which measuring devices are under study.

The studies are divided into three parts. The Introduction attempts to survey the 19 chapters that follow in Parts I, II, and III. Part I has seven chapters that discuss questions of item analysis and test design in what we shall call the classical framework. In this framework an underlying multivariate normal model is assumed for test-item variables and criterion variables. In the seven chapters of Part II, the usual multivariate normal assumptions of this structure are relaxed, and we observe the problem mainly from the viewpoint of dichotomous outcomes for both test-item and criterion variables. The five chapters of Part III return to the classical model to evaluate the properties of a classification statistic that has been proposed when the item variables are multivariate normal and the criterion variable is dichotomous.

The chapters, especially when those in one section are compared with chapters in another section, appear to be and are indeed quite different. However, they all resulted from studies made for a research project whose mission was an analysis of the design and the evaluation of tests. In this analysis paramount attention was given to the characteristics of test items and to the number of items in a test necessary to achieve efficient classification of an individual into one of several groups. The studies, even within one section, differ for two interacting reasons: (1) research efforts on the same topic will inevitably produce diverse analysis, and (2) different approaches were planned early in the research program. Much more has resulted than appears here, but the volume represents work that was at a publishable point. In fact, Chapters 4, 5, 6, 17, and 18 have been published previously and appear here in slightly revised form. All chapters have appeared in substantively the same form as technical reports prepared for the research project.

The program leading to these studies began in response to an invitation to Columbia University from the Biometrics Department, U.S. Air force School of Aviation Medicine, then located at Randolph Air Force Base, Texas, to propose a research attack on questions in item analysis and test design. This request was made in the spring of 1954 and led to the granting of a contract with Teachers College, Columbia University, which began on October 1 of that year. The research group was organized and then directed by the editor of this volume until September 1958. This program is still continuing at Columbia with the support of the School of Aviation Medicine under the direction of Professor Rosedith Sitgreaves. Recently the National Science Foundation also became a supporter of this research program.

Some of the studies were initially conceived as much as six or seven years ago. However, in the interest of publishing this volume at this time, the authors made only minor revisions for the older studies. While in all situations this does not affect the results, it is only fair to point out that in Chapter 12, Raiffa, who examines the item-selection and test-design problem from the point of view of statistical decision theory and the comparison of experiments, could have recast his exposition in the light of the advances in this topic since he prepared this chapter in 1956. However he agreed to allow his work to appear essentially in its original form so that publication would not be delayed.

The principal members of the research group were mathematical statisticians who came from the Columbia community and those who served it as visiting colleagues. They are Theodore W. Anderson, Raj R. Bahadur, Allan Birnbaum, Albert H. Bowker, Gustav Elfving, M. Vernon Johns, Howard Levene, Edward Paulson, Howard Raiffa, Herbert Robbins, Rosedith Sitgreaves, Herbert Solomon, and Daniel Teichroew. From the social science fraternity, Paul Lazarsfeld contributed by bringing his talents and his previous work on dichotomous systems to the problem of item selection. Irving Lorge provided psychological insight and guidance to our thinking. Many thanks are due all these people, and special thanks go to those who prepared the studies appearing in this volume.

What will strike the reader almost immediately is the amount and level of mathematical sophistication necessary to toy with even the simplest measurement ideas in psychology. The fact that we were somewhat successful is due to all who participated, but in particular to Rosedith Sitgreaves. She demonstrated the power of mathematical thinking and mathematical prowess on these unexplored subjects in psychology both wisely and well, with patience and good cheer; with enthusiasm and persistence, and with endurance and strength. Our visitors from overseas, Gustav Elfving from Finland and Raj Bahadur from India, contributed strongly to our thinking and left a high mark for international cooperation in research.

Sincere thanks and appreciation are extended to our colleagues in the Biometrics Department of the School of Aviation Medicine for their technical guidance, general helpfulness, and encouragement. In particular, we owe a large debt of thanks to Dr. M. Bryan Danford, who still serves as Scientific Monitor for the program, and to Dr. William F. Taylor, then Head of the Biometrics Department, for their unswerving support of our efforts. Dr. Saul B. Sells and Dr. Harry Hughes were always cooperative and helpful. To the United States Air Force School of Aviation Medicine we offer our gratitude and thanks for its financial support and cooperation in the publishing of this volume.

The editor wishes to acknowledge permission to reprint Chapter 4, which first appeared in *Psychometrika*; Chapter 6, which first appeared in Volume 1 of the *Proceedings of the Third Berkeley Symposium on Mathematical Statistics and Probability* (University of California Press); Chapter 5, which first appeared in *Societas Scientiarum Fennica*; Chapters 11 and 18, which first appeared in *Contributions to Probability and Statistics* (Stanford University Press); and Chapter 17, which first appeared in *Academia Scientiarum Fennica*.

The staff of the Stanford Press was very helpful in all the steps leading to the completion of a publication venture like this. Betty Jo Prine prepared the excellent drawings. Our appreciation and thanks are extended to them for their efforts.

HERBERT SOLOMON

Stanford, California
December 1, 1960

Contents

Studies in Item Analysis and Prediction

Introduction

HERBERT SOLOMON, Stanford University

The use of a test to measure behavior implies the existence of either a uni-dimensional or a multi-dimensional trait that is known and is capable of measurement. In reality one is rarely in this fortunate situation, and there can be many degrees of relevancy or association between the test and what it seeks to measure. In some situations, it is found, upon further investigation, that the test in no way measures what is sought, whereas in other cases there is at least a justifiable belief that the test is meeting some reasonable operating conditions of relevancy. These questions of the *validity* of a test are all-important but are extremely difficult to resolve. Not only is there required a measure of association between two variables, each of which may be multi-dimensional, but a complicating condition arises, since the set of test variables is observable (manifest) and the set of criterion variables is unobservable (latent). Another problem, which is usually more easily resolved, is the accuracy with which responses to the test are reproduced under parallel circumstances, and thus how *reliable* it is in achieving what it does measure. This characteristic does not depend on how accurately the latent variable is measured. Questions of reliability and validity are, of course, all-pervasive in science and are not confined to the province of psychological tests.

The validity and reliability of a test can be looked upon as two operational characteristics of a test. This has been the tradition in psychological testing. Thus in the design of a test, the items making up the "ideal" test are those chosen to maximize selected validity and reliability indexes. That is, the number of items, the characteristics of each item, and the characteristics of joint sets of items are selected to produce the best possible reliability and validity. This is easier said than done, but nevertheless apparently reasonable criteria are made available as targets.

Indexes of reliability and validity therefore can be used to compare tests. For example, a test of n_1 items with specific item characteristics and a test of n_2 items with another set of specific item characteristics can be suggested and the reliability and validity determined for each case. Also important from the point of view of test design is the fact that one can then seek the construction of a set of n_1 test items and another set of n_2 test items such that the reliability and validity of the two tests are equal. This would then force a choice between the two tests to be made by consideration of other important factors such as ease of administration or difficulty in construction of test items that have the specified characteristics. Once again we can add that actually accomplishing this may be rather difficult, but at least the notions of validity and reliability furnish possible guides to those who have a responsibility for designing tests. In this day and age of massive testing programs such as those administered by federal, state, and city civil service commissions and various national testing agencies such as the College Entrance Examination Board, the responsibility for the design of a test achieves an even greater importance than before because decisions based on test performance directly affect public policy in personnel selection, college admission, and so on.

Let us look into the ramifications of test design when reliability and validity are the indexes of worth and see what issues are raised by the classical assumptions and results. First let us remember that the motivation for early work in test design occurred over a half-century ago in connection with mental tests, and that Charles Spearman's work on the single-factor model provided the first conceptual framework for mental measurement through achievement or ability tests. Since then the theory of mental tests has borrowed the measuring tools developed by psychologists, physical anthropologists, and others interested in measurement.

Mental-test theorists usually operate under the following assumptions, although these assumptions are not always explicitly stated. A latent (unobservable) variable representing the human trait of mental ability is a uni-dimensional trait. Values of the variable in a population of human beings are normally distributed along this continuum with zero mean and unit standard deviation. These restrictions on mean and variance are in no way limiting at this juncture. Let Y denote the latent variable, then Y is $N(0, 1)$.[1] Since Y cannot be measured directly, we resort to a set of continuous variables X, each of which is related to Y in varying degrees and each of which is observable; we will call an element X_i of the set X a manifest (observable) variable. The elements X_i are the test item variables. If in other contexts Y is not uni-dimensional, we can think of Y as a set of latent variables with elements Y_i.

The classes in the population that are of interest can be viewed in terms of the Y-values of the individuals. For example, the fact that $Y = y$ for a given individual places him at a specific point in the uni-dimensional continuum. There are probably several decisions that interest the test designer which are based on the unknown y-value of the individual being tested, but all must await the gathering of information through the administration of a

[1] We use the symbol $N(0, 1)$ for a normal distribution with zero mean and unit variance.

test consisting, say, of k items obtained by tapping k elements of X. The individual takes the test, and the response to each item is usually scored 1 or 0, depending on whether it is right or wrong. This is a quick jump in our discussion from the continuous variables X_i to dichotomous variables, say S_i, which take on the values 0 or 1, and this is discussed in the next paragraph. In mental testing, the sum of the correct responses is called the total test score and this number is generally used as an index of the unknown y-value and consequently of the class to which the individual belongs. In attitude or personality testing the response can still be scored dichotomously with the values 1 or 0 determined by some rule.

A slight digression is in order here to discuss the somewhat heavy probabilistic structure developed by the more classical mental-test theorists for test design. The developments in the seven chapters of Part I of this volume require the notion of an item variable X_i with values which are assumed to be normally distributed. Yet in a number of cases we observe only a Bernoulli random variable S_i which takes on the value 1 or 0 as $X_i > \alpha_i$ or $X_i \leqq \alpha_i$. The value of α_i is fixed for the ith item in a specific test but increasing values of α suggest more difficult items. In this case, say,

$$\Pr\{S_i = 1\} = \Pr\{X_i > \alpha_i\} = P_i .$$

In test theory the quantity P_i is called the item difficulty of the ith item and is used to distinguish between items.

We may also write $\Pr\{S_i = 1 \mid Y = y\} = \Pr\{X_i > \alpha_i \mid Y = y\}$, where the conditional probabilities given by the function $\Pr\{S_i = 1 \mid Y = y\}$ is called the item characteristic curve for the ith item. For any fixed item i, a curve is computed by evaluating the specified probability for each value of y. This curve is useful in distinguishing among classes of test items.

This notion of an intervening variable X_i between Y, the criterion variable, and S_i, the observed item response which is scored as 0 or 1, does not appear in all measurement models which relate observed dichotomous responses to a latent criterion. As can be seen above, it is not essential. For example, in latent-structure analysis models proposed by Lazarsfeld in attitude measurement, the item characteristic curve, which is there named the traceline of the item, is frequently represented as a polynomial in the criterion value without recourse to any variable X_i. However, in the mental-test model the item characteristic curve is defined directly and uniquely as a normal ogive function of the criterion variable and involves two item parameters, but it is done through the intervening variable.

To some the notion of an intervening variable seems somewhat superfluous, and to others it appears to be a rather obfuscating idea. It is difficult to see why any battle lines at all should be drawn over this issue. The older discipline of measurement of ability arose in an era when assumptions of normality were current for intellective processes and when methodology, whatever the reason, seemed to dictate that all possible assumptions be made to produce some results. On the other hand, the more recent effort of, say, latent-structure analysis that stemmed from measurement of attitudes attempts to make predictions about Y from the dichotomous responses S_i with as few assumptions as possible. Like other recent investigations in sociology and psychology there is a more non-parametric flavor to latent-structure analysis, although Lazarsfeld's development could have arisen strictly from his own concepts of the model rather than from an attempt to minimize assumptions. However, as long as each model is specific about its assumptions and careful about its deductions from those assumptions the scholar looking into the matter can make his own decision in any particular situation.

A first glance at the classical test model and latent-structure analysis indicates a polarization of measurement into two extreme settings. But, however different these two approaches may seem, they have several things in common. First, they both use the condition of local independence. That is, given a point on the continuum Y, whether we are dealing with mental ability, attitude, etc., the responses to any pair of items for an individual at that point on the continuum are independent. For the classical mental-test theorist (1) this notion is assumed, and this in addition to the other assumptions in the probabilistic structure demonstrates that a Spearman single-factor model is operating for the item variables X_i and the criterion Y; or (2) the Spearman model is assumed, and from the other conditions the notion of local independence is deduced. The theorist is vague about whether (1) or (2) is the situation, but since it makes no difference, the statement that we have either local independence or the Spearman single-factor model can be made in the chapters that follow. In latent-structure analysis the condition of local independence is an assumption. Second, they both deal with observables which are dichotomous, and thus the algebra of dichotomous systems and its development is of methodological importance to both. In addition to these common features both models approach still more common ground as the mental-test theorist attempts to relax assumptions and still achieve his results, while the other finds it necessary to add assumptions to develop procedures.

Now to return to our central development. One of the interesting ramifications of the use of validity and reliability within the probabilistic structure of classical mental-test theory is the so-called "attenuation paradox." This paradox has received the attention of several writers in item analysis and test design and is the subject of Chapter 1 by Rosedith Sitgreaves. It seems a good jumping-off-point for studies in the theory of mental tests and is now briefly described: Given all the structure imposed by the model, it is discovered that if we allow inter-item correlations to increase, test reliability increases but test validity increases up to a maximum value and then decreases. This is considered a paradox, since increased correlation between test items is supposed to be tied directly to increased correlation between item and criterion. However, since reliability and validity need not be tied together in the first place, the psychologist has never carefully explained why this should be viewed as a paradox and, if it is, what one may do about it. An explanation can be given if we explicitly assume the single-factor model for item responses and then employ simple product moment correlations between test scores S (where $S = \sum S_i$) and between S and Y to measure reliability and validity. In Chapter 1, Sitgreaves presents this problem and develops all the details of the paradox.

This paradox could well be with us for all time and not cause any real setback in testing, but it does point up some interesting avenues of inquiry:

1. Should *test score*, i.e., the number of correct responses, be that summarization of the test responses which is to be used in predicting the position of an individual on the Y continuum? Is there another summarization of item responses which is "best" when judged by some reasonable criteria?

2. Should the product moment correlation, which is employed to define both reliability and validity, be replaced by other measures that are more meaningful or at least non-paradoxical?

3. What may one do if the single-factor structure assumption is replaced by a linear multiple-factor model?

4. Suppose as few assumptions as possible are made about the trait measured and item responses, as in latent-structure analysis. What can be achieved in a non-parametric situation?

The notion of test score, i.e., the number of correct responses, has a long tradition and is intuitively important. It is interesting to see how this notion can be reconciled with some formal principles in decision making. After all, test score is a most simple summary of the vector of item responses, and if it is used, decisions require only the distribution of a unidimensional variable. Ordinarily one would expect that the joint distribution of all the coordinates of the vector of item responses would be necessary for a reasonable decision procedure. However, for the underlying probability structure of classical mental-test theory and in the case of equivalent items (all item difficulties equal, all item intercorrelations equal), Lord [1] has shown that the test score is a sufficient statistic and thus is the most adequate summarization of the item responses. Birnbaum [2] has shown that when a logistic distribution rather than a normal distribution is assumed for Y, a more general but similar statement can be made, for then even when test items are not equivalent, a linear function of item responses, in which the weights depend on item validities (an item validity may be viewed as test validity where the test is composed of one item), is a sufficient statistic. In fact if the items are equivalent, this linear function is just test score multiplied by a constant. Notice, then, that a simple sum or simple weighted sum of item responses has desirable properties in some restricted situations where heavy assumptions are made about the underlying structure.

In Chapter 2, Sitgreaves develops a restricted model in which test score in the usual sense is the adequate summarization, but the classical use of product moment correlation as an index of reliability and validity, which led to the attenuation paradox, is ignored and another index is suggested.

She assumes that the test items satisfy a Guttman scale, thereby making the distribution of test score equivalent to the joint distribution of responses, and examines the use of an index that is a tried-and-true friend to statisticians, i.e., the index that minimizes the mean squared error of estimate of Y. She demonstrates that within a rather restricted but classical multivariate normal model the use of the minimum mean squared error of estimate produces an index that is the product of two meaningful factors. The first factor depends only on the observables and is a measure of reliability; the second is a correlation (validity coefficient) between the continuous variable Y and a vector-valued response variable whose components are item responses. The development is in terms of a vector-valued response variable, but in exploring it the author uses the aforementioned Guttman scale to achieve mathematical tractability. It turns out that this index can also be viewed as the square of a population correlation ratio between the latent variable and manifest set of variables, and thus varies between 0 and 1. However, it can be near 1 only when both factors are close to unity, thus neatly avoiding the attenuation paradox faced by previous workers in the field. It also becomes possible in the restricted situation studied by Sitgreaves to select directly the characteristics of optimal items. For example, given that a test is to contain, say, 5 items, the item difficulties can be obtained explicitly. The inter-item correlations are already determined by the very restricted nature of the model.

Since the conceptual development does not depend on the tight restrictions, Sitgreaves in Chapter 3 studies the same situation, i.e., the use of the new index for the classical multivariate model, but without the imposition of the Guttman scale on the item responses. This creates a great deal of tedious manipulation and then frustration, since integrals over the multivariate normal distribution are required and tables of such integrals are not available except in the bivariate and trivariate case. For the case of a two-item test, she demonstrates that the index developed in Chapter 2 is uniformly higher for any test within the general classical model than for any two-item test in this model which also obeys a Guttman scale. If the index is to have any merit, this result is to be expected; but demonstrating this is not easy. A study of Chapter 3 will show why this is so. We can expect this for any k-item test, but the lack of appropriate tables prevents its demonstration even for $k = 4$. Tables now exist to attempt this for $k = 3$, but this exercise is gladly given up by Sitgreaves to the next worker in the field.

Much has been made previously of the Spearman single-factor model and its implicit if not outright connection with the classical probabilistic structure. Its existence in the structure provided the attenuation paradox when reliability and validity were measured by product moment coefficients. Suppose this assumption is now replaced with a natural extension, namely, a linear multiple-factor model for item responses. This extension still contains the Spearman model as a special case. In a sense what we are doing is following one facet of the history of factor analysis, i.e., Thurstone's generalization of Spearman's work [3]. Suppose also that our item variables X_i are now directly observable. In Chapter 4, Elfving, Sitgreaves, and Solomon consider this new structure and employ the index of minimum mean squared error of estimate to provide procedures for item selection in test design. Here the criterion variable Y and the observables X_i are tied together by latent variables (factors), say z_j, in the following way. Each X_i and Y is a linear function of the z_j's, $j = 1, 2, \cdots, f$, where f is the number of common factors; $f = 1$ is the Spearman model. By assumption, the coefficients (factor loadings) are all known, and a prediction $\tilde{y}$ of Y, when the value of Y is actually y, is a linear function of the X_i's (item responses).

Elfving's theoretical work in Chapters 5, 6, and 7 is the forerunner to the exposition in Chapter 4 and is the kind of generalization that can be developed as soon as the employment of the Spearman single-factor assumption in the classical model is brought into clear focus. A study of Elfving's developments demonstrates the sophisticated mathematical level required to resolve the item-selection and test-design problem for the multiple-factor model for item responses. One obstacle in the use of this model for actual item selection is that all factor loadings must be known. This requires a large amount of data and a large amount of prior computational work, for rarely, if ever, will one be in the position of filling in the factor loadings by expert judgment.

However, one interesting phenomenon is produced by the model. If the index for item selection deduced from the model is analyzed for the Spearman single-factor situation, its use turns out to be equivalent to choosing those items such that the correlation between an item and the now single latent factor z_1 is maximized. Thus if n items are to be selected, we choose the item which has highest correlation with z_1, then the item with the next highest, etc., until n are selected. This procedure has always been followed by psychologists, except that the latent factor is not available. Psychologists usually resort to a manifest equivalent, namely, observed total test score. Thus a justification (at least in terms of minimum mean squared error of estimate) is produced by this model for what is usually done, provided that a Spearman single-factor model underlies item responses. Should the maximum correlation index for item selection be employed in a multifactor situation, it is possible that the item-selection process can be quite poor. One possible reason for the more serious problems encountered in item selection for personality inventories as contrasted with item selections for achievement tests may be the use of the maximum correlation index, since personality test items tend to have a larger common-factor structure. Naturally a still more important reason may be the relatively unexploited state of measurement of personality as contrasted with measurement of mental ability.

Suppose now we relax the assumption of the multivariate normal model. We touched on this point earlier in this chapter when we made the point that our observables are dichotomous. Even though all seven chapters of Part I study item selection and test design within the classical model, we have constantly turned to Bernoulli random variables for observed item responses, albeit the probabilities of responding correctly or incorrectly to an item are governed by the multivariate normal machinery. Now when we leave mental or achievement testing, we leave the protective comfort of the tradition of multivariate normal machinery in which they have been housed for some time. The newer measurement devices of attitude scales, personality inventories, projective tests, and biographical inventories must seek their own measurement frameworks. The blind assumption of the classical model can lead to more serious trouble here than the previously mentioned rote use of the maximum correlation index for item selection without regard to common factor structure.

To be on the ultra-safe side let us now consider probabilistic models in which item responses and the criterion variable are all dichotomous and no assumptions are made at first about the machinery governing the probability of the two values for each of the variables. First what is required here is an algebra for dichotomous systems. At the turn of the century the mathematical developments in social science for continuous variables took second place to the analysis of qualitative variables. However, the cumbersome methodology at hand for the development of an algebra for dichotomous variables, plus other scientific pressures, put the mathematical development of qualitative analysis in limbo until only recently. Then the quickening in the development of social research and its focus on variables that either are naturally dichotomous (such as sex) or are made dichotomous to make an analysis more manageable (age: old-young; income: rich-poor), plus the use of determinants, an appropriate notation, and the concept of symmetric parameters, brought about an improvement in the algebra of dichotomous systems and its consequent use in important problems in social research.

In Chapter 8, Lazarsfeld develops an algebra for dichotomous systems and imbeds it in several important social-research situations. Here he develops some new work and new insights and recalls his previous work that was stimulated by his efforts in latent-structure analysis. In Chapters 9 and 10, Bahadur analyzes representations of the fundamental set in the algebra of dichotomous systems and the use of these representations in classification procedures. By looking at different representations, approximations that have intuitive interest suggest themselves. We are viewing a dichotomous system of, say, m items in which each item response is coded 1 or 0, and this can be completely summarized by 2^m independent pieces of data. However, we can decide in what form we want to parametrize the problem, and both Lazarsfeld and Bahadur make good use of the notion of symmetric parameters to provide the fundamental set. For example, for each of 2^m possible response vectors we can assign the relative frequency of occurrence and thus have 2^m parameters (actually $2^m - 1$, since the sum of the relative frequencies must equal 1) defining the m-item dichotomous system; or we can have ${}^mC_1$ marginal frequencies of ones, $p_1, p_2, \cdots, p_m$; ${}^mC_2$ values $|ij| =$

$p_{ij} - p_i p_j$, where p_{ij} is the joint relative frequency of ones for two items: ${}^mC_3$ values $|ijk| = p_{ijk} - p_i p_j p_k$, where p_{ijk} is the joint relative frequency of ones for three items, etc.; and ${}^mC_1 + {}^mC_2 + {}^mC_3 + \cdots + {}^mC_m = 2^m - 1$. The latter are more instructive. For example, if there is independence among the items, then all $|ij| = 0$, yet we can have $|ij| = 0$ and have dependence in the model expressed by the higher-order joint frequencies. Moreover, all the higher-order parameters can be viewed as higher-order "correlation coefficients." In Chapter 11, Solomon demonstrates how these concepts are employed in an actual situation where dichotomous items and a dichotomous criterion were used in connection with a study of the scientific attitudes of high school students.

In addition to the Bahadur and Lazarsfeld representations, a classification procedure for placing the students into one of two groups, i.e., the likelihood-ratio criterion, which is analyzed by Bahadur in Chapter 10 for the dichotomous case, is employed by Solomon in Chapter 11. The likelihood-ratio procedure seems natural in this context and comes from a respectable tradition in statistical inference. Here one considers the probability (likelihood) of an occurrence (m-dimensional dichotomous response vector) under each of two alternatives (dichotomized criterion). If the ratio of the two probabilities is larger than some preassigned constant, the classification is made one way, otherwise the alternative is selected. The risks of this procedure are then measured by the two proportions of misclassification, i.e., the relative frequency of classification in Group A when the true position is Group B, and vice versa.

Here we are coming closer to the kind of study developed by Raiffa in Chapter 12. Raiffa employs the machinery of statistical decision theory and the comparison of experiments to study the item-selection and test-design problems for dichotomous items and a dichotomous criterion. For the sake of completeness he gives the basic concepts of statistical decision theory that are useful in evaluating possible classification procedures for a given experiment. Raiffa then considers the problem of item selection and test design in this framework. He does this for two situations: first, when the total number of available test items is small such as in medical diagnosis; second, when it is desired to select a small number of test items from a large battery of potential test items. The case of sequential selection is also studied. For example, it is quite realistic in some situations to have the use of a test item depend on the responses to the previously administered test items. Thus the question of optimal stopping rules, which depend on an analysis of the marginal cost of adding a specific item versus the marginal decrease in the risk of making incorrect predictions that can be attributed to the addition of the test item, are analyzed by Raiffa. In Raiffa's chapter we have an analysis of the probabilistic structure for the situation of dichotomous response test items and a dichotomous criterion variable in the nonparametric case. This can be contrasted with Lazarsfeld's chapter, which treats mainly the algebra of dichotomous systems for dichotomous response test items and a dichotomous criterion variable, and Bahadur's two chapters, which combine the algebra of dichotomous systems with probabilistic structure and notions of information for dichotomous systems.

In Chapter 13, Johns studies the two-way classification problem in the non-parametric case. At this point in Part II, through Chapter 14 by Paulson and all the chapters in Part III, the substance of the analysis is on the classification problem. In Chapter 14, a non-parametric classification procedure for deciding whether an individual belongs to one of several populations is developed. In Part III, only the two-population situation is discussed. Here when a classification procedure is employed, it becomes possible to evaluate the probabilities of misclassification.

Johns assumes the difficult task of finding satisfactory classification procedures when no *a priori* probabilities are known but where information becomes available either from observations previously made, or from individuals already selected from the same population as the new individual we wish to classify. This approach lies between the classical Neyman-Pearson procedure, which in no way takes into account the possible existence of *a priori* probabilities for the two categories, and the other extreme, which might be called the Bayesian approach, wherein all *a priori* considerations are known. The approach used by Johns is similar to the "empirical Bayes procedures" discussed and proposed by Robbins [4] for other problems in statistical inference. Within this approach Johns gives classification techniques for the two-way classification problem whose risk functions approach the Bayes risk as the number of *a priori* observations increases.

In the last chapter of Part II, Paulson branches out by seeking a classification procedure for selecting one of $(k+1)$ decisions, $D_0, D_1, D_2, \cdots, D_k$. For example, suppose that among k groups of students we wish to select the best one in mathematical ability and that D_0 is the decision that all students are the same, D_1 the decision that the first group is best, etc. Paulson develops a non-parametric procedure for comparing these k groups and for determining which is best. This procedure is optimum in the sense that it corresponds to the Bayes solution for selecting a procedure that maximizes the probability of selecting decision D_i when the ith group is the one that is best in mathematical ability.

When we enter Part III and observe its chapters, we leave the realm of new or modified conceptualizations in measurement and test design and return to one model in which we get heavily involved with a classification statistic and its sampling distribution. In Chapter 15, Sitgreaves describes the multivariate normal model and the classification statistic constructed from a sample from this model. This is the basis for all the remaining chapters. Briefly, an individual is to be classified as belonging to one of two populations on the basis of a p-dimensional vector of measurements made on him. It is assumed that in each population the measurements are jointly normally distributed with the same covariance matrix but with different mean values. The covariance matrix and the two vectors of mean values are unknown. However measurements on N_1 individuals known to belong to one population, π_1, and measurements on N_2 individuals known to belong to the other population, π_2, are available. From these observations a classification statistic now commonly known in the literature of multivariate analysis as W has been proposed by T. W. Anderson [5]. The p-dimensional measurements made on an unclassified individual are applied to the classification statistic W and if the observed value of W is greater than a preassigned cutoff point, the individual is assigned to one population; if W is less than or equal to the cutoff point, then the individual is assigned to the other population.

Notice here that a probabilistic model for classification has been established[2] and now total effort is given to either tests of hypotheses or estimation within the model. In short, problems of conceptualization in measurement are terminated and statistical inference is the only issue. This usually occurs in model building when a certain stability and comfort have been created in the employment of the model. In Chapter 15, Sitgreaves studies the sampling distribution of W under the hypothesis that the individual to be classified belongs to π_1, and under the alternative hypothesis that he belongs to π_2. She gives a series representation for these distributions when $N_1 = N_2$.

In subsequent chapters the same distribution problem is studied, for knowledge of it is necessary to determine the probabilities of misclassification associated with a given cutoff point and to compare these probabilities with corresponding probabilities of misclassification for other procedures. In Chapter 16, Sitgreaves and Teichroew provide a method for estimating the cumulative distribution of W by means of an empirical sampling experiment.

In Chapter 17, Elfving develops an asymptotic expansion for the cumulative distribution function of W for the uni-dimensional case; that is, $p = 1$. At the same time he uses this asymptotic expansion on the more familiar Student's t-distribution and obtains results that can be compared with previously computed exact values. These results are remarkably good. They are especially accurate in the tails of the distribution where many asymptotic expansions usually deteriorate. Thus reasonably good results for W should be expected from this asymptotic expansion.

Bowker, in Chapter 18, demonstrates how W can be represented in terms of simple statistics so that further analytical or computational work with W becomes more tractable. In Chapter 19, Bowker and Sitgreaves use this representation to develop an asymptotic expansion for the distribution function of W.

We have now sketched the problems under study from the classical item-analysis and test-design considerations of Part I, through the newer non-parametric procedures and dichotomous outcome models of Part II, to the sophisticated treatment of classification given in Part III. It appears that the most fertile fields for future research may be found in Part II. Here we are in a relatively unexploited area which still requires concerted attempts at

[2] Anderson's classification statistic W was developed in terms of the model. However, it should be noted that R. A. Fisher's linear discriminant function, to which W is closely related, was proposed earlier [6] without reference to a model.

conceptualizations and still more development of procedures. While important research should still go on in the subject matter of Part I, it has now received a great deal of detailed treatment. This is also true for the studies in Part III, except that there any interesting studies will relate only to problems in mathematical statistics rather than to psychological measurement.

REFERENCES

[1] Lord, F. M. An application of confidence intervals and of maximum likelihood to the estimation of an examinee's ability. *Psychometrika*, 1953, **18**, 57-76.

[2] Birnbaum, A. Efficient design and use of tests of mental ability for various decision-making problems, USAF SAM Series in Statistics, Report No. 58-16, Randolph AFB, Texas: School of Aviation Medicine, 1957.

[3] Solomon, H. A survey of mathematical models in factor analysis. Part III in *Mathematical Thinking in the Measurement of Behavior*. Glencoe, Ill.: Free Press, 1960.

[4] Robbins, H. An empirical Bayes approach to statistics. In J. Neman, ed., *Proceedings of the Third Berkeley Symposium on Mathematical Statistics and Probability*. Berkeley, Calif.: Univ. California Press, 1956.

[5] Anderson, T. W. Classification by multivariate analysis. *Psychometrika*, 1951, **16**, 31-50.

[6] Fisher, R. A. The use of multiple measurements in taxonomic problems. *Ann. Eugen.*, **7**, 179-88.

Part I. Item Selection: Multivariate Normal Structure

1

A Statistical Formulation of the Attenuation Paradox in Test Theory

ROSEDITH SITGREAVES, Columbia University

1. Introduction

In studying problems of discriminatory analysis and classification, we are often concerned with the following situation: A population of individuals is subdivided into a number of mutually exclusive and exhaustive classes. For each individual in the population, a number of variables can be observed; these include, depending on the particular problem, one or more whose values specify the class to which the individual belongs. Then, frequently, we are interested in selecting a set of these variables which best discriminate, in some sense, among the various classes; and in using observations on these variables, again in some optimal way, to assign individuals to various classes when their true classes are not known.

One situation of this kind which has been studied for some time by educators and psychologists is the case in which the population classes are defined in terms of a given mental ability, and the set of possible observables consists of responses to various test items. Each response is scored as either right or wrong, and the total test score is the number of correct responses. We formulate here an underlying probability model for this situation, and examine the resulting mathematical relation between two operating characteristics of the test; namely, its reliability and validity. This leads to an explanation of the so-called "attenuation paradox" in test theory [1, 2]. This explanation has been previously discussed, but in less detail, in [3].

2. Probability Considerations

Suppose we have the following situation: We assume that a given ability Y is a continuous variable taking on values y, with $-\infty < y < \infty$, which are normally distributed among individuals in a population Π. Without loss of generality we assume that the expected value of Y is zero and its variance is one. The classes of interest in Π are specified in terms of the y-values of the individuals. Suppose we want to assign an individual with an unknown y-value to one of these classes. To obtain information, we give him a test consisting of k items. The response to each item is scored either one or zero, depending on whether it is right or wrong. The sum of the correct responses is the total test score. This number is generally used as an index of the unknown y-value, and consequently of the class to which the individual belongs.

In selecting items for tests, certain item characteristics are usually taken into account, namely, the level of difficulty of the item, the item-characteristic curve (ICC), and the correlations between pairs of item responses. These are defined in the following way: Suppose $S_1, S_2, \cdots, S_k$ denote chance variables such that

$$S_g = 1 \text{ if item } g \text{ is answered correctly,} \quad S_g = 0 \text{ if item } g \text{ is answered incorrectly,} \tag{2.1}$$

and let

$$S = \sum_{g=1}^{k} S_g = \text{total test score.} \tag{2.2}$$

The level of difficulty of item g is defined by the probability that it is answered correctly, i.e.,

$$\Pr\{S_g = 1\} = P_g = E(S_g)\,, \tag{2.3}$$

where E denotes the expected value operator. The item-characteristic curve for item g is given by the probability that an item is answered correctly, given that an individual is at a point $Y = y$ on the Y continuum, or,

$$\text{ICC}(g, y) = \Pr\{S_g = 1 \mid y\} = E(S_g \mid y) \tag{2.4}$$

plotted as a function of y. If we denote the variance of S_g by σ_{gg} and the covariance between S_g and S_h by σ_{gh}, the correlation coefficient between S_g and S_h is defined by

$$\rho_{gh} = \frac{\sigma_{gh}}{\sqrt{\sigma_{gg}\sigma_{hh}}} = \frac{P_{gh} - P_g P_h}{\sqrt{(P_g[1 - P_g])(P_h[1 - P_h])}}\,, \tag{2.5}$$

where $P_{gh} = \Pr\{S_g = 1, S_h = 1\}$. It will be noted that $\rho_{gh} = 0$ when S_g and S_h are independent, and $\rho_{gh} = \pm 1$ when they are functionally related.

In terms of these item parameters, we have

$$E(S \mid y) = \sum_{g=1}^{k} E(S_g \mid y) = \sum_{g=1}^{k} \text{ICC}(g, y)\,, \tag{2.6}$$

$$E(S) = \sum_{g=1}^{k} E(S_g) = \sum_{g=1}^{k} P_g\,, \tag{2.7}$$

and

$$\sigma_{SS} = \sum_{g=1}^{k} \sum_{h=1}^{k} \sigma_{gh} = \sum_{g=1}^{k} \sigma_{gg} + 2 \sum_{g=1}^{k} \sum_{h=g+1}^{k} (\sigma_{gg}\sigma_{hh})^{\frac{1}{2}} \rho_{gh}\,. \tag{2.8}$$

Suppose now we postulate the following underlying probability structure:[1] Let X_g be a continuous chance variable such that item g is answered correctly whenever $X_g \geqq \alpha_g$, $g = 1, 2, \cdots, k$. In mental-test literature, the k items are usually measuring an underlying trait Y (assumed to be normally distributed with zero mean and unit variance) with the understanding that the item-intercorrelation matrix has rank one, since the items are saturated with the underlying ability only, and thus the Spearman single-factor model is operating between the items and the underlying trait. A corollary of this model is that for a fixed ability $Y = y$

$$\text{(2.9)} \qquad \begin{aligned} &\Pr\{S_g = 1, S_h = 1 \mid y\} = \Pr\{S_g = 1 \mid y\} \Pr\{S_h = 1 \mid y\}, \quad \text{or} \\ &\Pr\{X_g \geqq \alpha_g, X_h \geqq \alpha_h \mid y\} = \Pr\{X_g \geqq \alpha_g \mid y\} \Pr\{X_h \geqq \alpha_h \mid y\}, \end{aligned}$$

or the partial correlation $\overset{*}{\rho}_{gh.Y} = 0$. This also leads to $\overset{*}{\rho}_{gh} = \overset{*}{\rho}_{gY} \overset{*}{\rho}_{hY}$, and thus relates item intercorrelation to item-ability correlation. Since X_g and Y have bivariate normal distributions with known covariance matrices, the marginal distribution of X_g given $Y = y$ is normal with mean $(\overset{*}{\rho}_{gY} y)$ and variance $(1 - \overset{*}{\rho}{}^2_{gY})$. The joint distribution of $X_1, X_2, \cdots, X_g, \cdots, X_k, Y$ can now be written. Since

$$\text{(2.10)} \qquad p(X_1, X_2, \cdots, X_k, Y) = p(X_1, X_2, \cdots, X_k \mid Y = y) p(Y),$$

we get

$$\text{(2.11)} \qquad \begin{aligned} &p(X_1, X_2, \cdots, X_k, Y) \\ &= \frac{1}{(2\pi)^{\frac{1}{2}(k+1)} \prod_{g=1}^{k} (1 - \overset{*}{\rho}{}^2_{gY})^{\frac{1}{2}}} \exp\left\{-\frac{1}{2}\left[\sum_{g=1}^{k} \frac{(X_g - \overset{*}{\rho}_{gY} Y)^2}{1 - \overset{*}{\rho}{}^2_{gY}} + Y^2\right]\right\} \\ &\qquad \cdot dX_1\, dX_2, \cdots, dX_k\, dY. \end{aligned}$$

The various item characteristics are now completely determined in terms of the $2k$ parameters $\alpha_1, \alpha_2, \cdots, \alpha_k, \overset{*}{\rho}_{1Y}, \overset{*}{\rho}_{2Y}, \cdots, \overset{*}{\rho}_{kY}$. Thus, the level of difficulty for item g is

$$\text{(2.12)} \qquad \begin{aligned} P_g &= \int_{\alpha_g}^{\infty} \frac{1}{\sqrt{2\pi}} \exp[-\tfrac{1}{2} X_g^2]\, dX = \int_{-\infty}^{-\alpha_g} \frac{1}{\sqrt{2\pi}} \exp[-\tfrac{1}{2} X_g^2]\, dX_g \\ &= \Phi_1(-\alpha_g). \end{aligned}$$

The item-characteristic curve for item g is given by

$$\text{(2.13)} \qquad \begin{aligned} \text{ICC}(g, y) &= \int_{\alpha_g}^{\infty} \frac{1}{\sqrt{2\pi(1 - \overset{*}{\rho}{}^2_{gY})}} \exp\left[-\frac{(X_g - \overset{*}{\rho}_{gY} y)^2}{2(1 - \overset{*}{\rho}{}^2_{gY})}\right] dX_g \\ &= \Phi_1\left[\frac{\overset{*}{\rho}_{gY} y - \alpha_g}{(1 - \overset{*}{\rho}{}^2_{gY})^{\frac{1}{2}}}\right]; \end{aligned}$$

that is, the item-characteristic curve is a normal ogive function of the underlying ability. Also

[1] This model was considered earlier by Tucker [4] and Lord [2], and is discussed by Solomon in [3].

$$(2.14)\qquad P_{gh} = \int_{\alpha_g}^{\infty}\int_{\alpha_h}^{\infty} \frac{\exp\left[-\frac{1}{2(1-\rho_{gh}^{*2})}(X_g^2 - 2\rho_{gh}^{*}X_gX_h + X_h^2)\right]}{2\pi(1-\rho_{gh}^{*2})^{\frac{1}{2}}}\,dX_h\,dX_g$$
$$= \Phi_2(-\alpha_g, -\alpha_h, \rho_{gh}^{*}),$$

say, so that

$$(2.15)\qquad \rho_{gh} = \frac{\Phi_2(-\alpha_g, -\alpha_h, \rho_{gh}^{*}) - \Phi_1(-\alpha_g)\Phi_1(-\alpha_h)}{\sqrt{\Phi_1(-\alpha_g)(1-\Phi_1[-\alpha_g])\Phi_1(-\alpha_h)(1-\Phi_1[-\alpha_h])}}\,.$$

In (2.15), ρ_{gh} is a function of ρ_{gh}^{*}. This relationship is graphed in Figure 1 for three levels of item difficulty under the assumption that all item intercorrelations are equal.

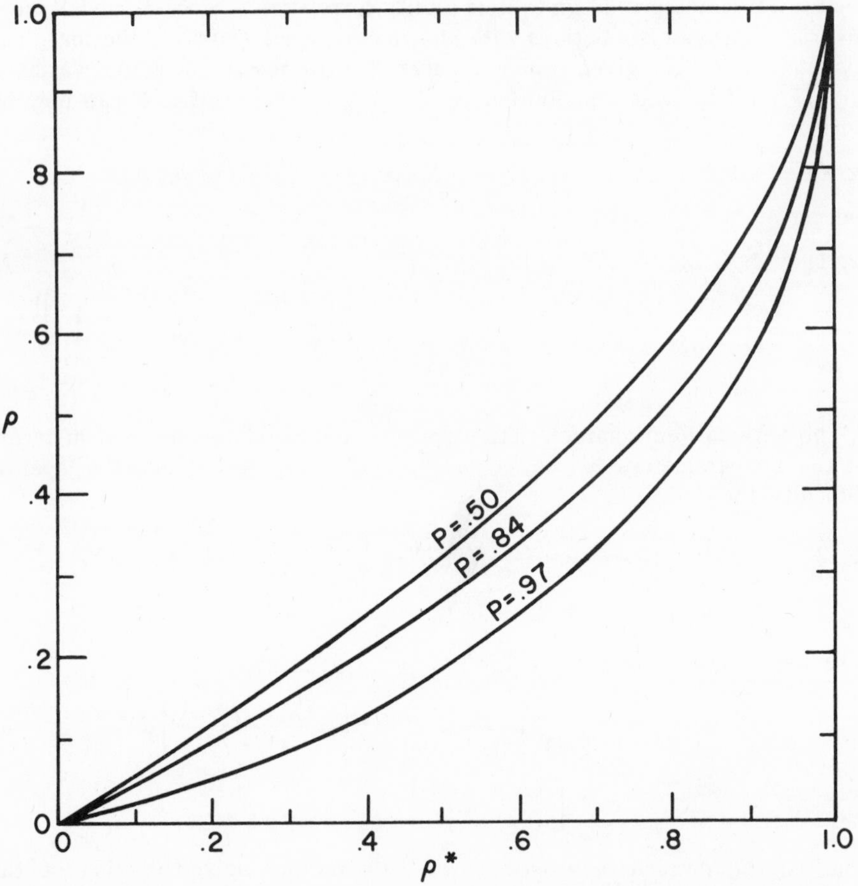

FIG. 1. Relation Between ρ and ρ^*, Where ρ Is the Correlation Between Two Item Scores and ρ^* Is the Correlation Between the Underlying Abilities to Answer These Items, for Three Levels of Item Difficulty

With these probability assumptions, Equations (2.6), (2.7), and (2.8) become

$$E(S \mid y) = \sum_{g=1}^{k} \Phi_1\left[\frac{(\rho_{gY}^* y - \alpha_g)}{(1 - \rho_{gY}^{*2})^{\frac{1}{2}}}\right], \tag{2.16}$$

$$E(S) = \sum_{g=1}^{k} \Phi_1(-\alpha_g), \tag{2.17}$$

and

$$\sigma_{SS} = \sum_{g=1}^{k} \Phi_1(-\alpha_g)(1 - \Phi_1[-\alpha_g]) + 2 \sum_{g=1}^{k} \sum_{h=g+1}^{k} \Phi_2(-\alpha_g, -\alpha_h, \rho_{gh}^*) - \sum_{g=1}^{k} \sum_{h=1}^{k} \Phi_1(-\alpha_g)\Phi_1(-\alpha_h). \tag{2.18}$$

We can also determine, at least theoretically, the probability distribution of S. For any integer j, $0 \leqq j \leqq k$, there are $\binom{k}{j}$ ways in which we can select j integers from the set $K = (1, 2, \cdots, k)$. We suppose that these ways are ordered, and let $J^{(r)}$ be the set of j integers chosen in the rth selection. Then

$$\Pr\{S = j \mid y\} = \sum_{r=1}^{\binom{k}{j}} \prod_{g \in J^{(r)}} \Phi_1\left(\frac{\rho_{gY}^* y - \alpha_g}{(1 - \rho_{gY}^{*2})^{\frac{1}{2}}}\right) \prod_{g \in K - J^{(r)}} \left[1 - \Phi_1\left(\frac{\rho_{gY}^* y - \alpha_g}{(1 - \rho_{gY}^{*2})^{\frac{1}{2}}}\right)\right] \tag{2.19}$$

and

$$\Pr\{S = j\} = \int_{-\infty}^{\infty} \Pr\{S = j \mid y\} \frac{\exp[-y^2/2]}{\sqrt{2\pi}} dy. \tag{2.20}$$

If we have $\rho_{1Y}^* = \rho_{2Y}^* = \cdots = \rho_{kY}^* = \rho^{*\frac{1}{2}}$, say, and $\alpha_1 = \alpha_2 = \cdots = \alpha_k = \alpha$, then

$$E(S \mid y) = k\Phi_1\left(\frac{\rho^{*\frac{1}{2}} y - \alpha}{(1 - \rho^*)^{\frac{1}{2}}}\right), \tag{2.21}$$

$$E(S) = k\Phi_1(-\alpha), \tag{2.22}$$

and

$$\sigma_{SS} = k\Phi_1(-\alpha)(1 - \Phi_1[-\alpha])(1 + [k - 1]\rho), \tag{2.23}$$

where ρ is the common value of the correlation between S_g and S_h. In this case, the conditional distribution of S, given y, is a binomial distribution, i.e.,

$$\Pr\{S = j \mid y\} = \binom{k}{j}\left[\Phi_1\left(\frac{\rho^{*\frac{1}{2}} y - \alpha}{(1 - \rho^*)^{\frac{1}{2}}}\right)\right]^j \left[1 - \Phi_1\left(\frac{\rho^{*\frac{1}{2}} y - \alpha}{(1 - \rho^*)^{\frac{1}{2}}}\right)\right]^{k-j}. \tag{2.24}$$

When k is large we have, given $Y = y$, that

$$z = \frac{\sqrt{k}\left[(S/k) - \Phi_1\left(\frac{\rho^{*\frac{1}{2}} y - \alpha}{(1 - \rho^*)^{\frac{1}{2}}}\right)\right]}{\left\{\Phi_1\left(\frac{\rho^{*\frac{1}{2}} y - \alpha}{(1 - \rho^*)^{\frac{1}{2}}}\right)\left[1 - \Phi_1\left(\frac{\rho^{*\frac{1}{2}} y - \alpha}{(1 - \rho^*)^{\frac{1}{2}}}\right)\right]\right\}^{\frac{1}{2}}} \tag{2.25}$$

is approximately normally distributed with zero mean and unit variance.

3. The Attenuation Paradox

In test construction, the two operating characteristics usually taken into account are the reliability and the validity of the test. By reliability, we mean essentially the precision of the test, i.e., the stability of an individual's test scores under repeated administrations of comparable forms of the test. By validity, we mean the accuracy of the test, i.e., how well it measures the underlying ability.

Conceptually, the reliability of a test is measured by the correlation between scores on two equivalent forms of a test. For our model this means that we are interested in the correlation between scores on two tests, each test consisting of k items with the parameters $(\alpha_1, \cdots, \alpha_k, \overset{*}{\rho}_{1Y}, \cdots, \overset{*}{\rho}_{kY})$. Theoretically, this correlation is given by

$$\rho_{S_1 S_2} = \frac{\sum_{g=1}^{k} \sum_{h=1}^{k} \sigma_{g^{(1)} h^{(2)}}}{\sum_{g=1}^{k} \sum_{h=1}^{k} \sigma_{gh}}, \tag{3.1}$$

where $\sigma_{g^{(1)} h^{(2)}}$ is the covariance between item g on the first test and item h on the second. For $g \neq h$, $\sigma_{g^{(1)} h^{(2)}} = \sigma_{gh}$. Practically, in order to obtain a reliability coefficient that depends only on the covariance matrix of the observable variables $S_1, \cdots, S_k$ and the number of items in the test, the quantity $\sigma_{g^{(1)} g^{(2)}}$ is approximated by (see [5])

$$\frac{1}{(k-1)} \sum_{\substack{h=1 \\ h \neq g}}^{k} \sigma_{gh} .$$

Thus, we obtain the usual definition of reliability, i.e.,

$$\begin{aligned} \rho_{SS} &= \frac{k}{k-1} \frac{\sum_{g=1}^{k} \sum_{\substack{h=1 \\ g \neq h}}^{k} \sigma_{gh}}{\sum_{g=1}^{k} \sum_{h=1}^{k} \sigma_{gh}} \\ &= \frac{k}{k-1} \frac{\sum_{g=1}^{k} \sum_{\substack{h=1 \\ g \neq h}}^{k} \rho_{gh} \sigma_{gg}^{\frac{1}{2}} \sigma_{hh}^{\frac{1}{2}}}{\sum_{g=1}^{k} \sigma_{gg} + \sum_{g=1}^{k} \sum_{\substack{h=1 \\ g \neq h}}^{k} \rho_{gh} \sigma_{gg}^{\frac{1}{2}} \sigma_{hh}^{\frac{1}{2}}} . \end{aligned} \tag{3.2}$$

If all the items are of equal difficulty, so that $P_g(1 - P_g) = P_h(1 - P_h) = \sigma^2$, say, and if all the intercorrelations are the same, i.e., $\rho_{gh} = \rho$, all g, h, then

$$\rho_{SS} = \frac{k}{k-1} \left[\frac{k(k-1)\sigma^2 \rho}{k\sigma^2 + k(k-1)\sigma^2 \rho} \right] = \frac{k\rho}{1 + (k-1)\rho} . \tag{3.3}$$

In this case,

$$\sigma_{g^{(1)}g^{(2)}} = \frac{1}{k-1} \sum_{\substack{h=1 \\ h \neq g}}^{k} \sigma_{gh} ,$$

so that Equation (3.1) gives us exactly (3.3).

The validity of a test is usually measured by the correlation between the ability Y and the test score S. Since we assume Y has mean zero and variance one, we have

$$\rho_{SY} = \frac{E(SY)}{\sigma_{SS}^{\frac{1}{2}}} = \frac{\sum_{g=1}^{k} E(S_g Y)}{\left[\sum_{g=1}^{k} \sum_{h=1}^{k} \sigma_{gh} \right]^{\frac{1}{2}}} . \tag{3.4}$$

For our model

$$E(S_g Y) = \int_{-\infty}^{\infty} \int_{\alpha_g}^{\infty} \frac{y \exp\left[-\frac{1}{2(1-\rho_{gY}^{*2})}(x_g^2 - 2\rho_{gY}^{*} x_g y + y^2) \right]}{2\pi(1-\rho_{gY}^{*})^{\frac{1}{2}}} dx_g\, dy \tag{3.5}$$

$$= \int_{\alpha_g}^{\infty} \frac{\rho_{gY}^{*} x_g \exp[(-\frac{1}{2})x_g^2]}{\sqrt{2\pi}} dx_g = \frac{\rho_{gY}^{*} \exp[(-\frac{1}{2})(\alpha_g^2)]}{\sqrt{2\pi}} .$$

Hence

$$\rho_{SY} = \frac{\sum_{g=1}^{k} \rho_{gY}^{*} \exp[-(\alpha_g^2)/2]}{\sqrt{2\pi} \left(\sum_{g=1}^{k} \sum_{h=1}^{k} \sigma_{gh} \right)^{\frac{1}{2}}} . \tag{3.6}$$

If $\alpha_g = \alpha_h = \alpha$, with $\sigma^2 = \Phi_1(\alpha)(1 - \Phi_1[\alpha])$ and $\rho_{gY}^{*} = \rho_{hY}^{*} = \rho^{*\frac{1}{2}}$, $g, h = 1, 2, \cdots, k$, then

$$\rho_{SY} = \frac{k\rho^{*\frac{1}{2}} \exp[-\alpha^2/2]}{\sqrt{2\pi}\,(k\sigma^2 + k[k-1]\sigma^2\rho)^{\frac{1}{2}}} \tag{3.7}$$

$$= \left[\frac{k\rho^{*} c(\alpha)}{1 + (k-1)\rho} \right]^{\frac{1}{2}} ,$$

where

$$c(\alpha) = \frac{\exp[-\alpha^2]}{2\pi\Phi_1(\alpha)(1 - \Phi_1[\alpha])} . \tag{3.8}$$

In studying the behavior of the reliability and validity coefficients, a number of writers (e.g., [1, 2]) have pointed out the so-called "attenuation paradox." That is, it has been observed that when the item intercorrelations are equal and all the item difficulties are the same, then as ρ increases from zero to one, the reliability increases from zero to one, but the validity coefficient increases to a maximum value less than one, and then decreases.

It is clear from Equation (3.3) that as ρ (the common value of the correlations between the observed responses) increases from zero to one, the reliability coefficient also increases from zero to one. In general, there appears to be no reason that measures of reliability and validity should be monotone increasing functions of each other, but for our model, as ρ (the correlation between the observed responses) increases from zero to one, ρ^* (the correlation between the underlying abilities to respond) is also increasing from zero to one. Since $\rho^* = \rho^*_{gY}\rho^*_{hY}$ for all g and h, we have $\rho^*_{gY} = \rho^{*\frac{1}{2}}$ for all g. It follows that as ρ^* increases from zero to one, the correlation between the ability Y and the underlying ability to answer each item is also increasing from zero to one. It seems reasonable, therefore, that since the accuracy and precision of each X_g as an index of Y is increasing, the validity of the test, in some sense, should continue to increase, and hence the observed behavior may be considered to be paradoxical. In Figures 2 and 3, this paradoxical behavior is demonstrated for $k = 1$, 10, 100, and two-item difficulties. Actually for $k = 1$, a one-item test, we can see that the paradox does not occur.

Mathematically, we can show that this paradoxical behavior results from the use of ρ_{SY} as a measure of validity. We suppose that all the inter-item

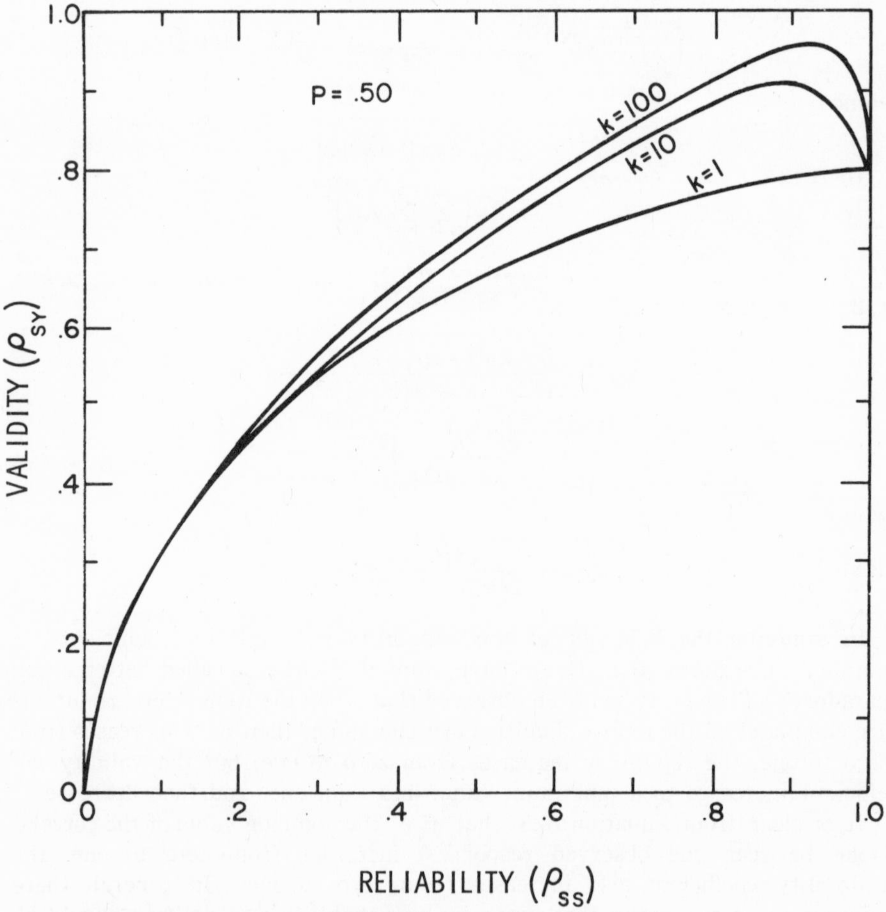

FIG. 2. Relation Between Reliability and Validity Coefficients When All Item Difficulties Are .50 and the Inter-Item Correlations Are Equal

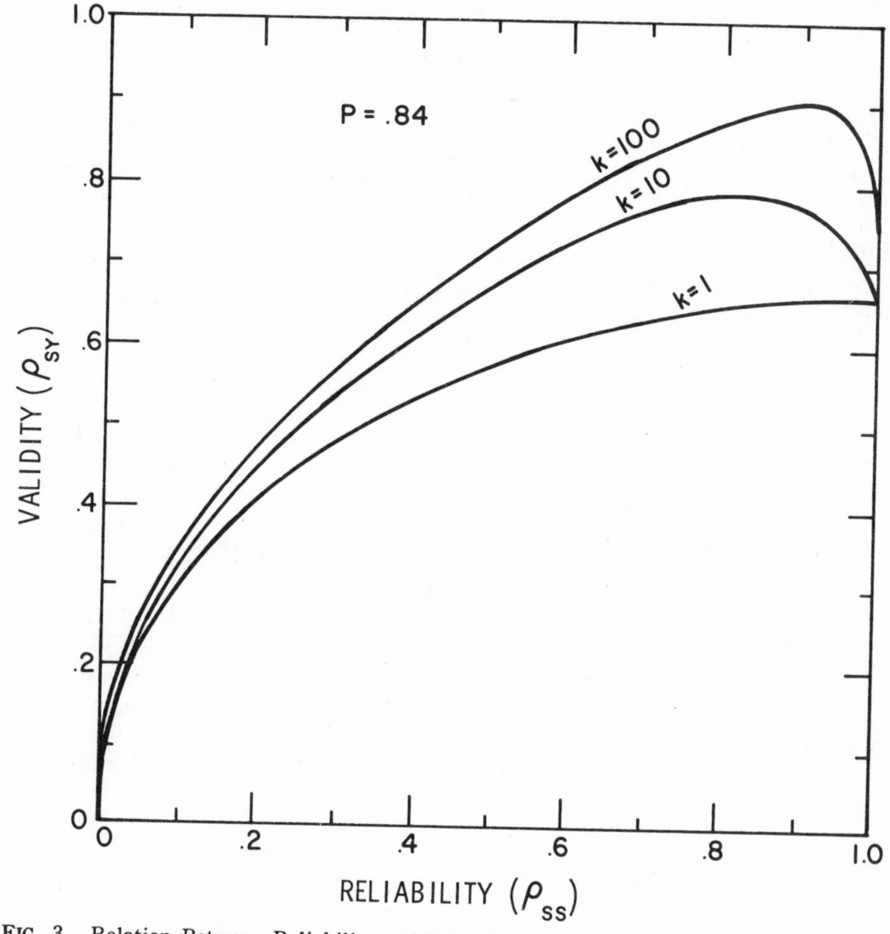

FIG. 3. Relation Between Reliability and Validity Coefficients When All Item Difficulties Are .84 and the Inter-Item Correlations Are Equal

correlations are equal to ρ, and all the item difficulties are equal to $\Phi_1(-\alpha)$. Writing $\rho = \Psi(\rho^*, \alpha)$, we can rewrite Equation (3.7) as

$$\rho_{SY} = \left[\frac{k\rho^* c(\alpha)}{1 + (k-1)\Psi(\rho^*, \alpha)}\right]^{\frac{1}{2}}. \tag{3.9}$$

It will be observed in (3.9) that when $\rho^* = 0$, then $\rho = 0$, and $\rho_{SY} = 0$, whereas when $\rho^* = 1$, then $\rho = 1$, and $\rho_{SY} = [c(\alpha)]^{\frac{1}{2}}$. The value of $c(\alpha)$ is a maximum when $\alpha = 0$, that is, when all the item difficulties are one-half. In this case, $c(0) = 2/\pi$, and $\rho_{SY} = (2/\pi)^{\frac{1}{2}} = .798$. For all α, $c(\alpha) = c(-\alpha)$, and $c(\alpha) \to 0$ as $|\alpha| \to \infty$. Thus, clearly, when the reliability coefficient is one, the validity coefficient has a value less than one.

It is of interest to note that when $\rho^* = 1$, the value of ρ_{SY} no longer depends on the number of items in the test. This is not unexpected, since when both ρ and ρ^* are equal to one, we are essentially in a test situation in which there is only one item.

To examine the behavior of ρ_{SY}, as ρ^* increases from zero to one, we consider

$$(3.10)\qquad \frac{\partial \rho_{SY}}{\partial \rho^*} = \frac{1}{2}\left[\frac{kc(\alpha)}{\rho^*[1+(k-1)\Psi(\rho^*,\alpha)]^3}\right]^{\frac{1}{2}} \cdot\left[1+(k-1)\Psi(\rho^*,\alpha)-(k-1)\rho^*\frac{\partial\Psi(\rho^*,\alpha)}{\partial\rho^*}\right].$$

From (2.15) we find that

$$(3.11)\qquad \frac{\partial\Psi(\rho^*,\alpha)}{\partial\rho^*} = \frac{\exp[-\alpha^2/(1+\rho^*)]}{2\pi\Phi_1(\alpha)(1-\Phi_1(\alpha)(1-\rho^{*2})^{\frac{1}{2}}} = c(\alpha)\frac{\exp[(\rho^*\alpha^2)/(1+\rho^*)]}{(1-\rho^{*2})^{\frac{1}{2}}}.$$

It follows that

$$(3.12)\qquad \frac{\partial \rho_{SY}}{\partial \rho^*} = \frac{1}{2}\left[\frac{kc(\alpha)}{\rho^*[1+(k-1)\Psi(\rho^*,\alpha)]^3}\right]^{\frac{1}{2}} \cdot\left[1+(k-1)\Psi(\rho^*,\alpha)-(k-1)\frac{c(\alpha)\rho^*\exp[(\rho^*\alpha^2)/(1+\rho^*)]}{(1-\rho^{*2})^{\frac{1}{2}}}\right].$$

If the test consists of only one item, i.e., $k=1$, $(\partial\rho_{SY})/(\partial\rho^*)$ is always positive so that the validity coefficient increases monotonically from zero to $[c(\alpha)]^{\frac{1}{2}}$ as ρ^* increases from zero to one. When $k>1$, however, $(\partial\rho_{SY})/(\partial\rho^*)$ is positive when ρ^* is zero and negative when ρ^* is one. Since $(\partial\rho_{SY})/(\partial\rho^*)$ is a continuous function of ρ^*, there is a value of ρ^*, say ρ_0^*, with $0<\rho_0^*<1$, for which ρ_{SY} is a maximum. This maximizing value is the value of ρ^* for which $(\partial\rho_{SY})/(\partial\rho^*)=0$, that is, ρ_0^* satisfies the equation

$$(3.13)\qquad 1+(k-1)\Psi(\rho_0^*,\alpha) = (k-1)\rho_0^*\frac{\partial\Psi(\rho_0^*,\alpha)}{\partial\rho^*} = (k-1)c(\alpha)\frac{\rho_0^*\exp[(\rho_0^*\alpha^2)/(1+\rho_0^*)]}{(1-\rho_0^{*2})^{\frac{1}{2}}}.$$

The maximized value of ρ_{SY} is

$$(3.14)\qquad \rho_{SY} = \left\{\frac{k(1-\rho_0^{*2})^{\frac{1}{2}}\exp[-(\rho_0^*\alpha^2)/(1+\rho_0^*)]}{k-1}\right\}^{\frac{1}{2}}.$$

To gain some insight into the meaning of Equations (3.13) and (3.14), we consider the case in which $\alpha=0$. First we have

$$(3.15)\qquad \rho = \Psi(\rho^*,0) = \frac{2}{\pi}\sin^{-1}\rho^*.$$

For $0 \leq \rho^* \leq 1$, the value of ρ is given by the convergent power series

$$(3.16)\qquad \rho = \sum_{\nu=0}^{\infty}\frac{\Gamma(\nu+\frac{1}{2})\Gamma(\nu+\frac{1}{2})}{\pi^{\frac{3}{2}}\Gamma(\nu+\frac{3}{2})\nu!}\rho^{*2\nu+1} = \frac{2\rho^*}{\pi}F(\tfrac{1}{2},\tfrac{1}{2};\tfrac{3}{2},\rho^{*2}),$$

where F is the hypergeometric function, i.e.,

$$F(a, b; c, z) = 1 + \frac{ab}{c} z + \frac{a(a+1)b(b+1)}{c(c+1)2!} z^2 \cdots . \tag{3.17}$$

It follows that

$$\frac{\partial \rho}{\partial \rho^*} = \frac{2}{\pi} F\left(\frac{1}{2}, \frac{1}{2}; \frac{3}{2}, \rho^{*2}\right) + \frac{2\rho^{*2}}{3\pi} F\left(\frac{3}{2}, \frac{3}{2}; \frac{5}{2}, \rho^{*2}\right). \tag{3.18}$$

Substituting in Equation (3.13), we find that the maximizing value of ρ^* satisfies either

$$\rho_0^{*3} F\left(\frac{3}{2}, \frac{3}{2}; \frac{5}{2}, \rho_0^{*2}\right) = \frac{3\pi}{2(k-1)} \tag{3.19}$$

or

$$\rho_0^{*3} + \frac{9}{10}\rho_0^{*5} + \frac{45}{56}\rho_0^{*7} + \cdots = \frac{3\pi}{2(k-1)}. \tag{3.20}$$

For $k = 1$, 10, 25, 50, and 100, the values of ρ_0^*, ρ, ρ_{SY}, and ρ_{SS} are as follows:

k	ρ_0^*	ρ	ρ_{SY}	ρ_{SS}
1	1.0000	1.0000	.7979	1.0000
10	.6754	.4720	.9052	.8994
25	.5279	.3540	.9407	.9320
50	.4311	.2762	.9717	.9502
100	.3487	.2268	.9729	.9670

Thus, for a test consisting of 10 items, each of difficulty level one-half, and with correlations between the item responses of .47, both the corresponding validity and reliability coefficients are of the order of .9. Moreover, this is the maximum validity that can be achieved for a test consisting of 10 items each of difficulty one-half and with equal inter-item correlations. If the inter-item correlations are all one, reflecting a perfect correlation between the underlying ability Y and the ability to answer each item, the validity of the test decreases to .8, although the reliability increases to one.

Clearly, even for this special case of equal item difficulties and equal item intercorrelations, a number of interesting questions remain to be explored. Two lines of inquiry immediately present themselves: One is the possibility of defining a measure of validity that continues to increase as the correlation between the ability Y and the underlying abilities X_g increases. The other is a study of the behavior of the distribution of test scores as ρ^* increases, with the thought that for some purposes of classification, there may be an optimal distribution, corresponding, in turn, to an optimal value of ρ^* which is less than one. In addition, the case of unequal item difficulties and unequal inter-item correlations also remain to be considered. Some of these questions will be considered in Chapters 3 and 4.

References

[1] Loevinger, J. The attenuation paradox in test theory. *Psych. Bull.*, 1954, **51**, 493–504.

[2] Lord, F. Theory of test scores and their relations to the trait measured. *Educational Testing Service Bulletin*, Princeton, 1951.

[3] Solomon, H. Probability and statistics in psychometric research with special regard to item analysis and classification techniques. In Vol. 5, J. Neyman, ed., *Proceedings of the Third Berkeley Symposium on Mathematical Statistics and Probability*, Berkeley, Calif.: Univ. California Press, 1956.

[4] Tucker, L. R. Maximum validity of a test with equivalent items. *Psychometrika*, 1946, **11**, 1–14.

[5] Kuder, G. F., and Richardson, M. W. The theory of the estimation of test reliability. *Psychometrika*, 1937, **2**, 151–60.

2

Optimal Test Design in a Special Testing Situation

ROSEDITH SITGREAVES, Columbia University

1. General Considerations

In many situations we are confronted with the problem of making one of several possible decisions about an individual, the preferred decision depending upon the amount of some specified ability he possesses. For example, it may be necessary to decide whether to assign a man entering the Air Force to pilot training, or whether to admit a high school graduate to a given college. In either case, the ability required to complete the indicated program successfully cannot be evaluated directly at the time the decision is to be made. A frequent procedure in situations of this kind is to give the individual some tests measuring related abilities, and to use the test results in reaching a decision.

In order to evaluate the usefulness of various tests and particularly to aid in the selection of items for a test, it seems desirable to construct a probability model for the testing situation. One such model, considered earlier by Tucker [1] and Lord [2], was developed in some detail in Chapter 1. In this chapter we shall examine this model, in a slightly different form.

In the model we assume that the variable of interest Y can be regarded as a continuous variable with values y, $-\infty < y < \infty$, which are normally distributed with zero mean and unit variance among individuals in a population Π. The set of possible observables consists of responses to test items which are scored as either right or wrong. It is postulated that to answer a given item correctly, say item g, requires an underlying ability X_g in an amount greater than a specified value α_g, and that this ability, which varies continuously over Π, has a correlation ρ^*_{gY} with Y, where $\rho^*_{gY} \geqq 0$, for all g. It is assumed further that among individuals for whom $Y = y$, any two such abilities, say X_g and X_h, are independently and normally distributed with means $\rho^*_{gY}\, y$, $\rho^*_{hY}\, y$, and variances $(1 - \rho^{*2}_{gY})$, $(1 - \rho^{*2}_{hY})$, respectively. These conditions arise from the fundamental assumption that the items obey a Spearman factor structure in which the sole common factor is the ability under examination. The reader is referred to the previous chapter for a more detailed account of the foregoing text.

Also we have a set of k variables, $X_1, \cdots, X_k$, which have a joint multivariate normal distribution over Π with zero means, unit variances, and correlations ρ^*_{gh}, $g, h = 1, \cdots, k$; moreover, because of the Spearman factor model, we have $\rho^*_{gh} = \rho^*_{gY}\rho^*_{hY}$.

For any test item g we define an associated observable binomial variable S_g such that $S_g = 1$ when item g is answered correctly, i.e., $X_g \geqq \alpha_g$, and $S_g = 0$ when item g is answered incorrectly, i.e., $X_g < \alpha_g$. With the above assumptions, the probability that $S_g = 1$ when $Y = y$ is given by

$$\Pr\{S_g = 1 \mid y\} = \Pr\{X_g \geqq \alpha_g \mid y\} . \tag{1.1}$$

Writing,[1]

$$\varphi_1(t) = \frac{1}{\sqrt{2\pi}} \exp\left[-\tfrac{1}{2}t^2\right] ,$$

$$\Phi_1(t) = \int_{-\infty}^{t} \varphi_1(u)\, du ,$$

we have

$$\Pr\{S_g = 1 \mid y\} = \Phi_1\left(\frac{\rho^*_{gY}\, y - \alpha_g}{\sqrt{1 - \rho^{*2}_{gY}}}\right) . \tag{1.2}$$

This probability, considered as a function of y, is known in test theory as the item-characteristic curve for item g. (In latent-structure analysis, this function is called the trace line of the item.)

Other item characteristics which are usually of interest are the item difficulties and the item intercorrelations. The level of difficulty of item g is defined as the probability in Π that $S_g = 1$. For our model, this is

$$\Pr\{S_g = 1\} = \Pr\{X_g \geqq \alpha_g\} = 1 - \Phi_1(\alpha_g) = \Phi_1(-\alpha_g) . \tag{1.3}$$

The inter-item correlation is defined as the product-moment correlation between the binomial variables S_g and S_h and is given by

$$\rho_{gh} = \frac{\Phi_2(-\alpha_g, -\alpha_h; \rho^*_{gh}) - \Phi_1(-\alpha_g)\Phi_1(-\alpha_h)}{\sqrt{\Phi_1(-\alpha_g)\Phi_1(\alpha_g)\Phi_1(-\alpha_h)\Phi_1(\alpha_h)}} , \tag{1.4}$$

where

$$\Phi_2(a, b; \rho) = \int_{-\infty}^{a}\int_{-\infty}^{b} \frac{\exp\{-[1/2(1-\rho^2)](x_1^2 - 2\rho x_1 x_2 + x_2^2)\}}{2\pi\sqrt{1-\rho^2}}\, dx_1\, dx_2 .$$

The inter-item correlation ρ_{gh} thus depends not only on the correlation ρ^*_{gh} between the underlying abilities X_g and X_h, but also on the difficulty levels of the two items.[2]

So far in the formulation we have assumed that the different test items measure different underlying abilities. It is clear, however, that the model

---

[1] The subscript 1 is used because φ and Φ here refer to a univariate normal. On the next page the subscript 2 indicates a bivariate normal. In the next chapter the subscript k will denote a k-variate normal.

[2] It will be observed that in the usual terminology, ρ_{gh} is a phi correlation coefficient, while ρ^*_{gh} is a tetrachoric correlation coefficient.

can be easily adapted to the case in which a subset of items measures the same underlying variable X_g, $(g = 1, 2, \cdots, k)$, the correct answers to these items requiring different amounts, say, $\alpha_{g_1}, \alpha_{g_2}, \cdots$, of X_g. For example, a test designed to gain information on general mathematical ability Y might contain five algebra problems and five geometry problems, all of varying difficulty, the two underlying variables X_1 and X_2 being, respectively, the ability to solve algebra problems and the ability to solve problems in geometry. In this connection, it might be mentioned that although presumably either set of problems can be ordered in terms of difficulty from a content point of view, in the present terminology the difficulty of a problem is specifically defined by a number, i.e., the probability that an individual, selected at random from the population of interest, can correctly solve the problem. In our model, this number uniquely defines the corresponding value of α_{g_i}.

For any two binomial variables S_{g_1} and S_{g_2}, both measuring the same underlying variable X_g, with $\alpha_{g_1} < \alpha_{g_2}$, we have, from (1.4),

$$(1.5) \qquad \rho_{g_1 g_2} = \frac{\Phi_2(-\alpha_{g_1}, -\alpha_{g_2}; 1) - \Phi_1(-\alpha_{g_1})\Phi_1(-\alpha_{g_2})}{\sqrt{\Phi_1(-\alpha_{g_1})\Phi_1(\alpha_{g_1})\Phi_1(-\alpha_{g_2})\Phi_1(\alpha_{g_2})}}$$

$$= \frac{\Phi_1(-\alpha_{g_2}) - \Phi_1(-\alpha_{g_1})\Phi_1(-\alpha_{g_2})}{\sqrt{\Phi_1(-\alpha_{g_1})\Phi_1(\alpha_{g_1})\Phi_1(-\alpha_{g_2})\Phi_1(\alpha_{g_2})}}$$

$$= \left[\frac{\Phi_1(\alpha_{g_1})\Phi_1(-\alpha_{g_2})}{\Phi_1(\alpha_{g_2})\Phi_1(-\alpha_{g_1})}\right]^{\frac{1}{2}} .$$

In the previous chapter the classical reliability and validity coefficients were examined in the framework of this model. Both these coefficients are product-moment correlation coefficients involving the total number of correct responses, i.e., the test score. The first is defined as the correlation between scores on two equivalent forms of a test, and the second as the correlation between the test score and the variable Y.

The use of the test score to evaluate the properties of a test seems justified only when the test items are symmetric, i.e., when all the items are equally difficult, and the item intercorrelations of each order are equal. Even in this case, it is not clear that the reliability and validity coefficients as defined are necessarily the best measures of the goodness of a test. As indicated in the previous chapter, their use results in the so-called "attenuation paradox" in test theory. That is, as ρ^* increases from 0 to 1, with α fixed, the reliability coefficient increases from 0 to 1, but the validity coefficient increases to a maximum less than one and then decreases. This behavior appears paradoxical, since increasing values of ρ^* reflect an increasing correlation between Y and each of the underlying variables X_g. However, in our model, such increasing correlations also result in higher correlations between X_g and X_h, for all g and h. It follows that as ρ^* approaches 1, with α fixed, an individual whose y-value is greater than α tends to answer all questions correctly, whereas an individual whose y-value is less than α tends to answer all questions incorrectly.

A test of this kind, of course—i.e., one with $\alpha_1 = \cdots = \alpha_k = \alpha$, and ρ^* close to 1—is extremely useful, regardless of the decline in value of the validity coefficient, if the purpose of the test is to select a number of individuals from Π with y-values greater than α. On the other hand, the test is not particularly helpful if it is desired, say, to rank a number of individuals from Π according to their y-values.

Clearly, in selecting a measure to evaluate a test's usefulness, we need to take into account the questions that the test's results are to aid in answering. If the basic decision problem concerning individuals from Π is sufficiently specified so that we can quantify losses associated with various wrong decisions when $Y = y$, then the minimum expected loss (i.e., the Bayes risk) to be attained with the use of a given test is a natural index to use.

In many instances, however, we may be able to specify only the particular decision that is preferred when $Y = y$. In such a situation it seems intuitively reasonable to use the results of a given test to estimate the individual's y-value and then make the decision assuming this is the exact value of Y. A possible procedure, therefore, is to determine, for a given test, an estimating procedure such that the resulting value of the estimate is "closest" to the true value in some selected metric, and to use a function of this "distance" as a measure of goodness of the test.

In this chapter and in the following one we adopt the expected squared error of the estimate as a measure of closeness of an estimation procedure. By this we mean that if $\hat{y}$ is the estimate of the value of Y, then the expected squared error of estimate is $E(\hat{y} - y)^2$. For any admissible estimation procedure, this expected value cannot be greater than 1, since if we estimate Y by its expected value of 0, without taking into account any test results, the expected squared error of the estimate is simply the population variance, which is 1. Any admissible procedure therefore must have an expected squared error not exceeding 1.

For a given test we find the procedure that minimizes the expected squared error of the estimate, and define 1 minus this minimum as a measure of goodness of the test. This number provides us with a means of comparing tests of different lengths, as well as tests of the same length but with different values of the parameters $\rho_{1Y}^*, \cdots, \rho_{kY}^*; \alpha_1, \cdots, \alpha_k$. It will be observed that this measure, or rather its square root, can be considered as a generalization of the notion of the correlation ratio. This will be demonstrated in Section 2.

In this chapter we consider the situation when the observable dichotomous variables, i.e., the item responses, all measure the same underlying variable X. In this case, a k-item test is defined by $(k+1)$ numbers, i.e., the correlation between X and Y, which we denote by $\sqrt{\rho^*}$, and the numbers $\alpha_1, \cdots, \alpha_k$, related to the item difficulties.[3] For a given test, we determine

[3] The notation $\sqrt{\rho^*}$ is used here, since in the general case if each of two or more abilities has correlation $\sqrt{\rho^*}$ with Y, the correlation in Π between any two of these abilities is ρ^*.

the estimating procedure for Y, namely $\tilde{Y}$, which minimizes the expected squared error of estimate, and find the value of this minimum, say $\tilde{S}^2(\rho^*; \alpha_1, \cdots, \alpha_k)$. The corresponding index for the test is given by

$$1 - \tilde{S}^2(\rho^*; \alpha_1, \cdots, \alpha_k) = h(\rho^*; \alpha_1, \cdots, \alpha_k) . \tag{1.6}$$

Various properties of h are demonstrated, and values of $(\rho^*; \alpha_1, \cdots, \alpha_k)$, which maximize h, are found.

2. Determination of $\tilde{Y}^*$ and $h(\rho^*; \alpha_1, \cdots, \alpha_k)$

We assume that we are given responses to k test items by an individual from a population Π, and on the basis of these responses we want to estimate, for the individual, the value of a variable Y in order to minimize the expected squared error of estimate. We assume also that a given item, say item g, is answered correctly if the individual possesses at least α_g units of an ability X, and that the variables X and Y are jointly normally distributed in Π, each with zero mean and unit variance, and with correlation coefficient $\sqrt{\rho^*}$.

Since the numbering of the items is arbitrary, we assume without loss of generality that $\alpha_1 \leqq \cdots \leqq \alpha_k$. In fact, we shall assume that strict inequality holds, since if, for some g and h, $\alpha_g = \alpha_h$, the corresponding item-characteristic curves coincide, and our test is essentially one of only $(k-1)$ items.

Let S_g denote the binomial variable associated with item g, i.e., $S_g = 1$ if item g is answered correctly and $S_g = 0$ otherwise. Then, in general, for a k-item test, there are 2^k possible values of the observation vector

$$V = (S_1, \cdots, S_k) .$$

Under the present assumptions, however, if an individual answers item g correctly, say $S_g = 1$, then for this individual

$$X \geqq \alpha_g > \alpha_{g-1} > \cdots > \alpha_1 ,$$

so that items $1, 2, \cdots, (g-1)$ are also answered correctly. It follows that only $(k+1)$ of the observation vectors have positive probability, namely, the vectors.

$$\begin{aligned} V_1 &= (0, 0, \cdots, 0) , \\ V_2 &= (1, 0, \cdots, 0) , \\ V_3 &= (1, 1, \cdots, 0) , \\ &\cdots\cdots\cdots\cdots\cdots\cdots \\ V_{k+1} &= (1, 1, \cdots, 1) . \end{aligned} \tag{2.1}$$

It should be observed in (2.1) that the total test score is a single-valued function of the response vectors, but since we want to keep the problem in a more general framework, we will not specifically make use of this relation. It should be noted also that the response vectors are of the form considered by Guttman [3] in his latent-distance model, but in that model the present underlying structure was not postulated.

We define $\alpha_0 = -\infty$, $\alpha_{k+1} = +\infty$, and note that V_j can occur only if $\alpha_{j-1} \leqq X < \alpha_j$. The conditional probability of V_j, given y, is thus

$$P(V_j \mid y) = \int_{\alpha_{j-1}}^{\alpha_j} \frac{1}{\sqrt{2\pi}\,(1-\rho^*)^{\frac{1}{2}}} \exp\{-[1/2(1-\rho^*)](X-\sqrt{\rho^*}\,y)^2\}\,dX$$
$$= \Phi_1\left(\frac{\alpha_j - y\sqrt{\rho^*}}{\sqrt{1-\rho^*}}\right) - \Phi_1\left(\frac{\alpha_{j-1} - y\sqrt{\rho^*}}{\sqrt{1-\rho^*}}\right).$$

The joint probability distribution of V_j and y is given by

$$p(V_j, y) = \left[\Phi_1\left(\frac{\alpha_j - y\sqrt{\rho^*}}{\sqrt{1-\rho^*}}\right) - \Phi_1\left(\frac{\alpha_{j-1} - y\sqrt{\rho^*}}{\sqrt{1-\rho^*}}\right)\right]\varphi_1(y)\,. \tag{2.2}$$

We may also write that the marginal distribution of the response vectors is

$$p(V_j) = \int_{-\infty}^{\infty} p(V_j, y)\,dy = \Phi_1(\alpha_j) - \Phi_1(\alpha_{j-1}) \qquad j = 1, 2, \cdots, k+1\,. \tag{2.3}$$

An estimation procedure $\hat{Y}$ is defined by the selection of $(k+1)$ numbers $\hat{y}_1, \cdots, \hat{y}_{k+1}$, such that Y is estimated by $\hat{y}_j$ when V_j is observed. The expected squared error of estimate associated with $\hat{Y}$ is

$$\sum_{j=1}^{k+1} \int_{-\infty}^{\infty} (\hat{y}_j - y)^2 p(V_j, y)\,dy\,. \tag{2.4}$$

To find the procedure $\tilde{Y}$ which minimizes (2.4), we differentiate under the integral sign with respect to $\hat{y}_j$, $j = 1, 2, \cdots, k+1$, and set the resulting equations equal to zero. From this, we obtain

$$\tilde{y}_j = \frac{\int_{-\infty}^{\infty} y p(V_j, y)\,dy}{\int_{-\infty}^{\infty} p(V_j, y)\,dy}\,. \tag{2.5}$$

(This result also comes directly from the general theory of Bayes estimation, e.g., see [4], p. 299.) We have

$$\int_{-\infty}^{\infty} y p(V_j, y)\,dy = \int_{-\infty}^{\infty} y\varphi_1(y)\left[\Phi_1\left(\frac{\alpha_j - y\sqrt{\rho^*}}{\sqrt{1-\rho^*}}\right) - \Phi_1\left(\frac{\alpha_{j-1} - y\sqrt{\rho^*}}{\sqrt{1-\rho^*}}\right)\right]dy$$
$$= -\sqrt{\rho^*}\int_{-\infty}^{\infty} \frac{\varphi_1(y)}{\sqrt{1-\rho^*}}\left[\varphi_1\left(\frac{\alpha_j - y\sqrt{\rho^*}}{\sqrt{1-\rho^*}}\right) - \varphi_1\left(\frac{\alpha_{j-1} - y\sqrt{\rho^*}}{\sqrt{1-\rho^*}}\right)\right]dy$$
$$= -\sqrt{\rho^*}\,[\varphi_1(\alpha_j) - \varphi_1(\alpha_{j-1})]\,.$$

It follows that

$$\tilde{y}_j = -\sqrt{\rho^*}\left[\frac{\varphi_1(\alpha_j) - \varphi_1(\alpha_{j-1})}{\Phi_1(\alpha_j) - \Phi_1(\alpha_{j-1})}\right]. \tag{2.6}$$

The value of the expected squared error of estimate for $\tilde{Y}$ is

$$(2.7)\qquad \tilde{S}^2(\rho^*;\alpha_1,\cdots,\alpha_k)=\sum_{j=1}^{k+1}\int_{-\infty}^{\infty}(\tilde{y}_j-y)^2p(V_j,y)\,dy$$
$$=\int_{-\infty}^{\infty}y^2\sum_{j=1}^{k+1}p(V_j,y)\,dy-\sum_{j=1}^{k+1}\tilde{y}_j^2\int_{-\infty}^{\infty}p(V_j,y)\,dy$$
$$=1-\rho^*\sum_{j=1}^{k+1}\frac{[\varphi_1(\alpha_j)-\varphi_1(\alpha_{j-1})]^2}{\Phi_1(\alpha_j)-\Phi_1(\alpha_{j-1})}\,.$$

The corresponding index for the test is

$$(2.8)\qquad h(\rho^*;\alpha_1,\cdots,\alpha_k)=\rho^*\sum_{j=1}^{k+1}\frac{[\varphi_1(\alpha_j)-\varphi_1(\alpha_{j-1})]^2}{\Phi_1(\alpha_j)-\Phi_1(\alpha_{j-1})}\,.$$

The index h can be considered to be a population value of the square of a correlation ratio. The sample correlation ratio between a dependent variable $Z^{(1)}$ and an independent variable $Z^{(2)}$ is used as a measure of relationship when the sample regression of $Z^{(1)}$ on $Z^{(2)}$ is markedly nonlinear, and the possible values of $Z^{(2)}$ are finite, say, $Z^{(2)}=z_1^{(2)},z_2^{(2)},\cdots,z_k^{(2)}$. Suppose in a sample of N pairs of observations there are N_i pairs for which $Z^{(2)}=z_i^{(2)}$, $i=1,2,\cdots,k$, $\sum_{i=1}^k N_i=N$, the corresponding values of $Z^{(1)}$ being $z_{i1}^{(1)},\cdots,z_{iN_i}^{(1)}$. Let

$$z_{i\cdot}^{(1)}=\frac{1}{N_i}\sum_{j=1}^{N_i}z_{ij}^{(1)}\qquad\text{and}\qquad z_{\cdot\cdot}^{(1)}=\frac{1}{N}\sum_{i=1}^{k}\sum_{j=1}^{N_i}z_{ij}^{(1)}\,.$$

Then the correlation ratio $E_{z_1z_2}$ is defined by the relation

$$(2.9)\qquad E^2_{Z^{(1)}Z^{(2)}}=1-\frac{\sum_{i=1}^{k}\sum_{j=1}^{N_i}(z_{ij}^{(1)}-z_{i\cdot}^{(1)})^2}{\sum_{i=1}^{k}\sum_{j=1}^{N_i}(z_{ij}^{(1)}-z_{\cdot\cdot}^{(1)})^2}\,.$$

The square root is taken with a positive sign.

Correspondingly, we can define a population value of the correlation ratio by the relation

$$(2.10)\qquad \eta^2_{Z^{(1)}Z^{(2)}}=1-\frac{E_{Z^{(2)}}(\sigma^2_{Z^{(1)}\cdot Z^{(2)}})}{\sigma^2_{Z^{(1)}}}\,,$$

where $E_{Z^{(2)}}(\sigma^2_{Z^{(1)}\cdot Z^{(2)}})$ denotes the expected value of the conditional variance of $Z^{(1)}$ given $Z^{(2)}$. Permitting $Z^{(2)}$ to be vector valued, we obtain h.

As an example of the determination of h, suppose we have a 5-item test with $\rho^*=.25$, $\alpha_1=-2$, $\alpha_2=-1$, $\alpha_3=0$, $\alpha_4=1$, and $\alpha_5=2$. The six observation vectors with positive probability are

$$V_1=(0,0,0,0,0)\,,\qquad V_4=(1,1,1,0,0)\,,$$
$$V_2=(1,0,0,0,0)\,,\qquad V_5=(1,1,1,1,0)\,,$$
$$V_3=(1,1,0,0,0)\,,\qquad V_6=(1,1,1,1,1)\,.$$

When a given vector V_j is observed ($j=1,\cdots,6$), the corresponding value of the estimate $\tilde{y}_j$ is

$$\tilde{y}_1 = -.5\left(\frac{.05399}{.02275}\right) = -.5(2.3732) = -1.186\,,$$

$$\tilde{y}_2 = -.5\left(\frac{.18798}{.13591}\right) = -.5(1.3831) = -0.692\,,$$

$$\tilde{y}_3 = -.5\left(\frac{.15697}{.34134}\right) = -.5(0.4599) = -0.230\,,$$

$$\tilde{y}_4 = .5\left(\frac{.15697}{.34134}\right) = .5(0.4599) = 0.230\,,$$

$$\tilde{y}_5 = .5\left(\frac{.18798}{.13591}\right) = .5(1.3831) = 0.692\,,$$

$$\tilde{y}_6 = .5\left(\frac{.05399}{.02275}\right) = .5(2.3732) = 1.186\,.$$

The value of h for this test is

$$h(.25; -2, -1, 0, 1, 2) = .25(2)\left[\frac{.05399^2}{.02275} + \frac{.18798^2}{.13591} + \frac{.15697^2}{.34134}\right] \tag{2.11}$$
$$= .25(.9206) = .2302\,.$$

3. Properties of $\tilde{Y}$ and h

The estimation procedure $\tilde{Y}$ and the associated test index h, for tests considered in this chapter, possess a number of interesting properties that are summarized in the following theorems:

THEOREM 3.1. *The estimation procedure $\tilde{Y}$ is such that*

$$\tilde{Y} = \tilde{X}\sqrt{\rho^*}\,,$$

where $\tilde{X}$ is the estimation procedure for X with minimum expected squared error of estimate.

PROOF. As in the case of Y, an estimation procedure $\hat{X}$ for X is also defined by the selection of $(k+1)$ numbers, $\hat{x}_1, \cdots, \hat{x}_{k+1}$ such that we estimate X by x_j when V_j is observed. The theorem is easily proved by considering estimation procedures for X as a special case of estimation procedures for Y with $\rho^* = 1$. The resulting estimates with minimum expected squared error are

$$\tilde{x}_j = -\frac{[\varphi_1(\alpha_j) - \varphi_1(\alpha_{j-1})]}{\Phi_1(\alpha_j) - \Phi_1(\alpha_{j-1})}\,, \tag{3.1.1}$$

and the theorem follows.

It is instructive, however, to prove the theorem by an alternative derivation of $\tilde{Y}$. For any estimation procedure $\hat{Y}$, we define a corresponding procedure $\hat{X}$ such that $\hat{x}_j = \hat{y}_j/\sqrt{\rho^*}$, $j = 1, 2, \cdots, k$. Then we can write

$$Y - \hat{Y} = Y - X\sqrt{\rho^*} + (X - \hat{X})\sqrt{\rho^*}\,. \tag{3.1.2}$$

The expected squared error of estimate for $\hat{Y}$ is

$$(3.1.3)\qquad \sum_{j=1}^{k+1}\int_{-\infty}^{\infty}(\hat{y}_j - y)^2 p(V_j, y)\,dy$$

$$= \sum_{j=1}^{k+1}\int_{-\infty}^{\infty}\int_{\alpha_{j-1}}^{\alpha_j}(y - x\sqrt{\rho^*}) + \sqrt{\rho^*}(x - \hat{x}_j)^2 \cdot \frac{\exp\{-[\frac{1}{2}(1-\rho^*)](x - 2\sqrt{\rho^*}\,xy + y^2)\}}{2\pi\sqrt{1-\rho^*}}\,dx\,dy$$

$$= \sum_{j=1}^{k+1}\int_{\alpha_{j-1}}^{\alpha_j}\frac{\exp[-\frac{1}{2}x^2]}{\sqrt{2\pi}}\left\{\left[\int_{-\infty}^{\infty}(y - x\sqrt{\rho^*})^2 + 2\sqrt{\rho^*}(y - x\sqrt{\rho^*})(x - \hat{x}_j) + \rho^*(x - \hat{x}_j)^2\right] \cdot \frac{\exp\{-[\frac{1}{2}(1-\rho^*)](y - x\sqrt{\rho^*})^2\}}{\sqrt{2\pi(1-\rho^*)}}\,dy\right\}dx$$

$$= \sum_{j=1}^{k+1}\int_{\alpha_{j-1}}^{\alpha_j}[1 - \rho^* + \rho^*(x - \hat{x}_j)^2]\frac{\exp[-\frac{1}{2}x^2]}{\sqrt{2\pi}}\,dx$$

$$= 1 - \rho^* + \rho^*\left\{\sum_{j=1}^{k+1}\int_{\alpha_{j-1}}^{\alpha_j}(x - \hat{x}_j)^2\frac{\exp[-\frac{1}{2}x^2]}{\sqrt{2\pi}}\,dx\right\}.$$

This quantity is minimized by choosing $\tilde{y}_j$ so as to minimize the quantity within the braces. But, clearly, this is accomplished by taking $\tilde{y}_j = \tilde{x}_j\sqrt{\rho^*}$, where $\tilde{X}$ is the estimation procedure for X with minimum expected squared error of estimate.

If we examine (2.8) and (3.1.3), we see that

$$(3.1.4)\qquad h(\rho^*; \alpha_1, \cdots, \alpha_k) = \rho^*\sum_{j=1}^{k-1}\frac{[\varphi_1(\alpha_j) - \varphi_1(\alpha_{j-1})]^2}{\Phi_1(\alpha_j) - \Phi_1(\alpha_{j-1})}$$

$$= \rho^*[1 - \tilde{S}_X^2(\alpha_1, \cdots, \alpha_k)]$$

$$= \rho^*\Psi(\alpha_1, \cdots, \alpha_k)\,.$$

We recall that h can be considered as the square of a population correlation ratio between the continuous variable Y and the vector-valued response variable V. We see here that this correlation ratio is the product of the usual correlation between Y and X, and the generalized correlation ratio between X and V. In other words, our test index is the product of two factors, one of which is an index of the information given by the test on the variable measured, whereas the other is an index of the information given by the measured variable on the latent variable (ability). In a rather broad sense, therefore, Ψ can be considered a measure of reliability and ρ^* a measure of validity. It will be observed that the value of h is close to 1 only if both ρ^* and Ψ are close to 1, whereas h is close to 0 if either ρ^* or Ψ is close to 0.

The value of h permits us to compare tests of different lengths as well as tests of the same length but with different values of $(\rho^*; \alpha_1, \cdots, \alpha_k)$. In general, let A and B be two tests specified by the parameter values $(\rho_A^*; \alpha_1, \cdots, \alpha_{k_A})$ and $(\rho_B^*; \beta_1, \cdots, \beta_{k_B})$, respectively. Then A is said to be equivalent to B if

$$h(\rho_A^*; \alpha_1, \cdots, \alpha_{k_A}) = h(\rho_B^*; \beta_1, \cdots, \beta_{k_B});$$

A is said to be better than B if

$$h(\rho_A^*; \alpha_1, \cdots, \alpha_{k_A}) > h(\rho_B^*; \beta_1, \cdots, \beta_{k_B}).$$

THEOREM 3.2. *Let A and B be two tests specified by the parameter values* $(\rho_A^*; \alpha_1, \cdots, \alpha_k)$ *and* $(\rho_B^*; \alpha_1, \cdots, \alpha_k)$ *with* $\rho_A^* > \rho_B^*$. *Then A is better than B.*

PROOF. This follows immediately from (3.1.4).

THEOREM 3.3. *Let A be a k-item test specified by the parameter values* $(\rho^*; \alpha_1, \cdots, \alpha_k)$. *Let* α_r^* *be any number such that* $\alpha_{r-1} < \alpha_r^* < \alpha_r$ $(r = 1, 2, \cdots, k+1)$. *Then, if* A^* *is the* $(k+1)$*-item test specified by the values* $(\rho^*; \alpha_1, \cdots, \alpha_{r-1}, \alpha_r^*, \alpha_r, \cdots, \alpha_k)$, A^* *is better than A.*

PROOF. From (3.1.4) it is sufficient to prove that

$$\Psi(\alpha_1, \cdots, \alpha_{r-1}, \alpha_r^*, \alpha_r, \cdots, \alpha_k) > \Psi(\alpha_1, \cdots, \alpha_{r-1}, \alpha_r, \cdots, \alpha_k).$$

However

$$\begin{aligned} (3.3.1)\quad & \Psi(\alpha_1, \cdots, \alpha_{r-1}, \alpha_r^*, \alpha_r, \cdots, \alpha_k) - \Psi(\alpha_1, \cdots, \alpha_{r-1}, \alpha_r, \cdots, \alpha_k) \\ &= \frac{[\varphi_1(\alpha_r^*) - \varphi_1(\alpha_{r-1})]^2}{\Phi_1(\alpha_r^*) - \Phi_1(\alpha_{r-1})} + \frac{[\varphi_1(\alpha_r) - \varphi_1(\alpha_r^*)]^2}{\Phi_1(\alpha_r) - \Phi_1(\alpha_r^*)} - \frac{[\varphi_1(\alpha_r) - \varphi_1(\alpha_{r-1})]^2}{\Phi_1(\alpha_r) - \Phi_1(\alpha_{r-1})}. \end{aligned}$$

Let

$$\begin{aligned} \varphi_1(\alpha_r^*) - \varphi_1(\alpha_{r-1}) &= a, & \Phi_1(\alpha_r^*) - \Phi_1(\alpha_{r-1}) &= c, \\ \varphi_1(\alpha_r) - \varphi_1(\alpha_r^*) &= b, & \Phi_1(\alpha_r) - \Phi_1(\alpha_r^*) &= d. \end{aligned}$$

Then, the right-hand side of (3.3.1) can be written as

$$(3.3.2)\qquad \frac{a^2}{c} + \frac{b^2}{d} - \frac{(a+b)^2}{c+d} = \frac{(ad-bc)^2}{cd(c+d)} > 0,$$

and the theorem follows.

Thus, the index h possesses two desirable consistency properties. That is (1) given two tests of the same length with equivalent item difficulties, the test that best measures the latent variable is preferred, and (2) if a new item is added to a test, the resulting test should be at least as informative as the original test. It is also symmetric in the following sense.

THEOREM 3.4. *For any k-item test A specified by the parameter values* $(\rho^*; \alpha_1, \cdots, \alpha_k)$, *there is an equivalent test B specified by the parameter values* $(\rho^*; -\alpha_k, \cdots, -\alpha_1)$.

PROOF. From (3.1.4), it is sufficient to prove that

$$(3.4.1)\qquad \Psi(\alpha_1, \cdots, \alpha_k) = \Psi(-\alpha_k, \cdots, -\alpha_1).$$

But since $\varphi_1(t) = \varphi_1(-t)$ and $\Phi_1(t) = 1 - \Phi_1(-t)$, we have

$$\begin{aligned}\Psi(\alpha_1, \cdots, \alpha_k) &= \sum_{j=1}^{k+1} \frac{[\varphi_1(\alpha_j) - \varphi_1(\alpha_{j-1})]^2}{\Phi_1(\alpha_j) - \Phi_1(\alpha_{j-1})} \\ &= \sum_{j=1}^{k+1} \frac{[\varphi_1(-\alpha_j) - \varphi_1(-\alpha_{j-1})]^2}{[1 - \Phi_1(\alpha_{j-1})] - [1 - \Phi_1(\alpha_j)]} \\ &= \sum_{j=1}^{k+1} \frac{[\varphi_1(-\alpha_{j-1}) - \varphi_1(-\alpha_j)]^2}{\Phi_1(-\alpha_{j-1}) - \Phi_1(-\alpha_j)} \\ &= \Psi(-\alpha_k, \cdots, -\alpha_1) .\end{aligned} \tag{3.4.2}$$

Consider again the 5-item test specified earlier. For this test the estimation procedure $\tilde{X}$ is such that

$$\begin{aligned} &\tilde{x}_1 = -2.3732 , \quad &&\tilde{x}_3 = -0.4599 , \quad &&\tilde{x}_5 = 1.3831 , \\ &\tilde{x}_2 = -1.3831 , \quad &&\tilde{x}_4 = 0.4599 , \quad &&\tilde{x}_6 = 2.3732 , \end{aligned}$$

with $\Psi(-2, -1, 0, 1, 2) = .9206$. If we add an item to the test, say one with $\alpha_3^* = .5$, we have $\Psi(-2, -1, 0, .5, 1, 2) = .9403$, and $h(.25; -2, -1, 0, .5, 1, 2) = .2351$. On the other hand, if we choose a variable X whose correlation with Y is .51 so that the corresponding value of ρ^* is .26, and select 5 test items for this variable with $\alpha_1 = -2$, $\alpha_2 = -1$, $\alpha_3 = 0$, $\alpha_4 = 1$, $\alpha_5 = 2$, we have $h(.26; -2, -1, 0, 1, 2) = .2394$.

4. Optimal Parameter Values for a Given k

It is clear that in constructing a k-item test to gain information on Y, in which all test items are measuring a related variable X, we have, at least conceptually, two basic choices to make. The first is the selection of the particular variable X to be measured, and the second is the selection of k items measuring X. That is, theoretically, we can conceive of a set of variables $\mathfrak{X}$, and for each $X \in \mathfrak{X}$, a set of potential items I_X. Each $X \in \mathfrak{X}$ can be characterized by a number, namely, the value of the correlation coefficient between X and Y. For each X, each item in I_X is also characterized by a number, namely, the probability that an individual chosen at random from the population under study will answer the item correctly, i.e., the item difficulty. In our model, this probability is equated to the probability that the individual's x-value is at least a given number, say α, and there is a one-to-one relationship between the value of the probability and α.

Mathematically, therefore, a test of this kind is completely specified by $(k + 1)$ numbers, namely, the correlation $\sqrt{\rho^*}$ between X and Y, and by the difficulty levels of the k items (or, in turn, the k numbers $\alpha_1, \cdots, \alpha_k$). We consider now the problem of finding the set of values $(\rho^*; \alpha_1, \cdots, \alpha_k)$ that maximizes our selected index h. When the optimal values have been found, we would hope to find an $X \in \mathfrak{X}$ and a set of items in I_X with the required properties. Admittedly this may not be possible in many practical situations, but it is useful nevertheless to know the specifications of the optimal test and the value of h associated with it.

It will be recalled that to evaluate a given test, we have adopted the measure

$$h = 1 - \tilde{S}_Y^2 , \tag{4.1}$$

where $\tilde{S}_Y^2$ is the minimum expected squared error of an estimate of Y attainable with the given test. We have shown that

$$h = \rho^* \Psi , \tag{4.2}$$

where ρ^* is the square of the correlation between X and Y and

$$\Psi = 1 - \tilde{S}_X^2 . \tag{4.3}$$

The quantity $\tilde{S}_X^2$ is the minimum expected squared error of an estimate of X based on the given test, and is a function only of the item difficulties.

It is clear from (4.2) that for purposes of maximizing h, the choice of the k-item difficulties is independent of the choice of X. Thus, we would like to choose X so that ρ^* is as close to 1 as possible, ideally taking $X = Y$. Regardless of the choice of X, however, the optimal item difficulties, i.e., the values $(\tilde{\alpha}_1, \cdots, \tilde{\alpha}_k)$ that maximize Ψ, remain the same, and we look for these now.

In finding the optimal values $(\tilde{\alpha}_1, \cdots, \tilde{\alpha}_k)$, it is useful to write

$$\Phi_1(\alpha_j) = q_j , \tag{4.4}$$

$$\varphi_1(\alpha_j) = v(q_j) , \tag{4.5}$$

i.e., for any number q, $0 \leqq q \leqq 1$, we define $\alpha = \Phi_1^{-1}(q)$ and

$$v(q) = \varphi_1[\Phi_1^{-1}(q)] . \tag{4.6}$$

We observe that corresponding to $\alpha_0 = -\infty$, $\alpha_{k+1} = \infty$, we have $q_0 = 0$, $q_{k+1} = 1$. Also, since we assume that $-\infty < \alpha_1 < \cdots \alpha_k < \infty$, it follows that $0 < q_1 < \cdots < q_{k+1} < 1$. We note that in this form, the level of difficulty of item j is $1 - q_j$.

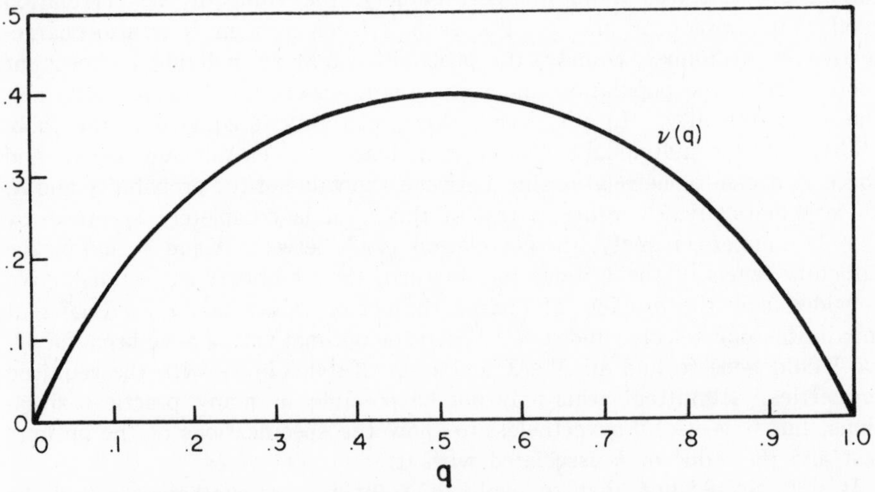

FIG. 1. Graph of the Function $v(q) = \phi_1(\Phi_1^{-1}(q))$.

The function v, shown graphically in Figure 1, is a continuous, differentiable function of q, with $v(q) = v(1 - q)$, and

$$v'(q) = -\Phi_1^{-1}(q) = -v'(1 - q)\,. \tag{4.7}$$

Thus as q increases from 0 to 1, the value of v' decreases monotonically from $+\infty$ to $-\infty$, with $v'(\frac{1}{2}) = 0$. It follows that v is a concave function of q, its values increasing from 0 for $q = 0$, to a maximum of .3989 for $q = \frac{1}{2}$, and then decreasing again to 0 for $q = 1$. Writing

$$\Psi(\alpha_1, \cdots, \alpha_k) = \lambda(q_1, \cdots, q_k)\,, \tag{4.8}$$

we have

$$\lambda(q_1, \cdots, q_k) = \sum_{j=1}^{k+1} \frac{[v(q_j) - v(q_{j-1})]^2}{q_j - q_{j-1}}\,. \tag{4.9}$$

Differentiating λ with respect to q_j, we obtain

$$\begin{aligned}\frac{\partial\lambda}{\partial q_j} &= 2v'(q_j)\left[\frac{v(q_j) - v(q_{j-1})}{q_j - q_{j-1}}\right] - \left[\frac{v(q_j) - v(q_{j-1})}{q_j - q_{j-1}}\right]^2 \\ &\quad - 2v'(q_j)\left[\frac{v(q_{j+1}) - v(q_j)}{q_{j+1} - q_j}\right] + \left[\frac{v(q_{j+1}) - v(q_j)}{q_{j+1} - q_j}\right]^2 \\ &= \left\{2v'(q_j) - \left[\frac{v(q_j) - v(q_{j-1})}{q_j - q_{j-1}} + \frac{v(q_{j+1}) - v(q_j)}{q_{j+1} - q_j}\right]\right\} \\ &\quad \cdot \left\{\left[\frac{v(q_j) - v(q_{j-1})}{q_j - q_{j-1}}\right] - \left[\frac{v(q_{j+1}) - v(q_j)}{q_{j+1} - q_j}\right]\right\} \\ &\qquad j = 1, 2, \cdots, k.\end{aligned} \tag{4.10}$$

A necessary condition that a set of values $\tilde{q}_1, \cdots, \tilde{q}_k$ maximize λ is that

$$\left.\frac{\partial\lambda}{\partial q_j}\right|_{q_1 = \tilde{q}_1, \cdots, q_k = \tilde{q}_k} = 0 \qquad j = 1, 2, \cdots, k, \tag{4.11}$$

Since v is a concave function of q, and we assume $q_{j-1} < q_j < q_{j+1}$, we have

$$\frac{v(q_j) - v(q_{j-1})}{q_j - q_{j-1}} > v'(q_j) > \frac{v(q_{j+1}) - v(q_j)}{q_{j+1} - q_j}\,. \tag{4.12}$$

It follows that the second term in the final expression of (4.10) can never be 0. For conditions (4.11) to hold, therefore, we must find k numbers, $0 < \tilde{q}_1 < \cdots < \tilde{q}_k < 1$, such that

$$\frac{1}{2}\left[\frac{v(\tilde{q}_j) - v(\tilde{q}_{j-1})}{\tilde{q}_j - \tilde{q}_{j-1}} + \frac{v(\tilde{q}_{j+1}) - v(\tilde{q}_j)}{\tilde{q}_{j+1} - \tilde{q}_j}\right] = v'(q_j) \qquad j = 1, 2, \cdots, k\,. \tag{4.13}$$

It is instructive to consider the meaning of these conditions in terms of Figure 1. Suppose a set of numbers satisfying the conditions has been found. Then if in the curve drawn in Figure 1 we draw the chords connecting successive pairs of points on the curve $v(0), \cdots, v(\tilde{q}_j), \cdots, v(1)$, the arithmetic mean of the slopes of any two successive chords is equal to the tangent to the curve at their common point.

For a given k there is only one set of values $0 < \tilde{q}_1 < \cdots < \tilde{q}_k < 1$ for which conditions (4.13) hold, and this set of values maximizes λ. This can be seen as follows: For each value of q_1, $0 < q_1 < \frac{1}{2}$, there is exactly one value of $q_2 > q_1$ for which the equation

$$\frac{v(q_1)}{q_1} + \frac{v(q_2) - v(q_1)}{q_2 - q_1} - 2v'(q_1) = 0 \tag{4.14}$$

holds. For any value of q_1, $\frac{1}{2} < q_1 < 1$, no such value of q_2 exists, since for every $q_2 > q_1$

$$\frac{v(q_1)}{q_1} + \frac{v(q_2) - v(q_1)}{q_2 - q_1} - 2v'(q_1) > 0\,. \tag{4.15}$$

For any q_1, $0 < q_1 \leqq \frac{1}{2}$, let $u_1(q_1)$ be the value of q_2 satisfying (4.14). The values of u_1 are shown graphically in Figure 2. It will be observed that u_1 is a monotone increasing function of q_1 with $u_1(0) = 0$ and $u_1(\frac{1}{2}) = 1$. In the case that $k = 1$, the condition for determining $\tilde{q}_1$ is given by (4.14) with $q_2 = 1$. But since u_1 is a single-valued monotone function of q, there is a unique inverse. For $k = 1$, therefore, $\tilde{q}_1 = u_1^{-1}(1) = \frac{1}{2}$.

Consider now the second equation of (4.13), namely,

$$\frac{v(q_2) - v(q_1)}{q_2 - q_1} + \frac{v(q_3) - v(q_2)}{q_3 - q_2} - 2v'(q_2) = 0\,. \tag{4.16}$$

For any pair of values $q_1, u_1(q_1)$ satisfying (4.14) with $0 < q_1 \leqq .27$, exactly one value of $q_3 = u_2(q_1) > u_1(q_1)$ satisfies (4.15). For values of $q_1 > .27$, no such value of q_3 exists. The values of u_2 are also shown graphically in Figure 2. Again it will be observed that u_2 is a monotone increasing function of q_1 with $u_2(0) = 0$ and $u_2(.27) = 1$.

In the case that $k = 2$, condition (4.16) holds with $q_3 = 1$. Thus, in this case, $\tilde{q}_1 = u_2^{-1}(1) = .27$ and $\tilde{q}_2 = u_1(.27) = .73$.

In a similar fashion, we find that for each succeeding value of j we have a function u_j of q_1 such that $q_1, u_1(q_1), \cdots, u_j(q_1)$ are a set of values of $q_1, \cdots, q_{j+1}$ satisfying the first j equations of conditions (4.13). For each j, u_j is a monotone increasing function of q_1, defined for $0 \leqq q_1 \leqq q_1^{(j)}$ with $q_1^{(j)} < q_1^{(j-1)}$, and such that $u_j(0) = 0$, $u_j(q_1^{(j)}) = 1$. In the case that $k = j$, the last equation of the set must be satisfied with $q_{j+1} = 1$. This means that for $k = j$, $\tilde{q}_1 = q_1^{(j)}$, $\tilde{q}_2 = u_1(q_1^{(j)})$, $\cdots$, and $\tilde{q}_j = u_{j-1}(q_1^{(j)})$.

It is easy to show that for each k, the values $\tilde{q}_1, \tilde{q}_2, \cdots, \tilde{q}_k$ are symmetric about $\frac{1}{2}$, that is $\tilde{q}_k = 1 - \tilde{q}_1$, $\tilde{q}_{k-1} = 1 - \tilde{q}_2, \cdots$. For consider any three values $q_{j-1} < q_j < q_{j+1}$, such that

$$\frac{v(q_j) - v(q_{j-1})}{q_j - q_{j-1}} + \frac{v(q_{j+1}) - v(q_j)}{q_{j+1} - q_j} - 2v'(q_j) = 0\,; \tag{4.17}$$

then, since $v(q) = v(1 - q)$ and $v'(q) = -v'(1 - q)$, we have

$$\frac{v(1 - q_j) - v(1 - q_{j+1})}{(1 - q_j) - (1 - q_{j+1})} + \frac{v(1 - q_{j-1}) - v(1 - q_j)}{(1 - q_{j-1}) - (1 - q_j)} - 2v'(1 - q_j) = 0\,. \tag{4.18}$$

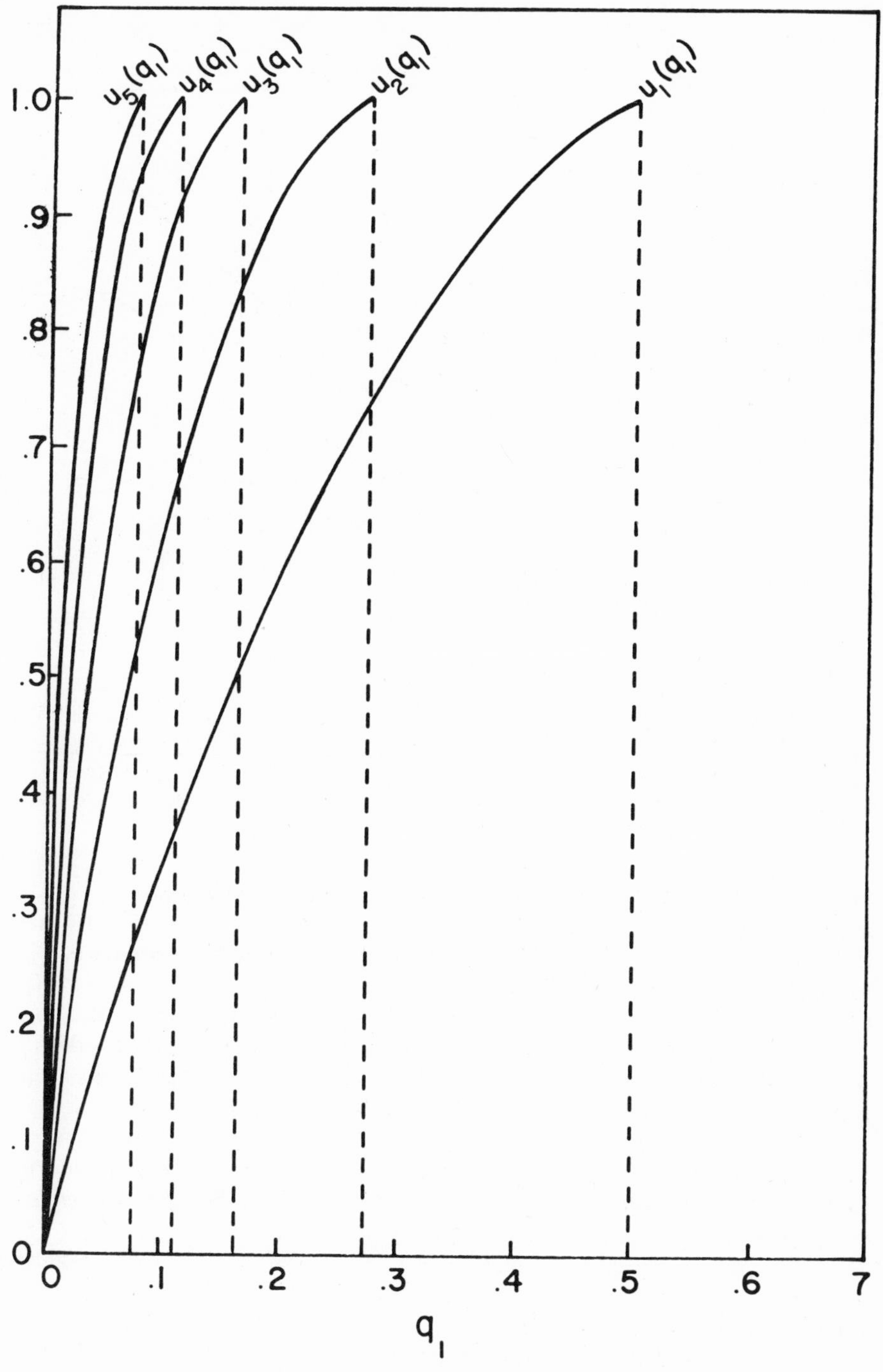

FIG. 2. Values of $u_j(q_1)$ for $j = 1(1)5$.

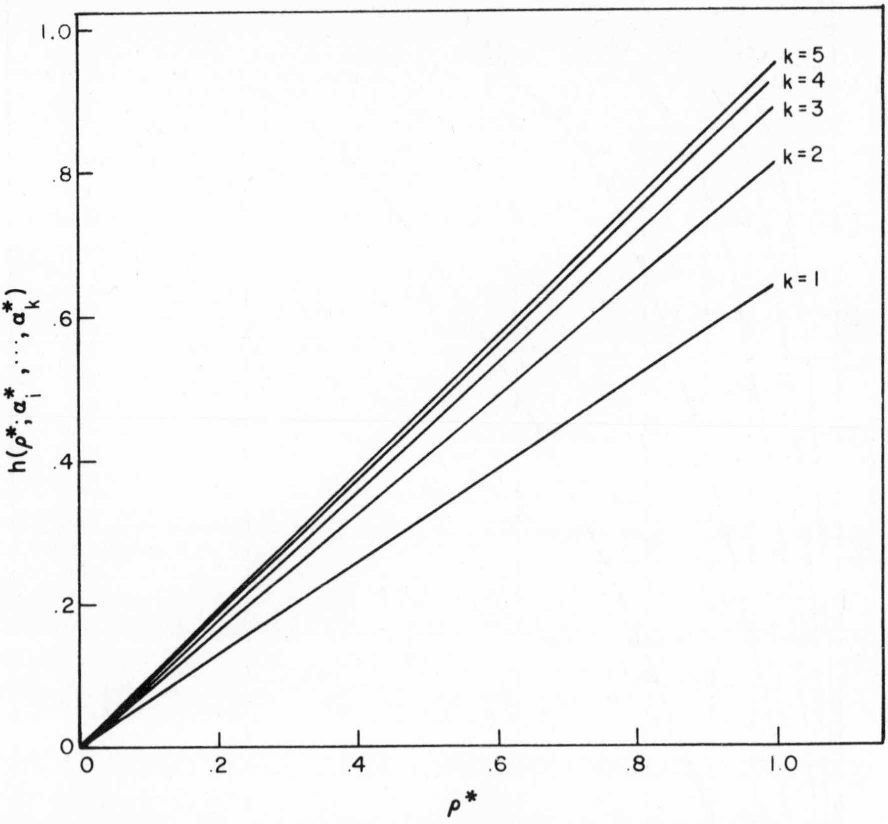

FIG. 3. Values of $h(\rho^*; \alpha_1^*, \cdots, \alpha_k^*) = \rho^* \Psi(\alpha_1^*, \cdots, \alpha_k^*)$ for $k = 1(1)5$.

Suppose now that k is even, i.e., $k = 2r$, and suppose that $q_1, u_1(q_1), \cdots, u_r(q_1)$ are the values of $q_1, \cdots, q_{r+1}$ satisfying the first r conditions of (4.13) such that $u_r(q_1) = 1 - u_{r-1}(q_1)$. Then, since (4.17) holds for the three values $u_{r-2}(q_1)$, $u_{r-1}(q_1)$, and $1 - u_{r-1}(q_1)$, the condition must also hold for $u_{r-1}(q_1)$, $1 - u_{r-1}(q_1)$, and $1 - u_{r-2}(q_1)$, that is, $u_{r+1}(q_1) = 1 - u_{r-2}(q_1)$. In turn, we find $u_{r+2}(q_1) = 1 - u_{r-3}(q_1), \cdots, u_{2r-1}(q_1) = 1 - q_1$, and $u_{2r}(q_1) = 1$. Similarly, if k is odd, i.e., $k = 2r + 1$, and $q_1, u_1(q_1), \cdots, u_r(q_r)$ are the values of $q_1, \cdots, q_{r+1}$ satisfying the first r conditions of (4.13) such that $u_r(q_r) = \frac{1}{2}$, then of necessity $u_{r+1}(q_1) = 1 - u_{r-1}(q_1), \cdots, u_{2r}(q_1) = 1 - q_1$, and $u_{2r+1}(q_1) = 1$.

That the values of $\tilde{q}_1, \cdots, \tilde{q}_k$ maximize Ψ can be seen by considering $\partial\Psi/\partial q_j$. For any fixed values $q_1, q_2, q_{j-1}, q_{j+1}, \cdots, q_k$, $\partial\Psi/\partial q_j$ is a monotone decreasing function of q_j, which is 0 for some point q_j', with $q_{j-1} < q_j' < q_{j+1}$. Thus, $\partial\Psi/\partial q_j$ considered as a function of q_j is positive for $q_j < q_j'$ and negative for $q_j > q_j'$. It follows that the set of values $\tilde{q}_1, \tilde{q}_2, \cdots, \tilde{q}_k$ are maximizing values.

Figure 2 shows values of the functions u_3, u_4, and u_5, in addition to those for u_1 and u_2 mentioned above. Thus, for a 5-item test the optimal item difficulties are

$$\begin{aligned} \tilde{q}_1 &= .074\,, &\quad \text{or} \quad \tilde{\alpha}_1 &= -1.447\,,\\ \tilde{q}_2 &= .255\,, & \tilde{\alpha}_2 &= -\ .659\,,\\ \tilde{q}_3 &= .500\,, & \tilde{\alpha}_3 &= \ 0\,,\\ \tilde{q}_4 &= .745\,, & \tilde{\alpha}_4 &= \ .659\,,\\ \tilde{q}_5 &= .926\,; & \tilde{\alpha}_5 &= \ 1.447\,. \end{aligned}$$

For these values $\Psi(-1.447, -.659, 0, .659, 1.447) = .9426$.

It will be recalled that for the test considered earlier, we had $\Psi(-2, -1, 0, 1, 2) = .9206$. For the optimal 4-item test, i.e., one with

$$\begin{aligned} \tilde{q}_1 &= .106\,, &\quad \text{or} \quad \tilde{\alpha}_1 &= -1.248\,,\\ \tilde{q}_2 &= .350\,, & \tilde{\alpha}_2 &= -\ .385\,,\\ \tilde{q}_3 &= .650\,, & \tilde{\alpha}_3 &= +\ .385\,,\\ \tilde{q}_4 &= .894\,; & \tilde{\alpha}_4 &= +1.248\,, \end{aligned}$$

we have $\Psi(-1.248, -.385, +.385, +1.248) = .9200$. Thus, the optimal 4-item test is almost as good as the 5-item test specified earlier.

In concluding our examination of this case, we present in Figure 3, for $k = 1(1)5$, values of $\rho^*\Psi$ as ρ^* increases from 0 to 1. Thus, for optimal choices of the item difficulties, we see that to attain an h-value of .6 for a one-item test requires a variable X whose correlation with Y is $\sqrt{.94} = .97$, while to attain this value with a 5-item test requires a variable whose correlation need be only $.80 = \sqrt{.64}$.

References

[1] Tucker, L. R. Maximum validity of a test with equivalent items. *Psychometrika,* 1946, **11**, 1–46.

[2] Lord, F. Theory of test scores and their relation to the trait measured. *Educational Testing Service Bulletin,* Princeton, 1951.

[3] Guttman, L. The quantification of a class of attributes: A theory and method for scale construction. In Horst, P., *et al., The Prediction of Personal Adjustment,* pp. 319–48. New York: Social Science Research Council, 1941.

[4] Blackwell, D., and Girshick, M. A. *Theory of Games and Statistical Decisions.* New York: Wiley, 1954.

3

Further Contributions to the Theory of Test Design

ROSEDITH SITGREAVES, Columbia University

1. Introduction

The general problem considered here and in the previous chapter is the following: A latent ability Y is regarded as a continuous chance variable with values y, $-\infty < y < \infty$, which are normally distributed with zero mean and unit variance among individuals in a population Π. It is necessary to make one of several possible decisions about an individual from Π, the preferred decision depending upon his y-value, which is unobservable. Consequently the decision for the individual is generally based on values of related and observable variables. Two questions naturally arise in such a situation: (1) How do we select the variables to be observed? and (2) How do we use the results of the observations to reach a decision?

In what follows, any potential observable is called a test item and any set of possible observables a test. An individual taking a test receives a score for his response to each item. We restrict ourselves here to the case in which each item response is scored dichotomously, for example, as either right or wrong. In comparing tests, that is, in evaluating various sets of possible observables, it is necessary to choose some operating characteristic of the test as a measure of worth in terms of which comparisons can be made. Some of these measures of worth, including the classical reliability and validity coefficients, have been discussed by Solomon in [1]. Here we shall investigate further the implications for test design of the measure proposed in the previous chapter.

There we suggested, as an intuitively reasonable solution to the second question raised above, that the results of a particular test be used to estimate the individual's y-value, and that the resulting decision be the one which would be made if the estimated value were the true value. It was also proposed that the estimation procedure adopted be the one for which

Supported by Grant C6118 from the National Science Foundation for psychometric research on the measurement of ability.

the expected squared error of the estimate is a minimum. For this procedure, some function of the minimum expected squared error seems a natural index of the goodness of the test. The suggested index was the number obtained by subtracting the minimum value from 1. This number increases as the expected squared error decreases, and, in this sense, larger values of the index represent "better" tests. Note that an expected squared error of 1 can always be attained if we estimate Y by its population mean of zero.

In the previous chapter a fairly restricted probability model was assumed to be operating between the observable item responses and the latent variable Y. Under the model, a test of k items was specified by k numbers $\alpha_1, \alpha_2, \cdots, \alpha_k$, related to the difficulty levels of the items, and one additional test parameter ρ^*. For a specified test, the desired estimate of Y and the value of the index were found to be functions of the $(k+1)$ test parameters. Properties of the index were examined, and optimizing parameter values were found.

In this chapter we consider a less restricted form of the probability model and obtain the desired estimate of Y and the value of the index for a specified test. Some implications for test design are examined, but the results generally involve integrals for the multivariate normal distribution for which tables are not available. Some comparisons between the present case and the restricted case of the previous chapter are made for tests of two items.

2. The Probability Model

Basic to the present discussion is the notion of a supply of test items from which items for a particular test can be drawn. Potentially, any k items, $k = 1, 2, \cdots$, can be taken from the supply and ordered from 1 to k to form a test. If the test is administered to an individual from Π, his k responses are scored dichotomously; for purposes of discussion we shall assume that each response is scored as right or wrong. For any selected set of items, that is, for any test, we have the (potentially) observable vector of item responses

$$V = \begin{pmatrix} S_1 \\ \vdots \\ S_k \end{pmatrix}, \tag{2.1}$$

where $S_g = 1$ if item g is answered correctly, and $S_g = 0$ if item g is answered incorrectly, $g = 1, 2, \cdots, k$. There are clearly 2^k values of the response vector V.

In postulating a probability model relating a set of test responses to the latent variable Y, we begin with assumptions similar to the assumptions of the previous chapter. Thus, we postulate a set of latent abilities $\mathfrak{X}$ such that each $X \in \mathfrak{X}$ is a continuous chance variable, normally distributed over Π with zero mean and unit variance. It is assumed that each $X \in \mathfrak{X}$ and Y are jointly normally distributed, and that among individuals for whom $Y = y$ any pair of variables from $\mathfrak{X}$ are independent. This is equivalent to assuming that any set of variables $X_1, X_2, \cdots, X_k$ from $\mathfrak{X}$ have a single factor structure, with Y as the sole common factor.

Consider now a k-item test with item variables $S_1, S_2, \cdots, S_k$. It is assumed that to answer item g correctly requires an ability $X_g \in \mathfrak{X}$ in an amount greater than a specified value $\alpha_g, g = 1, 2, \cdots, k$. Consequently, among individuals for whom $Y = y$

$$\Pr\{S_g = 1 \mid y\} = \Pr\{X_g > \alpha_g \mid y\} \qquad g = 1, 2, \cdots, k . \tag{2.2}$$

For an individual selected at random from Π

$$\Pr\{S_g = 1\} = \Pr\{X_g > \alpha_g\} \qquad g = 1, 2, \cdots, k . \tag{2.3}$$

The set of numbers

$$\boldsymbol{\alpha} = \begin{pmatrix} \alpha_1 \\ \vdots \\ \alpha_k \end{pmatrix} \tag{2.4}$$

is thus a set of item parameters related to the difficulty levels of the items.

So far, the assumptions of the model are similar to the assumptions made earlier. In Chapter 2, however, it was assumed that

$$X_1 = X_2 = \cdots = X_k = X . \tag{2.5}$$

That is, in the earlier model, it was assumed that all the test items were tapping the same latent ability from $\mathfrak{X}$. In the present model, we do not make this restriction. In fact, we assume specifically that each item is tapping a different latent ability from $\mathfrak{X}$.

Before we consider the implications of our assumptions for the joint distribution of Y and the observation vector V, it will be useful to introduce some symbols and to review some probability relations between Y and a selected set of variables from $\mathfrak{X}$. For any real number u, $-\infty < u < \infty$, let

$$\varphi_1(u) = \frac{\exp[-\frac{1}{2}u^2]}{\sqrt{2\pi}} \tag{2.6}$$

and

$$\Phi_1(u) = \int_{-\infty}^{u} \varphi_1(t)\, dt . \tag{2.7}$$

Also, for any n-dimensional vector of real numbers $\boldsymbol{u}$, and for any n-dimensional positive definite matrix Σ, let

$$\varphi_n(\boldsymbol{u} \mid \Sigma) = \frac{|\Sigma|^{-\frac{1}{2}} \exp[-\frac{1}{2}\boldsymbol{u}' \Sigma^{-1} \boldsymbol{u}]}{(2\pi)^{n/2}} \tag{2.8}$$

and

$$\Phi_n(\boldsymbol{u} \mid \Sigma) = \int_{-\infty}^{u_1} \cdots \int_{-\infty}^{u_n} \varphi_n(\boldsymbol{t} \mid \Sigma)\, dt_1 \cdots dt_n . \tag{2.9}$$

That is, φ_1 and φ_n are the univariate and multivariate normal densities, and Φ_1 and Φ_n are the integrals of these functions over the indicated regions. Note that if S is any region defined by

$$S = \{t_{i_1} < u_{i_1}, \cdots, t_{i_g} < u_{i_g}, t_{i_{g+1}} > u_{i_{g+1}}, \cdots, t_{i_n} > u_{i_n}\},$$

and if D is a diagonal matrix with

$$d_{i_\nu i_\nu} = 1, \quad \nu = 1, \cdots, g, \qquad d_{i_\nu i_\nu} = -1, \quad \nu = g+1, \cdots, n,$$

we have

$$\int_S \cdots \int \varphi_n(\boldsymbol{t} \mid \Sigma)\, dt_1 \cdots dt_n = \Phi_n(D\boldsymbol{u} \mid D\Sigma D'). \tag{2.10}$$

Let

$$\boldsymbol{\rho}^* = \begin{pmatrix} \rho^*_{1Y} \\ \vdots \\ \rho^*_{kY} \end{pmatrix} \tag{2.11}$$

denote the vector of correlations between the variables $X_1, X_2, \cdots, X_k$ from $\mathfrak{X}$ and Y, and let

$$R = \begin{bmatrix} 1 & \boldsymbol{\rho}^{*\prime} \\ \boldsymbol{\rho}^* & \boldsymbol{\rho}^*\boldsymbol{\rho}^{*\prime} + \Lambda \end{bmatrix} = \begin{bmatrix} 1 & \boldsymbol{\rho}^{*\prime} \\ \boldsymbol{\rho}^* & R^* \end{bmatrix}, \tag{2.12}$$

where

$$\Lambda = \begin{bmatrix} 1-\rho^{*2}_{1Y} & 0 & \cdots & 0 \\ 0 & 1-\rho^{*2}_{2Y} & \cdots & 0 \\ \vdots & \vdots & \vdots & \vdots \\ 0 & 0 & \cdots & 1-\rho^{*2}_{kY} \end{bmatrix}. \tag{2.13}$$

Then, for any value y of Y and any set of values

$$\boldsymbol{x} = \begin{pmatrix} x_1 \\ \vdots \\ x_k \end{pmatrix} \tag{2.14}$$

it follows from our assumptions that the joint density of $\boldsymbol{x}$ and y is given by

$$\begin{aligned} p(\boldsymbol{x}, y) &= p(\boldsymbol{x} \mid y)p(y) \\ &= \left[\prod_{g=1}^{k} \varphi_1\left(\frac{x_g - \rho^*_{gY}y}{\sqrt{1-\rho^{*2}_{gY}}}\right)(1-\rho^{*2}_{gY})^{-\frac{1}{2}}\right]\varphi_1(y) \\ &= \varphi_k(\boldsymbol{x} - \boldsymbol{\rho}^* y \mid \Lambda)\varphi_1(y) \\ &= \varphi_{k+1}\left(\begin{matrix}\boldsymbol{x} \\ y\end{matrix} \middle| R\right) \\ &= \varphi_k(\boldsymbol{x} \mid R^*)\varphi_1\left[\frac{y - \boldsymbol{\rho}^{*\prime}(R^*)^{-1}\boldsymbol{x}}{\sqrt{1-\boldsymbol{\rho}^{*\prime}R^{*-1}\boldsymbol{\rho}^*}}\right][1-\boldsymbol{\rho}^{*\prime}(R^*)^{-1}\boldsymbol{\rho}^*]^{-\frac{1}{2}}. \end{aligned} \tag{2.15}$$

Let us consider now the joint distribution of Y and

$$V = \begin{pmatrix} S_1 \\ \vdots \\ S_k \end{pmatrix}$$

for a test tapping the variables $X_1, X_2, \cdots, X_k$ from $\mathfrak{X}$. For a given value y of Y, we have

$$p(V \mid y) = \prod_{g=1}^{k} p(S_g \mid y) . \tag{2.16}$$

Since

$$\begin{aligned} p(S_g = 1 \mid y) &= \int_{\alpha_g}^{\infty} \varphi_1\left(\frac{x_g - \rho_{gY}^{*} y}{\sqrt{1 - \rho_{gY}^{*2}}}\right) \frac{dx_g}{\sqrt{1 - \rho_{gY}^{*2}}} \\ &= \Phi_1\left[(-1)\left(\frac{\alpha_g - \rho_{gY}^{*} y}{\sqrt{1 - \rho_{gY}^{*2}}}\right)\right], \end{aligned} \tag{2.17}$$

and

$$\begin{aligned} p(S_g = 0 \mid y) &= \int_{-\infty}^{\alpha_g} \varphi_1\left(\frac{x_g - \rho_{gY}^{*} y}{\sqrt{1 - \rho_{gY}^{*2}}}\right) \frac{dx_g}{\sqrt{1 - \rho_{gY}^{*2}}} \\ &= \Phi_1\left(\frac{\alpha_g - \rho_{gY}^{*} y}{\sqrt{1 - \rho_{gY}^{*2}}}\right), \end{aligned} \tag{2.18}$$

we can write

$$p(S_g \mid y) = \Phi_1\left[(-1)^{S_g}\left(\frac{\alpha_g - \rho_{gY}^{*} y}{\sqrt{1 - \rho_{gY}^{*2}}}\right)\right]. \tag{2.19}$$

It follows that

$$p(V \mid y) = \prod_{g=1}^{k} \Phi_1\left[(-1)^{S_g}\left(\frac{\alpha_g - \rho_{gY}^{*} y}{\sqrt{1 - \rho_{gY}^{*2}}}\right)\right]. \tag{2.20}$$

This expression for $p(V \mid y)$ can be given two other representations, which will also prove useful. Let D_V be the k-dimensional diagonal matrix with $(-1)^{S_g}$ as the gth diagonal element, $g = 1, \cdots, k$, and let D_V^{+} be the $(k+1)$-dimensional diagonal matrix defined by

$$D_V^{+} = \begin{bmatrix} 1 & 0 \\ 0 & D_V \end{bmatrix}.$$

Also, let S_V be the region in k-dimensional Euclidean space defined by

$$S_V = \{-\infty < x_1 < (-1)^{S_1}\alpha_1, \cdots, -\infty < x_k < (-1)^{S_k}\alpha_k\} .$$

Then

$$\begin{aligned} p(V \mid y) &= \prod_{g=1}^{k} \varphi_1\left[(-1)^{S_g}\left(\frac{\alpha_g - \rho_{gY}^{*} y}{\sqrt{1 - \rho_{gY}^{*2}}}\right)\right] \\ &= \int \cdots \int_{S_V} \varphi_k(\boldsymbol{x} - D_V \boldsymbol{\rho}^{*} y \mid \Lambda) \prod_{g=Y}^{k} dx_g \\ &= \Phi_k[D_V(\boldsymbol{\alpha} - \boldsymbol{\rho}^{*} y) \mid \Lambda] . \end{aligned} \tag{2.21}$$

Note that, since D_V is orthogonal and diagonal and Λ is diagonal, $D_V \Lambda D_V = \Lambda$.

Since

(2.22)
$$p(V, y) = p(V \mid y)\varphi_1(y)\,,$$

we have

(2.23)
$$\begin{aligned} p(V) &= \int_{-\infty}^{\infty} p(V \mid y)\varphi_1(y)\,dy \\ &= \int_{-\infty}^{\infty}\int \cdots \int_{S_V} \varphi_k(\boldsymbol{x} - D_V\boldsymbol{\rho}^* y \mid \Lambda)\varphi_1(y) \prod_{g=1}^{k} dx_g\,dy \\ &= \int \cdots \int_{S_V} \int_{-\infty}^{\infty} \varphi_{k+1}\left(\begin{matrix}\boldsymbol{x} \\ y\end{matrix} \mid D_V^+ R D_V^{+\prime}\right) \prod_{g=1}^{k} dx_g\,dy \\ &= \int \cdots \int_{S_V} \int \varphi_k(\boldsymbol{x} \mid D_V R^* D_V') \\ &\quad \cdot \int_{-\infty}^{\infty} \varphi_1\left(\frac{y - \boldsymbol{\rho}^{*\prime} R^{*-1} D_V' \boldsymbol{x}}{\sqrt{1 - \boldsymbol{\rho}^{*\prime} R^{*-1} \boldsymbol{\rho}^*}}\right) \frac{dy}{\sqrt{1 - \boldsymbol{\rho}^{*\prime} R^{*-1} \boldsymbol{\rho}^*}} \prod_{g=1}^{k} dx_g \\ &= \Phi_k(D_V \boldsymbol{\alpha} \mid D_V R^* D_V')\,. \end{aligned}$$

The matrix R^* [see Equations (2.12) and (2.13)] depends only on the vector $\boldsymbol{\rho}^*$. Under the assumptions of our model, therefore, a test is completely specified by the two vectors $\boldsymbol{\rho}^*$ and $\boldsymbol{\alpha}$. In the next section we shall determine the desired estimation procedure for Y, and the measure of worth for the test as functions of these $2k$ parameters. We denote by $\tilde{Y}$ the estimation procedure that minimizes the expected squared error of estimate, and by $g(\boldsymbol{\alpha}, \boldsymbol{\rho}^*)$ the index of worth for the test, namely, one minus the minimum expected squared error.

3. Determination of $\tilde{Y}$ and $g(\boldsymbol{\alpha}, \boldsymbol{\rho}^*)$

An estimation procedure $\hat{Y}$ for the latent variable Y is defined by 2^k numbers, one for each value of V such that Y is estimated by $\hat{y}_V$ when V is observed. The expected squared error of estimate associated with $\hat{Y}$ is

(3.1)
$$\sum_V \int_{-\infty}^{\infty} (\hat{y}_V - y)^2 p(V, y)\,dy\,.$$

The procedure $\tilde{Y}$, which minimizes (3.1), is given by (e.g., see [2], p. 299)

(3.2)
$$\begin{aligned} \tilde{y}_V &= \int_{-\infty}^{\infty} y p(y \mid V)\,dy \\ &= \frac{\int_{-\infty}^{\infty} y p(V, y)\,dy}{p(V)}\,. \end{aligned}$$

For our case, we write

(3.3)
$$\begin{aligned} \int_{-\infty}^{\infty} y p(V, y)\,dy &= \int_{-\infty}^{\infty} y \Phi_k[D_V(\boldsymbol{\alpha} - \boldsymbol{\rho}^* y) \mid \Lambda]\varphi_1(y)\,dy \\ &= -\,\Phi_k[D_V(\boldsymbol{\alpha} - \boldsymbol{\rho}^* y) \mid \Lambda]\varphi_1(y) \Big|_{y=-\infty}^{y=+\infty} \\ &\quad + \int_{-\infty}^{\infty} \frac{d}{dy} \varphi_k[D_V(\boldsymbol{\alpha} - \boldsymbol{\rho}^* y) \mid \Lambda]\varphi_1(y)\,dy\,. \end{aligned}$$

For any vector $\boldsymbol{u}$ let $\boldsymbol{u}_{[g]}$ be the vector derived from $\boldsymbol{u}$ by omitting the gth component, and for any square matrix U, let $U_{[g]}$ be the matrix derived from U by deleting the gth row and gth column. Similarly, for any region S_V [see Equation (2.20)], let

$$S_{V_{[g]}} = \{-\infty < x_1 < (-1)^{S_1}\alpha_1, \cdots, -\infty < x_{g-1} < (-1)^{S_{g-1}}\alpha_{g-1} \\ -\infty < x_{g+1} < (-1)^{S_{g+1}}\alpha_{g+1}, \cdots, -\infty < x_k (-1)^{S_k}\alpha_k\} . \tag{3.4}$$

Then

$$\begin{aligned} \frac{d}{dy}\Phi_k[D_V(\boldsymbol{\alpha} - \boldsymbol{\rho}^* y) \mid \Lambda] &= \frac{d}{dy}\prod_{g=1}^{k}\varphi_1\left[(-1)^{S_g}\left(\frac{\alpha_g - \rho^*_{gY} y}{\sqrt{1-\rho^{*2}_{gY}}}\right)\right] \\ &= -\sum_{g=1}^{k}\frac{(-1)^{S_g}\rho^*_{gY}}{\sqrt{1-\rho^{*2}_{gY}}}\varphi_1\left(\frac{\alpha_g - \rho^*_{gY} y}{\sqrt{1-\rho^{*2}_{gY}}}\right) \\ &\quad \cdot \prod_{h\neq g}\Phi_1\left[(-1)^{S_h}\left(\frac{\alpha_h - \rho^*_{hY} y}{\sqrt{1-\rho^{*2}_{hY}}}\right)\right] \\ &= -\sum_{g=1}^{k}\frac{(-1)^{S_g}\rho^*_{gY}}{\sqrt{1-\rho^{*2}_{gY}}}\varphi_1\left(\frac{\alpha_g - \rho^*_{gY} y}{\sqrt{1-\rho^{*2}_{gY}}}\right) \\ &\quad \cdot \Phi_{k-1}(D_{V_{[g]}}(\boldsymbol{\alpha}_{[g]} - \boldsymbol{\rho}^*_{[g]} y \mid \Lambda_{[g]}) . \end{aligned} \tag{3.5}$$

If we write [see Equation (2.12)]

$$\begin{aligned} R_{\cdot g} &= \begin{bmatrix} 1-\rho^{*2}_{gY} & (1-\rho^{*2}_{gY})\boldsymbol{\rho}^{*\prime}_{[g]} \\ (1-\rho^{*2}_{gY})\boldsymbol{\rho}^*_{[g]} & \Lambda_{[g]} + (1-\rho^{*2}_{gY})\boldsymbol{\rho}^*_{[g]}\boldsymbol{\rho}^{*\prime}_{[g]} \end{bmatrix} \\ &= \begin{bmatrix} 1-\rho^{*2}_{gY} & (1-\rho^{*2}_{gY})\boldsymbol{\rho}^{*\prime}_{[g]} \\ (1-\rho^{*2}_{gY})\boldsymbol{\rho}^*_{[g]} & R^*_{\cdot g} \end{bmatrix}, \end{aligned} \tag{3.6}$$

we have, from (3.5),

$$\begin{aligned} \int_{-\infty}^{\infty} y p(V, y)\, dy &= \int_{-\infty}^{\infty} -\sum_{g=1}^{k}\frac{(-1)^{S_g}\rho^*_{gY}}{\sqrt{1-\rho^{*2}_{gY}}}\varphi_1\left(\frac{\alpha_g - \rho^*_{gY} y}{\sqrt{1-\rho^{*2}_{gY}}}\right) \\ &\quad \cdot \Phi_{k-1}[D_{V_{[g]}}(\boldsymbol{\alpha}_{[g]} - \boldsymbol{\rho}^*_{[g]} y) \mid \Lambda_{[g]}]\varphi_1(y)\, dy \\ &= -\sum_{g=1}^{k}(-1)^{S_g}\rho^*_{gY}\varphi_1(\alpha_g) \\ &\quad \cdot \int_{-\infty}^{\infty}\int_{S_{V_{[g]}}}\cdots\int \varphi_{k-1}(\boldsymbol{x}_{[g]} - D_{V_{[g]}}\boldsymbol{\rho}^*_{[g]} y \mid \Lambda_{[g]}) \prod_{h\neq g} dx_h \\ &\quad \cdot \varphi_1\left(\frac{y - \rho^*_{gY}\alpha_g}{\sqrt{1-\rho^{*2}_{gY}}}\right)\frac{dy}{\sqrt{1-\rho^{*2}_{gY}}} \\ &= -\sum_{g=1}^{k}(-1)^{S_g}\rho^*_{gY}\varphi_1(\alpha_g)\int_{S_{V_{[g]}}}\cdots\int\int_{-\infty}^{\infty} \\ &\quad \cdot \varphi_{k-1}[\boldsymbol{x}_{[g]} - D_{V_{[g]}}\boldsymbol{\rho}^*_{[g]}\rho^*_{gY}\alpha_g - D_{V_{[g]}}\boldsymbol{\rho}^*_{[g]}(y - \rho^*_{gY} - \alpha_g) \mid \Lambda_{[g]}] \\ &\quad \cdot \varphi_1\left(\frac{y - \rho^*_{gY}\alpha_g}{\sqrt{1-\rho^{*2}_{gY}}}\right)\frac{dy}{\sqrt{1-\rho^{*2}_{gY}}}\prod_{h\neq g} dx_h \end{aligned} \tag{3.7}$$

$$= -\sum_{g=1}^{k}(-1)^{S_g}\rho_{gY}^{*}\varphi_1(\alpha_g)$$

$$\cdot \int_{S_{V_{[g]}}} \cdots \int_{-\infty}^{\infty} \varphi_k\left(\begin{matrix} \boldsymbol{x}_{[g]} - D_{V_{[g]}}\boldsymbol{\rho}_{[g]}^{*}\rho_{gY}^{*}\alpha_g \\ y - \rho_{gY}^{*}\alpha_g \end{matrix} \,\middle|\, D_{V_{[g]}}^{+} R_{\cdot g} D_{V_{[g]}}'\right)$$

$$\cdot\, dy \prod_{h \neq 1} dx_h$$

$$= -\sum_{g=1}^{k}(-1)^{S_g}\rho_{gY}^{*}\varphi_1(\alpha_g)$$

$$\cdot \int_{S_{V_{[g]}}} \cdots \int \varphi_{k-1}(\boldsymbol{x}_{[g]} - D_{V_{[g]}}\boldsymbol{\rho}_{[g]}^{*}\rho_{gY}^{*}\alpha_g \mid D_{V_{[g]}} R_{\cdot g}^{*} D_{V_{[g]}}')$$

$$\cdot \int_{-\infty}^{\infty} \varphi_1(t)\, dt \prod_{h \neq g} dx_h$$

$$= -\sum_{g=1}^{k}(-1)^{S_g}\rho_{gY}^{*}\varphi_1(\alpha_g)$$

$$\cdot\, \Phi_{k-1}[D_{V_{[g]}}(\boldsymbol{\alpha}_{[g]} - \boldsymbol{\rho}_{[g]}^{*}\rho_{gY}^{*}\alpha_g) \mid D_{V_{[g]}} R_{\cdot g}^{*} D_{V_{[g]}}'] \,.$$

It follows that the desired estimate is

$$(3.8) \qquad \tilde{y}_V = \frac{-1}{\Phi_k(D_V\boldsymbol{\alpha} \mid D_V R^* D_V')}\left\{\sum_{g=1}^{k}(-1)^{S_g}\rho_{gY}^{*}\varphi_1(\alpha_g) \cdot \Phi_{k-1}[D_{V_{[g]}}(\boldsymbol{\alpha}_{[g]} - \boldsymbol{\rho}_{[g]}^{*}\rho_{gY}^{*}\alpha_g) \mid D_{V_{[g]}} R_{\cdot g}^{*} D_{V_{[g]}}']\right\}.$$

The squared error of estimate is given by

$$(3.9) \qquad E(y - \tilde{y}_V)^2 = \sum_V \int_{-\infty}^{\infty} (y - \tilde{y}_V)^2 p(V, y)\, dy$$

$$= \sum_V \int_{-\infty}^{\infty} y^2 p(V, y)\, dy - 2\sum_V \tilde{y}_V \int_{-\infty}^{\infty} y p(V, y)\, dy + \sum_V \tilde{y}_V^2 \int_{-\infty}^{\infty} p(V, y)\, dy$$

$$= 1 - \sum_V \tilde{y}_V^2 p(V)\,.$$

Consequently

$$(3.10) \qquad g(\boldsymbol{\alpha}, \boldsymbol{\rho}^*) = \sum_V \frac{1}{\Phi_k(D_V\boldsymbol{\alpha} \mid D_V R^* D_V')}\left\{\sum_{g=1}^{k}(-1)^{S_g}\rho_{gY}^{*}\varphi_1(\alpha_g) \cdot \Phi_{k-1}[D_{V_{[g]}}(\boldsymbol{\alpha}_{[g]} - \boldsymbol{\rho}_{[g]}^{*}\rho_{gY}^{*}\alpha_g) \mid D_{V_{[g]}} R_{\cdot g}^{*} D_{V_{[g]}}']\right\}^2.$$

Note that [see (2.21), (2.23), (3.5), and (3.6)]

$$(3.11) \qquad \frac{\partial \Phi_k(D_V\boldsymbol{\alpha} \mid D_V R D_V')}{\partial \alpha_g} = \int_{-\infty}^{\infty} \frac{(-1)^{S_g}}{\sqrt{1 - \rho_{gY}^{*2}}}\,\varphi_1\!\left(\frac{\alpha_g - \rho_{gY}^{*} y}{\sqrt{1 - \rho_{gY}^{*2}}}\right) \cdot \prod_{h \neq g} \Phi_1\!\left[(-1)^{S_h}\left(\frac{\alpha_h - \rho_{hY}^{*} y}{\sqrt{1 - \rho_{hY}^{*2}}}\right)\right]\varphi_1(y)\, dy$$

$$= (-1)^{S_g}\varphi_1(\alpha_g)\Phi_{k-1}[D_{V_{[g]}}(\boldsymbol{\alpha}_{[g]} - \boldsymbol{\rho}_{[g]}^{*}\rho_{gY}^{*}\alpha_g) \mid \cdot\, D_{V_{[g]}} R_{\cdot g}^{*} D_{V_{[g]}}'] \,.$$

Hence we can write

$$\tilde{y}_V = \frac{-\sum \rho^*_{gY} \dfrac{\partial \Phi_k(D_V \boldsymbol{\alpha} \mid D_V R^* D'_V)}{\partial \alpha_g}}{\Phi_k(D_V \boldsymbol{\alpha} \mid D_V R^* D'_V)}, \tag{3.12}$$

and

$$g(\boldsymbol{\alpha}, \boldsymbol{\rho}^*) = \sum_V \frac{\left[\sum_{g=1}^{h} \rho^*_{gY} \dfrac{\partial \Phi_k}{\partial \alpha_g}(D_V \boldsymbol{\alpha} \mid D_V R^* D'_V)\right]^2}{\Phi_k(D_V \boldsymbol{\alpha} \mid D_V R^* D'_V)}. \tag{3.13}$$

When $k = 1$, we have two values for V, namely $V_1 = (0)$ and $V_2 = (1)$. In this case

$$\tilde{y}_1 = \frac{-\rho^*_{1Y} \varphi_1(\alpha_1)}{\Phi_1(\alpha_1)}, \tag{3.14}$$

and

$$\tilde{y}_2 = \frac{\rho^*_{1Y} \varphi_1(\alpha_1)}{\Phi_1(-\alpha_1)}. \tag{3.15}$$

The quantities $[-\varphi_1(\alpha_1)]/[\Phi_1(\alpha_1)]$ and $[\varphi_1(\alpha_1)]/[\Phi_1(-\alpha_1)]$ are the usual estimates for the dichotomized normal variable X_1. The corresponding estimates for Y are essentially estimating the regression of Y on X.

In the case $k = 2$, we have

$$\boldsymbol{\alpha} = \begin{bmatrix} \alpha_1 \\ \alpha_2 \end{bmatrix} \quad \boldsymbol{\rho}^* = \begin{bmatrix} \rho^*_{1Y} \\ \rho^*_{2Y} \end{bmatrix}, \tag{3.16}$$

with (see 2.12)

$$R = \begin{bmatrix} 1 & \rho^*_{1Y} & \rho^*_{2Y} \\ \rho^*_{1Y} & 1 & \rho^*_{1Y}\rho^*_{2Y} \\ \rho^*_{2Y} & \rho^*_{1Y}\rho^*_{2Y} & 1 \end{bmatrix}. \tag{3.17}$$

There are four possible values of the response vector V, i.e.,

$$V_1 = \begin{bmatrix} 0 \\ 0 \end{bmatrix}, \qquad V_2 = \begin{bmatrix} 0 \\ 1 \end{bmatrix}, \qquad V_3 = \begin{bmatrix} 1 \\ 0 \end{bmatrix}, \qquad V_4 = \begin{bmatrix} 1 \\ 1 \end{bmatrix}.$$

Correspondingly, we have

$$D_{V_1} = \begin{bmatrix} 1 & 0 \\ 0 & 1 \end{bmatrix}, \qquad D_{V_2} = \begin{bmatrix} 1 & 0 \\ 0 & -1 \end{bmatrix},$$

$$D_{V_3} = \begin{bmatrix} -1 & 0 \\ 0 & 1 \end{bmatrix}, \qquad D_{V_4} = \begin{bmatrix} -1 & 0 \\ 0 & -1 \end{bmatrix}.$$

If we write $\rho^*_{1Y}\rho^*_{2Y} = \rho^*$, our estimates of Y are

$$\tilde{y}_{V_1} = \frac{-\rho^*_{1Y}\varphi_1(\alpha_1)\Phi_1\left(\dfrac{\alpha_2 - \rho^*\alpha_1}{\sqrt{1-\rho^{*2}}}\right) - \rho^*_{2Y}\varphi_1(\alpha_2)\Phi_1\left(\dfrac{\alpha_1 - \rho^*\alpha_2}{\sqrt{1-\rho^{*2}}}\right)}{\Phi_2(D_{V_1}\boldsymbol{\alpha} \mid D_{V_1} R^* D'_{V_1}}, \tag{3.18}$$

$$\tilde{y}_{V_2} = \frac{-\rho_{1Y}^*\varphi_1(\alpha_1)\Phi_1\left(\frac{-(\alpha_2 - \rho^*\alpha_1)}{\sqrt{1-\rho^{*2}}}\right) + \rho_{2Y}^*\varphi_1(\alpha_2)\Phi_1\left(\frac{\alpha_1 - \rho^*\alpha_2}{\sqrt{1-\rho^{*2}}}\right)}{\Phi_2(D_{V_2}\boldsymbol{\alpha} \mid D_{V_2}R^*D'_{V_2})},$$

$$\tilde{y}_{V_3} = \frac{\rho_{1Y}^*\varphi_1(\alpha_1)\Phi_1\left(\frac{\alpha_2 - \rho^*\alpha_1}{\sqrt{1-\rho^{*2}}}\right) - \rho_{2Y}^*\varphi_1(\alpha_2)\Phi_1\left(\frac{-(\alpha_1 - \rho^*\alpha_2)}{\sqrt{1-\rho^{*2}}}\right)}{\Phi_2(D_{V_3}\boldsymbol{\alpha} \mid D_{V_3}R^*D'_{V_3})},$$

$$\tilde{y}_{V_4} = \frac{\rho_{1Y}^*\varphi_1(\alpha_1)\Phi_1\left(\frac{-(\alpha_2 - \rho^*\alpha_1)}{\sqrt{1-\rho^{*2}}}\right) + \rho_{2Y}^*\varphi_1(\alpha_2)\Phi_1\left(\frac{-(\alpha_1 - \rho^*\alpha_2)}{\sqrt{1-\rho^{*2}}}\right)}{\Phi_2(D_{V_4}\boldsymbol{\alpha} \mid D_{V_4}R^*D'_{V_4})}.$$

In general, it can be shown that our estimation procedure for Y is equivalent to obtaining minimum variance estimates for $X_1, \cdots, X_k$ and using these estimates in the multiple regression of Y on $X_1, X_2, \cdots, X_k$. This relation is also seen if we rewrite Equation (3.3) as

$$(3.19) \qquad \int_{-\infty}^{\infty} y p(V, y)\, dy$$

$$= \int_{-\infty}^{\infty} y \int_{S_V} \cdots \int \varphi_k(\boldsymbol{x} - D_V\boldsymbol{\rho}^* y \mid \Lambda) \prod_{g=1}^{h} dx_g\, \varphi_1(y)\, dy$$

$$= \int_{S_V} \cdots \int \varphi_k(\boldsymbol{x} \mid D_V R^* D'_V) \int_{-\infty}^{\infty} y\varphi_1\left(\frac{y - \boldsymbol{\rho}^{*\prime}R^{*-1}D'_V\boldsymbol{x}}{\sqrt{1 - \boldsymbol{\rho}^{*\prime}R^{*-1}\boldsymbol{\rho}^*}}\right) \cdot \frac{dy}{\sqrt{1 - \boldsymbol{\rho}^{*\prime}R^{*-1}\boldsymbol{\rho}^*}} \prod_{g=1}^{h} dx_g$$

$$= \int_{S_V} \cdots \int \boldsymbol{\rho}^{*\prime}R^{*-1}D'_V\boldsymbol{x}\varphi_k(\boldsymbol{x} \mid D_V R^* D'_V) \prod_{g=1}^{k} dx_g .$$

4. Optimal Values of $g(\boldsymbol{\alpha}, \boldsymbol{\rho}^*)$

In terms of our model, a k-item test is specified by the two vectors $\boldsymbol{\alpha}$ and $\boldsymbol{\rho}^*$. For a specified test, the estimation procedure for Y that minimizes the expected squared error of estimate is given by (3.8); the index of worth for the test, i. e., $g(\boldsymbol{\alpha}, \boldsymbol{\rho}^*)$, is given by (3.10).

Theoretically, the various possible test designs for a k-item test are generated by the various possible combinations of the vectors $\boldsymbol{\rho}^*$ and $\boldsymbol{\alpha}$. In practice, although the selection of the vector $\boldsymbol{\alpha}$ or, equivalently, the determination of the item difficulties, is generally at our disposal, we may frequently be limited in the values of $\boldsymbol{\rho}^*$ that can be attained. In considering possible test designs, therefore, we shall limit ourselves for the present to the problem of determining the value of $\boldsymbol{\alpha}$ that maximizes $g(\boldsymbol{\alpha}, \boldsymbol{\rho}^*)$ for a given vector $\boldsymbol{\rho}^*$.

We have seen earlier that

$$(4.1) \qquad g(\boldsymbol{\alpha}, \boldsymbol{\rho}^*) = \sum_V \frac{\left[\sum_{g=1}^{k} \rho_{gY}^* \frac{\partial \Phi_k(D_V\boldsymbol{\alpha} \mid D_V R^* D'_V)}{\partial \alpha_g}\right]^2}{\Phi_k(D_V\boldsymbol{\alpha} \mid D_V R^* D'_V)}.$$

Formally, the maximizing values $\alpha_1, \alpha_2, \cdots, \alpha_k$ satisfy the k equations

$$\frac{\partial g(\boldsymbol{\alpha}, \boldsymbol{\rho}^*)}{\partial \alpha_\nu} = 0 \qquad \nu = 1, 2, \cdots, k\,. \tag{4.2}$$

Remembering that

$$\tilde{y}_V = \frac{-\sum_{g=1}^{k} \rho_{gY}^* \dfrac{\partial \Phi_k(D_V\boldsymbol{\alpha} \mid D_V R^* D_V')}{\partial \alpha_g}}{\Phi_k(D_V\boldsymbol{\alpha} \mid D_V R^* D_V')}\,,$$

we have from (4.1)

$$\begin{aligned}\frac{\partial g(\boldsymbol{\alpha}, \boldsymbol{\rho}^*)}{\partial \alpha_\nu} = &-2\sum_V \left(\sum_{g=1}^{k} \rho_{gY}^* \frac{\partial^2 \Phi_k(D_V\boldsymbol{\alpha} \mid D_V R^* D_V')}{\partial \alpha_g \partial \alpha_\nu} \right) \tilde{y}_V \\ &- \sum_V \frac{\partial \Phi_k(D_V\boldsymbol{\alpha} \mid D_V R^* D_V')}{\partial \alpha_\nu} \tilde{y}_V^2\,.\end{aligned} \tag{4.3}$$

Now,

$$\begin{aligned}&\sum_{g=1}^{k} \rho_{gY}^* \frac{\partial^2 \Phi_k(D_V\boldsymbol{\alpha} \mid D_V R^* D_V')}{\partial \alpha_g \partial \alpha_\nu} \\ &\quad = \sum_{g=1}^{k} \rho_{gY}^* \frac{\partial}{\partial \alpha_\nu} \int_{-\infty}^{\infty} \frac{(-1)^{S_g}}{\sqrt{1-\rho_{gY}^{*2}}} \varphi_1\left(\frac{\alpha_g - \rho_{gY}^* y}{\sqrt{1-\rho_{gY}^{*2}}} \right) \\ &\qquad \cdot \prod_{h \neq g} \Phi_1(-1)^{S_h} \left(\frac{\alpha_h - \rho_{hY}^* y}{\sqrt{1-\rho_{hY}^{*2}}} \right) \varphi_1(y)\, dy\,.\end{aligned} \tag{4.4}$$

For $g = \nu$

$$\begin{aligned}&\frac{\partial}{\partial \alpha_\nu} \int_{-\infty}^{\infty} \frac{(-1)^{S_\nu}}{\sqrt{1-\rho_{\nu Y}^{*2}}} \varphi_1\left(\frac{\alpha_\nu - \rho_{\nu Y}^* y}{\sqrt{1-\rho_{\nu Y}^{*2}}} \right) \prod_{h \neq \nu} \Phi_1\left[(-1)^{S_h} \left(\frac{\alpha_h - \rho_{hY}^* y}{\sqrt{1-\rho_{hY}^{*2}}} \right) \right] \varphi_1(y)\, dy \\ &\quad = -\int_{-\infty}^{\infty} (-1)^{S_\nu} \frac{(\alpha_\nu - \rho_{\nu Y}^* y)}{(1-\rho_{\nu Y}^{*2})^{3/2}} \varphi_1\left(\frac{\alpha_\nu - \rho_{\nu Y}^* y}{\sqrt{1-\rho_{\nu Y}^{*2}}} \right) \\ &\qquad \cdot \prod_{h \neq \nu} \Phi_1\left[(-1)^{S_h} \left(\frac{\alpha_h - \rho_{hY}^* y}{\sqrt{1-\rho_{hY}^{*2}}} \right) \right] \varphi_1(y)\, dy \\ &\quad = -\alpha_\nu \int_{-\infty}^{\infty} \frac{(-1)^{S_\nu}}{\sqrt{1-\rho_{\nu Y}^{*2}}} \varphi_1\left(\frac{\alpha_\nu - \rho_{\nu Y}^* y}{\sqrt{1-\rho_{\nu Y}^{*2}}} \right) \\ &\qquad \cdot \prod_{h \neq \nu} \Phi_1\left[(-1)^{S_h} \left(\frac{\alpha_h - \rho_{hY}^* y}{\sqrt{1-\rho_{hY}^{*2}}} \right) \right] \varphi_1(y)\, dy \\ &\qquad + \int_{-\infty}^{\infty} (-1)^{S_\nu} \frac{\rho_{\nu Y}^* (y - \rho_{\nu Y}^* \alpha_\nu)}{(1-\rho_{\nu Y}^{*2} y)^{3/2}} \varphi_1(\alpha_\nu) \varphi_1\left(\frac{y - \rho_{\nu Y}^* \alpha_\nu}{\sqrt{1-\rho_{\nu Y}^{*2}}} \right) \\ &\qquad \cdot \prod_{h \neq \nu} \Phi_1\left[(-1)^{S_h} \left(\frac{\alpha_h - \rho_{hY}^* y}{\sqrt{1-\rho_{hY}^{*2}}} \right) \right] dy \\ &\quad = -\alpha_\nu \frac{\partial \Phi_k(D_V\boldsymbol{\alpha} \mid D_V R^* D_V')}{\partial \alpha_\nu} - \frac{(-1)^{S_\nu} \rho_{\nu Y}^* \varphi_1(\alpha_\nu)}{\sqrt{1-\rho_{\nu Y}^{*2}}} \varphi_1\left(\frac{y - \rho_{\nu Y}^* \alpha_\nu}{\sqrt{1-\rho_{\nu Y}^{*2}}} \right) \\ &\qquad \cdot \prod_{h \neq \nu} \Phi_1\left[(-1)^{S_h} \left(\frac{\alpha_h - \rho_{hY}^*}{\sqrt{1-\rho_{hY}^{*2}}} \right) \right]_{y=-\infty}^{y=+\infty}\end{aligned} \tag{4.5}$$

$$-\int_{-\infty}^{\infty}\sum_{g\neq\nu}\frac{(-1)^{S_\nu+S_g}\rho_{\nu Y}^{*}\rho_{gY}^{*}\varphi_1(\alpha_\nu)}{\sqrt{(1-\rho_{\nu Y}^{*2})(1-\rho_{gY}^{*2})}}\varphi_1\left(\frac{y-\rho_{\nu Y}^{*}\alpha_\nu}{\sqrt{1-\rho_{\nu Y}^{*2}}}\right)$$

$$\cdot\varphi_1\left(\frac{\alpha_g-\rho_{gY}^{*}}{\sqrt{1-\rho_{gY}^{*2}}}\right)\prod_{h\neq g,\nu}\Phi_1\left[(-1)^{S_h}\left(\frac{\alpha_h-\rho_{hY}^{*}y}{\sqrt{1-\rho_{hY}^{*2}}}\right)\right]dy$$

$$=-\alpha_\nu\frac{\partial\Phi_k(D_V\boldsymbol{\alpha}\mid D_VR^*D_V'}{\partial\alpha_\nu}$$

$$-\sum_{g\neq\nu}\int_{-\infty}^{\infty}\frac{(-1)^{S_\nu+S_g}\rho_{\nu Y}^{*}\rho_{gY}^{*}\varphi_1(\alpha_\nu)}{\sqrt{(1-\rho_{\nu Y}^{*2})(1-\rho_{gY}^{*2})}}\varphi_1\left(\frac{\alpha_g-\rho_{\nu Y}^{*}\rho_{gY}^{*}\alpha_\nu}{\sqrt{1-\rho_{\nu Y}^{*2}\rho_{gY}^{*2}}}\right)$$

$$\cdot\varphi_1\left\{\frac{\sqrt{1-\rho_{\nu Y}^{*2}\rho_{gY}^{*2}}}{(1-\rho_{\nu Y}^{*2})(1-\rho_{gY}^{*2})}\,\frac{\{y-[\rho_{\nu Y}^{*}(1-\rho_{gY}^{*})\alpha_\nu+\rho_{gY}^{*}(1-\rho_{\nu Y}^{*})\alpha_g]\}}{1-\rho_{\nu Y}^{*2}\rho_{gY}^{*2}}\right\}$$

$$\cdot\prod_{h\neq g,\nu}\Phi_1\left[(-1)^{S_h}\left(\frac{\alpha_h-\rho_{hY}^{*}y}{\sqrt{1-\rho_{hY}^{*2}}}\right)\right]dy\,.$$

For any vector $\boldsymbol{u}$ let $\boldsymbol{u}_{[\nu,g]}$ be the vector derived from $\boldsymbol{u}$ by omitting the νth and gth components, and for any matrix U let $U_{[\nu,g]}$ be the matrix derived from U by deleting the νth and gth rows and the νth and gth columns. Also, for any region S_V [see Equations (2.20) and (3.4)] let

$$\text{(4.6)}\quad S_{V[\nu,g]}=[-\infty<x_1<(-1)^{S_1}\alpha_1,\cdots,-\infty<x_{\nu-1}<(-1)^{S_{\nu-1}}\alpha_{\nu-1}$$
$$-\infty<x_{\nu+1}<(-1)^{S_{\nu+1}}\alpha_{\nu+1},\cdots,-\infty<x_{g-1}<(-1)^{S_{g-1}}\alpha_{g-1}$$
$$-\infty<x_{g+1}<(-1)^{S_{g+1}}\alpha_{g+1},\cdots,-\infty<x_k<(-1)^{S_k}\alpha_k]\,.$$

Further, let

$$\text{(4.7)}\qquad \boldsymbol{\alpha}_{\nu,g}=\begin{bmatrix}\alpha_\nu\\ \alpha_g\end{bmatrix}\qquad \boldsymbol{\rho}_{\nu,g}^{*}=\begin{bmatrix}\rho_{\nu Y}^{*}\\ \rho_{gY}^{*}\end{bmatrix},$$

$$R_{\nu g}^{*}=\begin{bmatrix}1 & \rho_{\nu Y}^{*}\rho_{gY}^{*}\\ \rho_{\nu Y}^{*}\rho_{gY}^{*} & 1\end{bmatrix},$$

$$R_{.\nu g}^{*}=R_{[\nu,g]}^{*}-\boldsymbol{\rho}_{[\nu,g]}^{*}\boldsymbol{\rho}_{\nu,g}^{*\prime}R_{\nu g}^{*-1}\boldsymbol{\rho}_{[\nu,g]}^{*}\boldsymbol{\rho}_{[\nu,g]}^{*\prime}\,.$$

In terms of the variables $X_1, X_2, \cdots, X_k$, $R_{g\nu}^{*}$ is the covariance matrix of the marginal distribution of X_ν and X_g; $R_{.\nu g}^{*}$ is the covariance matrix of the conditional distribution of $X_1,\cdots,X_{\nu-1}$, $X_{\nu+1},\cdots,X_{g-1}$, $X_{g+1},\cdots,X_k$, given X_ν and X_g.

Then

$$\text{(4.8)}\qquad \frac{\partial^2\Phi_k(D_V\boldsymbol{\alpha}\mid D_VR^*D_V')}{\partial\alpha_\nu^2}$$

$$=-\alpha_\nu\frac{\partial\Phi_k(D_V\boldsymbol{\alpha}\mid D_VR^*D_V')}{\partial\alpha_\nu}-\sum_{g\neq\nu}(-1)^{S_\nu+S_g}\rho_{\nu Y}^{*}\rho_{gY}^{*}\varphi_2(\boldsymbol{\alpha}_{\nu,g}\mid R_{\nu g}^{*})$$

$$\cdot\int_{-\infty}^{\infty}\int_{S_{V[\nu,g]}}\cdots\int\varphi_1\left\{\left(1+\frac{\rho_{\nu Y}^{*2}}{1-\rho_{\nu Y}^{*2}}+\frac{\rho_{gY}^{*2}}{1-\rho_{gY}^{*2}}\right)^{\frac{1}{2}}\left[y-\frac{\left(\frac{\rho_{\nu Y}^{*}}{1-\rho_{\nu Y}^{*2}}\alpha_\nu+\frac{\rho_{gY}^{*}}{1-\rho_{gY}^{*2}}\alpha_g\right)}{1+\frac{\rho_{\nu Y}^{*2}}{1-\rho_{\nu Y}^{*2}}+\frac{\rho_{gY}^{*2}}{1-\rho_{gY}^{*2}}}\right]\right\}$$

$$\cdot \varphi_{k-2}(\boldsymbol{x}_{[\nu,g]} - D_{V[\nu,g]}\boldsymbol{\rho}^*_{[\nu,g]}\, y \mid \Lambda_{[\nu,g]}) \prod_{h\neq\nu,g} dx_h$$

$$\cdot \left(1 + \frac{\rho^{*2}_{\nu Y}}{1-\rho^{*2}_{\nu Y}} + \frac{\rho^{*2}_{gY}}{1-\nu\rho^{*2}_{gY}}\right)^{\frac{1}{2}} dy$$

$$= -\alpha_\nu \frac{\partial \Phi_k(D_V\boldsymbol{\alpha} \mid D_V R^* D'_V)}{\partial \alpha_\nu} - \sum_{g\neq\nu} (-1)^{S_\nu + S_g} \rho^*_{\nu Y}\rho^*_{gY}\varphi_2(\boldsymbol{\alpha}_{\nu,g} \mid R^*_{\nu g})$$

$$\cdot \int_{S_{V[\nu,g]}} \cdots \int \varphi_{k-2}(\boldsymbol{x}_{[\nu,g]} - D_{V[\nu,g]}\boldsymbol{\rho}^*_{[\nu,g]}\boldsymbol{\rho}^{*\prime}_{[\nu,g]}\boldsymbol{\alpha}_{\nu,g} \mid D_{V[\nu,g]} R^*_{\cdot\nu g} D_{V[\nu,g]})$$

$$\cdot \int_{-\infty}^{\infty} \varphi_1 \left\{ \left(1 + \sum_{h=1}^{k} \frac{\rho^{*2}_{hY}}{1-\rho^{*2}_{hY}}\right)^{\frac{1}{2}} \left[y - \frac{\left(\frac{\rho^*_{\nu Y}\alpha_\nu}{1-\rho^{*2}_{\nu Y}} + \frac{\rho^*_{gY}\alpha_g}{1-\rho^{*2}_{gY}} + \sum_{h\neq\nu,g} \frac{\rho^*_{hY}x_h}{1-\rho^{*2}_{hY}}\right)}{1 + \sum_{h=1}^{k} \frac{\rho^{*2}_{hY}}{1-\rho^{*2}_{hY}}} \right] \right\}$$

$$\cdot \left(1 + \sum_{h=1}^{k} \frac{\rho^{*2}_{hY}}{1-\rho^{*2}_{hY}}\right)^{\frac{1}{2}} dy \prod_{h\neq\nu g} dx_h$$

$$= -\alpha_\nu \frac{\partial \Phi_k(D_V\boldsymbol{\alpha} \mid D_V R^* D'_V)}{\partial \alpha_\nu} - \sum_{g\neq\nu} (-1)^{S_\nu + S_g} \rho^*_{\nu Y}\rho^*_{gY}\varphi_2(\boldsymbol{\alpha}_{\nu,g} \mid R^*_{\nu g})$$

$$\cdot \Phi_{k-2}[D_{V[\nu,g]}(\boldsymbol{\alpha}_{[\nu,g]} - \boldsymbol{\rho}^*_{[\nu,g]}\boldsymbol{\rho}^{*\prime}_{\nu,g} R^{*-1}_{\nu g}\boldsymbol{\alpha}_{\nu,g}) \mid D_{V[\nu,g]} R^*_{\cdot\nu g} D'_{V[\nu,g]}]\,.$$

For $g \neq \nu$

$$\text{(4.9)} \quad \frac{\partial}{\partial\alpha_\nu} \int_{-\infty}^{\infty} \frac{(-1)^{S_g}}{\sqrt{1-\rho^{*2}_{gY}}} \varphi_1\left(\frac{\alpha_g - \rho^*_{gY}y}{\sqrt{1-\rho^{*2}_{gY}}}\right) \prod_{h\neq g} \Phi_1\left[(-1)^{S_h}\left(\frac{\alpha_h - \rho^*_{hY}y}{\sqrt{1-\rho^{*2}_{hY}}}\right)\right] \varphi_1(y)\, dy$$

$$= \int_{-\infty}^{\infty} \frac{(-1)^{S_\nu + S_g}}{\sqrt{(1-\rho^{*2}_{\nu Y})(1-\rho^{*2}_{gY})}} \varphi_1\left(\frac{\alpha_g - \rho^*_{gY}y}{\sqrt{1-\rho^{*2}_{gY}}}\right) \varphi_1\left(\frac{\alpha_\nu - \rho^*_{\nu Y}y}{\sqrt{1-\rho^{*2}_{\nu Y}}}\right)$$

$$\cdot \prod_{h\neq\nu,g} \Phi_1\left[(-1)^{S_h}\left(\frac{\alpha_h - \rho^*_{hY}y}{\sqrt{1-\rho^{*2}_{hY}}}\right)\right] \varphi_1(y)\, dy$$

$$= (-1)^{S_\nu + S_g}\varphi_2(\boldsymbol{\alpha}_{\nu,g} \mid R^*_{\nu g})$$

$$\cdot\, \Phi_{k-2}[D_{V[\nu,g]}(\boldsymbol{\alpha}_{[\nu,g]} - \boldsymbol{\rho}^*_{[\nu,g]}\boldsymbol{\rho}^{*\prime}_{\nu,g} R^{*-1}_{\nu g}\boldsymbol{\alpha}_{\nu,g}) \mid D_{V[\nu,g]} R^*_{\cdot\nu g} D_{V[\nu,g]}]\,.$$

Combining (4.8) and (4.9), we have

$$\text{(4.10)} \quad \sum_{g=1}^{k} \rho^*_{gY} \frac{\partial^2 \Phi_k(D_V\boldsymbol{\alpha} \mid D_V R^* D'_V)}{\partial\alpha_g \partial\alpha_\nu}$$

$$= -\rho^*_{\nu Y}\alpha_\nu \frac{\partial \Phi_k(D_V\boldsymbol{\alpha} \mid D_V R^* D'_V)}{\partial\alpha_\nu}$$

$$+ \sum_{g\neq\nu} \rho^*_{gY}(1-\rho^{*2}_{\nu Y}) \frac{\partial^2 \Phi_k(D_V\boldsymbol{\alpha} \mid D_V R^* D'_V)}{\partial\alpha_g \partial\alpha_\nu}$$

$$= -(-1)^{S_\nu}\rho^*_{\nu Y}\alpha_\nu\varphi_1(\alpha_\nu)\Phi_{k-1}[D_{V[\nu]}(\boldsymbol{\alpha}_{[\nu]} - \boldsymbol{\rho}^*_{[\nu]}\rho^*_{\nu Y}\alpha_\nu) \mid D_{V[\nu]} R^*_{\cdot\nu} D'_{V[\nu]}]$$

$$+ \sum_{g\neq\nu} (-1)^{S_\nu + S_g}\rho^*_{gY}(1-\rho^{*2}_{\nu Y})\varphi_2(\boldsymbol{\alpha}_{\nu,g} \mid R^*_{\nu g})$$

$$\cdot\, \Phi_{k-2}[D_{V[\nu,g]}(\boldsymbol{\alpha}_{[\nu,g]} - \boldsymbol{\rho}^*_{[\nu,g]}\boldsymbol{\rho}^*_{\nu,g} R^{*-1}_{\nu g}\boldsymbol{\alpha}_{\nu,g}) \mid D_{V[\nu,g]} R^*_{\cdot\nu g} D_{V[\nu,g]}]\,.$$

The maximizing values of $\alpha_1, \alpha_2, \cdots, \alpha_k$ must therefore satisfy the k equations

$$(4.11)\quad \begin{aligned}\sum_{V} \{ & 2(-1)^{S_\nu}\rho^*_{\nu Y}\alpha_\nu\varphi_1(\alpha_\nu)\Phi_{k-1}[D_{V_{[\nu]}}(\boldsymbol{\alpha}_{[\nu]} - \boldsymbol{\rho}^*_{[\nu]}\rho^*_{\nu Y}\alpha_\nu) \mid D_{V_{[\nu]}}R^*_{\cdot\nu}D'_{V_{[\nu]}}] \\ & - \sum_{g\neq\nu}(-1)^{S_\nu+S_g}\rho^*_{gY}(1-\rho^{*2}_{\nu Y})\varphi_2(\boldsymbol{\alpha}_{\nu,g} \mid R^*_{\cdot\nu g}) \\ & \cdot \Phi_{k-2}[D_{V_{[\nu,g]}}(\boldsymbol{\alpha}_{[\nu,g]} - \boldsymbol{\rho}^*_{[\nu,g]}\boldsymbol{\rho}^{*\prime}_{\nu,g}R^{*-1}_{\cdot\nu g}\boldsymbol{\alpha}_{\nu,g}) \mid D_{V_{[\nu,g]}}R^*_{\cdot\nu g}D'_{V_{[\nu,g]}}]\tilde{y}_\nu \\ & - (-1)^{S_\nu}\varphi_1(\alpha_\nu)\Phi_{k-1}[D_{V_{[\nu]}}(\boldsymbol{\alpha}_{[\nu]} - \boldsymbol{\rho}^*_{[\nu]}\rho^*_{\nu Y}\alpha \mid D_{V_{[\nu]}}R^*_{\cdot\nu}D'_{V_{[\nu]}}]\tilde{y}^2_V\} = 0\,,\end{aligned}$$

for $\nu = 1, 2, \cdots, k$. From Equation (3.8) we have

$$(4.12)\quad \begin{aligned}\tilde{y}_V = \frac{-1}{\Phi_k(D_V\alpha \mid D_V R^* D'_V)} & \sum_{g=1}^{k}(-1)^{S_g}\rho^*_{gY}\varphi_1(\alpha_g) \\ & \cdot \Phi_{k-1}[D_{V_{[g]}}(\boldsymbol{\alpha}_{[g]} - \boldsymbol{\rho}^*_{[g]}\rho^*_{gY}\alpha_g) \mid D_{V_{[g]}}R^*_{\cdot g}D'_{V_{[g]}}]\,.\end{aligned}$$

In general, these results are not very useful. However, they permit some comparisons of tests of two items for the present model with corresponding tests for the restricted model of Chapter 2.

5. Tests of Two Items

In the case $k = 2$, as indicated earlier, we have four possible values of the response vector V and corresponding four values of $\tilde{y}_V$. For purposes of comparison with the model examined in the previous chapter we assume that $\rho^*_{1Y} = \rho^*_{2Y} = \sqrt{\rho^*}$.

To simplify notation, we write

$$\Phi_1\left(\frac{\alpha_1 - \rho^*\alpha_2}{\sqrt{1-\rho^{*2}}}\right) = I_1\,, \qquad \Phi_1\left(\frac{\alpha_2 - \rho^*\alpha_1}{\sqrt{1-\rho^{*2}}}\right) = I_2\,,$$

and

$$\Phi_2(\boldsymbol{t} \mid R) = \Phi_2(t_1, t_2; \rho)\,,$$

where

$$R = \begin{pmatrix} 1 & \rho \\ \rho & 1 \end{pmatrix}.$$

With this notation, we have [see Equation (3.18)]

$$(5.1)\quad \begin{aligned} \tilde{y}_{V_1} &= -\sqrt{\rho^*}\,\frac{[\varphi_1(\alpha_1)I_2 + \varphi_1(\alpha_2)I_1]}{\Phi_2(\alpha_1, \alpha_2; \rho^*)}\,, \\ \tilde{y}_{V_2} &= -\sqrt{\rho^*}\,\frac{[\varphi_1(\alpha_1)(1-I_2) - \varphi_1(\alpha_2)I_1]}{\Phi_2(\alpha_1, -\alpha_2; -\rho^*)}\,, \\ \tilde{y}_{V_3} &= \sqrt{\rho^*}\,\frac{[\varphi_1(\alpha_1)I_2 - \varphi_1(\alpha_2)(1-I_2)]}{\Phi_2(-\alpha_1, \alpha_2; -\rho^*)}\,, \\ \tilde{y}_{V_4} &= \sqrt{\rho^*}\,\frac{[\varphi_1(\alpha_1)(1-I_2) + \varphi_1(\alpha_2)(1-I_1)]}{\Phi_2(-\alpha_1, -\alpha_2; \rho^*)}\,. \end{aligned}$$

The maximizing values of α_1 and α_2 must satisfy the two equations [see Equation (4.11)]

$$
\begin{aligned}
&2\sqrt{\rho^*}\,\alpha_1\varphi_1(\alpha_1)[I_2(\tilde{y}_{V_1}-\tilde{y}_{V_3})+(1-I_2)(\tilde{y}_{V_2}-\tilde{y}_{V_4})]\\
&\quad-2\sqrt{\rho^*}\,(1-\rho^*)\varphi_2(\alpha_1,\alpha_2;\rho^*)(\tilde{y}_{V_1}-\tilde{y}_{V_2}-\tilde{y}_{V_3}+\tilde{y}_{V_4})\\
&\qquad-\varphi_1(\alpha_1([I_2(\tilde{y}^2_{V_1}-\tilde{y}^2_{V_3})+(1-I_2)(\tilde{y}^2_{V_2}-\tilde{y}^2_{V_4})]=0\,;\\
&2\sqrt{\rho^*}\,\alpha_2\varphi_1(\alpha_2)[I_1(\tilde{y}_{V_1}-\tilde{y}_{V_2})+(1-I_1)(\tilde{y}_{V_3}-\tilde{y}_{V_4})]\\
&\quad-2\sqrt{\rho^*}\,(1-\rho^*)\varphi_2(\alpha_1,\alpha_2;\rho^*)(\tilde{y}_{V_1}-\tilde{y}_{V_2}-\tilde{y}_{V_3}+\tilde{y}_{V_4})\\
&\qquad-\varphi_1(\alpha_2)[I_1(\tilde{y}^2_{V_1}-\tilde{y}^2_{V_2})+(1-I_1)(\tilde{y}^2_{V_3}-\tilde{y}^2_{V_4})]=0\,.
\end{aligned}
\tag{5.2}
$$

In solving these equations, we shall consider only solutions for which $\alpha_1 \leqq \alpha_2$. Because of symmetry, if a pair (β_1, β_2) is a solution, the pair (β_2, β_1) is also a solution.

It is easy to see that the pair (0, 0) is a solution. In this case, $I_1 = I_2 = \frac{1}{2}$, and

$$
\tilde{y}_{V_1} = \frac{-\sqrt{\rho^*}\,\varphi_1(0)}{\Phi_2(0, 0; \rho^*)}\,, \quad \tilde{y}_{V_2} = \tilde{y}_{V_3} = 0\,, \quad \tilde{y}_{V_4} = \frac{\sqrt{\rho^*}\,\varphi_1(0)}{\Phi_2(0, 0; \rho^*)}\,. \tag{5.3}
$$

The question remains, however, whether this solution is the only solution and whether it maximizes $g(\boldsymbol{\alpha}, \boldsymbol{\rho}^*)$. Since the expressions on the left-hand side of Equations (5.2) are difficult to handle analytically, we offer the following heuristic and empirical considerations.

We know from Chapter 2 that when $\rho^* = 1$ the maximizing values of α_1 and α_2 are $-.61$ and $.61$, respectively. It seems reasonable, therefore, that the maximizing solution is of the form $(-\alpha, \alpha)$ with $\alpha \geqq 0$. For any pair $(-\alpha, \alpha)$ we have

$$
y_{V_1} = \frac{-\sqrt{\rho^*}\,\varphi_1(\alpha)}{\Phi_2(-\alpha, \alpha; \rho^*)}\,, \quad y_{V_2} = y_{V_3} = 0\,, \quad y_{V_4} = \frac{\sqrt{\rho^*}\,\varphi_1(\alpha)}{\Phi_2(-\alpha, \alpha; \rho^*)}\,. \tag{5.4}
$$

In this case

$$
g(\boldsymbol{\alpha}, \boldsymbol{\rho}^*) = \frac{2\rho^*[\varphi_1(\alpha)]^2}{\Phi_2(-\alpha, \alpha; \rho^*)} = g^*(\alpha, \rho^*)\,, \tag{5.5}
$$

say where $\alpha \geqq 0, 0 \leqq \rho^* \leqq 1$. Note that the minimum value of $g^*(\alpha, \rho^*)$ is zero, and this minimum is attained when $\rho^* = 0$ for all α. Also

$$
\lim_{\alpha \to \infty} g^*(\alpha, \rho^*) = 0 \quad \text{for all } \rho^*\,. \tag{5.6}
$$

To find the value of α, say α^*, which maximizes $g^*(\alpha, \rho^*)$, we can examine Equations (5.2) under the condition that $\alpha_1 = -\alpha, \alpha_2 = \alpha$. Equivalently, we can differentiatiate (5.5) directly with respect to α, obtaining

$$
\begin{aligned}
\frac{\partial g^*(\alpha, \rho^*)}{\partial \alpha} &= \frac{4\rho^*[\varphi,(\alpha)]^2}{\Phi_2(-\alpha, \alpha; \rho^*)}\left\{-\alpha + \frac{\varphi_1(\alpha)\left[\Phi_1\left(\alpha\sqrt{\dfrac{1+\rho^*}{1-\rho^*}}\right) - \dfrac{1}{2}\right]}{\Phi_2(-\alpha, \alpha; \rho^*)}\right\}\\
&= 2g^*(\alpha, \rho^*)\left\{-\alpha + \frac{\varphi_1(\alpha)\left[\Phi_1\left(\alpha\sqrt{\dfrac{1+\rho^*}{1-\rho^*}}\right) - \dfrac{1}{2}\right]}{\Phi_2(-\alpha, \alpha; \rho^*)}\right\}.
\end{aligned}
\tag{5.7}
$$

Since $g^*(\alpha, \rho^*) = 0$ is the minimum value, the value of α, say α^*, which maximizes $g^*(\alpha, \rho^*)$, must be such that

$$\alpha^* = \frac{\varphi_1(\alpha^*)\left[\Phi_1\left(\alpha^*\sqrt{\frac{1+\rho^*}{1-\rho^*}}\right) - \frac{1}{2}\right]}{\Phi_2(-\alpha^*, \alpha^*; \rho^*)} \tag{5.8}$$

$$= f_{\rho^*}(\alpha^*) \, ,$$

say.

Values of $f_{\rho^*}(\alpha)$ for the range $0 \leqq \alpha \leqq .7$ are shown graphically in Figure 1 for selected values of ρ^*. It will be seen in the figure that for values of $\rho^* < .7$ the function $f_{\rho^*}(\alpha)$ has only one value such that

$$\alpha = f_{\rho^*}(\alpha) \, ,$$

namely, the value $\alpha = 0$. For values of $\rho^* \geqq .7$ there are two values that

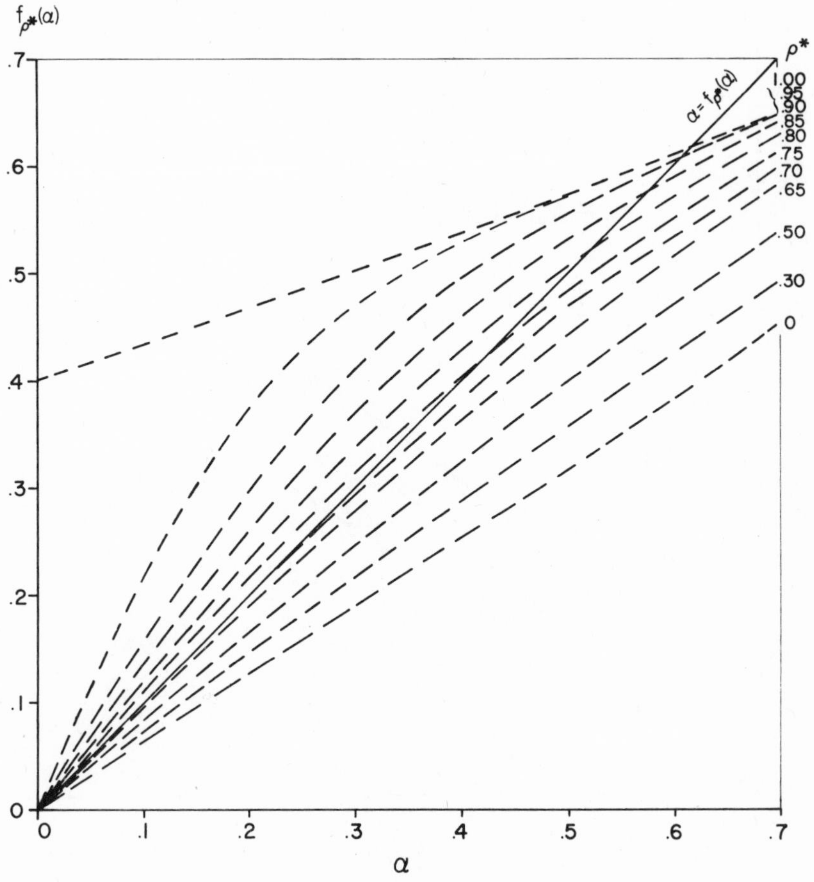

FIG. 1. Values of $f_{\rho^*}(\alpha)$ for Specified Values of ρ^*

satisfy Equation (5.8). One of these is $\alpha = 0$; the second depends on ρ^* and can be read from the graph, as follows:

(5.9)

ρ^*	$\alpha = f_{\rho^*}(\alpha)$
.70	.15
.75	.41
.80	.51
.85	.57
.90	.60
.95	.61
1.00	.61

An examination of $g^*(\alpha, \rho^*)$ for the values given in (5.9) shows that the non-zero value of α for $\rho^* \geqq .7$ is the desired maximizing value α^*.

Figure 2 gives values of $g^*(\alpha^*, \rho^*)$ and $g^*(0, \rho^*)$ for $0 \leqq \rho^* \leqq 1$. In addition, the corresponding optimal values of $1 - S_{\tilde{y}}^2$ for one- and two-item tests

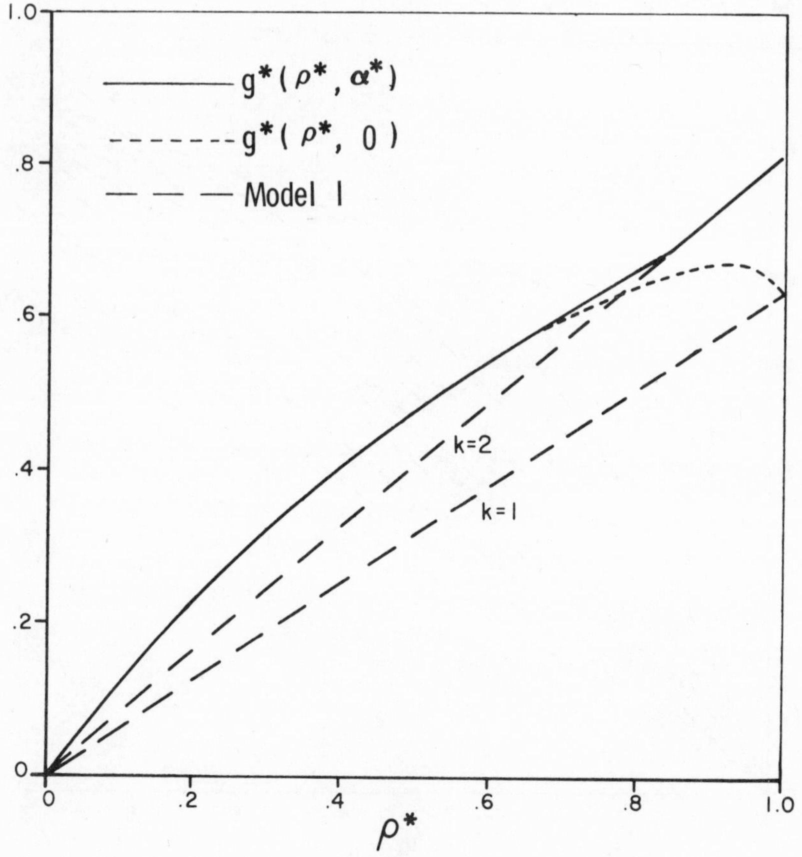

FIG. 2. Values of $(1-S_{\tilde{y}}^2)$ for Tests of One and Two Items

are shown for the case of the restricted model of Chapter 2. It will be recalled that in that chapter all items in the test are measuring the same latent variable X, which has a correlation of $\sqrt{\rho^*}$ with Y.

It was observed earlier that when $\rho^* = 1$, the two models are equivalent. Correspondingly the measures of worth for a two-item test are the same for this single value of ρ^*. For $0 < \rho^* < 1$ the two-item test with the present structure is uniformly better than the earlier one. Note that as ρ^* increases, the curve for $g^*(0, \rho^*)$ decreases to coincide, at $\rho^* = 1$, with the curve for the one-item test of the earlier model.

References

[1] Solomon, H. Measures of worth in item analysis and test design. Chap. 22 in Kenneth Arrow, Samuel Karlin, and Patrick Suppes, eds., *Mathematical Methods in the Social Sciences, 1959. Proceedings of the First Stanford Symposium.* Stanford, Calif.: Stanford Univ. Press, 1960.

[2] Blackwell, D., and Girshick, M. A. *Theory of Games and Statistical Decisions.* New York: Wiley, 1954.

4

Item-Selection Procedures for Item Variables with a Known Factor Structure

GUSTAV ELFVING, University of Helsinki; ROSEDITH SITGREAVES, Columbia University; HERBERT SOLOMON, Stanford University

1. Introduction

The question of type of item and number of items to be used in a test of mental ability, an attitude scale, or a personality or biographical inventory, is a familiar topic in psychological testing. In this chapter we shall attempt some resolution of the problem for the restricted situation in which the item variables obey a known factor structure. For simplicity we shall use the generic term "test" to represent a collection of items that deal with attitude, personality, etc. In addition we shall consider the classical situation in which test response is a linear function of the item responses. This, of course, may be somewhat unrealistic in some situations. Biographical inventories, for example, may call for non-classical approaches in item selection. On the other hand, even for what may be termed the classical situation the question has not been resolved.

We assume that the test response is to be used as a predictor of a criterion variable. The number and type of items selected for a test, therefore, are governed by the usefulness of the resulting test response for prediction purposes. In the usual techniques of item selection, the size of a correlation coefficient between an item response and the criterion is used to indicate how well the item aids in the prediction made by the test. Although the correlation index appears to have pragmatic value for tests of mental ability, it falls short in a number of other testing situations. It should be remembered that the correlation coefficient is a methodological tool borrowed from those who conceptualized its use in anthropometric settings, and it therefore may not be efficient in all psychometric situations. Here we shall consider a conceptualization of the problem leading toward a more general approach to item selection.

It is best now to become more specific. Suppose that, for prediction of a certain quantity z (criterion variable), a large number N of non-repeatable observations x_i (item variables) is potentially available. The quantities

This paper (except the Appendix) has previously been published in *Psychometrika*, 1959, **24**, 189–205.

$x_1, x_2, \cdots, x_N; z$ are assumed to be random variables, the joint distribution of which is known—except, perhaps, for certain parameters—either from past experience or by assumption. In other words, we completely disregard sampling questions, and *we restrict ourselves to a design problem only.*

For practical reasons, one wants to base the prediction of z on a restricted number, say $n < N$, of observations x_i. The problem that confronts us is how to choose them. In a psychological application we can think of the x_i's as scores obtained from the responses to items on a reading test; and the criterion z as a quantity indicating the intellectual maturity of a child. For concreteness, we can think of N as being of the order from 100 to 1000, and n from 10 to 50.

The proposed item-selection approach is based on the assumption that the variables $x_1, x_2, \cdots, x_N; z$ have a known factor structure, with a comparatively small number k of common factors; we assume that, practically speaking, k ranges from 1 to 5. The assumption of this latent-factor universe, and the conclusions concerning how the added information provides for item selection, mark a departure from other selection methods. As we shall see, the latent-factor universe also provides a rationale in one situation for the correlation index, which is used extensively at present. In this chapter, essentially we analyze and give an analytical and expository account of a method proposed by Elfving [1, 2], which is based on some prior work he did in different contexts [3, 4].[1]

An explanation of the principles leading to the steps of the method is given as we proceed, and the method is applied to two sets of data. One set of data comes from the Educational Testing Service in connection with aptitude testing for law school, where we seek the best two out of six items. The other set was artificially constructed, and we seek, respectively, from ten items the best four, the best five, and the best six. It can easily be demonstrated that the best $(n + 1)$ items need not contain the best set of n items. One reason for the scarcity of data on which to employ our item-selection procedure is not only that the factor structure for N items must be known completely but the factor loadings for the criterion variable z must be known or guessed realistically. The procedure we are going to describe is also useful for selecting tests from a battery of tests, and in these situations complete factor structures are available. However our language and demonstrations will stress the selection of items for a test.

2. The Factor Structure and Prediction Criterion

We shall consider the following factor structure for the x_i's and z. Naturally if the items are to have any validity in predicting the criterion, they should be composed of the same common factors and differ at most in factor loadings and specific factors. Thus we shall assume

---

1 Papers [1, 2] are reprinted with slight modifications as Chapters 5 and 6 in this volume. Chapter 7 is concerned with particular techniques for item selection. A brief survey of the aims of these three studies is given as an Appendix at the end of the present chapter.

$$x_i = a_{i1}y_1 + \cdots + a_{ik}y_k + \varepsilon_i \qquad i = 1, \cdots, N, \tag{2.1}$$

$$z = c_1 y_1 + \cdots + c_k y_k + \eta, \tag{2.2}$$

where

1) the *loadings* a_{ij}, c_j are known constants;

2) the (unobservable) *specific factors* $\varepsilon_1, \cdots, \varepsilon_N, \eta$ are random variables with mean zero, distributed independently of the unobservable (latent) common factors $y_1, \cdots, y_k$;

3) the ε_i have known covariance matrix (in most of what follows, this will be assumed to be diagonal);

4) η has variance σ_c^2 and is uncorrelated with the ε_i.

For the common factors y_j, we may consider two different models which, however, lead essentially to the same selection technique:

5a) Fixed-constants model: the y_j's are unknown constants.

5b) Random-factor model: the y_j's are random variables, with mean zero and a known non-singular covariance matrix T.

In model 5a, the y_j's may be thought of as factor values pertaining to the particular individual for which z has to be predicted. In 5b, the individual is thought of as belonging to a population with known characteristics.

In predicting z, we restrict ourselves to *linear unbiased minimum-variance predictors*; i.e., for any selected set of n items out of N items we take as a predictor the linear combination

$$\hat{z} = \sum_{i=1}^{n} q_i x_i, \tag{2.3}$$

which satisfies both $E(\hat{z} - z) = 0$, and $E(\hat{z} - z)^2 =$ minimum. This is a reasonable estimation criterion quite often used in classical multivariate analysis. Suppose for the selected set of n items we have in matrix notation

$$x = Ay + \varepsilon, \tag{2.4}$$

$$z = c'y + \eta, \tag{2.5}$$

and

$$\Sigma = \text{cov}\,\varepsilon = E(\varepsilon\varepsilon'). \tag{2.6}$$

Then, in the fixed-constants model, the best predictor of z on the basis of x is

$$\hat{z} = c'(A'\Sigma^{-1}A)^{-1}A'\Sigma^{-1}x, \tag{2.7}$$

with prediction variance

$$E(\hat{z} - z)^2 = c'(A'\Sigma^{-1}A)^{-1}c + \sigma_c^2; \tag{2.8}$$

whereas in the random-factor model the best predictor of z on the basis of x is

$$\hat{z} = c'(T^{-1} + A'\Sigma^{-1}A)^{-1}A'\Sigma^{-1}x, \tag{2.9}$$

with prediction variance

$$E(\hat{z} - z)^2 = c'(T^{-1} + A'\Sigma^{-1}A)^{-1}c + \sigma_c^2. \tag{2.10}$$

These results are merely stated, since they are well known in multivariate analysis.

3. The Selection Region

Let us now consider the selection problem. We wish to choose n out of N items. There are many possibilities, but we desire that set of n items which will minimize the prediction variance $E(\hat{z} - z)^2$. Naturally we do not want to have to look at all possible sets of n items to arrive at the proper choice. For small values of n and N, one can try all possibilities, but even when $N = 10$ and $n = 2$, it is quite tedious.

The prediction variance is given, for the two models considered, by (2.8) and (2.10). Since σ_c^2 does not depend on the selection, our problem reduces to the minimization of

$$V = c'M^{-1}c , \tag{3.1}$$

where

$$M = M_0 + A'\Sigma^{-1}A , \tag{3.2}$$

with $M_0 = 0$ in the parametric model, and $M_0 = T^{-1}$ in the random-factor model. The variable elements are, of course, in the $n \times k$ matrix A and the $n \times n$ matrix Σ, both of which depend on the choice of items.

From now on, we shall assume that the specific factors are uncorrelated, with variances σ_i^2. That is, for a selected set of n items,

$$A'\Sigma^{-1}A = \begin{bmatrix} \sum_{i=1}^{n} \frac{a_{i1}^2}{\sigma_i^2} & \sum_{i=1}^{n} \frac{a_{i1}a_{i2}}{\sigma_i^2} & \cdot\cdot & \sum_{i=1}^{n} \frac{a_{i1}a_{ik}}{\sigma_i^2} \\ \sum_{i=1}^{n} \frac{a_{i1}a_{i2}}{\sigma_i^2} & \sum_{i=1}^{n} \frac{a_{i2}^2}{\sigma_i^2} & \cdot\cdot & \sum_{i=1}^{n} \frac{a_{i2}a_{ik}}{\sigma_i^2} \\ \cdots & \cdots & \cdot\cdot & \cdots \\ \sum_{i=1}^{n} \frac{a_{i1}a_{ik}}{\sigma_i^2} & \sum_{i=1}^{n} \frac{a_{i2}a_{ik}}{\sigma_i^2} & \cdot\cdot & \sum_{i=1}^{n} \frac{a_{ik}^2}{\sigma_i^2} \end{bmatrix} . \tag{3.3}$$

Denote by a_i the ith row of A written as a column vector. We may then write

$$A'\Sigma^{-1}A = \sum_{i=1}^{n} \frac{a_i a_i'}{\sigma_i^2} = \sum_{i=1}^{n} u_i u_i' , \qquad \text{where } u_i = \frac{a_i}{\sigma_i} ; \tag{3.4}$$

and obviously,

$$u_i u_i' = \begin{bmatrix} \frac{a_{i1}^2}{\sigma_i^2} & \frac{a_{i1}a_{i2}}{\sigma_i^2} & \cdot\cdot & \frac{a_{i1}a_{ik}}{\sigma_i^2} \\ \frac{a_{i1}a_{i2}}{\sigma_i^2} & \frac{a_{i2}^2}{\sigma_i^2} & \cdot\cdot & \frac{a_{i2}a_{ik}}{\sigma_i^2} \\ \cdots & \cdots & \cdot\cdot & \cdots \\ \frac{a_{i1}a_{ik}}{\sigma_i^2} & \frac{a_{i2}a_{ik}}{\sigma_i^2} & \cdot\cdot & \frac{a_{ik}^2}{\sigma_i^2} \end{bmatrix} \tag{3.5}$$

is, for every i, a $k \times k$ matrix of rank 1. The sum $\sum_{i=1}^{n} u_i u_i'$ has for elements the moments of the k-dimensional "item population" consisting of the points $u_1, \cdots, u_n$, each with weight 1.

Returning to the original numbering of the items, $i = 1, \cdots, N$, and denoting by ω the selected set of n subscripts, we may now write (3.2) as

$$M = M_0 + \sum_{\omega} u_i u_i' . \tag{3.6}$$

The $k \times k$ matrix M is the *information matrix* of the experiment, i.e., of the selected set of observations. The sum $\sum u_i u_i'$ represents the information offered by the items in ω. In the random-factor model, $M_0 = T^{-1}$ may be said to represent the *a priori* information contained in the assumption that the factors are random variables with zero means and covariance matrix T. It may be noted, incidentally, that the constant term M_0 in (3.6) can also be used to take care of any *fixed* source of information, such as possible "compulsory" items.

It is seen that the effect of a particular item—say number i—depends solely on the vector u_i, i.e., on the "reduced loading vector" obtained by standardizing the item variable to have variance equal to 1. It should be noted that, in the fixed-constants case, one may multiply the u_i's by a common factor without affecting the minimization problem at hand. As a consequence, the item variables may actually be standardized to any common variance, not necessarily unity.

We also note that two items, one with vector u_i and the other with vector $-u_i$, yield the same contribution to the information matrix. For this reason and for reasons of symmetry which will become clearer later on, we shall usually describe each item by means of the *pair* of opposite points $\pm u_i$. These points, in k-space, will be referred to as *item points*.

It is natural to think of the selected set ω of item points as occupying a certain "selection region" S that will, of course, depend in some way on the totality of available item points. Before we attack the question of how to find this region, it may be useful to discuss briefly the cases $k = 1$ and $k = 2$.

When $k = 1$, all symbols in (3.1) and (3.6) denote scalars, and the problem reduces to that of minimizing

$$V = \frac{c^2}{m_0 + \sum_{\omega} u_i^2} \tag{3.7}$$

by a proper choice of ω. Thus we simply have to select the n items with largest $|u_i|$. If the x_i's and u_i's are standardized to variance 1 as often occurs in factor analysis, we have $a_i^2 + \sigma_i^2 = 1$, and hence $u_i^2 = a_i^2/\sigma_i^2 = a_i^2/(1 - a_i^2)$. The items with largest $|u_i|$ are then the same as those with largest $|a_i|$, i.e., those having largest loadings with respect to the single common factor. In this case, however,

$$\frac{a_i^2}{1 - a_i^2} = \frac{\rho_{x_i v_1}^2}{1 - \rho_{x_i v_1}^2} , \tag{3.8}$$

so that this procedure is equivalent to picking the n x_i's having the highest absolute correlation with y_1. This procedure is usually applied by psychologists, except that the latent factor is not available. Therefore, they resort to a manifest equivalent, usually to an observed total test score.

In the case $k = 2$, it is clear that, in general, if an item point happens to lie precisely on the straight line determined by the vector c, say $u_1 = \lambda_1 c$, then

$$x_1 = a_{11} y_1 + a_{12} y_2 + \varepsilon_1 = \sigma_1 \lambda_1 (c_1 y_1 + c_2 y_2) + \varepsilon_1 \,, \tag{3.9}$$

and $x_1/(\sigma_1\lambda_1)$ provides an unbiased estimate of $c'y$. The variance of this estimate is $\sigma_1^2/(\sigma_1\lambda_1)^2 = 1/\lambda_1^2$. Accordingly, item points on the line c may be expected to contribute more to the estimation of $c'y$, and hence to the prediction of z, the farther out they are along the line.

Similarly, suppose there are two item points located more or less symmetrically with respect to the line c. For example, suppose

$$\begin{aligned} u_1 &= \left(\frac{\lambda c_1}{\sqrt{c_1^2 + c_2^2}} + kc_2 \,, \quad \frac{\lambda c_2}{\sqrt{c_1^2 + c_2^2}} - kc_1\right), \\ u_2 &= \left(\frac{\lambda c_1}{\sqrt{c_1^2 + c_2^2}} - kc_2 \,, \quad \frac{\lambda c_2}{\sqrt{c_1^2 + c_2^2}} + kc_1\right). \end{aligned} \tag{3.10}$$

Then we have

$$\frac{1}{2}\left(\frac{x_1}{\sigma_1} + \frac{x_2}{\sigma_2}\right) = \frac{\lambda}{\sqrt{c_1^2 + c_2^2}}(c_1 y_1 + c_2 y_2) + \frac{1}{2}\left(\frac{\varepsilon_1}{\sigma_1} + \frac{\varepsilon_2}{\sigma_1}\right), \tag{3.11}$$

and the quantity

$$\frac{\sqrt{c_1^2 + c_2^2}}{2\lambda}\left(\frac{x_1}{\sigma_1} + \frac{x_2}{\sigma_2}\right) \tag{3.12}$$

is an unbiased estimate of $c'y$ with variance

$$\frac{c_1^2 + c_2^2}{2\lambda^2} \,. \tag{3.13}$$

Since λ is the distance from the origin to the point of intersection of the c-vector and the line joining u_1 and u_2, it is clear again that the two item points, after the elimination of the "orthogonal" component, provide a better estimator of $c'y$ the farther off in the $\pm c$-direction they lie.

These heuristic remarks make it plausible that the selection region S, which we are looking for, will have to comprise the "outer parts" of k-space with regard to the directions $\pm c$, and will have to fulfill the additional requirement that the item points in S should in some way balance each other with respect to that direction. It turns out (see Chapter 5) that S may be taken to consist of two symmetrical half-spaces (we shall say a twin half-space) bounded by two parallel planes, $t'u = \pm h$; the direction t of their common normal will depend in a certain way on the item points included in the selection region, which becomes in this way implicitly determined.

To formulate the result just sketched, we have to introduce a continuization device that will lead to a simple optimality criterion, which will help to solve our problem without essentially affecting the practical application. For this purpose we consider, instead of the previous M defined by (3.6), the generalized information matrix

$$M = M_0 + \sum_{i=1}^{N} p_i u_i u_i' , \tag{3.14}$$

where the allocation vector $p = (p_1, \cdots, p_N)$ is subject to the restrictions

$$0 \leqq p_i \leqq 1 , \quad \sum_{i=1}^{N} p_i = n . \tag{3.15}$$

Obviously, the set of matrices given by (3.14) and (3.15) contains the set of matrices (3.6). For any particular p, we shall refer to those items for which $p_i = 1$ as *totally selected*, those for which $p_i = 0$ as *non-selected*, and those for which $0 < p_i < 1$ as *fractionally selected*.

The following interpretation of the fractional p_i's (in the parametric case) may be instructive. Imagine for a moment that the observations x_i may be independently repeated, each of them at most r times, and assume that a total of rn observations is allowed. Let $n_1, \cdots, n_N$ $(0 \leqq n_i \leqq r;\ \sum n_i = rn)$ be the number of times that the different observations are repeated. The information matrix of the resulting experiment may be written

$$M = \sum n_i u_i u_i' = r \sum p_i u_i u_i' , \tag{3.16}$$

where the $p_i = n_i/r$ vary from 0 to 1 through multiples of $1/r$, subject to the condition $\sum p_i = n$. Since the factor r in M is obviously irrelevant to the minimization of (3.1), we are, for large r, faced essentially with the modified selection problem formulated above. In particular, if we take $n = 1$, and r large, we are concerned with the allocation problem treated by Elfving in [1]; the earlier problem thus appears to be a special case of the present one.

After these preparations, we are in a position to state the following propositions (see Chapter 5 and [1]):

THEOREM 3.1. *The scalar V, defined by*

$$V = c'M^{-1}c, \quad \text{where } M = M_0 + \sum_{i=1}^{N} p_i u_i u_i' \tag{3.17}$$

as a function of the vector p, has a minimum on the domain (3.15). *In order for the allocation vector p to yield this minimum, it is necessary and sufficient that, for a certain number $h > 0$,*

$$p_i = \begin{cases} 1 \\ 0 \end{cases} \text{whenever} \quad |c'M^{-1}u_i| \gtrless h . \tag{3.18}$$

Moreover, there always exists a minimizing p with at most k fractional components.

We recall that M is a $k \times k$ matrix, hence $c'M^{-1}$ is a k-dimensional row vector, and $c'M^{-1}u_i$ is a linear form in the components of the vector u_i. Essentially, the theorem says that the selection region consists mainly of the part of k-space that lies outside two parallel hyperplanes $c'M^{-1}u = \pm h$; the item points lying in the boundary planes will have to be totally or fractionally selected, or non-selected, as the case may be. Since the fractional p_i's (when they are taken to be as few as possible) will be at most k in number, and hence can total at most $k-1$, we will have from $n-k+1$ to n totally selected items. In practice, we may "round off" some or all of the fractional p_i's to 1's; i.e., we may select the corresponding items on an equal basis with the rest. In the latter case, at the expense of making at most $k-1$ more observations than originally planned, we will be sure of achieving a variance V not exceeding the smallest one that could be attained by any total selection of n items. When the optimal p contains only 1's and 0's, an exact solution of the original discrete problem is provided.

For a proof of Theorem 3.1 in the parametric case (the random-factor case goes quite similarly) we refer to Chapter 5 and to [1].

It should be noted that the theorem gives a necessary and sufficient criterion for optimum solutions, but no method for finding such a solution. When $k=2$ and n is small, a graphic picture of the item points may lead to a good guess. For more complex situations, a method has been suggested (see Chapter 6 and [2]) based on the idea that the population of item points may be approximately described by a k-dimensional normal distribution with the same second-order moments. The method may be condensed into the following practical rule:

(i) Find the matrix Λ with elements

$$\lambda_{jh} = \sum_{i=1}^{N} u_{ij}u_{ih} \qquad j, h = 1, \cdots, k. \tag{3.19}$$

(ii) Find the vector $\gamma = \Lambda^{-1}c$; i.e., solve the equations

$$\begin{aligned} \lambda_{11}\gamma_1 + \cdots + \lambda_{1k}\gamma_k &= c_1 , \\ &\cdots\cdots \\ \lambda_{k1}\gamma_1 + \cdots + \lambda_{kk}\gamma_k &= c_k . \end{aligned} \tag{3.20}$$

(iii) Find, for each i, the quantity

$$w_i = \gamma' u_i = \sum_j \gamma_j u_{ij} , \tag{3.21}$$

and select the n items with largest $|w_i|$.

The selection found in this way should provide a good first guess and of course may be checked by means of Theorem 3.1. If the criterion is not fulfilled, we may try to improve the solution by exchanging one or more of the selected item points for others in the neighborhood of the boundary planes. An example of such a procedure is given in Section 5.

In Chapter 7 we attempt a more refined selection technique for the case of a large and smoothly distributed population of items.

4. A Realistic Example When $k = 2$

To illustrate the meaning and use of Theorem 3.1, we consider two examples. Both involve a two-factor structure, and in each case we assume a fixed-constants model. The first example is based on data made available by the Educational Testing Service, Princeton, New Jersey. These data resulted from responses to six items used to measure aptitude for success in law school and a criterion variable that measured the actual success. Because of large-scale experience with the test and its predictive effect, we could secure factor loadings for the six items and the criterion variable. This resulted in two common factors plus specific factors. In this illustration we have

$$x_i = a_i'y + \varepsilon_i\,, \qquad z = c'y + \eta\,, \qquad i = 1, 2, \cdots, 6\,, \tag{4.1}$$

where

$$\begin{aligned} a_1' &= (.848, \ .225)\,, & a_4' &= (.481, \ -.216)\,,\\ a_2' &= (.833, \ .195)\,, & a_5' &= (.647, \ -.172)\,,\\ a_3' &= (.840, \ .122)\,, & a_6' &= (.869, \ .204)\,,\\ & & c' = (.641, \ -.205)\,. \end{aligned} \tag{4.2}$$

The (unobservable) specific factors $\varepsilon_1, \varepsilon_2, \cdots, \varepsilon_6; \eta$ are assumed to be independently distributed random variables with mean zero. The variances of $\varepsilon_1, \cdots, \varepsilon_6$ are

$$\begin{aligned} \sigma_1^2 &= .230\,, & \sigma_3^2 &= .280\,, & \sigma_5^2 &= .552\,,\\ \sigma_2^2 &= .268\,, & \sigma_4^2 &= .722\,, & \sigma_6^2 &= .203\,. \end{aligned} \tag{4.3}$$

The vector of (unobservable) common factors $y' = (y_1, y_2)$ is assumed to be a vector of unknown constants.

Then, if $u_i = a_i/\sigma_i$, we have

$$\begin{aligned} u_1' &= (1.767, \ .469)\,, & u_4' &= (\ .566, \ -.254)\,,\\ u_2' &= (1.608, \ .376)\,, & u_5' &= (\ .871, \ -.231)\,,\\ u_3' &= (1.588, \ .231)\,, & u_6' &= (1.927, \ .452)\,, \end{aligned} \tag{4.4}$$

and

$$\begin{aligned} u_1u_1' &= \begin{pmatrix} 3.122, & .829\\ .829, & .220 \end{pmatrix}, & u_4u_4' &= \begin{pmatrix} .320, & -.144\\ -.144, & .065 \end{pmatrix},\\ u_2u_2' &= \begin{pmatrix} 2.586, & .605\\ .605, & .141 \end{pmatrix}, & u_5u_5' &= \begin{pmatrix} .759, & -.201\\ -.201, & .053 \end{pmatrix},\\ u_3u_3' &= \begin{pmatrix} 2.522, & .367\\ .367, & .053 \end{pmatrix}, & u_6u_6' &= \begin{pmatrix} 3.713, & .871\\ .871, & .204 \end{pmatrix}. \end{aligned} \tag{4.5}$$

The item points $u_1, \cdots, u_6$, and the vector c are shown graphically in Figure 1.

For a given set of x's, say $x_{i_1}, \cdots, x_{i_n}$, the best predictor of z on the basis of x is

$$z = c' M_\omega^{-1} U_\omega x^* , \tag{4.6}$$

where ω denotes the selected set of subscripts, and

$$M_\omega = \sum_\omega u_i u_i' ,$$

$$U_\omega = (u_{i_1}, u_{i_2}, \cdots, u_{i_n}), \quad \text{a } 2 \times n \text{ matrix},$$

$$x^* = \left(\frac{x_{i_1}}{\sigma_{i_1}}, \frac{x_{i_2}}{\sigma_{i_2}}, \cdots, \frac{x_{i_n}}{\sigma_{i_n}}\right)' .$$

The variance of the estimate is

$$E(z - \hat{z})^2 = c' M_\omega^{-1} c + \sigma_c^2 . \tag{4.7}$$

We can consider that M_ω is the information matrix for the selected set of observations.

Let us now consider the generalized information matrix

$$M_p = \sum_{i=1}^{6} p_i u_i u_i' , \tag{4.8}$$

where the allocation vector $p' = (p_1, p_2, \cdots, p_6)'$ is subject to the restrictions

$$0 \leqq p_i \leqq 1 , \qquad \sum_{i=1}^{6} p_i = 2 . \tag{4.9}$$

That is, we desire two out of the six items.

Then, Theorem 3.1 states that as a function of the vector p,

$$V = c' M_p^{-1} c \tag{4.10}$$

has a minimum on the domain (4.9). For the allocation vector $p = p^*$ to yield this minimum, it is necessary and sufficient that for a certain number $h > 0$

$$p_i^* = \begin{cases} 1 \\ 0 \end{cases} \quad \text{whenever} \quad |c' M_{p^*}^{-1} u_i| \gtrless h ,$$

where p^* is the minimizing vector. That is, the wholly selected item points lie outside two parallel lines that are symmetric with respect to the origin, and the totally non-selected item points lie between these lines. (Totally selected and totally non-selected item points may also lie on the boundaries, i.e., the parallel lines.) Any fractionally selected item, say u_j, must be on one of the lines defined by

$$|c' M_{p^*}^{-1} u| = h .$$

At most, two items may need to be fractionally selected.

Suppose in the present example, where we have taken $n = 2$, we first limit ourselves to picking the best two wholly selected items; i.e., we do not permit the possibility of fractionally selected items. If we examine the 15 possible combinations of the six items in pairs, we find that items

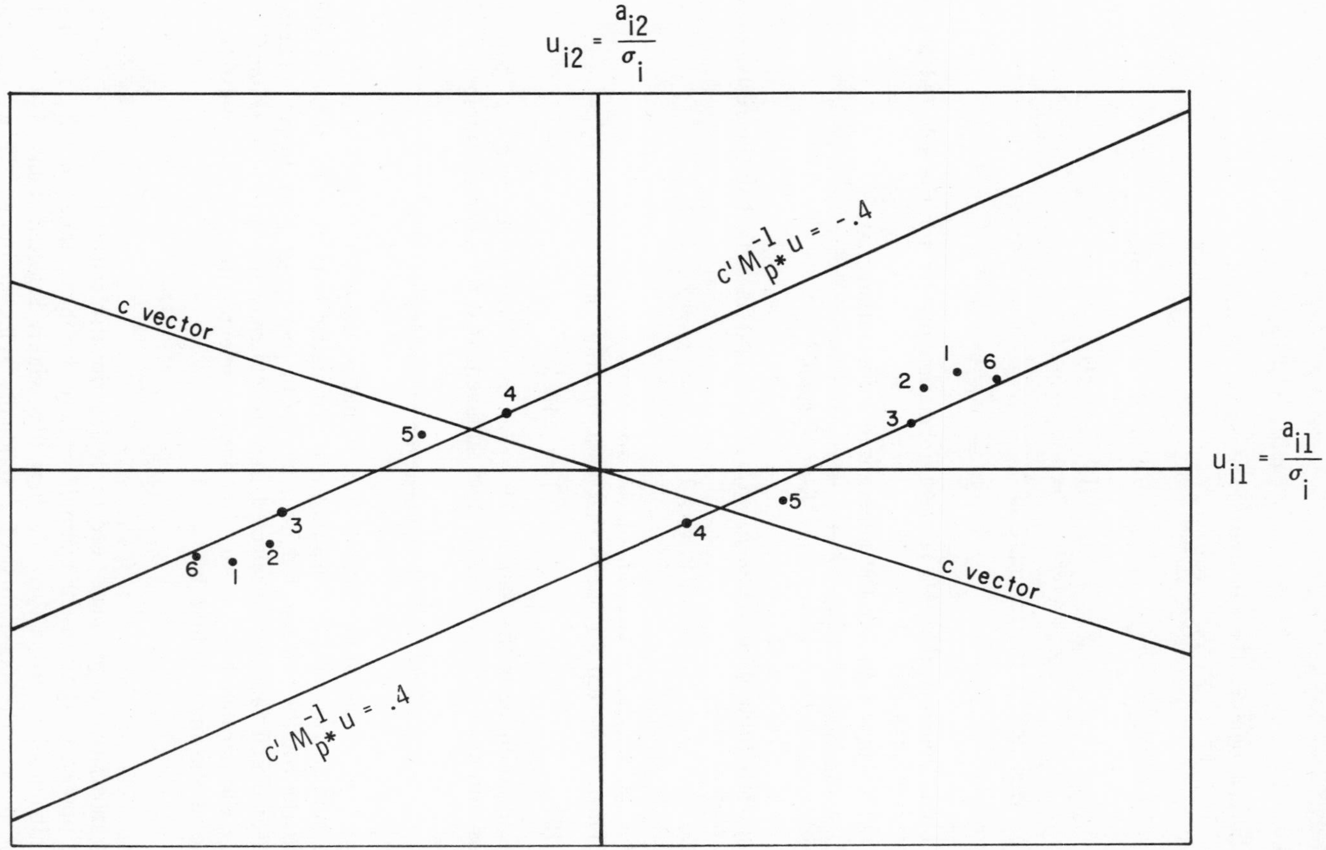

FIG. 1. Illustration of Solution for Realistic Data: Section 4

4 and 5 are best; i.e., they yield the estimate with the smallest variance. For $p_0 = (0, 0, 0, 1, 1, 0)$, the variance of this estimate is

$$c'M_{p_0}^{-1}c = .381 \,. \tag{4.11}$$

For the actual practical purpose, p_0 solves the selection problem. In order to illustrate the method, we shall, however, analyze the example as if p_0 were only a tentative solution, suggested, e.g., by Figure 1.

Theorem 3.1 states that if, in fact, p_0 is the minimizing vector when fractionally selected items are admitted, there is a number h such that

$$|c'M_{p_0}^{-1}u_4| \geqq h \,, \quad |c'M_{p_0}^{-1}u_5| \geqq h \,, \quad |c'M_{p_0}^{-1}u_j| \leqq h \,, \quad j = 1, 2, 3, 6 \,. \tag{4.12}$$

However, we find that

$$\begin{array}{lll} |c'M_{p_0}^{-1}u_1| = 1.043 \,, & |c'M_{p_0}^{-1}u_3| = .939 \,, & |c'M_{p_0}^{-1}u_5| = .517 \,, \\ |c'M_{p_0}^{-1}u_2| = .950 \,, & |c'M_{p_0}^{-1}u_4| = .337 \,, & |c'M_{p_0}^{-1}u_6| = 1.141 \,. \end{array} \tag{4.13}$$

It follows that p_0 is not the minimizing vector, and thus we must consider fractionally selected items.

Since items 4 and 5 are the best pair of items (the variance of the estimate based on items 2 and 6, for example, is 447.01), it seems reasonable to include these items when fractional selection is allowed. From the theorem we know that there must be a pair of parallel lines such that the two fractionally selected items lie on the line.

If we examine Figure 1, we see that if we draw the two parallel lines through items 3 and 4, we have item 5 lying outside the lines and items 1, 2, and 6 lying between them. This leads us to attempt a fractional solution of the form

$$p^* = (0, 0, r, 1-r, 1, 0) \,. \tag{4.14}$$

We determine r such that

$$c'M_{p^*}^{-1}u_3 = c'M_{p^*}^{-1}u_4 \,.$$

That is, we wish to have

$$\begin{aligned} (.641 \quad -.205)\begin{bmatrix} .118 - .012r & .345 - .511r \\ .345 - .511r & 1.079 + 2.202r \end{bmatrix}\begin{bmatrix} 1.588 \\ .231 \end{bmatrix} \\ = (.641 \quad -.205)\begin{bmatrix} .118 - .012r & .345 - .511r \\ .345 - .511r & 1.079 + 2.202r \end{bmatrix}\begin{bmatrix} .566 \\ -.254 \end{bmatrix} . \end{aligned} \tag{4.15}$$

From this equation we find that $r = .019$.

It follows that

$$p^* = (0, 0, .019, .981, 1, 0) \,; \tag{4.16}$$

$$M_{p^*} = \begin{bmatrix} 1.1208 & -.3353 \\ -.3353 & .1182 \end{bmatrix} ; \tag{4.17}$$

$$c'M_{p^*}^{-1} = (.3506 \quad -.7399)\,; \tag{4.18}$$

and

$$\begin{aligned} &c'M_{p^*}^{-1}u_1 = .273\,, \quad &&c'M_{p^*}^{-1}u_3 = .386\,, \quad &&c'M_{p^*}^{-1}u_5 = .476\,, \\ &c'M_{p^*}^{-1}u_2 = .286\,, \quad &&c'M_{p^*}^{-1}u_4 = .386\,, \quad &&c'M_{p^*}^{-1}u_6 = .341\,. \end{aligned} \tag{4.19}$$

Thus, the conditions of the theorem are satisfied, and p^* is the minimizing vector. The variance of the associated estimate is .376. Contrasting this with the variance when items 4 and 5 are used totally, namely .381, we see that the use of fractional allocation actually brings about a slight improvement in the solution of the modified problem.

It should be remembered, however, that modifying the problem by admitting fractional allocation is an *ad hoc* device, applying primarily when n is considerably larger than k; its justification is to be found in the paragraph following Theorem 3.1. Thus, in our present example, the *practical* problem is to find the best *integral* solution, i. e., the best pair of items. The fractional solution (4.16) suggests that items 4 and 5 are the best choice, which is actually the case, as has been checked by comparing the variances corresponding to all possible choices of two items.

5. An Artificial Example When $k=2$

In Section 4 we considered the selection of two out of six items. For this situation we actually could and did compute the variance of z for all 15 pairs in the two-factor structure; and we actually found that we could even improve on the best pair by fractional allocation. It was shown how Theorem 3.1, combined with graphical considerations, could be used to select the best pair of items without going through all possible pairs. This becomes especially important when N and n both increase, thus ruling out the examination of all possibilities. It also becames important when k, the number of common factors, increases.

To demonstrate the application of the theorem in a more complex situation we have generated the following artificial example. There are ten items, and we desire first the optimal set of 4 items, then the optimal set of 5 items, and finally the optimal set of 6 items. A common factor space in two dimensions is assumed. We take

$$x_i = a_i'y + \varepsilon_i\,, \qquad z = c'y + \eta\,, \qquad i = 1, \cdots, 10, \tag{5.1}$$

where $c' = (2, 1)$, and

$$\begin{aligned} u_1' &= (4, 0)\,, \qquad & u_6' &= (0, 3)\,, \\ u_2' &= (-2, 1)\,, & u_7' &= (3, 3)\,, \\ u_3' &= (3, 1)\,, & u_8' &= (6, 3)\,, \\ u_4' &= (1, 2)\,, & u_9' &= (5, 4)\,, \\ u_5' &= (4, 2)\,, & u_{10}' &= (2, 5)\,; \end{aligned} \tag{5.2}$$

$$
(5.3) \qquad
\begin{aligned}
u_1u_1' &= \begin{bmatrix} 16 & 0 \\ 0 & 0 \end{bmatrix}, & u_6u_6' &= \begin{bmatrix} 0 & 0 \\ 0 & 9 \end{bmatrix}, \\
u_2u_2' &= \begin{bmatrix} 4 & -2 \\ -2 & 1 \end{bmatrix}, & u_7u_7' &= \begin{bmatrix} 9 & 9 \\ 9 & 9 \end{bmatrix}, \\
u_3u_3' &= \begin{bmatrix} 9 & 3 \\ 3 & 1 \end{bmatrix}, & u_8u_8' &= \begin{bmatrix} 36 & 18 \\ 18 & 9 \end{bmatrix}, \\
u_4u_4' &= \begin{bmatrix} 1 & 2 \\ 2 & 4 \end{bmatrix}, & u_9u_9' &= \begin{bmatrix} 25 & 20 \\ 20 & 16 \end{bmatrix}, \\
u_5u_5' &= \begin{bmatrix} 16 & 8 \\ 8 & 4 \end{bmatrix}, & u_{10}u_{10}' &= \begin{bmatrix} 4 & 10 \\ 10 & 25 \end{bmatrix}.
\end{aligned}
$$

We shall apply the method indicated at the end of Section 3. We have

$$
(5.4) \qquad \Lambda = \sum_{i=1}^{10} u_iu_i' = \begin{pmatrix} 120 & 68 \\ 68 & 78 \end{pmatrix}.
$$

Then, indicating proportionality by the sign $\sim$, we obtain

$$
(5.5) \qquad \Lambda^{-1} \sim \begin{bmatrix} 78 & -68 \\ -68 & 120 \end{bmatrix}
$$

and

$$
(5.6) \qquad \gamma' = c'\Lambda^{-1} \sim (88, \quad -16).
$$

In (5.5) and (5.6) we need not concern ourselves with the proportionality factors.

The item points are plotted graphically in Figure 2. If we plot the direction of γ in Figure 2, and imagine a straight line perpendicular to it moving from right to left, the order in which the item points are swept over by this line indicates their order of preference in our first approximation.

If $n = 4$, i.e., four items are to be selected, we are thus led to the selection I : 1, 5, 8, 9. Forming the corresponding product sums, we find that

$$
(5.7) \qquad M_1^{-1} \sim \begin{bmatrix} 29 & -46 \\ -46 & 93 \end{bmatrix}, \qquad \gamma_1' \sim (12, 1).
$$

In the direction of γ_1, the four outermost item points are still numbers 1, 5, 8, and 9. The theorem tells us, then, that choice I is optimal.

Next, take $n = 5$. Using the approximate selection determined by the γ-direction, we shall have to try the set $\text{II}_1 : 1, 3, 5, 8, 9$. From the corresponding product sums, we find as above that $\gamma_1' \sim (11, 4)$. In this direction, however, the five outermost item points are $\text{II}_2 : 1, 5, 7, 8, 9$. On the other hand, if we try the latter set, we get the direction $\gamma_2' \sim (21, -8)$, and the five outermost points are 1, 3, 5, 8, and 9, i.e., the set first attempted. This mutuality makes it plausible that a selection of form $\text{II}_3 : 1, 3^*, 5, 7^*, 8, 9$ (* indicating fractional selection) might give an optimal solution of the problem. Introducing unknown weights p_3, p_7 with sum 1, we find that

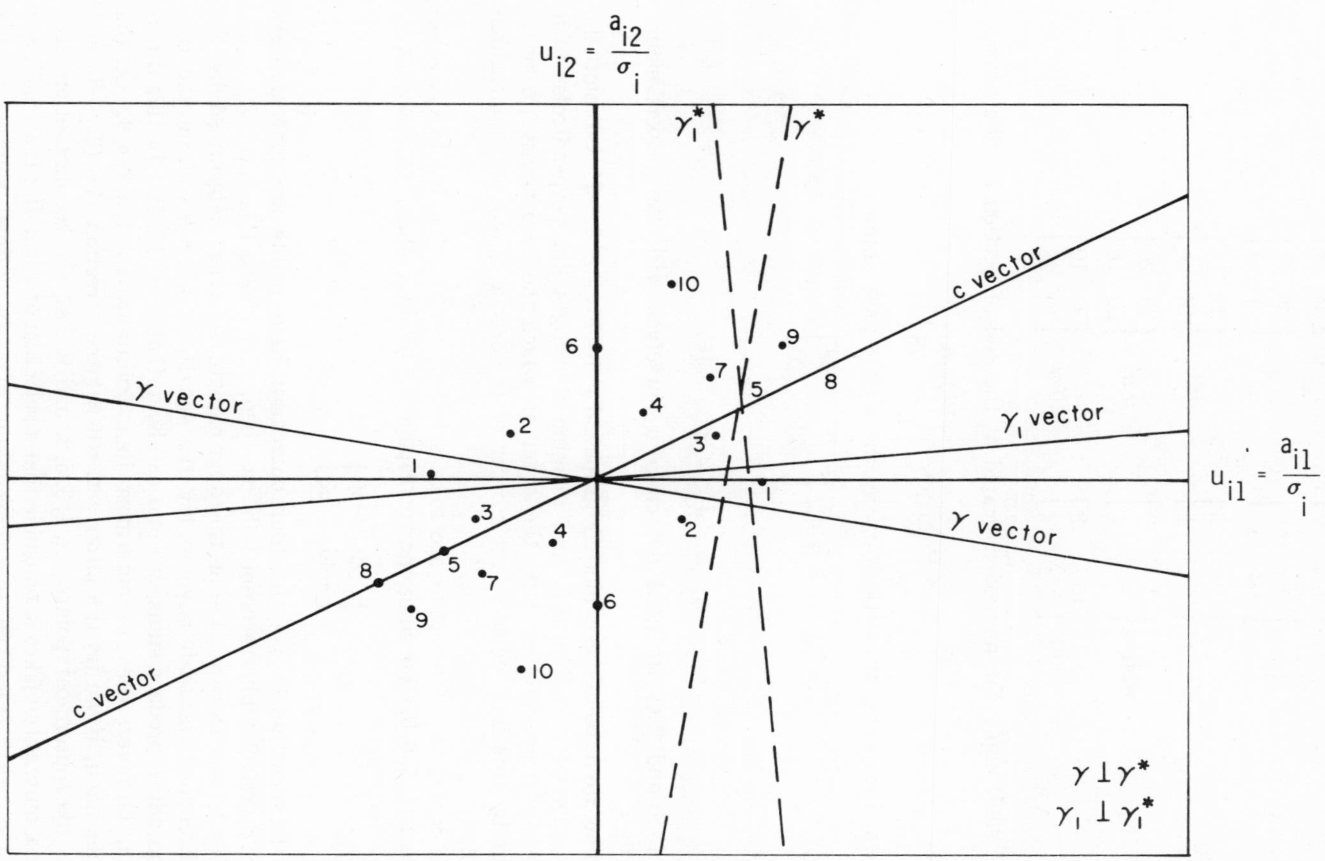

FIG. 2. Illustration of Solution for Artificial Data: Section 5

(5.8) $$M_3 \sim \begin{bmatrix} 93 + 9p_3 + 9p_7 & 46 + 3p_3 + 9p_7 \\ 46 + 3p_3 + 9p_7 & 29 + p_3 + 9p_7 \end{bmatrix}.$$

In order for the points 3 and 7 to lie on the boundary line of the selection region, the vector $\gamma = M^{-1}c$ must have direction (1, 0), which gives the condition

(5.9) $$-2(46 + 3p_3 + 9p_7) + (93 + 9p_3 + 9p_7) = 0 ,$$

and hence (noting that $p_3 + p_7 = 1$), $p_3 = \frac{2}{3}$, $p_7 = \frac{1}{3}$. Thus the optimum allocation vector is $p^* = (1, 0, \frac{2}{3}, 0, 1, 0, \frac{1}{3}, 1, 1, 0)$. In practice, we have to make a choice between selections II_1 and II_2. The corresponding variance $V = c'M^{-1}c$ are as follows (note that the factors $1/|M|$ cannot be omitted at this point):

$$V_1 = \frac{30(2^2) - 2(49)(2)(1) + 102(1^2)}{102(30) - 49(49)} = \frac{26}{659} = 0.03945 ,$$

$$V_2 = \frac{38(2^2) - 2(55)(2)(1) + 102(1^2)}{102(38) - 55(55)} = \frac{34}{851} = 0.03995 .$$

Thus, there will be a slight preference for the former choice.

Finally, if we wish to include $n = 6$ items, it seems reasonable, from the figure, to try the set III : 1, 3, 5, 7, 8, 9. It leads to $\gamma_1' \sim (20, -5)$. In this case, the moving boundary line will hit points 2 and 7 at the same time. Nevertheless, the set III still fulfills the condition of the theorem, and hence is optimal. We note that in this example, of the two item points on the boundary line, item 7 has weight 1, and item 2 has weight 0.

Early in the chapter we stated that the optimal $(n + 1)$ set of items need not completely contain the optimal set of n items. However in many practical situations this will occur, as the foregoing exercise demonstrates.

APPENDIX

The theory behind the method presented and illustrated above is more fully developed in Chapters 5 to 7, to which this Appendix is to serve as a clue.

The fundamental Theorem 3.1 is illustrated and proved in Chapter 5; its development is built around the realistic, but analytically troublesome, case of a discrete item population.

In Chapter 6 there is an attempt to work out a selection method for the case of a large and smoothly distributed population of item points, replacing the actual discrete distribution by a continuous and, particularly, by a normal (or quasi-normal) one. This approach leads to the practical procedure described at the end of Section 3 in this chapter.

Chapter 7 is devoted to refinements of the continuous method of the previous chapter. It treats the following questions: (1) How can a normal distribution be fitted to the relevant outer parts of the item-point population? (2) When a nearly optimal selection region has been found, how can it be improved by slightly varying its boundary planes? The answers given are perhaps not too attractive from a practical point of view; they are reported simply as attempts that may prove useful in *some* situations.

References

[1] Elfving, G. A selection problem in experimental design. *Soc. Sci. Fenn. Comment. Phys.-Math.*, 1957, **20**, 2. See also this volume, Chapter 5.

[2] Elfving, G. Selection of non-repeatable observations for estimation. In Vol. 1, J. Neyman, ed., *Proceedings of the Third Berkeley Symposium on Mathematical Statistics and Probability*, Berkeley, Calif.: Univ. California Press, 1956. See also this volume, Chapter 6.

[3] Elfving, G. Optimum allocation in linear regression theory. *Ann. Math. Stat.*, 1952, **23**, 255-62.

[4] Elfving, G. Geometric allocation theory. *Skand. Aktuarietidskr.*, 1954, **37**, 170-90.

5

The Item-Selection Problem and Experimental Design

GUSTAV ELFVING, University of Helsinki

1. Introduction

In this chapter we shall be concerned with the following type of statistical design problem. Let $\alpha_1, \cdots, \alpha_k$ be unknown parameters, and denote by $\alpha = (\alpha_1, \cdots, \alpha_k)'$ the parameter vector. Let the aim of the planned experiment be to estimate a particular linear form $\theta = c'\alpha$ in the parameters. Assume that for this purpose a finite set of potential observations ("items") is available, each in the following form:

$$x_i = u_i'\alpha + \xi_i , \qquad i = 1, \cdots, N . \tag{1.1}$$

Here, the ξ_i's are uncorrelated error terms with zero expectation and (for convenience) variance 1, whereas the u_i's are known $m \times 1$ coefficient vectors. The experimenter is allowed to perform $n < N$ of the observations (1.1), each of them *once*. The design problem, then, is to select a set $w = (i_1, \cdots, i_n)$ from the subscripts $i = 1, \cdots, N$ so as to minimize the variance of the least-squares estimator $\hat{\theta}$ derived from the corresponding observations.

The question is closely related to the allocation problem treated in [1], [2]; the difference is that in the allocation problem repetition of the observations is allowed. An "idealized" version of the present question is treated in Chapter 6 and in [3]; there the discrete set $\{u_i\}$, $i = 1, \cdots, N$, of coefficient vectors ("item points") is replaced by a continuous distribution.

2. Main Theorem

For any particular selection ω of subscripts the estimation properties of the corresponding set of observations are essentially described by the information matrix

$$M = \sum_{\omega} u_i u_i' . \tag{2.1}$$

This paper has previously been published in *Soc. Sci. Fenn. Comment. Phys.-Math.*, 1957, **22**, 2.

In order to avoid unnecessary complications, throughout this chapter we shall assume that for *any* set ω of n observations the matrix M is non-singular. This will generally be the case when the coefficient vectors u_i are empirically determined, e.g., by factor analysis. The variance of the least-squares estimator $\hat{\theta}$ corresponding to ω is, then,

$$V = D^2(\hat{\theta}) = c'M^{-1}c . \tag{2.2}$$

We shall now introduce a "continuization" device that greatly facilitates the solution of our selection problem without, as we shall see, essentially impairing its practical applicability. For this purpose we consider, instead of the matrix (2.1), the generalized information matrix

$$M = \sum_{i=1}^{N} p_i u_i u_i' , \tag{2.3}$$

where the *allocation vector* $p = (p_1, \cdots, p_N)$ is subject to the restrictions

$$0 \leqq p_i \leqq 1 ; \qquad \sum_1^N p_i = n . \tag{2.4}$$

Obviously the set of matrices (2.3) contains the set of matrices (2.1). For a given p, we shall characterize those items for which $p_i = 1$ as *totally selected*, those for which $p_i = 0$ as *excluded*, and those for which $0 < p_i < 1$ as *fractionally selected*. It will be seen below that the optimal allocation (when properly chosen) will contain at most k fractionally selected items. Since the corresponding p_i's can total at most $k - 1$, there will be from $n - k + 1$ to n totally selected items. In practice, we may "round off" the fractional p_i's to 1's, i.e., select the corresponding items on an equal basis with the rest. Then, at the expense of making at most $k - 1$ more observations than originally planned, we will be sure to have a variance $D^2(\hat{\theta})$ not exceeding the smallest one that could be obtained by any selection of n items. In many cases, the optimal p will contain only 1's and 0's, and hence provide an exact solution of the original discrete problem.

The following interpretation of the fractional p_i's may be instructive. Imagine that the observations (1.1) may be independently *repeated*, each of them at most r times. The information matrix of the resulting experiment may then be written as $M = r \sum p_i u_i u_i'$, where the p_i's vary from 0 to 1 through multiples of $1/r$. The factor r in M is obviously irrelevant for the minimization problem. In particular, if we take $n = 1$, and if r is very large, we shall be concerned with the allocation problem treated in [1], which thus appears as a special case of the present one.

After these preparations, we are in a position to state the following main

THEOREM 1. *The function V of p, defined by* (2.2–3) *on the set* (2.4), *has a minimum. In order for an allocation vector p to yield this minimum, it is necessary and sufficient that for a certain non-negative number h*

(2.5) $$p_i = \begin{cases} 0 \\ 1 \end{cases} \quad \textit{whenever } |c'M^{-1}u_i| \lesseqgtr h \,,$$

where M denotes the matrix (2.3) *corresponding to p.*

What this theorem says is, roughly, that the "selection region" consists of that part of k-space lying outside the twin hyperplanes $c'M^{-1}u = \pm h$; the item points lying in the boundary planes may have to be totally selected, fractionally selected, or not selected at all.

PROOF. From our general assumption that $M = \sum_\omega u_i u_i'$ is non-singular for any choice ω of n item points, it follows that $M = \sum p_i u_i u_i'$ is non-singular on (2.4). Actually, if p_0 denotes the smallest positive p_i, we may write

$$M = p_0 \sum_{p_i > 0} u_i u_i' + \sum_{p_i > 0} (p_i - p_0) u_i u_i' \,.$$

The first sum consists of at least n terms, and hence is non-singular. This property is not destroyed by adjoining the second sum, whose terms are non-negative definite. It follows that $V = c'M^{-1}c$ is continuous on the closed set (2.4), and hence attains its greatest lower bound.

Necessity of (2.5). Let p be an allocation vector for which the minimum of V is attained, and let i and j be two items such that $p_i > 0$ and $p_j < 1$, respectively. Then, for any small enough $\delta p > 0$, the variation $dp_i = -\delta p$, $dp_j = \delta p$, $dp_h = 0$ $(h \neq i, j)$ is admissible with regard to (2.4). Since p was assumed to make V a minimum, the corresponding differential

$$dV = \frac{\partial V}{\partial p_i} dp_i + \frac{\partial V}{\partial p_j} dp_j = \left(-\frac{\partial V}{\partial p_i} + \frac{\partial V}{\partial p_j} \right) \delta p$$

must be $\geqq 0$, and hence

(2.6) $$-\frac{\partial V}{\partial p_i} \geqq -\frac{\partial V}{\partial p_j} \qquad p_i > 0,\ p_j < 1 \,.$$

If $0 < p_j, p_i < 1$, then i and j are interchangeable in (2.6), and it follows that $-\partial V / \partial p_i = h^2$, say, for all fractionally selected items, if any (the non-negativity of $-\partial V / \partial p_i$ will be proved below). Applying (2.6) to a fractionally selected item combined with either a totally selected or an excluded one, we see that $-\partial V / \partial p_i \geqq h^2$ for the former and $\leqq h^2$ for the latter type. Finally, if p comprises no p_i with $0 < p_i < 1$, there will exist, according to (2.6), a number h^2 (not uniquely determined) that is smaller than every $-\partial V / \partial p_i$, with $p_i = 1$ and larger than every $-\partial V / \partial p_j$ with $p_j = 0$. Thus, in any case, we have

(2.7) $$p_i = \begin{cases} 0 \\ 1 \end{cases} \quad \text{whenever } -\frac{\partial V}{\partial p_i} \lesseqgtr h^2 .$$

We must now calculate $-\partial V / \partial p_i$. By well-known matrix operations, we find for a variation dp_i of p_i alone

$$-dV = -c'dM^{-1}c = c'M^{-1}\cdot dM\cdot M^{-1}c$$
$$= c'M^{-1}\cdot u_i u_i' dp_i \cdot M^{-1}c = |c'M^{-1}u_i|^2\, 2dp_i\,,$$

and hence

$$-\frac{\partial V}{\partial p_i} = |c'M^{-1}u_i|^2\,. \tag{2.8}$$

This result combined with (2.7) gives the necessary condition (2.5).

Sufficiency of (2.5). Assume that the allocation vector p^0, together with a number $h \geqq 0$, satisfies (2.5). Let p^1 be another vector in (2.4), and consider the convex combinations $p(\lambda) = (1-\lambda)p^0 + \lambda p^1$ [also in (2.4)] the corresponding information matrices

$$M_\lambda = \sum p_i(\lambda)u_i u_i' = (1-\lambda)M_0 + \lambda M_1\,,$$

and the variances $V(\lambda) = c'M_\lambda^{-1}c$. Obviously, $V(0)$ and $V(1)$ are the variances corresponding to p^0 and p^1, respectively. In order to prove that $V(0) \leqq V(1)$, we shall show that $V'(0) \geqq 0$, and $V''(\lambda) \geqq 0$ in $0 \leqq \lambda \leqq 1$.

By the same matrix differentiation that was used above, we find

$$-V'(\lambda) = c'M_\lambda^{-1}(M_1 - M_0)M_\lambda^{-1}c\,, \tag{2.9}$$

and hence

$$-V'(0) = c'M_0^{-1}\cdot \sum (p_i^1 - p_i^0)u_i u_i' \cdot M_0^{-1}c$$
$$= \sum (p_i^1 - p_i^0)\,|c'M_0^{-1}u_i|^2\,.$$

Replacing the second factor in this sum by h^2 will, owing to (2.5), increase the sum, because when $|c'M_0^{-1}u_i| > h$ the first factor will be $p_i^1 - 1 \leqq 0$, and when $|c'M_0^{-1}u_i| < h$ the first factor will be $p_i^1 - 0 \geqq 0$. Hence $-V'(0) \leqq h^2 \sum (p_i^1 - p_i^0) = h^2(n-n) = 0$, or $V'(0) \geqq 0$.

Differentiating (2.9) once more and using the symmetry of all M's, we find that

$$V''(\lambda) = 2c'M_\lambda^{-1}(M_1 - M_0)M_\lambda^{-1}(M_1 - M_0)M_\lambda^{-1}c$$
$$= 2[(M_1 - M_0)M_\lambda^{-1}c]'M_\lambda^{-1}[(M_1 - M_0)M_\lambda^{-1}c]\,.$$

Since M_λ, and hence M_λ^{-1}, is positive definite for $0 \leqq \lambda \leqq 1$, it follows that $V''(\lambda) \geqq 0$. This completes the proof of Theorem 1.

3. Illustration

Let $N = 3$, $n = 2$, $u_1' = (1, 0)$, $u_2' = (\frac{1}{2}, \frac{\sqrt{3}}{2})$, $u_3' = (\frac{1}{2}, -\frac{\sqrt{3}}{2})$. The vector $c' = (\cos\gamma, \sin\gamma)$ will be considered as variable. Any optimal allocation must consist of either (i) one item point, totally selected, together with its two neighbors, fractionally selected; or (ii) two neighbor points, totally selected. Note that any point u_i may be replaced by its opposite point $-u_i$, which yields the same contribution to the information matrix.

Take first the allocations of form $(1, p_2, p_3)$. One finds that

$$M = \frac{1}{4}\begin{bmatrix} 5 & \sqrt{3}\,(p_2 - p_3) \\ \sqrt{3}\,(p_2 - p_3) & 3 \end{bmatrix},$$

$$M^{-1} = \frac{4}{15 - 3(p_2 - p_3)^2}\begin{bmatrix} 3 & \sqrt{3}\,(p_3 - p_2) \\ \sqrt{3}\,(p_3 - p_2) & 5 \end{bmatrix}.$$

In order for the boundary line $c'M^{-1}u = h$ to be the line joining u_2 and u_3, the vector $M^{-1}c$ has to be proportional to $(1, 0)$, which gives the condition

$$\sqrt{3}\,(p_3 - p_2)\cos\gamma + 5\sin\gamma = 0\,,$$

and together with $p_2 + p_3 = 1$,

$$p_2 = \frac{1}{2} + \frac{5}{2\sqrt{3}}\tan\gamma\,, \qquad p_3 = \frac{1}{2} - \frac{5}{2\sqrt{3}}\tan\gamma\,.$$

This gives non-negative p_2, p_3 if and only if $|\tan\gamma| \leqq \sqrt{3}/5$, i.e., when γ is between $\pm 19°6'$.

Next we consider the allocation $(1, 1, 0)$, and find

$$M = \frac{1}{4}\begin{bmatrix} 5 & \sqrt{3} \\ \sqrt{3} & 3 \end{bmatrix}, \qquad M^{-1} = \frac{1}{3}\begin{bmatrix} 3 & -\sqrt{3} \\ -\sqrt{3} & 5 \end{bmatrix}.$$

For direction angle the vector $M^{-1}c$ (normal to the boundary line) has the angle Θ determined by

$$\tan\Theta = \frac{-\sqrt{3}\cos\gamma + 5\sin\gamma}{3\cos\gamma - \sqrt{3}\sin\gamma}\,. \tag{3.1}$$

In order for the boundary line $c'M^{-1}u = h$ to cut off precisely the selected points u_1, u_2, the angle Θ has to be between $0°$ and $60°$, which implies that γ lies between $19°6'$ and $40°54' = 60° - 19°6'$. These are then the γ for which $(1, 1, 0)$ is the optimal allocation. By analogy with the case $(1, p_2, p_3)$, one finds that the γ's between $60° \pm 19°6'$ lead to optimal allocations of form $(p_1, 1, p_3)$, and so on.

4. Number of Fractionally Selected Items

In general the $(k-1)$-dimensional boundary plane $c'M^{-1}u = h$ will contain at most k item points (note that opposite points $\pm u_i$ are always counted as equivalent), and hence in general there will be at most k fractionally selected items. When the boundary plane happens to contain more than k points, there may well be optimal allocations with more than k fractional p_i's. It will be seen, however, that one can always find an equivalent allocation with at most k weights p_i between 0 and 1. This is the content of

THEOREM 2. *The function V defined by* (2.2–3) *can always be minimized on* (2.4) *by means of an allocation vector p with at most k fractional p_i's.*

PROOF. The proof rests on a continuity argument. Consider, together with the given set $\{u_i\}$ of item points, a sequence of sets $\{u_i^j\}$ $(i = 1, \cdots, N;$

$j = 1, 2, \cdots$) such that (i) $u_i^j \to u_i$ as $j \to \infty$, and (ii) for each j, no $k+1$ points u_i^j lie in the same $(k-1)$-dimensional hyperplane. The sequence $\{u_i^j\}$ can be constructed, e.g., by choosing an arbitrary set $\{u_i^*\}$ $(i = 1, \cdots, N)$ with property (ii), forming $u_i(\lambda) \equiv (1-\lambda)u_i + \lambda u_i^*$, and taking $u_i^j = u_i(\lambda_j)$ for a sequence $\lambda_1, \lambda_2, \cdots \to 0$. In order for (ii) to hold, we must choose the λ_j in such a way that all $(k+1) \times (k+1)$ determinants of type

$$\begin{vmatrix} u_{i_1}(\lambda) \cdots u_{i_1 k}(\lambda) & 1 \\ \cdots\cdots\cdots\cdots\cdots\cdots & \\ u_{i_{k+1}1}(\lambda) \cdots u_{i_{k+1}k}(\lambda) & 1 \end{vmatrix} \tag{4.1}$$

are different from zero for $\lambda = \lambda_j$. Now, each such determinant is a polynomial in λ_j and cannot be identically zero, since in that case the set $\{u_i^*\}$ to which $\{u_i^j\}$ reduces for $\lambda = 1$ would not have property (ii). To make sure that (ii) holds for all $\{u_i^j\}$, we only have to choose the λ_j in order to avoid the finitely many roots of all polynomials (4.1).

For each set $\{u_i^j\}$ $(j = 1, 2, \cdots)$ our allocation problem (with c and n fixed once and for all) is solvable according to Theorem 1: there exists an allocation vector $p^j = \{p_1^j, \cdots, p_N^j)$ in (2.4) and a corresponding information matrix $M_j = \sum_i p_i^j u_i^j u_i^{j\prime}$ such that $c' M_j^{-1} c = \min$; moreover, there exists a number $h_j \geqq 0$ such that the hyperplanes $c' M_j^{-1} u = \pm h_j$ separate the totally selected and the excluded item points, and contain all u_i^j for which $0 < p_i^j < 1$. By the construction of the sequence $\{u_i^j\}$, there are, for each j, at most k points u_i^j in any hyperplane, and hence at most k fractionally selected items.

Since there are only finitely many ways to subdivide N elements into three classes, i.e., ω_+ (totally selected), ω_0 (fractionally selected) and ω_- (excluded), at least one such partition must repeat itself for infinitely many j's. By a first elimination, we exclude all other j's, thus obtaining fixed sets $\omega_+, \omega_-, \omega_0$ of selected, excluded, and fractionally selected i's, the last group containing at most k elements.

Since the set (2.4) is closed, we construct by a well-known procedure a new subsequence $\{j\}$ such that on this sequence p^j converges to a limiting allocation vector p; this is still in (2.4), and the subscripts of its fractional components, if any, still belong to ω_0. If M denotes the information matrix corresponding to p, we have $M_j \to M$; also, M^{-1} exists, and $M_j^{-1} c \to M^{-1} c$, which implies that $\| M_j^{-1} c \|$ is bounded.

Finally, since $h_j \leqq | c' M_j^{-1} u_i^j |$ for some i, and since all norms $\| u_i^j \|$ have a common bound, we conclude that the h_j are bounded. Thus, applying once more the selection procedure, we find that $h_j \to h$.

For the sets $\{h_i^j\}$ constructed in this way we have by the necessity part of Theorem 1

$$p_i^j = \begin{cases} 0 \\ 1 \end{cases} \text{whenever } | c' M_j^{-1} u_i^j | \lessgtr h_j . \tag{4.2}$$

Now, consider the limiting p, h. If for some subscript i, $|c'M^{-1}u_i| > h$, then from some j_0 on, $|c'M_j^{-1}u_i^j| > h_j$, hence by (4.2) $p_i^j = 1$, and $p_i = \lim p_i^j = 1$; similarly, if for some i, $|c'M^{-1}u_i| < h$, we conclude that $p_i = 0$. The sufficiency part of Theorem 1 then proves that p minimizes $c'M^{-1}c$ on (2.4). Since p has at most k fractional components, this completes the proof of Theorem 2.

References

[1] Elfving, G. Optimum allocation in linear regression theory. *Ann. Math. Stat.*, 1952, **23**, 255–62.

[2] Elfving, G. Geometric allocation theory. *Skand. Aktuarietidskr.*, 1954, **37**, 170–90.

[3] Elfving, G. Selection of nonrepeatable observations for estimation. In Vol. 1, J. Neyman, ed., *Proceedings of the Third Berkeley Symposium on Mathematical Statistics and Probability*, Berkeley, Calif.: Univ. California Press, 1956. See also this volume, Chapter 6.

6

Item Selection and Choice of Nonrepeatable Observations for Estimation

GUSTAV ELFVING, University of Helsinki

1. Introduction and Summary

This paper deals with the following particular type of design problem. Let there be given a set of possible observations, of the form

$$x_i = u_{i1}\alpha_1 + \cdots + u_{ik}\alpha_k + \xi_i = u_i'\alpha + \xi_i\,, \qquad i = 1, \cdots, N\,, \tag{1.1}$$

where the coefficient vectors u_i are known, the parameter vector α is unknown, and the error terms ξ_i are uncorrelated random variables with mean zero and variance one. The last requirement can obviously be met by a change of scale if the original error variances are known. Let the aim of the investigator be to estimate a particular parametric form $\theta = c'\alpha$. If it is necessary to do this on the basis of a subset comprising, say, $n < N$ observations, and if N and n are too large to permit trying out all possible combinations, one has to find some feasible selection procedure leading to a least-squares estimator $\hat{\theta}$ with the smallest possible variance.

A practical situation in which this problem is encountered is the following one in psychology. Let the x_i's be the scores associated with various possible test items, and assume that a factor analysis has been performed, yielding a more or less approximate representation of the scores in terms of certain common factors $\alpha_1, \cdots, \alpha_k$ and mutually uncorrelated specific factors ξ_i. If the scores are normalized to specific variance one, and if the common factors are considered as parameters characteristic of the individual, we are concerned with the model (1.1). Further, let z be a "criterion score" measuring, for example, some ability of particular interest, for which, by the same factor analysis, a representation $z = c'\alpha + \zeta$ has been found. For practical reasons, a planned routine prediction of z often has to be based on a moderate-size subset of the original large set of items. The question then arises how to select this subset.

This paper has previously been published in *Proceedings of the Third Berkeley Symposium on Mathematical Statistics and Probability*, J. Neyman, ed., Berkeley, Calif.: Univ. California Press, Vol. I, 1956.

Our problem is closely connected with the allocation problem, which, in its simplest form, can be stated as follows: Given a set (1.1) of possible observations, each of which can be independently *repeated* as many times as we please, which of them should we select for estimating $\theta = c'\alpha$, and how many times should we repeat the selected ones when a fixed total n of actual observations is allowed? This problem may be considered as a special case of the previous one, namely, the case that all different coefficient vectors u_i occur in the given set with at least multiplicity n. This is approximately the situation when the "item points" u_i, in k-space, appear in clusters. In such a case it is possible to make use of certain geometric allocation methods developed in [1] and [2].

In this chapter we shall be concerned with the opposite situation, where the u_i's are more or less smoothly distributed, so as to permit an idealized description by means of a density function. With this idealization, we shall show (i) that the question of selection reduces to a variational problem, the varied element being a region S in k-space; (ii) that this problem leads to conditions (3.2), which essentially constitute a system of $[k(k+1)/2]+1$ equations with equally many unknowns; (iii) that, if the above-mentioned density function is spherically symmetric, or can be reduced to such symmetry by a linear transformation of the argument, Equations (3.2) admit a unique solution, obtained by taking for S a twin half-space $\{u\colon |g'u| > \kappa\}$.

It seems very likely that these results will prove modifiable and will cover also the original discrete problem.

2. The Variational Problem

Let ω denote any subset of the set $(1, \cdots, N)$ of integers. Every ω determines a set of observations (1.1), and a corresponding system of normal equations in $\alpha_1, \cdots, \alpha_k$, with information matrix

$$M = \sum_{\omega} u_i u_i' \,.$$

The least-squares estimator $\hat{\theta}$ for $\theta = c'\alpha$ has variance $D^2(\hat{\theta}) = c'M^{-1}c$. Thus, in the discrete case, our problem is a restricted minimum problem in ω, viz.,

$$c'\Big(\sum u_i u_i'\Big)^{-1} c = \min_{\omega}; \qquad \sum_{\omega} 1 = n \,. \tag{2.1}$$

Before proceeding to the idealization referred to in Section 1, it is useful to introduce what might be called a symmetry convention. The contribution of any observation (1.1) to the information matrix M depends solely on the vector ("item point") u_i in k-space. Items with opposite u_i's obviously yield the same contribution. For reasons of symmetry we shall henceforth describe each item by means of the *pair* of opposite points $\pm u_i$. Denoting by S the centrally symmetric set of all points u_i and $-u_i$ corresponding to a particular selection ω, we note that the sums in (2.1) may be written as sums over S divided by 2. Introducing for convenience a constant factor $1/N$, which obviously does not affect the minimization, we may rewrite the problem (2.1) as

$$c'\left(\frac{1}{2N}\sum_S uu'\right)^{-1}c = \min_S ; \qquad \frac{1}{2N}\sum_S 1 = \delta , \tag{2.2}$$

where $\delta = n/N$ is the selection rate.

Now, let $f(u)$ denote a centrally symmetric probability density function in k-space, with finite second-order moments, and assume that $f(u)$ provides a reasonably accurate description of the distribution of the item points $\pm u_i$; i.e., the number of such points in a region A is approximately $2N\int_A f(u)\,du$, where du denotes the volume element. With this idealization, our problem (2.2) turns into the variational problem

$$c'M^{-1}c = \min_S ; \tag{2.3}$$

$$\int_S f(u)\,du = \delta , \tag{2.4}$$

where S is the "selection region" sought for, and M denotes the $k \times k$ information matrix

$$M = \int_S uu'f(u)\,du , \tag{2.5}$$

with elements

$$\mu_{ij} = \int_S u_i u_j f(u)\,du . \tag{2.6}$$

In what follows we shall confine ourselves to this continuous problem, returning to the original discrete one only to establish the practical procedure presented at the end of the chapter.

3. Necessary Conditions for Extremal Regions

By an argument somewhat similar to that of the Neyman-Pearson lemma, we are led to

THEOREM 3.1. *Any extremal region of the problem presented in Equations* (2.3), (2.4), *and* (2.5) *is, aside from a set of f-measure* 0, *a twin half-space of the following form:*

$$S = \{u\colon |c'M^{-1}u| > h\} , \tag{3.1}$$

where the matrix M in turn depends on S according to (2.5).

We note that (2.5), (2.4), and (3.1) constitute a system

$$M = \int_S uu'f(u)\,du , \qquad \int_S f(u)\,du = \delta , \qquad S = \{u\colon |c'M^{-1}u| > h\} , \tag{3.2}$$

of equations in M, h, S; upon insertion of S from the last equation, the two first ones make $[k(k+1)/2] + 1$ equations in the equally many unknowns $\mu_{11}, \mu_{12}, \cdots, \mu_{kk}, h$.

PROOF. Let the set S be a solution of the problem (2.3–5), and S^* its complement. It is no restriction to assume that any neighborhood of a point $u \in S$ contains a subset of S with positive f-measure, and similarly for S^*. Take $u \in S$ and $u^* \in S^*$ such that $f(u) \neq 0, f(u^*) \neq 0$, but otherwise arbitrary. At each of these points, take a differential set, either $du \in S$ or $du^* \in S^*$, of non-vanishing Euclidean measure (we use, for simplicity, the same notation for the sets and their measures), such that

$$f(u)\,du = f(u^*)\,du^* . \tag{3.3}$$

The variation $S - du + du^*$ then obviously is admissible with respect to the size condition (2.4). Since S yields a minimum of $c'M^{-1}c$, with M depending on S according to (2.5), the corresponding variation of the first-mentioned quantity must be non-negative. Using the differential formula $dM^{-1} = -M^{-1}\cdot dM\cdot M^{-1}$ and noting that the differential of (2.5) is the integration element, we find that the effect on $c'M^{-1}c$ of subtracting du is

$$\begin{aligned} -\delta(c'M^{-1}c) &= c'M^{-1}\cdot dM\cdot M^{-1}c \\ &= c'M^{-1}\cdot uu'f(u)\,du\cdot M^{-1}c \\ &= (c'M^{-1}u)^2 f(u)\,du , \end{aligned} \tag{3.4}$$

and we find a similar expression for the effect of adding du^*. By the minimum property of S, we thus have

$$(c'M^{-1}u)^2 f(u)\,du \geqq (c'M^{-1}u^*)^2 f(u^*)\,du . \tag{3.5}$$

Dividing (3.5) by (3.3), we realize that $|c'M^{-1}u| \geqq |c'M^{-1}u^*|$ as soon as $u \in S \cap (f > 0)$ and $u^* \in S^* \cap (f > 0)$. It follows that there exists a constant $h > 0$ (in case $f = 0$ in some parts of u-space, h may not be uniquely determined) such that

$$|c'M^{-1}u| \begin{cases} \geqq h & \text{in} \quad S \cap (f > 0) \\ \leqq h & \text{in} \quad S^* \cap (f > 0) . \end{cases} \tag{3.6}$$

This completes the proof of Theorem 3.1.

We do not as yet know whether, in the general case, the system (3.2) possesses a solution, or whether this, if existing, is unique and constitutes a solution of the variational problem presented in Equations (2.3), (2.4), and (2.5). It seems likely that some iterative procedure might be designed for solving the system mentioned. Here we shall only discuss a special case in which an explicit solution is easily obtainable. The resulting procedure will probably be useful as an approximate solution also in more general cases.

4. A Transformation Lemma

Before proceeding to the special case referred to above, we shall prove the following simple

LEMMA 4.1. *Let $v = Lu$ be a linear transformation of k-space onto itself, with $|L| = 1$. If M, S, c satisfy* (3.2), *then*

$$\bar{M} = LML' , \qquad \bar{S} = LS , \qquad \bar{c} = Lc \tag{4.1}$$

satisfy the same system, with u replaced by v and $f(u)$ *by* $\bar{f}(v) = f(L^{-1}v)$; *and conversely.*

PROOF. Applying the transformation $v = Lu$ to the second integral in (3.2), we find that the second part of (3.2) remains true when S and f are replaced by $\bar{S}$ and $\bar{f}$, respectively. Applying the same transformation to the first part of (3.2), we find

$$M = L^{-1}\cdot\int_{\bar{S}} vv'\bar{f}(v)\,dv\cdot L'^{-1} ; \tag{4.2}$$

it follows that the matrix $\bar{M} = LML'$, together with $\bar{S}$ and $\bar{f}$, satisfies the first part of (3.2). For the third equation of (3.2), we have

$$\bar{S} = LS = \{v: |\, c'M^{-1}L^{-1}v \,| > h\} ; \tag{4.3}$$

replacing c by $L^{-1}\bar{c}$ and M by $L^{-1}\bar{M}L'^{-1}$, we find that $\bar{S}, \bar{M}, \bar{c}$ satisfy the third part of (3.2). The converse is proved in the same way, replacing L by L^{-1}.

5. The Spherically Symmetric Case

When the density function $f(u)$ is spherically symmetric with respect to the origin, it is intuitively almost obvious that the twin half-space of Theorem 3.1 has to be symmetric with respect to the "relevant direction" determined by the vector c. This is the content of the following proposition.

THEOREM 5.1. *If* $f(u)$ *is constant on every sphere* $u'u = C$, *then the system* (3.2) *has a unique solution, determined by the region*

$$S = \{u: |\, c'u \,| > \kappa\} , \tag{5.1}$$

where κ *has to be chosen in order to satisfy the second part of* (3.2).

PROOF. (i) We shall first prove that the solution (5.1) is sufficient in the standardized case $c = \gamma e$, where e is the first coordinate vector $(1, 0, \cdots, 0)'$ and γ any positive constant.

Take S according to (5.1), determine κ in order to satisfy the second part of (3.2), and M from the first part of (3.2). It remains to show that for an appropriate h the third part of (3.2) is satisfied. For this purpose, we first note that in the present case M takes the form

$$M = \begin{bmatrix} m_1 & 0 & \cdots & 0 \\ 0 & m & \cdots & 0 \\ \cdot & \cdot & \cdot & \cdot \\ 0 & 0 & \cdots & m \end{bmatrix} , \tag{5.2}$$

which follows from (2.6); we note that (a) S is now of the form $\{u = |\, u_1 \,| < c\}$, (b) $f(u)$ is an even function of each variable u_j separately, and hence (c) the integral from $-\infty$ to $+\infty$ of $u_j f(u)\,du_j$, $j = 2, \cdots, k$, vanishes. It follows from (5.2) that the coefficient row vector appearing in the third part of (3.2) may be written as

$$c'M^{-1} = \gamma e'M^{-1} = \frac{\gamma e'}{m_1} = \frac{c'}{m_1} . \tag{5.3}$$

Hence, the region S may be written as

$$S = \left\{ u: |c'M^{-1}u| > \frac{\kappa}{m_1} \right\} , \tag{5.4}$$

and the third part of (3.2) is satisfied if we choose $h = \kappa/m_1$.

(ii) Next, we shall prove that the solution (5.1) is sufficient for a general c. For this purpose, take an *orthogonal* transformation $v = Lu$, mapping c onto a vector along the first coordinate axis, such that $c = \gamma L'e$, $\gamma > 0$. From (i) we know that the entities

$$\bar{c} = \gamma e , \qquad \bar{S} = \left\{ v: |e'v| > \frac{\kappa}{\gamma} \right\} , \qquad \bar{M} = \int_{\bar{S}} vv' \bar{f}(v)\, dv , \tag{5.5}$$

with appropriate choice of κ, satisfy (3.2). Applying Lemma 4.1 and noting that in the spherically symmetric case $\bar{f}(v) = f(v)$, we conclude that the entities $c = L'\bar{c}$, $S = L'\bar{S}$, and $M = L'\bar{M}L$ satisfy the same system (3.2). Moreover,

$$S = L'\bar{S} = \left\{ u: |e'Lu| > \frac{\kappa}{\gamma} \right\} = \{ u: |c'u| > \kappa \} \tag{5.6}$$

is actually the region (5.1).

(iii) Finally, we shall show that a region S which, together with the corresponding M and h, satisfies (3.2) is necessarily of form (5.1); i.e., that the coefficient vector $c'M^{-1}$ in the third part of (3.2) is proportional to c'.

For this purpose, take an orthogonal transformation $v = Lu$ that takes the vector $M^{-1}c$ onto γe, $\gamma > 0$, such that

$$M^{-1}c = \gamma L'e . \tag{5.7}$$

This transformation takes the region $S = \{ u: |c'M^{-1}u| > h \}$ into

$$\bar{S} = LS = \left\{ v: |v_1| > \frac{h}{\gamma} \right\} . \tag{5.8}$$

By Lemma 4.1 the transformed matrix $\bar{M} = LML'$ satisfies

$$\bar{M} = \int_{\bar{S}} vv' f(v) dv , \tag{5.9}$$

and hence, by the argument of (i), it takes the form of (5.2) with first diagonal element, say, $\bar{m}_1$. From (5.7) it follows that

$$c = \gamma ML'e = \gamma \cdot L'\bar{M}L \cdot L'e = \gamma L'\bar{M}e = \gamma \bar{m}_1 L'e , \tag{5.10}$$

and hence, again by (5.7), $c = \bar{m}_1 M^{-1}c$. But this is the proportionality that we set out to establish, and so the proof of Theorem 5.1 is complete.

6. The Quadrically Symmetric Case

Theorem 5.1 is easily generalized to the case that $f(u)$ can be made spherically symmetric by a linear transformation of the argument.

Assume that there is a non-singular linear transformation $v = Lu$ such that $\bar{f}(v) = f(L^{-1}v)$ is spherically symmetric. Since a constant factor in the argument does not affect this property, we may without restriction assume $|L| = 1$. Our assumption says that f remains constant whenever the squared distance

$$(L^{-1}v)'(L^{-1}v) = v'(LL')^{-1}v \tag{6.1}$$

remains constant, i.e., on each member of a certain family of homothetic ellipsoids. We shall refer to this situation as the quadrically symmetric case.

Consider any set of entities c, S, M in u-space and their counterparts $\bar{c} = Lc, \bar{S} = LS, \bar{M} = LML'$ in v-space. According to Lemma 4.1, the former set satisfies (3.2) if and only if the latter set satisfies the same equations, with u replaced by v and $f(u)$ by $\bar{f}(v) = f(L^{-1}v)$. Since $\bar{f}(v)$ is spherically symmetric, we know from Theorem 5.1 that the latter system has a unique solution generated by the region

$$\bar{S} = \{v\colon |\bar{c}'v| > \kappa\}\,, \tag{6.2}$$

where κ has to be determined to meet the size condition. It then follows that the original system (3.2) has a unique solution generated by the transformed region

$$S = L^{-1}\bar{S} = \{u\colon |\bar{c}'Lu| > \kappa\} = \{u\colon |c'(L'L)u| > \kappa\}\,. \tag{6.3}$$

The matrix $L'L$ can be expressed in terms of the convariance matrix Λ of the distribution $f(u)$. Integrating over the whole u-space, we have

$$\Lambda = \int uu'f(u)\,du = L^{-1}\cdot \int vv'\bar{f}(v)\,dv \cdot L'^{-1}. \tag{6.4}$$

Since $\bar{f}(v)$ is spherically symmetric, the last integral is of form θI, where θ is a positive scalar. It follows that $\Lambda = \theta(L'L)^{-1}$ and $L'L = \theta\Lambda^{-1}$. Inserting this result in (6.3) and denoting $\kappa/\theta = \lambda$, we have the following theorem:

THEOREM 6.1. *If $f(u)$ is quadrically symmetric, then the system* (3.2) *has a unique solution generated by the region*

$$S = \{u\colon |c'\Lambda^{-1}u| > \lambda\}\,, \tag{6.5}$$

where Λ is the covariance matrix of the f-distribution, and where λ has to be determined in order to satisfy the size condition of the second part of (3.2).

7. Practical Procedure

We now finally return to our original discrete problem. If the distribution of the item points in u-space is regular enough to justify a description by means of a quadrically symmetric density function, then we may apply Theorem 6.1 and use for Λ the empirical covariance matrix of the item points. The size requirement may be met simply by counting off from the "outer end," i.e., in order of decreasing $|c'\Lambda^{-1}u|$, as many items as desired. We thus end up with the following practical procedure:

(i) Compute the moment matrix Λ with elements

$$\lambda_{jh} = \frac{1}{N}\sum_{i=1}^{N} u_{ij}u_{ih}\,, \qquad j, h = 1, \cdots, k\,. \tag{7.1}$$

(ii) Compute the vector $g = \Lambda^{-1}c$, i.e., solve the equations

$$\begin{aligned} \lambda_{11}g_1 + \cdots + \lambda_{1k}g_k &= c_1\,, \\ \cdots\cdots & \cdots\cdots \\ \lambda_{k1}g_1 + \cdots + \lambda_{kk}g_k &= c_k\,. \end{aligned} \tag{7.2}$$

(iii) Compute, for each item i, the quantity

$$w_i = g'u_i = \sum_{j=1}^{k} g_j u_{ij} \tag{7.3}$$

and select the n items with largest $|w_i|$.

REFERENCES

[1] Elfving, G. Optimum allocation in linear regression theory. *Ann. Math. Stat.*, 1952, **23**, 255-62.

[2] Elfving, G. Geometric allocation theory. *Skand. Aktuarietidskr.*, 1954, **37**, 170-90.

7

Contributions to a Technique for Item Selection

GUSTAV ELFVING, University of Helsinki

1. Introduction and Summary

This chapter may be considered as a continuation of Chapter 6. It presents a tentative technique for finding and improving a selection region in the item-point space when the simplifying assumption that the item population be "quadrically symmetric" is not fulfilled.

The main result (Theorem 3.1) of Chapter 6 may be re-stated as follows. We use u as a generic notation for vectors (points) in R^k. Let $f(u)$ be a centrally symmetric density function and c a constant vector in that space, and let S be a (variable) region in R^k subject to the size condition

$$\int_S f(u)\,du = \delta\,; \tag{1.1}$$

finally, let M denote the moment matrix

$$M = M(S) = \int_S uu'f(u)\,du\ . \tag{1.2}$$

Then, in order for the function $c'M^{-1}c$ to be a minimum with respect to S, it is necessary that S be (aside from a set of f-measure 0) a twin half-space, of the following form:

$$S = \{u : |\,c'M^{-1}u\,| > h\}\ , \tag{1.3}$$

where M denotes the matrix (1.2).

The relations (1.1–3) constitute a system of $[k(k+1)/2] + 1$ equations with equally many unknowns. When $f(u)$ is a normal or, more generally, a quadrically symmetric, density function, an exact solution of this system is easily found (see Chapter 6, Theorem 6.1). In the general case, then, a natural way to find an approximate solution would be to fit a normal distribution to the f-distribution. However, since the fulfillment of (1.1–3) is independent of the behavior of $f(u)$ between the boundary planes of S, it seems reasonable first to find a preliminary S^* (including in this region perhaps a little more than the required probability mass δ), and then to fit a truncated normal distribution to the truncated population contained in S^*. The fitting may be performed by using the second-order moments. In practice, of course, one will be concerned with a discrete item-point distribution instead of the idealized f-distribution. It should be noted that the relative size of the "outer" part of the population must be treated as unknown, since the "inner" part is entirely disregarded. The above considerations lead to the problem posed and solved in Section 2.

On the other hand, once an approximate solution of (1.1–3) has been found in one way or another, one may try to improve it by appropriate variation of the boundary planes of S (i.e., of the direction cosines of their normal). This idea is carried out in Section 3 by means of the multidimensional analog of Newton's *regula falsi*.

2. Reconstruction of a Multivariate Normal Distribution from a Truncated Part of It

Let Λ be a positive definite $k \times k$ matrix determining the normal density function

$$f(u) = (2\pi)^{-k/2} \,|\Lambda|^{-1/2} \exp\{-\tfrac{1}{2}u'\Lambda^{-1}u\} . \tag{2.1}$$

Let g be a $k \times 1$ vector and h a positive scalar. Denote

$$\delta = \int_{|g'u|>h} f(u)\,du , \tag{2.2}$$

$$\bar{\Lambda} = \delta^{-1}\int_{|g'u|>h} uu'f(u)\,du . \tag{2.3}$$

Then, if $\bar{\Lambda}$, g, and h are given, is it possible to "reconstruct" Λ and δ, and if so, how? Furthermore, if $\bar{\Lambda}$ is the moment matrix of some arbitrary (e.g., empirical) distribution in $|g'u| > h$, is it possible to find Λ and δ such that (2.1–3) are fulfilled? The answer to these questions is given by the following theorem.

THEOREM 2.1. *For given $\bar{\Lambda}$, g, and $h > 0$ ($\bar{\Lambda}$ is subject to the sole condition of being the moment matrix of* some *non-singular symmetric distribution confined to the domain $|g'u| > h$), Equations* (2.1–3) *have a unique solution in Λ and δ, which is determined as follows:*

Let K be a solution of the factorization equation $KK' = \bar{\Lambda}$, subject to the normalization that $g'K$ be of form $\kappa e'$, where $e' = (1, 0, \cdots, 0)$, $\kappa > 0$ (this implies that $\kappa^2 = g'\bar{\Lambda}g$). Further, let b be the unique positive solution of the transcendental equation

$$\frac{1}{b^2} = \frac{\kappa^2}{h^2} - \frac{\varphi(b)}{b\Phi(-b)} , \tag{2.4}$$

and let

$$n_1^2 = 2[\Phi(-b) + b\varphi(b)], \qquad n^2 = 2\Phi(-b) , \tag{2.5}$$

$$N = \begin{bmatrix} n_1 & 0 & \cdots & 0 \\ 0 & n & \cdots & 0 \\ 0 & 0 & \cdots & n \end{bmatrix} \qquad (n_1, n > 0) . \tag{2.6}$$

Then the solution of (2.1–3) *mentioned above is*

$$\delta = n^2 , \tag{2.7}$$

$$\Lambda = \delta K N^{-2} K' . \tag{2.8}$$

Necessity. Assume that Λ, δ, and $\bar{\Lambda}$ satisfy (2.1–3). Let $\Lambda = LL'$ be a factorization of Λ; since L is determined only up to an orthogonal matrix factor to the right, we may normalize L so that the vector $L'g$ is of form λe, $\lambda > 0$. Now perform the transformation $u = Lv$ in (2.2) and (2.3). The density function turns into the normalized density function

$$\bar{f}(v) = (2\pi)^{-k/2} \exp\{-\tfrac{1}{2}v'v\} ,$$

and—owing to the property $L'g = \lambda e$—the integration domain is mapped onto the region $|v_1| > b$, where

$$b = h/\lambda . \tag{2.9}$$

Hence

$$\delta = \int_{|v_1|>b} \bar{f}(v)\, dv = 2\Phi(-b) , \tag{2.10}$$

and

$$\bar{\Lambda} = \delta^{-1} L N^2 L' , \quad \text{where } N^2 = \int_{|v_1|>b} vv'\bar{f}(v)\, dv . \tag{2.11}$$

It is easily seen that all non-diagonal elements of N^2 vanish, whereas the diagonal elements n_1^2 and $n_2^2 = \cdots = n_k^2 = n^2$ (say) are

$$\begin{aligned} n_1^2 &= \int_{|v_1|>b} v_1^2 \varphi(v_1)\, dv_1 \int_{-\infty}^{+\infty} \cdots \int \varphi(v_2) \cdots \varphi(v_k)\, dv_2 \cdots dv_k \\ &= 2[\Phi(-b) + b\varphi(b)] , \end{aligned} \tag{2.12}$$

$$\begin{aligned} n^2 &= \int_{|v_1|>b} \varphi(v_1)\, dv_1 \int_{-\infty}^{\infty} v_2^2 \varphi(v_2)\, dv_2 \int_{-\infty}^{+\infty} \cdots \int \varphi(v_3) \cdots \varphi(v_k)\, dv_3 \cdots dv_k \\ &= 2\Phi(-b) . \end{aligned} \tag{2.13}$$

Thus, the scalar δ and the matrix N^2 are exactly those mentioned in the theorem, except that we still have to prove that b [as defined by (2.9)] is the root of (2.4).

In order to establish the representation (2.8), compare (2.11) to the factorization $KK' = \bar{\Lambda}$ mentioned in our theorem. Due to the quasi-uniqueness of factorization, we must have

$$\delta^{-1/2} L N = K R , \tag{2.14}$$

where R is orthogonal. Moreover, multiplying the left-hand side of (2.14) by g', and noting the normalization of L and K, we find

$$\delta^{-1/2}\lambda n_1 e' = \kappa e' R \; ; \tag{2.15}$$

since the orthogonal factor R does not affect the length of the preceding vector, we conclude, first, that

$$\lambda = \delta^{1/2}\kappa n_1^{-1} \tag{2.16}$$

and, second, that $e'R = e'$, which implies that

$$R = \begin{bmatrix} 1 & : & 0 \\ \cdots & \cdots & \cdots \\ 0 & : & R_1 \end{bmatrix}, \quad R_1 \text{ orthogonal} . \tag{2.17}$$

We may now solve (2.14) for L, finding $\Lambda = LL' = \delta KRN^{-2}R'K'$. Due to the form (2.6) of N and (2.17) of R, it is easily seen that $RN^{-2}R' = N^{-2}$. This establishes (2.8).

What remains is to prove that the constant b on which δ, n and n_1 depend, and which was defined above in (2.9), actually fulfills (2.4). This follows from Equations (2.9), (2.10), (2.12), and (2.16) by elimination of n_1, λ, and δ.

Sufficiency. Assume, now, that $\bar{\Lambda}$ is the moment matrix of some non-singular symmetric m-variate distribution confined entirely to the domain $|g'u| > h$; say,

$$\bar{\Lambda} = E(uu') . \tag{2.18}$$

We wish to prove that Λ and δ can be found as described in Theorem 2.1, and that the density function (2.1) determined by Λ fulfills (2.2–3).

First, we must show that (2.4) has a unique solution $b > 0$. For this purpose, we notice that according to (2.18)

$$\kappa^2 = g'\bar{\Lambda}g = E(g'uu'g) = E(|g'u|^2) > h^2 ,$$

since the distribution generating $\bar{\Lambda}$ is confined to the domain $|g'u| > h$. Hence, the first term on the right-hand side in (2.4) is > 1. According to a well-known asymptotic representation of the normal distribution function, the term $\varphi(b)/[b\Phi(-b)]$ approaches 1 from above as $b \to \infty$; actually, as b increases from 0 to ∞, this term decreases monotonically[1] from ∞ to 1, and hence the right-hand side of (2.4) increases from $-\infty$ to $\kappa^2/h^2 - 1 > 0$. Since, at the same time, $1/b^2$ decreases from $+\infty$ to 0, the existence of a unique solution follows. A numerical solution can be obtained by iteration.

Once (2.4) is solved, we may calculate K, κ, N, δ as described in Theorem 2.1, and finally

$$\Lambda = \delta KN^{-2}K' . \tag{2.19}$$

[1] This statement is, as one may find by logarithmic differentiation, equivalent with the inequality $\Phi(-x) / \varphi(x) > x/(x^2+1)$ for $x > 0$, which has been proved by R. D. Gordon, *Ann. Math. Stat.*, 1941, **12**, 364-66.

With this Λ, we may form the density function $f(u)$ according to (2.1) and the integrals corresponding to (2.2–3), i.e.,

$$\delta^* = \int_{|g'u|>h} f(u)\,du \,, \tag{2.20}$$

$$\bar{\Lambda}^* = \delta^{-1}\int_{|g'u|>h} uu'f(u)\,du \,. \tag{2.21}$$

We wish to prove that $\delta^* = \delta$ and $\bar{\Lambda}^* = \bar{\Lambda}$; this will imply that δ and Λ constitute a solution of (2.1–3).

For this purpose, (2.19) suggests the factorization $\Lambda = LL'$, with $L = \delta^{1/2}KN^{-1}$. Since

$$g'L = \delta^{1/2}g'KN^{-1} = \delta^{1/2}\kappa e'N^{-1} = \delta^{1/2}\kappa n_1^{-1}e' \,,$$

the matrix L possesses the property $g'L = \lambda^* e'$, with

$$\lambda^* = \delta^{1/2}\kappa n_1^{-1} \,. \tag{2.22}$$

Precisely as in the necessity proof, we may apply the transformation $u = Lv$ to the integrals in (2.20–21). Denote for a moment by $b^* = h/\lambda^*$ the integration limit corresponding to (2.9). We shall show that b^* coincides with b, which is defined as the root of (2.4). Actually, the elimination of $\varphi(b)$, $\Phi(-b)$, and n from (2.4), (2.5), and (2.7) gives

$$b = \frac{h}{\delta^{1/2}\kappa n_1^{-1}} \,,$$

and this combined with (2.22) gives $b = h/\lambda^* = b^*$. The transformation of (2.20) then gives

$$\delta^* = 2\Phi(-b) = \delta \,,$$

and the transformation of (2.21) gives

$$\bar{\Lambda}^* = \delta^{-1}LN^2L' \,,$$

where N is the same diagonal matrix as was defined by (2.5–6). Inserting $L = \delta^{1/2}KN^{-1}$ and noting that $KK' = \bar{\Lambda}$, we conclude that $\bar{\Lambda}^* = \bar{\Lambda}$. This completes the proof of Theorem 2.1.

3. A Method for Improving a Non-Optimal Selection

Given a symmetrical "item density function" $f(u)$, the fundamental problem of the present theory is to solve Equations (1.1–3) in the Summary of this chapter. In a slightly different way, this problem can be formulated as follows: Let p denote a vector of length 1 and r denote a positive scalar; denote by S the twin half-space

$$S = \{u : |p'u| > r\} \,, \qquad ||p|| = 1 \,, \quad r > 0 \,, \tag{3.1}$$

and by P, M the corresponding probability mass and moment matrix

$$P = P(S) = \int_S f(u)\,du \,, \tag{3.2}$$

(3.3) $$M = M(S) = \int_S uu'f(u)du .$$

We want to find p and r, subject to the condition $P(S) = \delta$, such that the region

$$S' = \{u : |c'M^{-1}u| > h\} , \qquad P(S') = \delta ,$$

which in any case depends on S through M, coincides with S; shortly, we wish the vector p and the vector $M^{-1}c$ to be proportional. If we write

(3.4) $$q = \frac{M^{-1}c}{||M^{-1}c||} ,$$

Equations (3.1), (3.3), and (3.4), together with the condition $P = \delta$, define q as a function $q = q(p)$ of p. The problem, then, is to solve the equation $q(p) = p$.

If we start with an approximate p (found, e.g., by the method described at the end of Chapter 5), we usually find $q(p) \neq p$. However, if p is a fair approximation, both p and q will presumably be close to the required p_0, for which $q(p_0) = p_0$. To any differential variation dp of p, there will correspond a differential variation $dq = Qdp$, where Q is the matrix derivative $[(\partial q_i)/(\partial p_j)]$ of $q(p)$. In particular, we have

(3.5) $$q - p_0 \approx Q_0(p - p_0) ,$$

and hence

(3.6) $$p_0 \approx (I - Q_0)^{-1}(q - Q_0 p) .$$

Of course, $Q_0 = Q(p_0)$ is not known, but we may, as will be shown below, calculate $Q = Q(p)$ for the given p, and then find a new—presumably an improved—approximation for p_0 from

(3.7) $$p_0 \approx (I - Q)^{-1}(q - Qp) .$$

This equation obviously constitutes the vector analog of Newton's *regula falsi*.

We now turn to the problem of calculating $Q = [(\partial q_i)/(\partial p_j)]$, i.e., of calculating dq when dp is given. In view of the formula (3.4) we notice, to begin with, that for an arbitrary vector variable x,

(3.8) $$\begin{aligned} d\frac{x}{||x||} &= \frac{||x||\,dx - x\,d||x||}{||x||^2} \\ &= ||x||^{-2}\left\{||x||\,dx - x\frac{x'dx}{||x||}\right\} \\ &= ||x||^{-1}\left\{I - \frac{xx'}{||x||^2}\right\}dx . \end{aligned}$$

If we denote

(3.9) $$q_1 = M^{-1}c ,$$

the formula (3.8) gives us

$$dq = \frac{I - qq'}{||M^{-1}c||} dq_1 . \tag{3.10}$$

By the well-known formula, $dM^{-1} = -M^{-1} \cdot dM \cdot M^{-1}$ we have

$$dq_1 = -M^{-1} \cdot dM \cdot M^{-1}c , \tag{3.11}$$

where dM is the differential of M corresponding to the given differential dp. Our next and main problem will be to find dM in terms of dp.

Here, we have to observe that M depends on p both directly and through r, since r is connected with p by the size condition $P = \delta$. Accordingly, we have

$$dM = \frac{\partial M}{\partial p} dp + \frac{\partial M}{\partial r} dr , \tag{3.12}$$

where dr has to be expressed in dp according to the equation

$$\frac{\partial P}{\partial r} dr + \frac{\partial P}{\partial p} dp = 0 . \tag{3.13}$$

Here, $\partial P/\partial r$ is a scalar, $\partial P/\partial p$ a row vector, $\partial M/\partial r$ an $m \times m$ matrix, and $\partial M/\partial p$ a three-dimensional matrix, with the two first subscripts corresponding to those of dM, the last to that of dp. Of course, Equation (3.12) is nothing but a condensed form for m^2 equations, one for every element $d\mu_{ij}$ of dM. In the latter presentation, the $\partial \mu_{ij}/\partial p$ would be row vectors.

The derivatives occurring in (3.12–13) are obtained from the two lemmas given below. In both, $g(u)$ denotes a scalar function of a k-dimensional vector argument. This function must fulfill certain regularity conditions, e.g., the following, which could probably be considerably weakened.

1) $g(u)$ is differentiable, with gradient (row) vector $g'_u(u)$, and with the second-order remainder term bounded according to the inequality

$$| g(u + h) - g(u) - g'_u(u) \cdot h | \leqq \varphi(||u||) \cdot ||h||^2 ,$$

where $\varphi(t)$ is a function of one variable;

2) $$g(u) \to 0 \quad \text{as} \quad ||u|| \to \infty ;$$

3) $$|g(u)|, \qquad ||g'_u|| \cdot ||u||, \qquad \varphi(||u||) \cdot ||u||^2$$

are integrable. We notice that the above properties are invariant under any rotation of the argument space; i.e., for any orthogonal L, the function $g(v) = g(Lv)$ has the same properties, with bounds on the above-mentioned integrals that do not depend on L.

The symbol p (and similarly $p + dp$) always denotes a vector of length 1, and r means a positive number.

Lemma 3.1. *The function*

$$\gamma(p, r) = \int_{p'u > r} g(u) \, du \tag{3.14}$$

has for derivative with respect to r

(3.15)
$$\frac{\partial \gamma}{\partial r} = -\int_{p'u=r} g(u)\, du^* ,$$

where the integration is over the $(k-1)$*-dimensional hyperplane* $p'u = r$*, of which* du^* *is the volume element.*

PROOF. Take an orthogonal matrix L such that $p = Le$, where $e = (1, 0, \cdots, 0)'$. Perform in (3.14) the transformation $u = Lv$. Then

(3.16)
$$\gamma(p, r) = \int_r^\infty dv_1 \int_{-\infty}^\infty \cdots \int_{-\infty}^\infty g(Lv)\, dv_2 \cdots dv_k ,$$

(3.17)
$$\frac{\partial \gamma}{\partial r} = -\int_{-\infty}^{+\infty} \cdots \int g(Lv)\, dv_2 \cdots dv_k , \qquad v = (r, v_2, \cdots, v_k)'.$$

In the last integral we apply the transformation $Lv = u$, this time considered as a measure-preserving mapping from the hyperplane $v_1 = r$ to the hyperplane $p'u = r$. This gives us (3.15).

LEMMA 3.2. *With the notations of Lemma* 3.1, *we have*

(3.18)
$$d\gamma = \int_{p'u=r} g(u)u'\, du^* \cdot dp ,$$

where the integral is a row vector.

PROOF. Consider a fixed p and a particular differential variation dp. Let L' be an orthogonal matrix taking p onto e, and $p + dp$ onto a vector $e + d\bar{p} = (1 + d\bar{p}_1, d\bar{p}_2, 0, \cdots, 0)$ in the plane of the two first coordinates. Further, let R be the orthogonal transformation mapping e onto $e + d\bar{p}$ and leaving the 3d, $\cdots$, kth coordinates invariant. It is easily verified that R is of form

(3.19)
$$R = I + \left[\begin{array}{cc:c} d\bar{p}_1 & -d\bar{p}_2 & \\ d\bar{p}_2 & d\bar{p}_1 & 0 \\ \hdashline \multicolumn{2}{c:}{0} & 0 \end{array}\right] = I + D(\text{say}) .$$

Obviously, then, $L'p = e$ and $R'L'(p + dp) = e$. In the integrals (3.14) representing $\gamma(p, r)$ and $\gamma(p + dp, r)$, we now perform the substitutions $u = Lv$, $u = LRv$, respectively. The difference of these integrals can then be written as a single integral over $\{e'v > r\} = \{v_1 > r\}$,

(3.20)
$$\begin{aligned} \Delta\gamma &= \int_{v_1 > r} [g(LRv) - g(Lv)]\, dv \\ &= \int_{v_1 > r} [\bar{g}(v + Dv) - \bar{g}(v)]\, dv , \end{aligned}$$

where

(3.21)
$$\bar{g}(v) = g(Lv) .$$

We now use our assumptions concerning $g(u)$; as already remarked, they hold true for $\bar{g}(v)$ as well. According to Assumption 1,

(3.22)
$$\bar{g}(v + Dv) - \bar{g}(v) = \bar{g}'_0 Dv + \vartheta\varphi(\| v \|)\| Dv \|^2 \quad (|\vartheta| \leqq 1) .$$

Here,

$$Dv = \begin{bmatrix} v_1 d\bar{p}_1 - v_2 d\bar{p}_2 \\ v_1 d\bar{p}_2 + v_2 d\bar{p}_1 \\ 0 \\ \cdot \\ \cdot \\ 0 \end{bmatrix}, \tag{3.23}$$

$$\| Dv \| \leqq 2 \| v \| \cdot \| d\bar{p} \| = 2 \| v \| \cdot \| dp \| , \tag{3.24}$$

$$\bar{g}_v' Dv = \left(-\frac{\partial \bar{g}}{\partial v_1} v_2 + \frac{\partial \bar{g}}{\partial v_2} v_1\right) d\bar{p}_2 + \left(\frac{\partial \bar{g}}{\partial v_1} v_1 + \frac{\partial \bar{g}}{\partial v_2} v_2\right) d\bar{p}_1 . \tag{3.25}$$

Due to the relation

$$(1 + d\bar{p}_1)^2 + (d\bar{p}_2)^2 = \| p + dp \|^2 = 1 ,$$

we have

$$| d\bar{p}_1 | = \tfrac{1}{2}(| d\bar{p}_1 |^2 + | d\bar{p}_2 |^2) = \tfrac{1}{2} \| dp \|^2 ;$$

hence, the last term in (3.25) is absolutely less than $\frac{1}{2} \| \bar{g}_v' \| \cdot \| v \| \cdot \| dp \|^2$. Using this fact, the relation (3.24), and our Assumption 3 about $g(u)$, we obtain on integrating (3.22)

$$\Delta r = \int_{v_1 > r} \left(-\frac{\partial \bar{g}}{\partial v_1} v_2 + \frac{\partial \bar{g}}{\partial v_2} v_1\right) dv \cdot d\bar{p}_2 + O(\| dp \|^2) . \tag{3.26}$$

The integral of the second term vanishes, since integration with respect to v_2 gives

$$v_1 \bar{g}(v_1, \infty, \cdots) - v_1 \bar{g}(v_1, -\infty, \cdots) = 0 ,$$

by Assumption 2. The integral of the first term with respect to v_1 is $\bar{g}(r, v_2, \cdots, v_k) \cdot v_2$. Hence, using again the fact that $| d\bar{p}_1 | = \frac{1}{2} \| dp \|^2$, we have

$$\begin{aligned} \Delta r &= \int_{-\infty}^{+\infty} \cdots \int \bar{g}(r, v_2, \cdots, v_k) v_2 d\bar{p}_2 \, dv_2 \cdots dv_k + O(\| dp \|^2) \\ &= \int_{-\infty}^{+\infty} \cdots \int \bar{g}(r, v_2, \cdots, v_k) v' d\bar{p} \, dv_2 \cdots dv_k + O(\| dp \|^2) . \end{aligned} \tag{3.27}$$

Performing here the transformation $u = Lv$, considered as a measure-preserving mapping of the hyperplane $v_1 = r$ onto the hyperplane $p'u = r$, and noticing that $Ld\bar{p} = dp$, we have

$$\Delta r = \int_{p'u = r} g(u) u' \, du^* \cdot dp + O(\| dp \|^2) . \tag{3.28}$$

This proves Lemma 3.2.

We are now in a position to find the differential dM in (3.12). (Notice the relation (3.13) between dr and dp.)

Because of the symmetry of $f(u)$, the integrals in (3.2) and (3.3) equal twice the same integrals taken over the half-space $p'u > r$. Applying Lemmas 3.1 and 3.2, with $g(u) = f(u)$, we obtain

$$\frac{\partial P}{\partial r} = -2\int_{p'u=r} f(u)\, du^* , \tag{3.29}$$

$$\frac{\partial P}{\partial p} = 2\int_{p'u=r} f(u)u'\, du^* , \tag{3.30}$$

and hence, by (3.13),

$$dr = \int_{p'u=r} f(u \mid p'u = r)u' du^*\, dp = \xi' dp \text{ (say)} ; \tag{3.31}$$

ξ is obviously the center of gravity of the conditional distribution generated by $f(u)$ in the hyperplane $p'u = r$.

On the other hand, we apply the same lemmas with $g(u) = u_i u_j \cdot f(u)$ $(i, j = 1, \cdots, k)$. The conditions on $g(u)$ are fulfilled, e.g., when $f(u)$ is a normal density function. Lemma 3.1 yields

$$\frac{\partial \mu_{ij}}{\partial r} = -2\int_{p'u=r} u_i u_j f(u)\, du^* , \tag{3.32}$$

and Lemma 3.2 yields

$$\frac{\partial \mu_{ij}}{\partial p} = 2\int_{p'u=r} u_i u_j f(u)\, u'\, du^* . \tag{3.33}$$

Inserting (3.31–33) in (3.12), we find for the differentials of the elements of M

$$d\mu_{ij} = 2\int_{p'u=r} u_i u_j (u - \xi)' f(u) du^*\, dp , \tag{3.34}$$

and for the matrix M

$$dM = 2[C^{(1)} dp_1 + \cdots + C^{(k)} dp_k] , \tag{3.35}$$

where

$$C^{(h)} = \int_{p'u=r} uu' (u_h - \xi_h) f(u)\, du^* . \tag{3.36}$$

Inserting (3.35) in (3.11), we find

$$dq_1 = -2[M^{-1}C^{(1)}M^{-1}c\, dp_1 + \cdots + M^{-1}C^{(k)}M^{-1}c\, dp_k] ,$$

or

$$dq_1 = -2C\, dp , \tag{3.37}$$

where C is the matrix with columns $M^{-1}C^{(h)}M^{-1}c$ $(h = 1, \cdots, k)$:

$$C = [M^{-1}C^{(1)}M^{-1}c \cdots M^{-1}C^{(k)}M^{-1}c] . \tag{3.38}$$

Combining this result with (3.10), we are able to state:

THEOREM 3.1. *Let $f(u)$ be an even density function on R_k such that $f(u)$ as well as all functions $u_i u_j f(u)$ fulfill the assumptions* (1–3) *on p.* 102. *Let $q = q(p)$ be the function (from the unit sphere in R^k to the same unit sphere) defined by* (3.1–4), *with r determined by the condition $P = \delta$. Then $dq = Q\,dp$, where*

$$Q = -\frac{2}{\|M^{-1}c\|}(I - qq')C\,, \tag{3.39}$$

the matrix C being given by (3.38) *and* (3.36).

A simplification. The computation of Q is, in the general case, relatively complicated. We shall now derive a straightforward expression for Q in a simple, yet important, special case.

As seen from the considerations in Chapter 6, the problem of finding the optimal selection region can always be reduced to a situation in which the covariance matrix of $f(u)$ is of form κI, and the vector c of form γe. In fact, let

$$\Lambda = \int uu' f(u)\,du\,, \tag{3.40}$$

and let $\Lambda = |\Lambda|\cdot LL'$ $(|L| = 1)$ be a factorization of Λ, chosen in such a way that the vector $L'c$ is of form γe. Consider the mapping $u = Lv$. It is readily verified (cf. Lemma 4.1 in Chapter 6) that if the matrix M and the region

$$S = \{u : |c'M^{-1}u| > h\} \tag{3.41a}$$

satisfy the relations

$$M = \int_S uu' f(u)\,du\,, \qquad \int_S f(u)\,du = \delta\,, \tag{3.41b}$$

then the matrix $N = L^{-1}ML'^{-1}$ and the region

$$T = \{v : |d'N^{-1}v| > h\} \tag{3.42a}$$

satisfy the relations

$$N = \int_T \bar{f}(v)\,dv\,, \qquad \int_T \bar{f}(v)\,dv = \delta\,, \tag{3.42b}$$

where $\bar{f}(v) = f(Lv)$ and $d = L'c = \gamma e$. On the other hand, multiplying (3.40) by L^{-1} and L'^{-1} to the left and right, respectively, we find that

$$|\Lambda|\,I = \int_T vv'\bar{f}(v)\,dv\,; \tag{3.43}$$

thus, the transformed distribution is "spherical up to the second order," and the transformed "relevant direction" is that of the vector e.

Let us assume that this situation is brought about and that the original notation is resumed. If $f(u)$ were *strictly* spherically symmetric, it would be intuitively evident (and is formally proved in Section 5 of Chapter 6) that the solution of (3.41), with $c = e$, would be given by a region $S = \{u : |u_1| > h_1\}$ and a diagonal matrix M; i.e., the function $q(p)$ defined at the outset of this section would satisfy $q(e) = e$. Now, when $f(u)$ is not strictly, but only "up to the second-order" spherically symmetric we may expect $q(e)$ to be close to e, and M (as computed from (3.3) with $p = e$ and with r satisfying the size condition) to be close to the matrix

$$\bar{M} = \begin{bmatrix} \mu_{11} & 0 & \cdot & \cdot & 0 \\ 0 & \mu_{22} & \cdot & \cdot & 0 \\ \cdot & \cdot & \cdot & \cdot & \cdot \\ 0 & 0 & \cdot & \cdot & \mu_{kk} \end{bmatrix} \tag{3.44}$$

with the same diagonal element as M. Under these circumstances, a reasonable procedure seems to be the following:

(i) Take $p = e$ and find M and q from (3.3–4) in conjunction with the size condition $P = \delta$; (ii) find Q approximately, replacing q by e in Theorem 3.1, and M by the diagonal matrix $\bar{M}$ in (3.44); (iii) apply the interpolation formula (3.7).

For the purpose of carrying out this idea, let us see what the formulas (3.36), (3.38), and (3.39) reduce to when $p = q = e$ and M is replaced by the diagonal matrix $\bar{M}$. We first notice that

$$I - qq' = \begin{bmatrix} 0 & 0 & \cdot\cdot & 0 \\ 0 & 1 & \cdot\cdot & 0 \\ \cdot & \cdot & \cdot\cdot & \cdot \\ \cdot & \cdot & \cdot\cdot & \cdot \\ 0 & \cdot & \cdot\cdot & 1 \end{bmatrix} \tag{3.45}$$

and

$$M^{-1}c = \begin{bmatrix} \mu_{11}^{-1} & \cdot\cdot & 0 \\ \\ \cdot & \cdot\cdot & \cdot \\ \\ 0 & \cdot\cdot & \mu_{kk}^{-1} \end{bmatrix} \cdot \begin{bmatrix} 1 \\ 0 \\ \cdot \\ \cdot \\ 0 \end{bmatrix} = \begin{bmatrix} \mu_{11}^{-1} \\ 0 \\ \cdot \\ \cdot \\ 0 \end{bmatrix}, \tag{3.46}$$

and hence $||M^{-1}c|| = \mu_{11}^{-1}$. From (3.46) we see that, for the computation of $C^{(h)}M^{-1}c$, only the first column of $C^{(h)}$ is relevant. By (3.36) we see that the elements of this column are

$$\begin{aligned} C_{i1}^{(h)} &= r\int_{u_1=r} u_i(u_h - \xi_h)f(u)\,du^* \\ &= r\int_{u_1=r} (u_i - \xi_i)(u_h - \xi_h)f(u)\,du^* \\ &= rf_1(r)\operatorname{cov}(u_i, u_h \mid u_1 = r)\,, \end{aligned} \tag{3.47}$$

where $f_1(u)$ is the density function of u_1. Denoting

$$\lambda_{ih} = \operatorname{cov}(u_i, u_h \mid u_1 = r), \tag{3.48}$$

we thus have

$$C^{(1)} = 0, \quad C^{(h)} = rf_1(r)\begin{bmatrix} 0 & \cdot & \cdot & \cdot \\ \lambda_{2h} & \cdot & \cdot & \cdot \\ \cdot & \cdot & \cdot & \cdot \\ \lambda_{kh} & \cdot & \cdot & \cdot \end{bmatrix} \quad (h \neq 1), \tag{3.49}$$

$$M^{-1}C^{(h)}M^{-1}c = \frac{rf_1(r)}{\mu_{11}}\begin{bmatrix} 0 \\ \lambda_{2h}/\mu_{22} \\ \cdot\cdot \\ \lambda_{kh}/\mu_{kk} \end{bmatrix} \quad (h \neq 1), \tag{3.50}$$

and resuming the notation (3.38), we have

$$C = \frac{rf_1(r)}{\mu_{11}}\begin{bmatrix} 0 & 0 \\ 0 & C_{11} \end{bmatrix}, \quad C_{11} = \begin{bmatrix} \lambda_{22}/\mu_{22} & \cdot\cdot & \lambda_{2k}/\mu_{22} \\ \cdot & \cdot\cdot & \cdot \\ \lambda_{k2}/\mu_{kk} & \cdot\cdot & \lambda_{kk}/\mu_{kk} \end{bmatrix}. \tag{3.51}$$

Finally, we obtain by (3.45) and (3.38)

$$Q = -2rf_1(r)\begin{bmatrix} 0 & 0 \\ 0 & C_{11} \end{bmatrix}. \tag{3.52}$$

In particular, if $k = 2$, then C_{11} reduces to the element λ_{22}/μ_{22}. In Equation (3.7) we now have $Qp = 0$, whereas for $k = 2$ we have

$$(I - Q)^{-1} = \begin{bmatrix} 1 & 0 \\ 0 & (1 + 2rf_1(r)\lambda_{22}/\mu_{22})^{-1} \end{bmatrix}.$$

The *regula falsi* then gives

$$p_{01} = q_1, \quad p_{02} = \frac{q_2}{1 + 2rf_1(r)\lambda_{22}/\mu_{22}}. \tag{3.53}$$

Practical procedure. In practice, we are not concerned with a density function $f(u)$ but with a population of $2N$ item points $\pm u_i$. For any selection region S, the corresponding matrix M is then the matrix with elements

$$\mu_{jh} = (2N)^{-1} \sum_{u_i \in S} u_{ij}u_{ih}.$$

For the matrices $C^{(h)}$, we must of course replace the plane $p'u = r$ by an appropriately chosen "layer," say $R = \{u : r - \varepsilon < p'u < r + \varepsilon\}$. The integrals (3.36) then have to be replaced by the corresponding sums over R, divided by the total number of item points, and by the "thickness" 2ε of the layer. In (3.52), we see that $f_1(r)$ is the relative number of item points in R divided by 2ε.

Part II. Item Selection: Several Non-Parametric Situations

8

The Algebra of Dichotomous Systems

PAUL F. LAZARSFELD, Columbia University

1. Observations on Dichotomous Systems

The statistics of attributes has made little progress since Yule [1] gave it a standard form in the first chapters of his famous textbook. Investigators have concentrated on problems that required the use of continuous variables. Only in recent years has the development of social research focused attention on dichotomies, like yes-no answers to questionnaires on sex and American citizenship of respondents. Survey analysis has to take into account so many variables that a reverse process has set in; even continuous variables, like age and income, are often treated as dichotomies: old-young and rich-poor.

As a result, it seemed worthwhile to develop new ideas on the treatment of what might be called "dichotomous systems": the set of relative frequencies by which a sample of people is partitioned into 2^m classes which come about if they are classified by m dichotomous observations. The following sections develop first a number of significant theorems that exist between three dichotomies, and then extend some of them to more general systems.

2. The Cross Product

Two dichotomies lead to the well-known fourfold table:

(2.1)

		Attribute j +	Attribute j −	
Attribute i	+	p_{ij}	$p_{i\bar{j}}$	p_i
	−	$p_{\bar{i}j}$	$p_{\bar{i}\bar{j}}$	$p_{\bar{i}}$
		p_j	$p_{\bar{j}}$	1

The symbolism is obvious. For any dichotomy one of the two observations or "responses" is arbitrarily designated as positive (+), the other as negative (−). The corresponding frequencies will be designated as p_i and $p_{\bar{i}}$, respectively,[1] and $p_i + p_{\bar{i}} = 1$. For the response pattern + + the joint frequency is p_{ij}, for the response pattern + − it is $p_{i\bar{j}}$, etc. The items are listed and numbered in an arbitrary sequence, which remains fixed in the course of one investigation.

The association between the two attributes in (2.1) can be "measured" by a variety of coefficients. They all have in common that they compare the association with statistical independence, which is characterized by the vanishing of the so-called cross product

$$(2.2) \qquad |ij| = \begin{vmatrix} p_{ij} & p_{i\bar{j}} \\ p_{\bar{i}j} & p_{\bar{i}\bar{j}} \end{vmatrix} = \begin{vmatrix} p_{ij} & p_i \\ p_j & 1 \end{vmatrix} = p_{ij} - p_i p_j .$$

The three well-known indices of association all have the cross product as a nucleus. They differ only by the way they introduce the marginal frequency of the two dichotomies; i.e.,

$$(2.3) \qquad \phi = \frac{|ij|}{\sqrt{p_i p_{\bar{i}} p_j p_{\bar{j}}}} , \qquad \chi^2 = \phi^2 , \qquad f_{ij} = \frac{|ij|}{p_i p_{\bar{i}}} .$$

A word may be added about the third coefficient, which is often used in connection with controlled experiments. People are divided into two groups, one of which is exposed to some stimulus (i). Then some reaction of theirs (j) is ascertained. The effect of the stimulus is measured by comparing the relative frequencies in which the response appears in the two groups; i.e.,

$$(2.4) \qquad f_{ij} = \frac{p_{ij}}{p_i} - \frac{p_{\bar{i}j}}{p_{\bar{i}}} = \frac{1}{p_i p_{\bar{i}}} \begin{vmatrix} p_{ij} & p_{\bar{i}j} \\ p_i & p_{\bar{i}} \end{vmatrix} = \frac{|ij|}{p_i p_{\bar{i}}} .$$

It should be noted that $f_{ji} = |ij|/p_j p_{\bar{j}}$, and therefore differs from f_{ij}. The product $f_{ij} \times f_{ji}$ obviously equals ϕ^2.

The frequencies can be ordered by their "level," that is, p_i is of first order, p_{ij} of second order. When we consider three attributes at a time, there are eight third-order class proportions. These eight elements can be thought of as occupying the eight positions formed by cutting a cube by three normal planes, just as the four cells of the fourfold table were formed by cutting a square from two directions. This *dichotomous cube*, the extension of the fourfold table to three dimensions, will be discussed in some detail.

For convenience of language we shall often talk as if the cross product itself were the measure of association. However, none of the formulas we shall develop will prejudice what measure of association should actually be used. In subsequent sections of this paper we shall give examples to show this point. It can be made conclusively only after the reader is acquainted with some substantive results.

[1] For brevity's sake, the word "relative" will be omitted. We shall always deal with proportion of the total sample and not with absolute frequencies.

3. The Dichotomous Cube

The relation between two dichotomous attributes was summarized in the fourfold table, a two-dimensional array with four cells, one for each of the four second-order class proportions. Such a dichotomous cube consists of eight smaller cubes, each corresponding to one of the third-order proportions. We shall arrange these proportions in such a way that the four proportions having the subscript 1 in common, p_{123}, $p_{1\bar{2}3}$, $p_{12\bar{3}}$, and $p_{1\bar{2}\bar{3}}$, are in the left section of the cube, while those proportions having the subscript $\bar{1}$ in common lie in the right section of the cube. Similarly, the four proportions with the subscript 2 in common are in the upper layer, and those with $\bar{2}$ in common are in the lower layer. The front sheet contains the four proportions having the subscript 3 in common; the back sheet, those with $\bar{3}$ in common.

The dichotomous cube and the relative position of the third-order frequencies are shown in Figure 1.

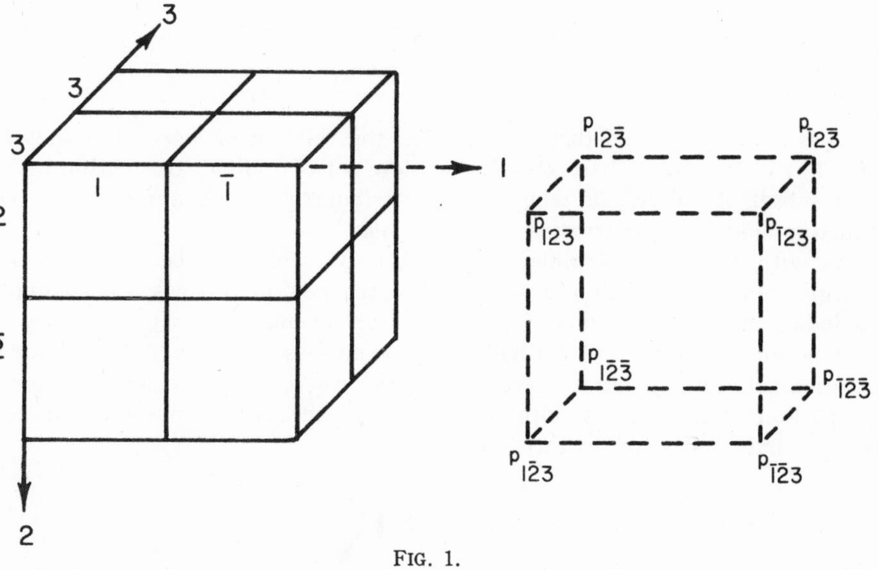

FIG. 1.

A second-order frequency can be *expanded* in terms of its third-order component. Thus, e.g., $p_{1\bar{2}} = p_{1\bar{2}3} + p_{1\bar{2}\bar{3}}$. No frequency can be negative. Therefore *if a second-order frequency vanishes, so do its components.* If, e.g., $p_{\bar{1}2} = 0$, then it follows that $p_{\bar{1}23} = p_{\bar{1}2\bar{3}} = 0$.

If we deal with $m > 3$ dichotomies, we could talk of a cube of m dimensions; but little is gained from such a terminology. The rules of handling indices, however, apply quite directly to such an extension. A word may be added about an alternative possibility and why it has been discarded.

Some authors use the symbols 1 and 2 for positive and negative responses, respectively; and they assign to each item a fixed position in the frequency symbol. Thus $p_{1\cdot 2}$ would be the frequency of a positive response to the first item and a negative to the third, irrespective of the response to the second item. In our symbolism this would be $p_{1\bar{3}}$, because we take the order of the item from a numbered list, fixed for the whole study. With a larger number of dichotomies this makes for considerable saving in space. Furthermore, as the reader will see, the use of bars for negative responses puts better into relief a number of basic theorems.

4. Stratified Fourfold Tables

Consider now the elements that lie in the front sheet of the dichotomous cube. Keeping them in their same relative position, they are

	1	$\bar{1}$	
2	p_{123}	$p_{\bar{1}23}$	p_{23}
$\bar{2}$	$p_{1\bar{2}3}$	$p_{\bar{1}\bar{2}3}$	$p_{\bar{2}3}$
	p_{13}	$p_{\bar{1}3}$	p_{3}

This is a fourfold table that summarizes the relation between attributes 1 and 2 within only a part of the complete set of individuals—within only that subset of individuals who possess attribute 3. Such a table will be called a *conditional or stratified fourfold table.*[2]

As with the fourfold table, the conditional table can be bordered by marginal entries, which are the sums of the respective rows and columns as indicated in the margins of the preceding schema.

If within the subset of individuals who possess attribute 3 there is no relation between attributes 1 and 2, then we would expect to find the same proportion of individuals with attribute 1 in the entire subset as in the subset that also possesses attribute 2. That is,

$$\frac{p_{13}}{p_3} = \frac{p_{123}}{p_{23}} \,,$$

or

$$\begin{vmatrix} p_{123} & p_{23} \\ p_{13} & p_3 \end{vmatrix} = 0 \,.$$

This determinant will be taken as the definition of the partial cross

[2] The term "conditional" emphasizes the fact that we are concerned with the relation between two attributes under the condition that a third attribute is present (or absent). "Stratified" emphasizes the fact that all entries in such a table carry the index of the attribute by which the population has first been sorted; the role of this "stratifier" is very important for many purposes. We shall use the two terms interchangeably.

product between attributes 1 and 2 within the subset possessing attribute 3. The symbol $|12;3|$ will be used for this cross product. In general, then, we shall define $|ij;k|$ by

$$|ij;k| = \begin{vmatrix} p_{ijk} & p_{jk} \\ p_{ik} & p_k \end{vmatrix}. \tag{4.1}$$

Suppose now we consider the elements in the back sheet of the dichotomous cube. They make up the following conditional fourfold table:

	1	$\bar{1}$	
2	$p_{12\bar{3}}$	$p_{\bar{1}2\bar{3}}$	$p_{2\bar{3}}$
$\bar{2}$	$p_{1\bar{2}\bar{3}}$	$p_{\bar{1}\bar{2}\bar{3}}$	$p_{\bar{2}\bar{3}}$
	$p_{1\bar{3}}$	$p_{\bar{1}\bar{3}}$	$p_{\bar{3}}$

This table summarizes the relation between attributes 1 and 2 within the subset of individuals lacking attribute 3. The cross product of this stratified fourfold table will be denoted by $|12;\bar{3}|$, where

$$|12;\bar{3}| = \begin{vmatrix} p_{12\bar{3}} & p_{2\bar{3}} \\ p_{1\bar{3}} & p_{\bar{3}} \end{vmatrix} = \begin{vmatrix} p_{12\bar{3}} & p_{\bar{1}2\bar{3}} \\ p_{1\bar{2}\bar{3}} & p_{\bar{1}\bar{2}\bar{3}} \end{vmatrix}.$$

In general we shall define $|ij;\bar{k}|$ by

$$|ij;\bar{k}| = \begin{vmatrix} p_{ij\bar{k}} & p_{j\bar{k}} \\ p_{i\bar{k}} & p_{\bar{k}} \end{vmatrix}. \tag{4.2}$$

It should be noted that Equation (4.1) suffices to define both $|ij;k|$ and $|ij;\bar{k}|$ if in (4.1) we allow the index k to range through both barred and unbarred integers designating particular attributes.[3]

[3] It is difficult to decide how the symbol introduced by Equation (4.1) should be used. The stratified cross product pertains to a subset of the total sample. To make it comparable with the unstratified cross product, it should really be standardized for the size of the subset, and therefore be divided by (p_k^2). This, however, yields a very clumsy notation. The standardization, as will be seen, can always be introduced after a theorem has been developed. Only occasionally will we use the standardized conditional cross product and then indicate it by a prime, i.e.,

$$|ij;k|' = \frac{|ij;k|}{p_k^2}.$$

There is also a problem of terminology. Cross products can have levels of stratification. We shall designate the level by reference to the level of the subset. Thus, a zero-order cross product pertains to the total sample; a first-order cross product pertains to a subset, which is a result of partitioning the original sample by one dichotomy; and so on. Thus, the cross product appearing in Equation (4.1) is called of first order although it comprises frequencies up to the third order.

5. A Single Parameter Characterizing the Dichotomous Cube as a Whole

Six fourfold tables can be formed, each from the elements on one of the six faces of the dichotomous cube. Each of these conditional fourfold tables can be characterized by its cross product. Thus, six partial cross products, $|12;3|$, $|12;\bar{3}|$, $|23;1|$, $|23;\bar{1}|$, $|13;2|$, and $|13,\bar{2}|$, can be formed from the data of a dichotomous cube.

It is well known that eight independent pieces of information are necessary to form a *fundamental set* for a system of three dichotomies. The eight ultimate frequencies form one such set. The frequencies on all levels that have no barred indices, together with the size of the sample, form another. (These are the two investigated by Yule.) Another could be formed from the following elements: let n be the total number of individuals; let p_1, p_2, p_3 be the first-order proportions; and let $|12|$, $|23|$, $|13|$ be the three possible cross products. But these are only seven elements, and so far we have utilized no third-order data. The eighth element must be of the third order, somehow characterizing the dichotomous cube as a whole.

We might choose our eighth element from among the six conditional cross products, but there is no good reason for choosing one in preference to another. Also, any one of these would lack the symmetry that one can reasonably require of a parameter representing the whole cube.

Our choice of the eighth parameter will be determined by three criteria:

a) The parameter should be *symmetric*, i.e., its value should not be affected by the numbering of the three attributes from which it is formed. The cross product, characterizing the fourfold table as a whole, has the following property of symmetry: the value assigned to the symbol $|12|$, i.e., $|12| = p_{12} - p_1 p_2$, is not changed by an interchange of the subscripts.

b) The parameter should be *homogeneous* of the third order, i.e., each of its terms should involve three subscripts. What is meant by this requirement is best seen by examining the cross product, which is homogeneous of the second order. The cross product between attributes 1 and 2, as shown above, has two terms on the right, each of which involves two subscripts. In this sense each of these terms is of the second order.

c) The parameter should be such that we can use it, together with lower-order class proportions, to evaluate any third order class proportion. That the cross product has the corresponding property can be easily shown.

$$(5.1)\qquad \begin{aligned} p_{12} &= p_1 p_2 + |12|\,, & p_{1\bar{2}} &= p_1 p_{\bar{2}} - |12|\,, \\ p_{\bar{1}2} &= p_{\bar{1}} p_2 - |12|\,, & p_{\bar{1}\bar{2}} &= p_{\bar{1}} p_{\bar{2}} + |12|\,. \end{aligned}$$

These four equations can be condensed into a single equation if in the equation $p_{ij} = p_i p_j + |ij|$ we allow the indices i and j to range over both unbarred and barred numbers. This equation thus defines the new symbols $|i\bar{j}|$, $|\bar{i}j|$, and $|\bar{i}\bar{j}|$. That this is true is easily seen when we recognize that the definition $|ij| = p_{ij} - p_i p_j$ implies that

$$(5.2)\qquad |\bar{i}j| = -|ij|\,, \qquad |i\bar{j}| = -|ij|\,, \qquad |\bar{i}\bar{j}| = |ij|\,.$$

For example, by letting $i = 1$ and $j = \bar{2}$, we obtain

$$p_{1\bar{2}} = p_1 p_{\bar{2}} + |1\bar{2}| = p_1 p_{\bar{2}} - |12| .$$

A homogeneous, symmetric parameter of third order can be built up from lower-order data as follows:

$$p_{ijk} = p_i p_j p_k + p_i |jk| + p_j |ik| + p_k |ij| + |ijk| . \tag{5.3}$$

The quantity $|ijk|$, implicitly defined by this equation, quite evidently satisfies the criteria of homogeneity and symmetry; that it can be used together with lower-order data to compute any third-order class proportion will be shown in Section 7.

6. The Intuitive Meaning of the Symmetric Parameter in a Dichotomous Cube

It is possible to give the symmetric parameter a first intuitive meaning by looking at the case where zero-order cross products vanish. Then the parameter is the difference between an actual third-order frequency and its chance value. From Equation (5.3) we find in this case that

$$p_{ijk} - p_i p_j p_k = |ijk| .$$

It is not too difficult to think of a concrete example. Suppose we are dealing with a community in which the educational system is fairly stabilized. Among the adult population we shall then find educational differences due to ability and social background; but the probability that a person went beyond high school would not be related to age as it is now in the United States, where the high-school system is still expanding from year to year. In such an adult population there would be no association between age (1) and education (2). Consider now the relation between age and interest in serious music (3). Empirical studies indicate that people who never go beyond high school reach the peak of their cultural taste right after they leave school because from then on their taste becomes corroded by their work and their environment. College graduates, on the other hand, who live and work in a middle-class environment develop further cultural taste as they grow older and lose the vitality of their youth. These two trends may compensate each other, and in a mixed population we therefore have no relation between age and interest in serious music, for $|13| = 0$.

To this we have to add one more assumption, which is considerably less realistic: no relation exists between education (2) and interest in serious music (3). This could be approximated in an ethnically mixed community, i.e., one in which the poorly educated Italians are mainly interested in opera while the more highly educated Germans are mainly interested in classical symphony. In this kind of situation all three zero-order cross products would vanish. But because of the differential age trend for the two educational groups, the third order symmetric parameter would still have a positive value.

It is possible to represent this situation by a coin-throwing experiment. We represent education by a regular penny (1) and age by a regular nickel (2). Interest in serious music (3) is represented by a biased coin with the probability of .8 to fall heads. In the case of the two regular coins, a showing of heads is considered equivalent to a positive response; in the case of age, this will signify "old"; and in the case of education, it will signify having gone beyond high school. For the third coin we have a conditional scoring.

If (1) and (2) are either (++) or (−−), then heads for the third coin scores (+); if (1) and (2) are either (+−) or (−+), then heads for the third coin scores (−). If the three coins are thrown often enough, the distribution of scores will approach the following scheme:

1 +	3 +	3 −	
2 +	.20	.05	.25
2 −	.05	.20	.25
	.25	.25	.5

1 −	3 +	3 −	
2 +	.05	.20	.25
2 −	.20	.05	.25
	.25	.25	.5

The reader can easily satisfy himself that in this scheme $|12| = |13| = |23| = 0$. However, $p_{123} = .20$, and therefore

$$|123| = p_{123} - p_1 p_2 p_3 = .20 - (\tfrac{1}{2})^3 = .075 .$$

In our example the two sides of the scheme would correspond to educated and uneducated people, respectively. The left (educated) side shows a positive association of age and interest in serious music. The right (uneducated) side shows a negative association. The vanishing of the cross products $|13|$ and $|23|$ can be seen from the fact that the two fourfold tables have the same distribution in corresponding marginal rows and columns. That $|12| = 0$ can be seen from adding the two tables cell by cell.

We shall presently find additional interpretations of the third-order symmetric parameter. In general it makes sense to think of it as an index of association between three attributes, just as the cross product indicates the association between two attributes.[4]

7. Use of the Parameter $|ijk|$ to Compute Third-Order Class Proportions

If we again allow the indices i, j, and k to range through any three different barred or unbarred numbers, it is easily shown that the symbols $|ij\bar{k}|$, $|i\bar{j}\bar{k}|$, etc., thus defined are not independent but are related as follows:

$$(7.1) \qquad |ij\bar{k}| = -|i\bar{j}\bar{k}|, \qquad |\bar{i}\bar{j}\bar{k}| = |ij\bar{k}|, \qquad |i\bar{j}k| = -|\bar{i}\bar{j}k| .$$

[4] Again a terminological issue has to be clarified. The level of cross products is determined by the level of the subset to which they belong (see footnote 3). Symmetric parameters are better described by the number of items they feature. This makes $|ij|$ a zero-order cross product but a second-order symmetric parameter. The anomaly is due to the desire to keep in tune with corresponding terminology in correlation analysis. Maybe after a while it will be advisable to agree on a more consistent terminology, which systematically starts with the idea of stratification levels.

In words: if in $|ijk|$ an odd number of indices is barred, the symmetric parameter changes its sign; if an even number is barred, the value of $|ijk|$ remains unchanged. To prove this we show that $|ijk| + |ij\bar{k}| = 0$.

The index k in this equation appears in each term and only either inside or outside a symmetric parameter. If inside, the bar causes a change in sign, and the addition cancels (e.g., $p_k|ij| + p_k|i\bar{j}| = 0$). The bar outside the symmetric parameter causes (after addition) the index to disappear (e.g., $p_k|ij| + p_{\bar{k}}|ij| = |ij|$).

To choose a specific case:

$$|123| = p_{123} - p_1p_2p_3 - p_1|23| - p_2|13| - p_3|12|,$$
$$|12\bar{3}| = p_{12\bar{3}} - p_1p_2p_{\bar{3}} + p_1|23| + p_2|13| - p_{\bar{3}}|12|.$$

If we add the two equations, the third and the fourth terms on the right-hand side cancel because the bar *inside* the cross products makes for a change in sign. The first, second, and last terms have the bar *outside* the cross products; by adding the corresponding terms in the two equations, we see that the coefficients add up to unity. As a result

$$|123| + |12\bar{3}| = p_{12} - p_1p_2 - |12| = p_{12} - p_{12} = 0.$$

Thus $|123| = -|12\bar{3}|$. This mode of computation will presently turn out to have very general applications, which is the main advantage of symmetric parameters.

Once we define and compute a symmetric parameter by Equation (5.3), we can compute any desired third-order class proportion. For example,

(7.2)
$$\begin{aligned} p_{\bar{1}2\bar{3}} &= p_{\bar{1}}p_2p_{\bar{3}} + p_{\bar{1}}|2\bar{3}| + p_2|\bar{1}\bar{3}| + p_{\bar{3}}|\bar{1}2| + |\bar{1}2\bar{3}| \\ &= p_{\bar{1}}p_2p_{\bar{3}} - p_{\bar{1}}|23| + p_2|13| - p_{\bar{3}}|12| + |123|. \end{aligned}$$

We note in passing that subtracting (7.2) from (5.3) yields

(7.3)
$$\begin{aligned} p_{123} - p_{\bar{1}2\bar{3}} &= p_2(p_1p_3 - p_{\bar{1}}p_{\bar{3}}) + |23| + |12| \\ &= p_2(p_1 - p_{\bar{3}}) + |23| + |12| = p_2(p_3 - p_{\bar{1}}) + |23| + |12|. \end{aligned}$$

Actually a general formula, which we shall find useful later, can be derived without the use of the third-order symmetric parameters; i.e.,

(7.4)
$$\begin{aligned} p_{ijk} - p_{i\bar{j}\bar{k}} &= p_{ijk} - p_{i\bar{j}} + p_{i\bar{j}k} = p_{ik} - p_{i\bar{j}} \\ &= p_i(p_k - p_{\bar{j}}) + |ik| + |ij|. \end{aligned}$$

But the parameter enters into another important relation, i.e.,

(7.5)
$$p_{ijk} - p_kp_{ij} = p_i|jk| + p_j|ik| + |ijk|.$$

The computation is straightforward. (The reader is invited to carry it out as an exercise.)

With the introduction of the third-order symmetric parameter a three-attribute dichotomous system can now be completely summarized by the fundamental set of eight parameters:

$$n, p_1, p_2, p_3, |12|, |13|, |23|, |123|.$$

8. The Transformation of Stratified Cross Products

We introduce symmetric parameters into the form

$$|ij;k| = \begin{vmatrix} p_{ijk} & p_{ik} \\ p_{jk} & p_k \end{vmatrix}$$

$$= \begin{vmatrix} p_ip_jp_k + p_i|jk| + p_j|ik| + p_k|ij| + |ijk| & p_ip_k + |ik| \\ p_jp_k + |jk| & p_k \end{vmatrix}.$$

We subtract in the last determinant the second *row* multiplied by p_i from the first row; then we subtract the second *column* multiplied by p_j from the first column. This leaves us on the right-hand side of (5.2) with

$$\begin{vmatrix} |ijk| + p_k|ij| & |ik| \\ |jk| & p_k \end{vmatrix}.$$

Thus

$$|ij;k| = p_k|ijk| + p_k^2|ij| - |ik||jk|. \tag{8.1}$$

By a similar computation we arrive at

$$|ij;\bar{k}| = -p_{\bar{k}}|ijk| + p_{\bar{k}}^2|ij| - |ik||jk|. \tag{8.2}$$

The last two formulas are of course related to each other by the general rule of barred indices expressed above.

It is worth while to give intuitive meaning to Equations (8.1) and (8.2). Suppose we study the relation between political interest (i) and voting (j), computed separately for men and women (k). The cross product for voting and interest as it prevails among men alone is $|ij;k|$. According to Equation (8.1), this conditional interrelation is the cross product $|ij|$ as it prevails in the total population, corrected for relation of sex to both voting and interest, that is, the product $|ik||jk|$. But an additional correction has to be considered, the triple interaction between all three attributes, to wit, $|ijk|$.

Equation (8.1) can be used to compute the relation between different conditional cross products within the same dichotomous cube. Suppose, e.g., we are interested in the relation between $|12;3|$ and $|13;2|$. The answer can be found in a variety of ways, e.g., by writing down $|12;3|$ from Equation (8.1) and substituting into it the value of $|123|$ obtained from the same equation specified for $|13;2|$. But a more revealing way is to compute the determinant

$$\begin{vmatrix} p_3 & |12;3| \\ p_2 & |13;2| \end{vmatrix}. \tag{8.3}$$

We substitute Equation (8.1) twice in the second column, specifying the proper indices. This gives a new determinant, the second column of which consists of three additive terms. It can therefore be separated into the following form:

$$\begin{vmatrix} p_3 & p_3|123| \\ p_2 & p_2|123| \end{vmatrix} + \begin{vmatrix} p_3 & p_3^2|12| \\ p_2 & p_2^2|13| \end{vmatrix} - \begin{vmatrix} p_3 & |13||23| \\ p_2 & |12||23| \end{vmatrix} .$$

The first of these three terms vanishes. The other two are obviously

$$\begin{vmatrix} p_2 & |12| \\ p_3 & |13| \end{vmatrix} \cdot \{p_3 p_2 + |23|\}$$

This expression is equal to (8.3). By equating and rearranging terms, we finally obtain

$$|13;2| = \frac{p_2}{p_3}|12;3| + \frac{p_{23}}{p_3} \cdot \{p_2|13| - p_3|12|\} . \tag{8.4}$$

The relation between any other two conditional cross products can be found either by a similar computation or by rotating indices and bars in Equation (7.4).

9. The Sum of Two Conditional Cross Products—"Partial Association"

By dividing (8.1) and (8.2) by p_k and $p_{\bar{k}}$, respectively, we obtain

THEOREM 1.

$$\frac{|ij;k|}{p_k} + \frac{|ij;\bar{k}|}{p_{\bar{k}}} = |ij| - \frac{|ik||jk|}{p_k p_{\bar{k}}} . \tag{9.1}$$

The formula on the left-hand side is analogous to the traditional notion of partial correlation: a weighted average of the two conditional cross products. We may call it the partial association between (i) and (j) with (k) partialed out.

It is very important to *distinguish between the partial and conditional associations*. A partial association, for instance, can be zero, whereas the two conditional ones can have numerical values, one positive and one negative. This is exactly what happened in our example in Section 6, which should be reread in the present context.

Equation (9.1) is of considerable importance in the theory of survey analysis. It can be made the basis for systematic analysis of what is usually called interpretation. A more detailed discussion will be found in Appendix B.

We are now in a position to answer a question raised in Section 2. Suppose someone likes to express associations between dichotomies in terms of the ϕ-coefficient. How would we use the theorem just derived? The ϕ-coefficient between two attributes is

$$\phi_{12} = \frac{|12|}{\sqrt{p_1 p_{\bar{1}} p_2 p_{\bar{2}}}} .$$

The coefficient for a conditional association, for example, would be

$$\phi_{12\cdot 3} = \frac{|12;3|}{\sqrt{p_{13} p_{\bar{1}3} p_{23} p_{\bar{2}3}}} .$$

Theorem 1 can be restated in the following form:

$$\phi_{12} = \frac{\phi_{12\cdot 3}}{p_3}\sqrt{\frac{p_{13}p_{\bar{1}3}p_{23}p_{\bar{2}3}}{p_1p_{\bar{1}}p_2p_{\bar{2}}}} + \frac{\phi_{12\cdot\bar{3}}}{p_{\bar{3}}}\sqrt{\frac{p_{1\bar{3}}p_{\bar{1}\bar{3}}p_{2\bar{3}}p_{\bar{2}\bar{3}}}{p_1p_{\bar{1}}p_2p_{\bar{2}}}} + \phi_{13}\cdot\phi_{23}\,. \tag{9.2}$$

The only change that occurred affects the weights of the algebraic sum on the right-hand side. Similar adjustments can be made in all other theorems and formulas we shall subsequently derive. It is doubtful whether anything is gained by introducing these conventional coefficients.[5]

Theorem I has an important *corollary*, which was pointed out by David Gold of the University of Iowa (personal communication). Let us introduce for the left side of (9.1) the symbol $|ij;\hat{k}|$. It can be shown that if in a dichotomous cube $|12;3| = 0$, then neither $|13;\hat{2}|$ nor $|23;\hat{1}|$ can vanish as long as none of the zero-order cross products $|ij|$ vanish. Take, e.g.,

$$|23;\hat{1}| = |23| - \frac{|12|\,|13|}{p_1p_{\bar{1}}}\,. \tag{9.3}$$

Because of the original assumption

$$|12| = \frac{|13|\,|23|}{p_3p_{\bar{3}}}\,. \tag{9.4}$$

Substituting (9.4) in (9.3), we obtain

$$|23;\hat{1}| = |23| - \frac{|13|^2\,|23|}{p_1p_{\bar{1}}\,p_3p_{\bar{3}}} = |23|\{1 - \phi_{13}^2\}\,. \tag{9.5}$$

Except if items (1) and (3) are identical, we will always have $\phi_{13} < 1$, which proves the corollary. Let it be noticed that ϕ_{13} in (9.5) is not a "coefficient" invented to "measure" something, but is shorthand for a term that evolved from the general algebraic relation just demonstrated.

10. The Difference Between Two Conditional Cross Products—the Meaning of $|ijk|$

Subtracting Equation (8.2) from Equation (8.1) and rearranging terms, we obtain

THEOREM 2.

$$|ijk| = |ij;k| - |ij;\bar{k}| - |ij|(p_k - p_{\bar{k}})\,. \tag{10.1}$$

The symmetric parameter thus "measures" in a way the difference in the degree of association between $|ij|$, under the condition of k, and $\bar{k}$. This would be especially true if $p_k = p_{\bar{k}}$, that is, if the two conditions are repre-

[5] If one likes to carry out analogies, the following observation may be made. $p_{i3}p_{\bar{i}3}/p_3$ is the variance of item (i) in the subset of people who give a positive response to item (3) and may be symbolized by $\sigma_{i.3}^2$. In the same way $\sigma_{i.\bar{3}}^2$ may be defined for the subset whose response to item (3) is negative. The variance of item (i) for the whole sample is $\sigma_i^2 = p_ip_{\bar{i}}$. The coefficient of $\phi_{12.3}$ in Equation (9.2) is therefore $\sigma_{1.3}\sigma_{2.3}/\sigma_1\sigma_2$. A corresponding reinterpretation can be made for the coefficient of $\phi_{12.\bar{3}}$.

sented equally often. Thus in the example given in Section 7, if we had an equal number of men and women, $|ijk|$ would tell how different the association between vote and interest is, comparing the two sex groups. The conditional relations concealed by (9.1) are brought into focus by (10.1). The numerical scheme of Section 5 permits a check on (10.1). The cross products for the two conditional fourfold tables are .0375 and $-.0375$, respectively. There difference is .075, a value for $|123|$ that we had found previously in a different way. (In this example $p_3 = p_{\bar{3}} = .5$.)

Such an intuitive interpretation of the symmetric parameter can be put still in another way. Let us think of a controlled experiment where item (i) is the stimulus applied under conditions k and $\bar{k}$ with the purpose of measuring the effect on item (j). In such an experiment the experimental and the control groups are matched, which means that by definition the stimulus (i) is uncorrelated with any other factor, and therefore $|ik| = 0$. Consequently, $p_{ik}p_{\bar{i}k} = p_{i\bar{k}}p_{\bar{i}\bar{k}} = c$. (We maintain the presumption that $p_k = p_{\bar{k}}$, which means that the two groups are alike in size.) In this situation the coefficients $f_{ij.k}$ and $f_{ij.\bar{k}}$ mentioned early in the chapter are appropriate measures of the effect of (i) on (j) under the two specified conditions. Theorem 2 tells us that

$$f_{ij.k} - f_{ij.\bar{k}} = \frac{|ijk|}{c}, \tag{10.2}$$

and thus $|ijk|$ expresses the difference it makes whether the effect of (i) on (j) is studied under condition k or $\bar{k}$.[6]

This is a good place to say a word about the relation between the Yule tradition and the tenor of the present paper. The original objective of Yule's attribute statistics was very similar to a logician's presentation of Boolean algebra; to this he added the study of joint frequencies and their deviation from chance values. In a later edition Yule added one page on "relations between partial association." He did not attach much importance to this approach:

> In practice the existence of these relations is of little or no value. They are so complex that lengthy algebraic manipulation is necessary to express those which are not known in terms of those which are.

The few computations Yule presented were indeed rather clumsy. It is easy to see what brought about improvement: the use of determinants, an index notation, and most of all the symmetric parameters. Still it has to be acknowledged that Yule drew attention to the program that is here being carried out to a certain extent. Incidentally, Yule reported the theorem on the weighted sum of stratified cross products. It appeared in

[6] It is hoped that by now the introduction of conventional indices of association into the formulas developed here has become familiar. We shall not continue this line of argument for the rest of this chapter.

earlier editions only as an exercise, but in later editions it was called "the one result which has important theoretical consequences." The consequences he had in mind were the roles of spurious factors in causal analysis, which he called "illusory associations."

11. Application to Panel Analysis

Theorem 2 has various applications to the type of studies in which a sample of people is repeatedly interviewed. One question of interest is the stability of responses. Suppose a first response (1) and a second one (2) to the same question is recorded separately for men and women (3). The stability of their responses is well indicated by the conditional cross products $|12;3|$ and $|12;\bar{3}|$. Theorem 2 shows that the difference in their stability depends essentially upon the parameter $|123|$.

The panel idea—the analysis of repeated responses—requires the notion of trend, i.e., the ratio between the frequency of the first and the second responses.

In the case of propoganda studies the notion of differential trend becomes especially important. Suppose we classify people according to whether they are interested or not in an election, say in August (1). Then we watch whether they were contacted or not by a party worker (2). Finally, we repeat the question on interest, say in October (3). We first compare the people who were contacted (p_2) with those who were not ($p_{\bar{2}}$). Their interest in October relative to their interest in August is p_{32}/p_{12} and $p_{3\bar{2}}/p_{1\bar{2}}$, respectively. If intervening contact is effective, we should find that $p_{32}/p_{12} > p_{3\bar{2}}/p_{1\bar{2}}$. This is tantamount to saying that

$$D = \begin{vmatrix} p_{32} & p_{3\bar{2}} \\ p_{12} & p_{1\bar{2}} \end{vmatrix} = \begin{vmatrix} p_{32} & p_3 \\ p_{12} & p_1 \end{vmatrix} > 0\,. \tag{11.1}$$

It can now happen that $D = 0$, i.e., the trend for the two groups is the same. From this one might conclude that contact with party workers had no effect on interest. This, however, could be a mistake. We develop

$$D = \begin{vmatrix} p_3p_2 + |23| & p_3 \\ p_1p_2 + |12| & p_1 \end{vmatrix} = \begin{vmatrix} |23| & p_3 \\ |12| & p_1 \end{vmatrix},$$

or

$$|23| = \frac{D + p_3|12|}{p_1}\,.$$

On the left-hand side we substitute for $|23|$ the stratified cross products according to Theorem 1. This gives us

$$\frac{|23;1|}{p_1} + \frac{|23;\bar{1}|}{p_{\bar{1}}} = \frac{D + p_3|12|}{p_1} - \frac{|12|\,|13|}{p_1p_{\bar{1}}}\,,$$

and finally

THEOREM 3.

$$\frac{|23;1|}{p_1} + \frac{|23;\bar{1}|}{p_{\bar{1}}} = \frac{p_{\bar{1}}D + |12|\,p_{3\bar{1}}}{p_1 p_{\bar{1}}}, \tag{11.2}$$

with D, the differential trend, defined in Equation (11.1).

Specific indices are used to remind the reader that the notion of a differential trend D hinges on the idea that items (1) and (3) are comparable observations made at different times and that item (2) occurs between (1) and (3). But even so, Theorem 3 needs further discussion before its utility becomes evident.

What is the meaning of $|23;1|$? It refers to the people who had a positive interest in the beginning. It reports their responses at the second interview, which establishes whether or not they have meanwhile been exposed to the party workers. It will usually be found that some defection has occurred from the positive position, but this happens less often among the exposed people. We might loosely talk of a *preserving effect* of the exposure. Numerically this is represented by $p_{1\bar{2}3}/p_{13} < p_{1\bar{2}\bar{3}}/p_{1\bar{3}}$, which is tantamount to saying that

$$\begin{vmatrix} p_{1\bar{2}3} & p_{1\bar{2}\bar{3}} \\ p_{13} & p_{1\bar{3}} \end{vmatrix} < 0,$$

or that $|23;1| > 0$. (The reader is urged to carry out the details as an exercise.)

How about $|23;\bar{1}|$? Here we deal with the subset of people who originally had a negative response. Some of them will have changed to a positive interest the second time. In the same way as before it can be shown that if such conversions are more frequent among exposed people, $|23;\bar{1}|$ will be positive. In this case we shall talk of a *generating effect* of the exposure.

Now Equation (11.2) can be properly interpreted. The two conditional "effects" on the left-hand side depend upon the differential trend D and a term that is positive if $|12| > 0$ and $p_{3\bar{1}} > 0$. The latter is necessarily the case. No frequency can be negative. The frequently observed case of *selective exposure* is signified by $|12| > 0$; people tend to expose themselves to the propaganda with which they tend to agree anyhow.

If the last term in (11.2) is positive, then D can vanish, and the conditional effects on the left-hand side of (11.2) still exist. This is an interesting result. The trend in people's attitude might be the same whether or not they are exposed to a certain piece of propaganda; and yet the latter might have a generating and preserving effect. This however is only the case if the exposure to the propaganda is selective, and is found more frequently among the people who favor its side to begin with; i.e., $|12| > 0$. Obviously the two differential effects are needed to maintain this positive association between the respondent's attitude and his exposure to propaganda.

The following numerical scheme illustrates the situation:

		Contacted (2) October Interest (3) High	Low			Not Contacted ($\bar{2}$) October Interest (3) High	Low	
August Interest (1)	High	40	10	50	High	30	10	40
	Low	20	30	50	Low	18	42	60
		60	40	100		48	52	100

In both fourfold tables high interest increases by twenty percent from August to October, as can be seen from comparing the marginals. The trend is the same for contacted and uncontacted people. And, therefore, $D = 0$. But if we compare the first line of four figures in the above scheme with the second line, we find the following *conditional effects* of contact: Among people with high initial interest, contact *preserves* interest, i.e., there are relatively fewer losses on the left- than on the right-hand side; among people of initially low interest, contact *generates* interest, i.e., there are relatively more gains on the left- than on the right-hand side. For full understanding, the reader is urged to insert the figures of this scheme into Equation (11.2) and consider its separate terms numerically.

Theorem 3 is of interest in still another context. Suppose that (1) is an intended action (e.g., the intention to become a physician); (3) is the action actually carried out some time later; (2) is a condition favorable to the intention (e.g., the father's being a physician). Then $|12| > 0$, and Theorem 3 predicts that most often the following proposition will be found: if a condition favors a certain intention, then this intention is also more likely actually to be carried out if the same condition prevails. To stay with our example: sons of doctors have a tendency toward wanting to be doctors too; among all the people who want to become doctors the sons of doctors will more often carry this intention to a successful end. Findings of this kind are very frequent in social research, and their implications are much discussed. Theorem 3 specifies when they are bound to occur and under what condition exceptions will be found.

12. The Simultaneous "Effect" of Two Attributes on a Third

So far we have examined the effect of stratification by one dichotomy on the association of two others. But the dichotomous cube permits still another application. Often one wants to study a problem like this: How does a certain attitude (1) differ if we compare people of high education (2) and high income (3) with people of low education and low income. Here we deal with two stratifiers and their effect upon presence or absence of a third attribute, in this case sometimes called the criterion. Essentially this comes down to a study of the determinant

$$(12.1) \qquad E = \begin{vmatrix} p_{123} & p_{1\bar{2}\bar{3}} \\ p_{\bar{1}23} & p_{\bar{1}\bar{2}\bar{3}} \end{vmatrix} = \begin{vmatrix} p_{123} & p_{1\bar{2}\bar{3}} \\ p_{23} & p_{\bar{2}\bar{3}} \end{vmatrix}.$$

We now subtract in (12.1) the first column from the second, applying Equation (7.4). This gives

$$E = \begin{vmatrix} p_{123} & -p_1(p_2 - p_{\bar{3}}) - |13| - |12| \\ p_{23} & -(p_2 - p_{\bar{3}}) \end{vmatrix} . \tag{12.2}$$

(The reader should confirm that $p_{\bar{2}\bar{3}} - p_{23} = p_{\bar{2}}p_{\bar{3}} - p_2p_3 = p_{\bar{3}} - p_2$). Now in (12.2) we multiply the second row by p_1 and subtract it from the first row. Using Equation (7.5) we obtain

$$E = -|123|(p_2 - p_{\bar{3}}) - E_1 , \tag{12.3}$$

where

$$E_1 = \begin{vmatrix} p_2|13| + p_3|12| & |13| + |12| \\ p_{23} & (p_2 - p_{\bar{3}}) \end{vmatrix} . \tag{12.4}$$

Now E_1 can be looked upon as a third-order determinant expanded along its third row (or by pivotal condensation around $|13|$), i.e.,

$$E_1 = \begin{vmatrix} |13| & p_3 & 1 \\ -|12| & p_2 & 1 \\ 0 & p_{23} & (p_2 - p_{\bar{3}}) \end{vmatrix} . \tag{12.5}$$

But E_1 can also be expanded along its first column. The unsigned cofactor of $|13|$ is

$$\begin{vmatrix} p_2 & 1 \\ p_2p_3 + |23| & (p_2 - p_{\bar{3}}) \end{vmatrix} = \begin{vmatrix} p_2 & 1 \\ |23| & p_2 - 1 \end{vmatrix} = -(p_2t_{\bar{2}} + |23|) .$$

The unsigned cofactor of $-|12|$ in (12.5) is

$$\begin{vmatrix} p_3 & 1 \\ p_{23} & p_2 - p_{\bar{3}} \end{vmatrix} = \begin{vmatrix} p_3 & 1 \\ |23| & -p_{\bar{3}} \end{vmatrix} = -(p_3p_{\bar{3}} + |23|) ;$$

therefore (12.5) becomes

$$E_1 = \begin{vmatrix} p_3p_{\bar{3}} + |23| & |13| \\ p_2p_{\bar{2}} + |23| & -|12| \end{vmatrix} . \tag{12.6}$$

We obtain

THEOREM 4.

$$\begin{vmatrix} p_{123} & p_{1\bar{2}\bar{3}} \\ p_{\bar{1}23} & p_{\bar{1}\bar{2}\bar{3}} \end{vmatrix} = |123|(p_{\bar{3}} - p_2) - E_1 ,$$

where E_1 *is given by Equation* (12.6).

The third-order symmetric parameter does not enter the theorem if $p_2 = p_{\bar{3}}$. This can often be achieved by making $p_2 = p_3 = .5$; this means choosing an equal number of people with, say, high and low income (2) and with high and low education (3) in the original sample. Then the joint effect of these two attributes upon the attitude (3) under study would be measured by an index, the nucleus of which would be $\{.25 + |23|\}\{|12| + |13|\}$.

The joint effect is greater when the stronger two stratifiers are associated among themselves and each singly with the "criterion" (3).

The use of third-order determinants also facilitates greatly the computation of another form:

$$G = \begin{vmatrix} p_{12\bar{3}} & p_{1\bar{2}3} \\ p_{\bar{1}2\bar{3}} & p_{\bar{1}\bar{2}3} \end{vmatrix} .$$

This form comes up when we ask which of two attributes has a stronger effect on a third. For the record we present the appropriate expression of G in terms of symmetric parameters, leaving it to the reader to carry out the proof as a very useful exercise. The necessary computations are completely parallel to those carried out in this section, i.e.,

$$G = |123|(p_2 - p_3) + G_1 ,$$

$$G_1 = \begin{vmatrix} p_3 p_{\bar{3}} - |23| & |13| \\ p_2 p_{\bar{2}} - |23| & |12| \end{vmatrix} .$$

It is important to see the difference between Theorem 4 and Theorem 2, especially in the derived form of Equation (9.2). The "both-or-neither effect" of, say, income and education does not essentially depend on $|123|$ as shown by E_1 in Theorem 4. What is it then that the third-order parameter describes according to Theorem 2? Staying with the same substantive example, the answer is as follows. The two attributes of education (2) and income (3) divide the whole group into four subsets, to wit, $(--)$, $(-+)$, $(+-)$, and $(++)$. Suppose that the proportion of people in each subset who have attitude (3) increases in the direction just indicated: the proportion is lowest in subset $(--)$, highest in subset $(++)$, and somewhere in between in the other two subsets. This means that both education and income increase the probability of attitude (3). This still leaves the question of whether the effect of one of these factors as compared to none is the same as the effect of two of the factors as compared to one. If the two factors are "linearly additive" in this sense, then $|123|$ will vanish. If the symmetric parameter does not vanish, then the "jump" in the attitude between $(--)$ and $(-+)$ is greater (or smaller) than the "jump" between $(+-)$ and $(++)$. The sign of $|123|$ decides whether "greater" or "smaller" applies. An exact computation shows that the result is the same whether we start with the order $(-+)(+-)$ or with the order $(+-)(-+)$. The reader can easily formalize the general argument by restudying Equation (9.2) in the light of this new interpretation of $|123|$. The matter becomes practically obvious if we assume the weak restriction that $p_2 = p_3$ and $|23| = 0$.

In the light of all this, Theorem 4 then states that the joint effect of two attributes is essentially the same, irrespective of whether they are linearly additive or not.

13. Hybrid Stratification

For certain problems it is necessary to substitute into $|ij|$ one after another the corresponding columns of $|ij; k|$. This leads to the *compound*, which is defined as

$$C = \begin{vmatrix} p_{ijk} & p_j \\ p_{ik} & 1 \end{vmatrix} + \begin{vmatrix} p_{ij} & p_{kj} \\ p_i & p_k \end{vmatrix} .$$

Each of these determinants can be derived from $|ij|$ by stratifying one column at a time, i.e., by adding the index k. This is why we talk here of hybrid stratification.

Inserting the symmetric parameters and using Equation (7.5), we obtain

$$C = |ijk| + p_i|jk| + p_k|ij| + p_k|ij| - p_i|jk| = |ijk| + 2p_k|ij| .$$

From (10.1) we can express $|ijk|$ in terms of two stratified cross products and obtain

$$C = |ij; k| - |ij; \bar{k}| + |ij| .$$

This result is interesting because it shows that C is dependent upon cross products only, and not upon p_k; this is not the case for $|ijk|$ if it is expressed in terms of cross products.

The compound C appears in the determinantal equation

$$\begin{vmatrix} p_{ijk} - tp_{ij} & p_{jk} - tp_j \\ p_{ik} - tp_i & p_k - t \end{vmatrix} = 0 ,$$

which plays an important role in latent-structure analysis. The equation has the form

(13.1) $$|ij; k| - Ct + |ij|t^2 = 0 .$$

The reader can easily verify this result by expanding the determinantal equation. We shall come back to it in Section 17.

14. Symmetric Parameters in General

We have discussed so far symmetric parameters of the second order—the familiar cross products—and symmetric parameters of the third order. The criteria by which the third-order symmetric parameter was chosen suggest the form of a fourth-order parameter. The symbol $|ijkl|$ will be used to denote the fourth-order symmetric parameter, which will be defined implicitly by

(14.1) $$p_{ijkl} = p_ip_jp_kp_l + p_ip_j|kl| + p_ip_k|jl| + p_ip_l|jk| + p_jp_k|il| + p_jp_l|ik| + p_kp_l|ij| + p_i|jkl| + p_j|ikl| + p_k|ijl| + p_l|ijk| + |ijkl| .$$

This equation can be written more concisely in the form

$$p_{ijkl} = p_ip_jp_kp_l + \sum p_ip_j|kl| + \sum p_i|jkl| + |ijk| ,$$

where the summation sign indicates summation over all possible permutations of the four indices. In general the symmetric parameter of order m will be defined implicitly by

(14.2) $$p_{12\cdots m} = p_1p_2\cdots p_m + \sum p_1p_2\cdots p_{m-2}\,|(m-1)\,m| + \sum p_1p_2\cdots p_{m-3}\,|(m-2)(m-1)\,m| + \cdots + \sum p_1\,|23\cdots(m-1)| + |12\cdots m|\,.$$

A dichotomous system of m attributes can be completely summarized by 2^m independent pieces of data. The *fundamental set* using symmetric parameters consists of the following data:

Order of term	Number of terms	Parameters of given order
0	1	n
1	m	$p_1, p_2, \cdots, p_m$
2	$\frac{m}{2!(m-2)!}$	$\|12\|, \|13\|, \cdots, \|(m-1)m\|$
3	$\frac{m}{3!(m-3)!}$	$\|123\|, \cdots, \|(m-2)(m-1)m\|$
$\vdots$	$\vdots$	$\vdots$
$m-1$	m	$\|12\cdots(m-1)\|, \cdots, \|23\cdots m\|$
m	1	$\|12\cdots m\|$

The numbers of terms of the various orders above are the coefficients of the binomial expansion of $(a+b)^m$. If we let $a = b = 1$, it then follows that the total number of such parameters of all orders is 2^m.

It can be seen easily that these higher-order symmetric parameters can be used to compute simply all ultimate frequencies. *Thus, e.g., a formula for $p_{\bar{i}jkl}$ can be obtained by changing in* (14.1) *any p_i into $p_{\bar{i}}$ and by changing the sign of any symmetric parameter in which a barred index appears.* The proof from frequency level 3 to level 4 is exactly the same that was given above for frequency level 3. The general rule is obvious, and can be obtained by induction from any level to the next.

Insight into the symmetric parameters is strengthened by the following observation. Suppose in the parametric expression of $p_{1234\ldots}$ we want to collect all the terms that have p_1 as a factor. What than would X and Y be in the following form?

(14.3) $$p_{1234\ldots} = p_1X + Y + |1234\cdots|\,.$$

Since no term in Y has p_1 as a factor, Y has to comprise all and only those terms *that have the index* (1) *in brackets.* For the four-level case, e.g., we would have

(14.4) $$Y = p_2\,|134| + p_3\,|124| + p_4\,|123| + |12|\,p_3p_4 + |13|\,p_2p_4 + |14|\,p_2p_3\,.$$

On the other hand, X comprises all the terms that do not contain the index (1) at all but otherwise comprises all the combinations within and outside brackets of all the other indices. Therefore $X = p_{234\ldots}$.

In the 4-item case we obtain the useful formula

(14.5) $$p_{1234} - p_1p_{234} = |1234| + Y\,,$$

where Y is defined by (14.4). This is, of course, a generalization of Equation (7.5), which dealt with 3 items.

15. Some Problems of Fourth Order

The dichotomous cube represented two situations: the effect of stratification by one attribute upon the relation between the two others; or the effect of double stratification upon the third attribute alone. With four dichotomies we can combine the two ideas.[7]

The cross product of items (3) and (4) stratified for items (1) and (2) is

$$|\,34;12\,| = \begin{vmatrix} p_{1234} & p_{124} \\ p_{123} & p_{12} \end{vmatrix}. \tag{15.1}$$

For purpose of illustration, the stratifiers might be taken as sex (1) and race (2). Two abilities, mathematical (3) and language (4) might be the associated attributes. Then equation (1) would be the cross product between the two abilities for white men—if male sex and white race are arbitrarily symbolized as positive. The same association for white women would be indicated by $|\,34;\bar{1}2\,|$ etc.

We shall develop four different combinations of such cross products, which will lead to some theorems corresponding to the ones we have developed for the dichotomous cube. (We could talk here of a four-dimensional cube, but little would be gained.)

One combination of interest is obviously the weighted average of the four conditional cross products taken over the four subsets partitioned by the two stratifiers: white men, Negro men, white women, Negro women. This would be an obvious extension of the notion of partial association developed in Section 9.

Two more results can be derived from the notion of differential association developed in Section 10. We can first compute whether the association between the two abilities is greater for white men than for white women. The same difference can be computed for Negro men and Negro women. If the two differences are in some way averaged, then we know the differential effect of sex on the association between the two abilities with the role of race "partialed out." Obviously, the same computation can be performed taking the two stratifiers in reverse order. This would give the differential effect of sex on the association of the two abilities with race partialed out.

A fourth result leads into new territory. We can develop the idea of a second-order differential effect. The wording of it becomes rather clumsy: What is the differential effect of race upon the differential effect of sex upon the association between the two abilities? Mathematically, however, this second-order difference turns out to be especially simple and throws considerable light on the meaning of the fourth-order symmetric parameter. It will also be seen that in this case the order of the two stratifiers is irrelevant. The weighted difference between conditional associations is a notion which we are not accustomed to because traditional correlation analysis considers only weighted sums. But one of the purposes of this chapter

[7] Hereafter the word "effect" will not be quoted.

is to show that differences are equally interesting and to provide an appropriate algorithm to deal with them.

In order to underscore the main ideas and not be burdened with irrelevant computations, we shall develop our theorems under some simplifying assumptions. We shall assume that a sample has been arbitrarily selected so that the four subsets engendered by the two stratifiers are of equal size. In terms of our example this means that we start with equal numbers of white and Negro men and women. This makes

$$p_1 = p_2 = .5\,, \qquad p_{12} = .25\,, \qquad |12| = 0\,,$$

from which numerous other constants can be derived, such as $p_{\bar{2}} = .5$, $p_{\bar{1}2} = .25$, etc.

Under this assumption the questions just raised boil down to the translation of four forms in terms of symmetric parameters. The main purpose of Section 16 will be to show computing devices by which the symmetry of these forms can be utilized. As a matter of fact, we shall develop a procedure that permits computing all four forms simultaneously. Meantime the reader is asked to check carefully that the following algebraic definitions correspond to the verbal definitions given above.

Form I. $|34;12| + |34;\bar{1}2| + |34;1\bar{2}| + |34;\bar{1}\bar{2}|\,.$

Form IIa. $\{|34;12| - |34;\bar{1}2\} + \{|34;1\bar{2}| - |34;\bar{1}\bar{2}|\}\,.$

Form IIb. $\{|34;12| - |34;1\bar{2}|\} + \{|34;\bar{1}2| - |34;\bar{1}\bar{2}\}\,.$

Form III. $\{|34;12| - |34;\bar{1}2|\} - \{|34;1\bar{2}| - |34;\bar{1}\bar{2}|\}$

$$= |34;12| - |34;\bar{1}2| - |34;1\bar{2}| + |34;\bar{1}\bar{2}|\,.$$

16. The Derivation of Fourth-Order Relations

The four forms just listed are all algebraic sums of the same four terms. They differ only in the sequence of signs by which the four terms are added or subtracted. The four terms, in turn, differ only in the digits of the barred indices. We know in advance, therefore, how these four terms will differ once they are developed further: the symmetric parameters will change signs, and their coefficients will have sometimes barred and sometimes unbarred indices. The problem is how to take best advantage of all this symmetry.

We first take Equation (15.1) and transform the determinant on the right-hand side in the usual way: we subtract the last column, multiplied by p_3, from the first column; then we subtract the last row, multiplied by p_4, from the first row. This gives the expression

$$(16.1)\quad \begin{vmatrix} p_1p_2|34| + p_1|234| + p_2|134| + |1234| & p_1|24| + p_2|14| + |124| \\ p_1|23| + p_2|13| + |123| & p_1p_2 + |12| \end{vmatrix}.$$

Because our forms require the adding or subtracting of four such expressions, it is advantageous to develop (16.1) right away. Taking into account our limitations on the stratifiers, we get

$$(16.2)\qquad |34;12| = (.5)^4|34| + (.5)^2\{.5|234| + .5|134| + |1234|\} - \{.5|23| + .5|13| + |123|\}\{.5|24| + .5|14| + |124|\}.$$

The expression on the left-hand side of (16.2) consists of three parts, which we shall designate separately by introducing the following *definitions*.

The first term $(.5)^4|34| = A$ remains obviously the same, irrespective of what stratification subset we use.

We shall designate $(.5)^2\{.5|234| + .5|134| + |1234|\}$ by B_{12}. A barred stratifier will be indicated correspondingly; thus $B_{\bar{1}2}$ would be the middle part of $|34;\bar{1}2|$.

The remaining part of (16.2) will be designated by C_{12}; it is the product of the two sets in braces. Again, if $|34;1\bar{2}|$ were under discussion, the necessary changes in signs inside the braces would be made, and the product would be symbolized by $C_{1\bar{2}}$.

All the forms set out in the previous section are linear algebraic sums of the same four cross products, differing only in the sign patterns attached to $|34;ij|$; they, in turn, are the sums of A, B_{ij}, and C_{ij}. We first carry out the summations over the latter terms and then proceed to the forms themselves. Thus the contribution of A to Form I is $4 \times (.5)^4|34|$. For Forms IIa, IIb, and III the contribution of A vanishes, because the same expression appears twice with the negative and twice with the positive sign.

To compute the contribution of B_{ij} to the four forms we set up Schema 1.

	$.5\|234\|$	$.5\|134\|$	$\|1234\|$
$\|34;12\|$	(+)	(+)	(+)
$\|34;\bar{1}2\|$	(+)	(−)	(−)
$\|34;1\bar{2}\|$	(−)	(+)	(−)
$\|34;\bar{1}\bar{2}\|$	(−)	(−)	(+)

SCHEMA 1. The Contribution of B_{ij} to the Four Forms

On top we write out in full the three symmetric parameters of B_{ij}. On the left side we list the four possible ways that $|34;ij|$ can occur. For each symmetric parameter the schema indicates the sign with which it enters into the stratified cross product listed on the left.

We can now easily ascertain the contribution of B_{ij} to a form by noting the signs in the last three columns of Schema 1 by considering how the cross products enter a form. In *Form I* all cross products are positive, and therefore the sign pattern in the scheme does not change. Adding B_{ij} for the four cross products means adding the symmetric parameters with the original signs. Each element of the top row enters into the summation twice with a positive and twice with a negative sign. The contribution of B_{ij} vanishes in this case.

The algebraic sum of *Form IIa* reverses the signs in the second and fourth rows since $|34; \bar{1}2|$ and $|34; \bar{1}\bar{2}|$ enter into this form with the negative sign. This leaves again two positive and two negative signs in the column for $|234|$ and $|1234|$ of Schema 1. But in the $|134|$ column all signs are now positive, and therefore the contribution of B_{ij} to Form IIa is $4 \times .5|134| = 2 \times |134|$.

In *Form IIb* the third and fourth rows change signs. This leaves only the $|234|$ column with four positive signs, and in this case then the contribution of B_{ij} is $2 \times |234|$. Notice that at this point Forms IIa and IIb differ only by exchanging indices (1) and (2).

In *Form III* the signs in the second and third rows are reversed because $|34; \bar{1}2|$ and $|34; \bar{1}3|$ enter into it with reversed signs. This makes all the signs in the $|1234|$ column positive. Therefore B_{ij} contributes $4 \times |1234|$. The sums in the other two columns vanish.

This leaves us with C_{ij} in Equation (16.2). To simplify this part of the computation we set up Schema 2. The cells correspond to the nine products that evolve from the multiplication of the two expressions in the braces of C_{ij}. We have now four signs in each cell corresponding to the four stratified cross products in the following arrangement:

$$\begin{matrix} |34; 12| & |34; 1\bar{2}| \\ |34; \bar{1}2| & |34; \bar{1}\bar{2}|\,. \end{matrix}$$

	$.5\|24\|$	$.5\|14\|$	$\|124\|$
$.5\|23\|$	+ + + +	+ − − +	+ − + −
$.5\|13\|$	+ − − +	+ + + +	+ + − −
$\|123\|$	+ − + −	+ + − −	+ + + +

SCHEMA 2. The Contribution of C_{ij} to the Four Forms

What in Schema 1 were listed in the first column are now listed *within* each of the nine cells. And the additions performed previously in the second, third, and fourth columns of the four signs now have to be performed in each cell in the arrangement just indicated. Again, the forms will differ only inasmuch as the various cross products $|34; ij|$ enter into them with a different sign pattern.

For *Form I* all terms have a positive sign. Therefore, only those cells in which all signs are alike have to be considered; this is the case for the three cells in the main diagonal of Schema 2. The contribution of C_{ij} to Form I is therefore $.25|24||23| + .25|13||14| + |123||124|$.

In *Form IIb* the signs corresponding to $|34; 1\bar{2}|$ and $|34; \bar{1}\bar{2}|$ are reversed, and are indicated by the second column in each cell. This restricts the contributions of C_{ij} to the upper-right and the lower-left cells; in all other cells we have two positive and two negative signs, which cancel each other. The contribution to Form IIb is therefore $.5\,|\,23\,||\,124\,| + .5\,|\,123\,||\,24\,|$.

Applying the same procedure to *Form IIa*, we find the contribution of C_{ij} in this case is $.5\,|\,13\,||\,124\,| + .5\,|\,123\,||\,14\,|$. The result is the same as in Form IIb but indices (1) and (2) are exchanged.

Finally, in *Form III* the signs corresponding to $|\,34; \bar{1}2\,|$ and $|\,34; 1\bar{2}\,|$ are reversed; they occur in the minor diagonal of each cell. Thus in Schema 2 all signs in the second cell of the first row and all signs in the first cell of the second row are positive. The contribution to Form III is therefore $.25\,|\,23\,||\,14\,| + .25\,|\,13\,||\,24\,|$.

It follows from Equation (16.2) that the contributions from Schema 1 have to be multiplied by .25 and the contributions from Schema 2 must be taken with a negative sign. We are now in a position to evaluate all forms.

We thus find that for

Form I. $.25\,|\,34\,| - .25\{|\,24\,||\,23\,| + |\,13\,||\,14\,|\} - |\,123\,||\,124\,|$.

Form IIa. $.5\{|\,134\,| - |\,13\,||\,124\,| - |\,14\,||\,123\,|\}$.

Form IIb. $.5\{|\,234\,| - |\,23\,||\,124\,| - |\,24\,||\,123\,|\}$.

Form III. $|\,1234\,| - .25\{|\,23\,||\,14\,| + |\,13\,||\,24\,|\}$.

Forms I and III are of special substantive interest; we shall cast them slightly differently and discuss them in more detail in the next section.

17. Some Fourth-Order Theorems

From Section 10 we know that in the case of $p_1 = p_{\bar{1}}$

$$|\,134\,| = |\,34; 1\,| - |\,34; \bar{1}\,| .$$

The third-order symmetric parameter is then the differential effect of stratification: the difference in the association of the two items (2) and (3) for the two sides of (1). The interesting feature of this formula is that no second-order parameters appear. In the case of two stratifiers we have the following second-order differential effect:

(17.1) $$S = (34; 12 - 34; 1\bar{2}) - (34; \bar{1}2 - 34; \bar{1}\bar{2}) .$$

The meaning of the fourth-order parameter can be seen from Form III recast into

THEOREM 5. *If two stratifiers* (1) *and* (2) *are uncorrelated and each partitions a sample into two equal parts, then*

$$|\,1234\,| = S + .25\{|\,23\,||\,14\,| + |\,31\,||\,24\,|\} ,$$

where S is defined by Equation (17.1).

Here no third-order parameters appear. As a matter of fact not even $|\,34\,|$ enters this formula. We can go one step further. Referring back to our example, we find that $|\,1234\,| = S$ under one of two conditions: either that one of the two abilities is unrelated to both stratifiers, which means, e.g., $|14| = |24| = 0$, or that one stratifier is unrelated to both abilities, e.g., $|23| = |24| = 0$.

In general, then, the symmetric parameters permit two interpretations. They indicate the higher-order interrelations of dichotomies on their own level. But they also indicate the distortions that are introduced by stratification on lower levels. In this sense they play the same shape-describing role that mixed moments play in the analysis of multivariate distribution functions.

Form I is equivalent to the findings of Section 8. If we assumed there that $p_1 = p_{\bar{1}}$, we found

$$|34| = \frac{|34;1|}{.5} + \frac{|34;\bar{1}|}{.5} + \frac{|13||14|}{.25}.$$

Here it is the third-order parameter that does not appear, and we stressed the relation of this theorem to the notion of partial association. Now with Form I we can again introduce this idea by concentrating on the average stratified cross product

$$P = \frac{|34;12|}{.25} + \frac{|34;1\bar{2}|}{.25} + \frac{|34;\bar{1}2|}{.25} + \frac{|34;\bar{1}\bar{2}|}{.25}. \tag{17.2}$$

Form I furnishes then

THEOREM 6. *Under the same restrictions that were introduced in Theorem* 5, $|34| = P + |13||14| + |23||24| + (|123||124|/.25)$, *where* P *is defined by* (17.2).

Here the fourth-order symmetric parameter does not enter, and we notice an interesting additivity of the correction factors. The second-order association $|34|$ is composed of P plus the terms $|i3||i4|$(which we found in the third-order case) plus an analogous new term $|123| \cdot |124|$. If $P = 0$, we now have quite a variety of "spurious correlations" to take care of in the interpretation of survey findings. (See Appendix A.)

Because of Theorem 6, the first of our four forms is by far the most useful one. It is therefore worth while to show that Form I can be derived more directly and by a procedure that introduces a new idea.

Suppose that a sample is now partitioned by a polytomy, say the total score of a test. On each score level we then cross-tabulate two dichotomous items. Since such data are seldom investigated, we give a concrete example.

Our material comes from a public-relations study in which 560 respondents were questioned regarding their attitudes to the oil industry. Do oil companies treat their workers fairly; do they make too much profit; are they wasteful of our natural resources, etc.? To each question the respondent could give one of five answers, which ranged from firmly favorable to firmly unfavorable (from the oil industry's point of view). There were ten questions in all, and eight of them were combined into an arbitrary score in the following way: a firmly favorable answer was given a weight of 4, and so on down to the firmly unfavorable, which got a weight of 0. Then all the weights were added so that a respondent's general-attitude score could range from 0 to 32. This score was used as the "outside continuum," or base variable. Against it the answers to the remaining two questions were plotted. These two were:

Item 1. Do the big oil companies control too much of the oil business?

Item 2. Is the oil industry wasteful of our natural resources?

The interrelation of the two test items for the five subclasses of respondents classified according to the general attitude score derived from the eight other questions is shown in Table 1.

TABLE 1

	Item 2 +	Item 2 −		Item 2 +	Item 2 −		Item 2 +	Item 2 −		Item 2 +	Item 2 −		Item 2 +	Item 2 −	
Item 1 +	3	14	17	15	27	42	35	26	61	40	18	58	67	17	84
Item 1 −	30	59	89	32	61	93	34	29	63	13	21	34	12	7	19
Total	33	73	106	47	88	135	69	55	124	53	39	92	79	24	103
General attitude score	0 to 16			17 to 20			21 to 23			24 to 26			27 to 32		

A response favorable to the oil industry is indicated by a + sign.

A positive reply (from the industry's point of view) was one in which a respondent expressed at least some disagreement (score class 3 and 4). The joint positive response required such disagreement with both items. In Table 1 we now have the absolute frequencies for each item alone and for the joint responses. After dividing by the number of cases in each fourfold table (106, 135, etc.), we have now in this table the conditional marginals and joint frequencies for the two items on five levels of the general score. The joint positive frequencies for the two items are $3/106 = .03$ on the lowest level and $67/103 = .65$ on the highest level.

Now we move to a general formulation. On each of the m levels x of a polytomy we have a conditional cross product for two items (3) and (4), i.e.,

$$|\,34; x\,| = \begin{vmatrix} p_{x34} & p_{x3} \\ p_{x4} & p_x \end{vmatrix} \qquad x = 1, \cdots, m\,.$$

Then

$$p_{x34} = \frac{|\,34; x\,| + p_{x3}p_{x4}}{p_x} \tag{17.3}$$

and

$$\sum_{x=1}^{m} p_{34x} = p_{34}\,, \qquad \sum_{x=1}^{m} p_{3x} = p_3\,, \qquad \sum_{x=1}^{m} p_{4x} = p_4\,. \tag{17.3a}$$

We now introduce (17.3) into $|\,34\,|$ and obtain

$$|\,34\,| = \begin{vmatrix} \sum_{x=1}^{m} \frac{|\,34;\,x\,|}{p_x} + \sum_{x=1}^{m} \frac{p_{x3}p_{x4}}{p_x} & p_4 \\ p_3 & 1 \end{vmatrix} = \sum_{x=1}^{m} \frac{|\,34;\,x\,|}{p_x} + W\,,$$

where

$$W = \sum_{x=1}^{m} \frac{p_{x3}p_{x4}}{p_x} - p_3p_4\,.$$

To make the meaning of W more obvious, we introduce the symbols

$$\frac{p_{xi}}{p_x} = \pi_i^x\,.$$

The expressions π_i^x are now the proportion of people who in each subset x provide a positive response to item i. The difference between π_i^x and p_{xi} is obvious: the former is computed on the basis of the size of the subset, while the latter is computed on the basis of the total sample. In order to facilitate a subsequent discussion, the subset x is now indexed as a superscript, while the item i remains a subscript. W then becomes

$$W = \sum_{x=1}^{m} p_x \pi_3^x \pi_4^x - p_3 p_4\,. \tag{17.4}$$

Thus π_i^x can also be looked upon as the probability of a person in subset x to supply a positive response to item i. The expectation of π_i^x or its average over the whole sample is

$$\sum_{x=1}^{m} p_x\pi_i^x = \sum_{x=1}^{m} \frac{p_x p_{xi}}{p_x} = p_i\,.$$

Now we can apply a well-known formula about covariances to the effect that

$$W = \sum_{x=1}^{m} (\pi_3^x - p_3)(\pi_4^x - p_4)\,.$$

W thus turns out to be the covariance of the marginal frequencies p_{x3} and p_{x4} of the fourfold tables as we move along the polytomy. This in itself is a useful result and deserves to be listed as

THEOREM 7. *If a sample is partitioned by a polytomy x into m sections, then the cross product between two dichotomies (i) and (j) is*

$$|\,ij\,| = \sum_{x=1}^{m} \frac{|\,ij;\,x\,|}{p_x} + W\,,$$

where W is the covariance of the conditional marginals as defined by Equation (17.4).

The reader should satisfy himself that Theorem 1 in Section 9 is a special case of Theorem 7 for the case when $m = 2$, and x therefore is itself a dichotomy.[8]

[8] If all $|\,ij;\,x\,| = 0$, we have the case of "local independence," which is so important in latent-structure analysis. This point will be pursued elsewhere.

But x can also be a four-part polytomy generated by two dichotomous stratifiers. The 4 values of p_x then become our usual $p_{12}, p_{1\bar{2}}, p_{\bar{1}2}$ and $p_{\bar{1}\bar{2}}$. If we assume that $p_1 = p_2 = .5$ and $|12| = 0$, we should come back from Theorem 7 to our Form I and the related Theorem 6. And this is indeed the case.

Equation (17.4) is now the sum of four expressions of the form

$$\frac{(p_{ij3} - p_3 p_{ij})(p_{ij4} - p_4 p_{ij})}{p_{ij}}, \tag{17.5}$$

where the summation is extended over all combinations of bars on i and j. Equation (7.5) converts (17.5) into

$$\frac{\{p_i|3j| + p_j|3i| + |ij3|\}\{p_i|4j| + p_j|4i| + |ij4|\}}{p_{ij}}. \tag{17.6}$$

We now write again the product of the two braces in the form of Schema 3, remembering our restrictions on the stratifiers.

	.5 | 32 |	.5 | 13 |	| 123 |
.5 | 42 |	+ + + +	+ − − +	+ + − −
.5 | 41 |	+ − − +	+ + + +	+ − + −
| 124 |	+ + − −	+ − + −	+ + + +

SCHEMA 3. Computing the Value of (17.6) for Four Subsets

In order to get all four combinations of (17.6) for the summation needed in Theorem 7, we indicate again the signs which the terms of the products in (17.6) take on if we consider the stratified subsets in the following arrangement:

$$\begin{matrix} |34; 12| & |34; 1\bar{2}| \\ |34; \bar{1}2| & |34; \bar{1}\bar{2}| \end{matrix}. \tag{17.7}$$

The reader familiar with the procedure from the preceding section should have no difficulty in checking the signs inserted in Schema 3. The product in the last cell of the first row, e.g., is positive for $|42||123|$ and $|4\bar{2}||1\bar{2}3|$; it is negative for $|42||\bar{1}23|$ and $|4\bar{2}||\bar{1}\bar{2}3|$. In summing the cross product listed in (17.7), we find that all the terms disappear which have two positive and two negative cell entries in Schema 3. Thus only the cells in its main diagonal remain. The sum of their values is

$$.25|23||24| + .25||13||14| + |123||124|.$$

We have now only to remember from (17.6) that for the final result this expression has to be divided by $p_{12} = .25$. Then Theorem 7 gives

$$|\,34\,| = \sum_{ij} \frac{|\,34; ij\,|}{p_{ij}} + |\,23\,||\,24\,| + |\,13\,||\,24\,| + \frac{|\,123\,||\,124\,|}{.25}\,,$$

which is indeed identical with Theorem 6.

18. Special Dichotomous Systems

In various applications sets of dichotomies that are subject to certain restrictions occur. The most obvious is the *homogeneous system* H, characterized by the condition that all symmetric parameters vanish. Then $p_{ij} = p_i p_j$, $p_{ijk} = p_i p_j p_k$, and so on. In other words the higher-order frequencies can be computed from the marginals by probability considerations. Another restricted joint-distribution dichotomy will be called the *Guttman system* G, because it derives from what he has called the "perfect scale." It consists of a set of m-ordered dichotomies so that $p_1 > p_2 \cdots > p_i > p_{i+1} \cdots > p_m$. The marginals in this case are the frequencies of positive responses to the questionnaire item. It is assumed that every person gives a positive response up to a certain item i and a negative response for all subsequent items in the series. This means that among the ultimate frequencies all are zero except those having an unbroken series of unbarred indices followed by the remaining indices barred. To exemplify with four items, we have the following:

$$p_{1234} \neq 0\,, \quad p_{123\bar{4}} \neq 0\,, \quad p_{12\bar{3}\bar{4}} \neq 0\,, \quad \cdots, \text{etc.},$$

but, e.g.,

$$p_{12\bar{3}4} = 0\,, \quad p_{\bar{1}\bar{2}3\bar{4}} = 0\,, \quad \cdots, \text{etc.}$$

It is easily seen that in the non-vanishing frequencies all the indices but the last can be dropped. Thus

$$p_{\underline{234}} = p_{24} - p_{2\bar{3}4} = p_{\underline{24}} = p_4 - p_{\bar{2}4} = p_{\underline{4}}\,.$$

The frequencies subtracted in this example all vanish because they have an inadmissable bar pattern.

If two items satisfy the condition that $p_{\bar{i}j} = 0$ $(i > j)$, we shall call them *cumulative*, which in test terms means that all the people who give a positive reply to item (j) are part of the set with a positive reply to item (i) as follows:

$$p_i = p_{ij} + p_{i\bar{j}} = p_j - p_{\bar{i}j} + p_{i\bar{j}} = p_j + p_{i\bar{j}}\,.$$

We then can easily prove

THEOREM 8. *If in a set of ordered dichotomies any two* adjacent *items are cumulative then they form a Guttman system.*

We first prove the theorem for three items. Assume that $p_{\bar{1}2} = p_{\bar{2}3} = 0$. Then obviously $p_{\bar{1}23} + p_{\bar{1}\bar{2}3} = 0$, and because frequencies cannot be negative, each of these two terms vanishes. The same is true for $p_{1\bar{2}3} + p_{\bar{1}\bar{2}3} = 0$. Therefore $p_{\bar{1}3} = p_{\bar{1}23} + p_{\bar{1}\bar{2}3} = 0$. This shows that items (1) and (3) are also cumulative, although they are not adjacent. Extending this proof step by step we see that if all *adjacent* items have the property $p_{\bar{i}j} = 0$, then for *any* pair $p_{\bar{a}b} = 0$.

Furthermore, if $p_{\bar{a}b} = 0$, then any frequency with the signature $p_{x\bar{a}by}$ has to vanish because it is the non-negative part of a zero sum. But any ultimate frequency with an "inverted" sign pattern is obviously of this type. Thus all such ultimate frequencies vanish, which is the definition of a Guttman system.

Our next example is taken from latent-structure analysis. Under what conditions can a general dichotomous system S be the sum of two homogeneous systems H_1 and H_2? If we designate the marginals of these two systems by superscripts, i.e., by p_i^1 and p_i^2, and the total proportion of people in the two systems by V^1 and V^2, then the frequencies of S have to satisfy equations of the type

$$
\begin{aligned}
p_i &= V^1 p_i^1 + V^2 p_i^2 \\
p_{ij} &= V^1 p_i^1 p_j^1 + V^2 p_i^2 p_j^2 \\
&\;\vdots \qquad\qquad \vdots \\
p_{ijk}\cdots & V^1 p_i^1 p_j^1 p_k^1 \cdots + V^2 p_i^2 p_j^2 p_k^2 \cdots .
\end{aligned}
\tag{18.1}
$$

We shall summarize this equation by the symbolic form

$$S = H_1 + H_2 , \tag{18.2}$$

and say that S is a *latent dichotomous* system LD. With m items there are $2^m - 1$ equations with $2m + 1$ unknowns, and they therefore set restrictions on the frequencies of S. Elsewhere we have proven

THEOREM 9. *For a dichotomous system S to be reducible to two H systems the symmetric parameters of S have to satisfy the following condition:*

$$| 123 \cdots m | = k_m \cdot S_1 \cdot S_2 \cdot S_3 \cdot \cdots ,$$

where $k_m k_{m-2} = (k_{m-1})^2 + (-1)^m$ *and* $k_2 = k_3 = 1$.

It may be noted that this is a kind of generalization of a Spearman system. The zero-order cross products are $| ij | = S_i S_j$, and their matrix therefore is of rank 1. But the higher-order frequencies have no parallel in correlation analysis. From Theorem 9 one can deduce the following property of an LD system: it has m free marginals, m free cross products $| ij |$, and one free third-order parameter—all together $2m + 1$ degrees of freedom. All other frequencies, including all symmetric parameters of order 4 and higher, can be computed from the basic $2m + 1$ degrees of freedom. A G system has only m degrees of freedom. All higher-order frequencies can be computed from the m marginals; the same is true for an H system.

It is important to see the difference between an H system and an LD system. In the former the *joint frequencies* are products of a set of basic terms (p_i); in the latter the *symmetric parameters* are the products of basic terms (S_i). The frequencies in an LD do not have this property. It can easily be seen that here

$$p_{ij} = p_i p_j + S_i S_j\,, \qquad p_{ijk} = p_i p_j p_k + \sum_{ijk} p_i S_j S_k + k_3 S_i S_j S_k\,, \cdots .$$

Incidentally, the roots of Equation (13.1) are p_k^1 and p_k^2 as defined by (18.1).

There are many other systems that deserve investigation. One may assume, for example, that all the symmetric parameters above a certain level vanish, which means that beginning at this level the system becomes homogeneous. Or one might follow latent-structure analysis into more complicated models; it can be shown that generally the symmetric parameters are the covariances of the trace lines.

A somewhat different application is the relation between dichotomous systems and the typologies developed in empirical social research. Many of these types are combinations of cells in a multidimensional dichotomous cube. The operation by which a typology is carved out from a given S has been called *reduction*. Inversely, if a typology is presented by an author, one can try to reconstruct the dichotomous system from which it might have derived; this inverse process is called *substruction*. No new mathematical problems develop with these operations. But they give a vivid picture of the general importance of dichotomous systems in empirical research. Therefore a number of examples are discussed in Appendix B.

APPENDIX A

The Use of Theorem 1 in the Interpretations of Survey Findings

In a series of earlier papers the author showed how Theorem 1 can be used to clarify some logical problems arising from "cross tabulations" of survey findings. The question "When is a correlation a true causal relation?" can at least be formulated more precisely by using this theorem. Readers interested in the substantive application of dichotomous algebra might be helped by a recent summary [2]. The symbolism used there was somewhat different from the one used in this chapter. The stratifier is (t) and the two interrelated dichotomies are (x) and (y).

The stratifier was called the *test variable*. The excerpt pertinent here started with the two correlative operations of *mixture* and *elaboration*. It then continued as follows.

A numerical example of *mixture* is given in Schema 1 as follows:

	t present x	$\bar{x}$				t absent x	$\bar{x}$				total group x	$\bar{x}$	
y	9	3	12	+	y	1	3	4	=	y	10	6	16
$\bar{y}$	3	1	4		$\bar{y}$	3	9	12		$\bar{y}$	6	10	16 .
	12	4				4	12				16	16	

SCHEMA 1

In the two tables on the left-hand side the variables x and y are unrelated. But if we mix the two groups originally separated according to t, we do find that people who are y are also more likely to be x than those who are not y.

Elaboration is mixture in reverse order. It consists of decomposing the group on the right-hand side into two subgroups and studying the relation of x and y separately for people who are and are not t. Elaboration is clearly not a unique operation. We could obtain the right-hand side, for example, by mixing the two subgroups as shown in Schema 2.

$$\begin{array}{c} t \text{ present} \\ \begin{array}{c|c|c|c} & x & \bar{x} & \\ \hline y & 5 & 3 & 8 \\ \hline \bar{y} & 3 & 5 & 8 \\ \hline & 8 & 8 & \end{array} \end{array} + \begin{array}{c} t \text{ absent} \\ \begin{array}{c|c|c|c} & x & \bar{x} & \\ \hline y & 5 & 3 & 8 \\ \hline \bar{y} & 3 & 5 & 8 \\ \hline & 8 & 8 & \end{array} \end{array} = \begin{array}{c} \text{total group} \\ \begin{array}{c|c|c|c} & x & \bar{x} & \\ \hline y & 10 & 6 & 16 \\ \hline \bar{y} & 6 & 10 & 16 \\ \hline & 16 & 16 & \end{array} \end{array} .$$

SCHEMA 2

There is one important difference between Schema 1 and Schema 2. Both attributes x and y were formerly related to t. Neither $[xt]$ nor $[yt]$ were zero. In Schema 2 we find that the proportion of x and y is the same for people who are and are not t:

$$[xt] = 0 \,, \quad \text{and} \quad [yt] = 0 \,.$$

We shall call the relations on the left-hand side of the schemas stratified relations (depending on t), and symbolize them by $[xy; t]$ and $[xy; \bar{t}\,]$, respectively. Elaboration then consists of studying how $[xy]$ depends upon $[xy; t]$ and $[xy; \bar{t}\,]$ under varying conditions of $[xt]$ and $[yt]$. An algebraic development of the problems leads to the following general formula:

FORMULA 1:

$$[xy] = \frac{[xy; t]}{P_t} + \frac{[xy; \bar{t}\,]}{P_{\bar{t}}} + \frac{[xt] \cdot [ty]}{P_t \cdot P_{\bar{t}}} \,.$$

The original relationship can be described as the sum of the two stratified relations and an additional factor, which is the product of what are called the marginal relations between the test factor and each of the two original variables.

This elaboration leads to two major forms. Either the two stratified relations may vanish; then Formula 1 reduces to

FORMULA 2a:

$$[xy] = \frac{[xt] \cdot [ty]}{P_t \cdot P_{\bar{t}}} \,,$$

or the test factor t might be unrelated to x (this means that $[xt] = 0$), and we then have

FORMULA 2b:

$$[xy] = \frac{[xy; t]}{P_t} + \frac{[xy; \bar{t}\,]}{P\bar{t}} \,,$$

a form that will turn out to be of interest only if one of these two stratified relations is markedly stronger than the other. We shall call this the S-form (emphasis on the stratified cross products), while Formula 2a will be called the M-form (emphasis on the "marginals").

To this formal distinction we now add a substantive one: the time order of the three variables. Assuming that x is prior to y, then either t can be located *between* x and y in time, or it can *precede* both. In the former case we talk of an intervening test variable, in the latter case of an antecedent one. We thus have four major possibilities:

	Statistical Form	
Position of t	S	M
Antecedent	SA	MA
Intervening	SI	MI

We are now ready to present the decisive point. It is claimed that there are essentially four operations that can be performed with two original and one test variable. It makes no difference whether this is done with actual data or whether they take the form of theoretical analyses. If a relation between two variables is analyzed in the light of a third, only these four operations or combinations thereof will occur, irrespective of whether they are called interpretation, understanding, theory, or anything else.

We now turn to some concrete examples that will clarify what these four types of elaboration stand for. In cases of the type SA, we usually call the test variable t a "condition." General examples easily come to mind, although in practice they are fairly rare and are a great joy to the research man when they are found. For example, the propaganda effect of a film is greater among less educated than among highly educated people. Unemployment had worse effects on authoritarian families than on other types.

Three general remarks can be made about this type of finding or reasoning: (i) It corresponds to the usual stimulus-disposition-response sequence, with x being the stimulus and the antecedent t being the disposition. (ii) The whole type might best be called *specification*. One of the two stratified associations will necessarily be larger than the original relationship. We specify, so to speak, the circumstances under which the original relationship holds true more strongly. (iii) Usually we will go on from there and ask why the relationship is stronger on one side of the test dichotomy. This might then lead into one of the other types of analysis. Durkheim uses type SA in discussing why married people commit suicide less than unmarried people. He introduces as a test variable "a nervous tendency to suicide, which the family, by its influence, neutralizes or keeps from developing." This is type SA exactly. We do not take it to be a convincing explanation because the introduction of the hypothetical test variable (tendency to suicide) sounds rather tautological; rather we want to know why the family keeps this tendency from developing, which leads to type MI, as we shall see later.

The type SI is also easily exemplified. We study the relationship between job success (y) and progressive-school background (x). We find that if the progressively educated people come into an authoritarian job situation (t), they do less well in their work than the others; on the other hand, if they come into a democratic atmosphere, their job success is greater.

The relation between type of education and job success is elaborated by an intervening test factor, i.e., the work atmosphere. We call such a test factor a "*contingency*." In many prediction studies, the predicted value depends upon subsequent circumstances that are not related to the predictor—for example the relation between occupational status and participation in the life of a housing community. White-collar people participate more if they are dissatisfied, whereas manual workers participate more if they are satisfied with their jobs.

Type MA is used mainly when we talk of rectifying what is usually called a *spurious relationship*. It has been found that the more fire engines that come to a fire (x), the larger is the damage (y). Because fire engines are used to reduce damage, the relationship is startling and requires elaboration. As a test factor (t) the size of the fire is introduced. The partials then become zero and the original result appears as the product of two marginal relationships; the larger the fire, the more engines, and also the more damage.

When we encounter a relationship that is psychologically puzzling, we usually stop at that point; but this same mode of elaboration can also be used under different psychological circumstances. More people commit suicide during the summer than during the winter. Durkheim suggests, as a t factor for elaboration, that increased social activities are going on during the summer. Our general knowledge tells us that x (the season) is indeed related to t in this way.

Our interest immediately shifts to the $[ty]$ relationship, namely, the presumed fact that greater intensity of social life leads to more suicides. Actually, of course, whether this explanation (which comes from Durkheim) is correct would depend upon a disappearance of the stratified cross products. Durkheim would have to show that if intensity of social life is kept constant, the season does not make any difference in suicides. Because he has no data on this point, he looks for other situations in which he can presume the intensity of social life to vary. He finds that there are more suicides during the day compared with the number during the night, which he again explains with the help of the same test factor. This leads into the whole question of probability of inference, which we do not follow up here.

We now turn to type MI, for which we shall use the term "*interpretation*." The difference between "explanation" and "interpretation" in this context is related to the time sequence between x and t. In an interpretation, t is an intervening variable situated between x and y in the time sequence.

Examples of type MI are numerous. Living in a rural community rather than in a city (x) is related to a lower suicide rate (y). We introduce the greater intimacy of rural life (t) as an intervening variable. If we had a good test of cohesion, we should undoubtedly find that a community's being rural rather than urban (x) is positively correlated with its degree of cohesion (t), and that greater cohesion (t) is correlated with lower suicide rates (y). But obviously some rural communities will have less cohesion that some urban communities. If cohesion is kept constant as a statistical device, then the partial relationship between the rural-urban variable and the suicide rate would have to disappear.

It might be useful to illustrate the difference between types MA and MI in one more example. During the war it was found that married women working in factories had a higher rate of absence from work than single women. Here are a number of possible elaborations:

a) *Test factor:* more responsibilities at home. This is an intervening variable. If it is introduced and the two partial relationships—between marital status and absenteeism—disappear, we have an elaboration of type MI. We interpret the relation by showing what intervening variable connects the original two variables.

b) *Test factor:* physical infirmity as crudely measured by age. Age is an antecedent variable. The *older* women are more likely to be married, and to have less physical strength, both as a result of their age. If it turns out, when age is kept constant, that the relation between marital status and absenteeism disappears, we would have an explanation, and probably call it a spurious effect; i.e., type MA.

The second case suggests again an important point. After having explained the original relationship, our attention might shift to $[ty]$, which is the fact that older people show a higher absentee rate. This, in turn, might lead to new elaborations: Is it true that older women have less physical resistance, whether they are married or single? Or, could it be simply that older women were born in a time when work was not as important for women as it is today, and therefore they have a lower work morale? In other words, after one elaboration is completed, we will, as good scientists, immediately turn to a new one; but the basic analytical processes will always be the same.

One final point can be cleared up, at least to a certain degree, by this analysis. We can suggest a clear-cut definition of the *causal* relation between two attributes. If we have a relationship between x and y, and if for any *antecedent* test factor the partial relationships between x and y do *not* disappear, then the original relationship should be called a causal one. It makes no difference here whether the necessary operations are actually carried out or made plausible by general reasoning. In a controlled experiment we have two matched groups: the experimental exposure corresponds to the variable x, and the observed effect corresponds to the variable y. By matching the two groups, we make sure that for any antecedent t we shall have $[xt] = 0$. If then $[xy] \neq 0$, in the light of the preceding analysis we can always be sure that there is a causal relation between exposure x and effect y.

This has special bearing on the following kind of discussion. It is well known that in densely populated areas the crime rate is higher than in sparsely populated areas. Although some authors state that this could not be considered a true causal relationship, such a remark is often used in two very different ways. Assume an intervening variable, for instance the increased irritation that results from crowded conditions. Such an interpretation does not detract from the causal character of the original relationship. On the other hand, the argument might go this way: crowded areas have cheaper rents, and therefore attract poorer, partly demoralized people. Here the character of the inhabitants is antecedent to the characteristics of the area. In this case the original relationship is indeed explained as a spurious one, and should not be called causal.

Explanation consists of the formal aspect of elaboration and some substantive ordering of variables. We have here focused on ordering by time sequence. But not all variables can be ordered this way. We can distinguish orders of complexity such as variables characterizing persons, collectives, and sets of collectives. Other ordering principles could be introduced, e.g., degree of generality, exemplified by the instance of a specific opinion, a broader attitude, and a basic value system. It is necessary to combine the formalism of elaboration with a classification of variables according to different ordering principles. This would cover a great part of what needs to be known about the logic of explanation and inference in contemporary survey analysis.

APPENDIX B

Typologies and Property Spaces in Social Research[9]

1. Introduction

A survey characterizes people by a number of variates, which might be continuous (age), qualitatively ordered (upper, middle, and lower class), mere listings (state of birth), and so on. All the variates together can be considered a Cartesian product, which puts each person into a *property space*.

When we chart the property space formed by two qualitative characteristics, the result is not, of course, a continuous plane but an array of cells, each representing one combination of values on two properties. For example, a study of the 1952 election described people's "political position" in October 1952 in terms of the two dimensions of "usual party affiliation" and "degree of political interest." When Americans are questioned about their usual

[9] The notion of property space for the explanation of typologies was originally suggested in a German monograph by Hempel and Oppenheim: "Der Typusbegriff im Lichte der modernen Logik." There also the notion of *reduction* was developed. The reverse operation of *substruction* was introduced by the present author in a paper [3], which contains the only available English summary of the important Hempel-Oppenheim monograph. This Appendix explains the two notions of reduction and substruction with the help of examples taken from a larger collection provided by Allen Barton.

party affiliations, almost everyone answers one of three categories: Republican, Democratic, and independent. These are natural divisions. Degree of interest on the other hand can be divided into any number of ranked categories we wish, depending on the alternatives we offer the respondent. In the present case they could rate themselves as having high, medium, or low interest. These two trichotomous dimensions then define a ninefold property space as shown in Table B1.

TABLE B1

A QUALITATIVE PROPERTY SPACE OF POLITICAL POSITION

		Usual Party Affiliation		
		Republican	Democratic	Independent
Degree of Political Interest	High			
	Medium			
	Low			

In dealing with qualitative property spaces that have limited numbers of categories on each dimension, we can chart the property space on paper even though it is three-dimensional or even higher-dimensional. Let us take the two dimensions of occupation, dichotomized as manual/non-manual, and political preference, dichotomized as Democratic/Republican. These give us a fourfold table. If we add the dimension of father's occupation, again dichotomized as manual/non-manual, we now have a "two-story" fourfold table: (1) occupation and party of sons of manual workers and (2) occupation and party of sons of non-manually employed people. This can be physically represented by a cube having eight cells, with the original fourfold table repeated on both the "first floor" and the "second floor" (see Table B2).

TABLE B2

A FOUR-DIMENSIONAL ATTRIBUTE SPACE LAID OUT IN TWO DIMENSIONS

		Father Manual Occupation			Father Non-Manual Occupation	
		Son's Occupation			Son's Occupation	
		Manual	Non-Manual		Manual	Non-Manual
Father Democrat	Son Democrat			Son Democrat		
	Republican			Republican		
		Son's Occupation			Son's Occupation	
		Manual	Non-Manual		Manual	Non-Manual
Father Republican	Son Democrat			Son Democrat		
	Republician			Republican		

To suggest how far the use of very high-dimension property spaces has actually developed in social research, we need only note that the results of each interview in a survey are normally punched on an IBM card containing 80 columns, each with twelve rows. Such a card provides for an 80-dimensional property space, with each property having twelve classes. In practice one never uses all eighty dimensions simultaneously to characterize a respondent; however, they are all available to use in whatever smaller combinations we select.

An interesting application of a high-dimensioned property space is found in W. J. Goode's *Religion Among the Primitives* [4]. He first picks out five elements, which he considers basic to the description of primitive religious systems: (1) personnel; (2) societal matrix; (3) sacred entities; (4) ritual; and (5) belief. These are not all single dimensions; each is what might be termed an "attribute area." "Personnel" is thus described in two dimensions: (*a*) extent of formal religious training (both leaders and followers trained, leaders only, or neither); and (*b*) extent of identification of the sacred with the secular leadership of the community. The "societal matrix" is described initially by five dimensions: rationality/traditionalism, self-interest/other-interest, universalism/particularism, specificity of relationships/diffuseness, and impersonality/emotional involvement in daily interaction. These are reduced to form two polar types, labeled "basic-rural" and "basic-urban", and societies located along a range between the two poles. The "sacred entities" are described as ranging from a highly abstract and distant entity, through broad, natural forces like the sun and the rain, various anthropomorphic entities such as ancestral spirits, to the concrete and prosaic entities of animals, plants, and other natural objects. "Ritual" is described by the degree of elaboration and symbolism. "Belief" turns out to be a highly complex element, involving, among others, beliefs about the soul, beliefs relating to the ritual, beliefs about punishment for violation of norms, and beliefs about the origin of gods, men, and the world.

In his final classification Goode described five particular societies by their position on these dimensions, omitting "belief", which was apparently too complex to permit a simple set of categories. The use of the property space makes clear that these five prolonged and intensive studies of different cultures only fill a very small portion of the whole range of possible types.

2. The Reduction of a Property Space

One of the uses to which the concept of property space can be applied is to clarify the operation of reduction. By reduction we mean the combining of classes in order to obtain a smaller number of categories. This is often done for purely practical purposes to keep the number of groups to be compared small enough so that each will have enough cases in a limited sample. It may also be done for theoretical reasons. We shall discuss the types of reduction that occur rather frequently in social research, although their methodological characteristics often are not recognized.

One obvious type of reduction occurs if we simplify continuous variables to ranked classes, or a set of classes to a dichotomy. Let us return to the two-dimensional property space of "political position" represented in Table 1. It was considered that for some purposes the major distinction of the dimension of party affiliation was between those who identified with either party on the one hand and the independent voters on the other. It was also believed that the most important distinction of the interest dimension was between the highly interested voters and those with medium or low interest. With each dimension reduced to a dichotomy, the property space as a whole was reduced to the four cells of a fourfold table (see Table B3).

TABLE B3

REDUCTION OF A PROPERTY SPACE BY SIMPLIFYING THE DIMENSIONS

		Usual Party Affiliation		
		Republican	Democratic	Independent
Degree of Political Interest	High	Partisans		Independents
	Medium	Habituals		Apathetics
	Low			

Those who have some party identification and high interest were labeled "partisans"; those who were independent and had high interest were labeled "independents." Those who identified with a party but had only medium or low interest were called "habitual party voters," and those who identified with no party and had only medium or low interest were called "apathetics". What has been gained by this is the elimination of distinctions that were considered less relevant for certain purposes, thus making it easier—especially with a limited number of cases in the sample—to examine the separate and joint effects of the two dichotomies of "party identification/non-identification" and "high interest/less than high interest." It was expected that each of the four groups might show distinctive behavior on certain attributes.

A study of mass-communication habits might rate reading, radio listening, and movie attendance each as "high," "medium," and "low" according to certain cultural standards. This creates a three-dimensional property space of twenty-seven cells.

We can observe three "pure types" that present no difficulty: those who are high in all three communications habits, those who are medium in all, and those who are low in all. We now have the problem of classifying the remaining combinations. We might add to the "pure high-brows" those three groups that were high on two and medium on only one communications channel. Likewise we might add to the middle-brows all those who make two middle-brow choices and one either high or low choice. To the low-brows we could add those who were low on two and middle on one.

But what should be done with those groups with two preferences at one extreme and one at the other? These may constitute special types that should be kept separate. Those with two highs and one low might be labeled, somewhat unkindly, "slummers." They might include people who find a "primitive" beauty in certain low-brow material, like New Orleans jazz or sporting prints, as well as those who abandon themselves to soap opera or Mickey Spillane. If we feel that in spite of these lapses they are still essentially high-brows, we would put them along with all the others making two or more high-brow choices. The people with two low preferences and one high may be a still more significant group. They might be a distinctive type, perhaps like the old ideal of the self-educated workingman who skipped standardized, middle-class popular culture to enjoy the classics. We might call them, somewhat awkwardly, "looking-up brows." There remain, finally, six groups with one high, one middle, and one low preference. From the given data we cannot tell whether they are broad-minded or indiscriminate, or what the reason might be for such a peculiar set of choices. We might call these the "broad-brows." The results of this reduction are shown in Table B4.

TABLE B4

PRAGMATIC REDUCTION OF A THREE-DIMENSIONAL PROPERTY SPACE OF LEVELS OF TASTE

Movie Preference	High in Reading			Medium in Reading			Low in Reading		
	Radio Listening			Radio Listening			Radio Listening		
	H	M	L	H	M	L	H	M	L
High	*High*	High	Slum.	High	Mid.	Broad	Slum.	Broad	L.U.
Middle	High	Mid.	Broad	Mid.	*Mid.*	Mid.	Broad	Mid.	Low
Low	Slum.	Broad	L.U.	Broad	Mid.	Low	L.U.	Low	*Low*

This pragmatic reduction of the twenty-seven possible patterns gives us a set of six types. It appears that we are classifying on the one hand by the predominate level preferred, and on the other according to the amount of "spread" of a person's choices. The three pure types run diagonally through a cube which has been cut into thirds on each side to give twenty-seven smaller cubes, from the "high-high-high" corner to the "low-low-low" corner. Adjacent to them are the groups that deviate only one step from a pure type and that have also been classified with the highs, the middles, and the lows. The other three types deviate still further from the main axis of the cube as marked by the three pure types. The "slummers" and the "looking-uppers" are the purest deviants.

3. Substruction of a Property Space for a Typology

In discussing reduction, we have employed the concept of property space to clarify the operations by which initially complex classifications are simplified and in some cases formed into rank-ordered categories. We shall now apply the property-space concept to another problem: the clarification of typologies.

It is common practice for both intuitive analysts and empirical researchers to think in terms of a few outstanding "types" of people, situations, or institutions. A study of community leadership is based on the distinction between the "cosmopolitan" versus the "locally oriented" type of leader. Analysts of social norms traditionally classify them as "folkways," "mores," and "law." Psychologists speak of extroverted and introverted personalities; anthropologists, of folk and urban communities.

These types when examined in detail turn out to be defined as clusters of many different attributes. The cosmopolitan leader is distinguished from the local leader by his geographical mobility, his education, his channels of becoming a leader, his interests, his communications behavior. Folkways, mores, and law are distinguished in terms of how they originated, how they are enforced, how deeply they are felt, and so on for each set of types. It appears that the types must represent a reduction or selection of categories from a fairly complex property space. The understanding of such types will often be assisted if we reconstruct the entire property space and see how they were derived from it. The procedure of finding, for a given set of types, the property space in which they are located and the reduction that has implicitly been used in their formation has been termed "*substruction.*"

It is not claimed that this formal analysis will necessarily help in the initial creation of sets of types that are fruitful in disclosing new relationships. Neither is it claimed that it describes the actual mental processes of those who creat typologies. It is rather intended to assist us in understanding and working with the typologies that are created by someone's fruitful insight. If a typology leads us toward understanding whole networks of related variables—as for instance the "cosmopolitan/local" typology, which helped to organize meaningfully a wide range of data—it should be worth while to break it down into its components, to study the part played by each. In this process we may also find combinations of properties that we overlooked in constructing the initial typology, and bring to light the assumptions that led us to bypass certain combinations or ignore certain distinctions.

For an example we may turn to Kingsley Davis's presentation of the traditional typology of social norms [5]. Among the types he distinguished are the following: *folkways*, *mores*, *law*, *customary law*, *enacted law*, *customs*.

Folkways are defined as norms that are considered obligatory in the proper situation, but not tremendously important or supported by very strong social sanctions. They are enforced by informal social controls rather than by formal control agencies, and originate through the gradual growth of tradition rather than by deliberate enactment.

Mores are norms that are believed to be extremely important for the welfare of the society, and are therefore very strongly sanctioned. Folkways and mores are similar, however, in originating in tradition rather than in deliberate enactment, and in being enforced by informal sanctions, depending on the spontaneous reactions of the group rather than on the reactions of officials acting in some official capacity.

Law arises when some formal machinery of enforcement is present. If the norms enforced in this way have originated in an unplanned manner through tradition, and there is no legislative agency to enact new rules or change old ones, we may speak of a system of *customary law*. On the other hand, what we regard as fully developed law is the product of thought and planning, of deliberate formulation, and subject to change through regular institutional procedures. This may be called *enacted law*.

Custom is a broad term embracing all the norms classified as folkways and mores. It connotes long-established usage—practices repeated by generation after generation, and enforced by spontaneous community pressures.

In his discussion, Davis suggests a great many attributes of the various types of norms. Some of these, however, seem to be more basic, in that others are expressly stated to be derivative from them. Others seem to be so closely related that there is little need to distinguish them—strength of sanctions, for example, seems to vary with the mechanism by which the norm originates. This represents in itself a form of functional reduction. The types listed here seem to have been defined basically in terms of the three dimensions: *how originated* (tradition versus organized enactment); *how enforced* (informal versus formal sanctions); and *strength of group feeling* (strong versus mild). The property space that is formed when we put these three dimensions together is shown in Table B5.

TABLE B5

A PROPERTY SPACE SUBSTRUCTED FOR A TYPOLOGY OF NORMS

How Originated	How Enforced			
	Informal Enforcement		Formal Enforcement	
	Group Feeling		Group Feeling	
	Strong	Mild	Strong	Mild
	Customs			
Tradition	MORES	FOLKWAYS	CUSTOMARY	LAWS
Enactment	XX	XX	ENACTED	

It will be noted that some of the types embrace more than one cell; i.e., they leave one or more dimensions unspecified. "Customs" is thus a generic term for informally enforced, traditional norms, regardless of the group feeling; if we want to distinguish the latter dimension, we talk of "mores" or "folkways." "Laws" cover four cells, while the notions of customary and enacted law do not distinguish the actual strength of the group feeling regarding the content of the law. This is of course an important distinction in the sociology of law and of crime.

It also appears that certain combinations have been left out, i.e., those involving formal enactment with only informal enforcement. Perhaps this omission is based on a certain evolutionary assumption, whereby a society first develops formal enforcement machinery for its traditional norms and only then develops institutions for enacting new norms or changing old ones. It might be, however, that certain types of norms are enacted in a modern society without any provision for formal enforcement; this is possibly true of some "laws" against ethnic and religious discrimination in employment and public service, which affirm the principle but provide no enforcement. We might want to formulate a new term for such legislation, since it is not exactly "law" in the sociological sense.

Another example of the substruction of a property space for a typology can be based on a study of the structure of authority in the family, which was conducted by the Institute of Social Research in Germany in the early 1930's. Erich Fromm, the director of the study, suggested as a theoretical basis for classifying the questionnaire data the following four types of authority relationships: *complete authority*, *simple authority*, *lack of authority*, *rebellion*.

By using the procedure of substruction and reduction, it is possible to attain a thorough research procedure and at the same time exhaust the possible significance of Fromm's types. The authority relationship in a family is determined by the way in which the parents exercise their authority, and by the way in which the children accept it. Through questionnaires, the parental exercise of authority was rated as either strong, moderate, or weak; likewise the children's acceptance of authority was rated as high, medium, or low. This makes logically possible nine combinations (Table B6).

TABLE B6

A PROPERTY SPACE SUBSTRUCTED FOR A TYPOLOGY OF FAMILY RELATIONSHIPS

	Children's Acceptance		
Parents Exercise	High	Medium	Low
Strong	1	2	3
Moderate	4	5	6
Weak	7	8	9

The above scheme can be related to Fromm's four types, which were, of course, originally conceived by a quite different procedure (Table B7).

TABLE B7

RELATION OF THE SUBSTRUCTED PROPERTY SPACE TO THE ORIGINAL TYPOLOGY

Fromm's type	Attribute Combination	Exercise	Acceptance
I Complete Authority	1 and 2	Strong	High or Medium
II Simple Authority	4 and 5	Moderate	High or Medium
III Lack of Authority	8	Weak	Medium
IV Rebellion	3 and 6	Strong or Moderate	Low

Combinations 7 and 9 are not covered. Apparently it was assumed that neither very high nor very low acceptance was possible for an authority which was scarcely exercised at all. The substruction, however, may be used as a tool for discovery. It points out the logical possibility that there might be children who want an authority which is not actually exercised over them—combination 7. These discovered combinations suggest further research.

The reader may disagree with the above substruction, and may think that other combinations should be matched with Fromm's types; or he may feel that there are certain contradictions between the combinations and the types. Then he may try to improve the types on the basis of the general scheme suggested above. He will see for himself that the procedure of substruction, which has been constructed on the basis of theoretical considerations or intuitions, may very probably lead to improvements in topologies. The proof of the success of the procedure lies, of course, in concrete applications which lie beyond the scope of the present exemplification.

The problem comes up whether, to every given system of types, only one attribute space and the corresponding reduction can be substructed. The answer is probably "no." The typological classifications used in current social research are often somewhat vague, and therefore more than one logical substruction can usually be provided for them. The different attribute spaces originating this way can be transformed one into another, however. The procedure of tranformation is very important because it is the logical background of what is generally understood to be an interpretation of a statistical result. It could be shown that such an interpretation is often nothing else than transforming a system of types from one attribute space into another with different coordinates, and therewith changing simultaneously one reduction into another.

APPENDIX C

Symmetric Parameters and Tracelines in Latent-Structure Analysis

The general problem of latent-structure analysis can be put in the following way. Given a dichotomous system S, how can it be decomposed into a sum of fully homogenous systems $\sum_x H^x$. Once a solution is found, we know the proportion of people v^x belonging to each "latent class"; and for any given item (i) we obtain a sequence of latent probabilities p_i^x indicating what proportion in class x give a positive response [6]. It has become conventional to call this sequence the *traceline* of item i; the probabilities trace, so to say, the latent continuum through this indicator.

By definition the manifest proportion p_i of all the positive responses is the weighted sum of the latent probabilities

$$\sum_x v^x p_i^x = p_i \,.$$

If we have two items, it is possible to compute the covariance between their latent probabilities, which is

$$\text{Cov}\,(ij) = \sum_x v^x (p_i^x - p_i)(p_j^x - p_j)\,.$$

Extending this notion, we can define the higher-order covariances as follows:

$$\text{Cov}\,(ijk\cdots) = \sum_x v^x (p_i^x - p_i)(p_j^x - p_j)(p_k^x - p_k)\cdots\,.$$

Now these *covariances can be expressed directly by manifest data, without actual knowledge of the latent probabilities.*

To show this we have to draw upon a general theorem about covariances. Assume a set of functions $f_i(x)$ and a density distribution of $\phi(x)$ for a given population. The average value[10] of each function is $P_i = \int f_i(x)\phi(x)\,dx$.

The covariances between the $f_i(x)$ on a given level, say the third, are defined by

$$\text{Cov}\,(123) = \int [f_1(x) - p_1][f_2(x) - p_2][f_3(x) - p_3]\,\phi(x)\,dx\,.$$

Now any such covariance can be expressed by the covariances on the lower levels and the averages for the individual functions.

In order not to overburden this Appendix with symbolism, we restrict our demonstration to four functions. It is easy to show that

$$\begin{aligned}\text{Cov}\,(1234) &= \int [f_1(x) - p_1][f_2(x) - p_2][f_3(x) - p_3][f_4(x) - p_4]\,\phi(x)\,dx \\ &= \int f_1(x)f_2(x)f_3(x)f_4(x)\,\phi(x)\,dx - p_1p_2p_3p_4 \\ &\qquad - \sum_{ijk} p_e\,\text{Cov}\,(ijk) - \sum_{ij} p_kp_e\,\text{Cov}\,(ij)\,,\end{aligned}$$

where the summations are extended over all possible combinations of triplets and pairs of indices, respectively.

This formula can be converted into one holding for symmetric parameters. Let us first note that in view of the general accounting equations

$$\int f_1(x)f_2(x)f_3(x)f_4(x)\,\phi(x)\,dx = p_{1234}\,.$$

Let us then compute the lowest covariance

$$\begin{aligned}\text{Cov}\,(ij) &= \int [f_i(x) - p_i][f_j(x) - p_j]\,\phi(x)\,dx \\ &= \int f_i(x)f_j(x)\,\phi(x)\,dx - p_i \int f_j(x)\,\phi(x)\,dx - p_j \int f_i(x)\,\phi(x)\,dx + p_ip_j \\ &= p_{ij} - p_ip_j = |\,ij\,|\,.\end{aligned}$$

In other words the second-order covariances are identical with the second-order symmetric parameters. Proceeding now step by step we can show that Cov $(ijk = |\,ikk\,|$ and this converts the equation defining the fourth-order covariance into

$$\text{Cov}\,(1234) = p_{1234} - p_1p_2p_3p_4 - \sum_{ijk} p_l\,|\,ijk\,| - \sum_{ij} p_kp_l\,|\,ij\,|\,.$$

Now the right-hand side of this equation is identical with the definition of

[10] The integration extends over the interval where people may be located and will not be specified.

$|ijkl|$, the fourth-order symmetric parameter (see Section 14). Therefore

$$\text{Cov}\,(1234) = |1234|\,.$$

The generality of the proof is easily seen: *the symmetric parameters are the covariances of the traceline.*

References

[1] Yule, G. U., and Kendall, M. G. *An Introduction to the Theory of Statistics.* New York: Hafner. 14th ed. rev. 1950.

[2] Lazarsfeld, P. F. Evidence and inference in social research. *Daedalus*, 1958, **87**, No. 4, pp. 99–130.

[3] Lazarsfeld, P. F. Some remarks on the typological procedure in social research. *Z. für Sozialforschung*, 1937.

[4] Goode, W. J. *Religion Among the Primitives.* Glencoe, Ill.: Free Press, 1951.

[5] Davis, K. *Human Society.* New York: Macmillan, 1950.

[6] Lazarsfeld, P. F. "Latent-Structure Analysis" in *Psychology, the State of a Science.* Vol. 3. New York: Wiley, 1960.

9

A Representation of the Joint Distribution of Responses to *n* Dichotomous Items

R. R. BAHADUR, Indian Statistical Institute

1. Introduction

Consider a specified set of n dichotomous items, and let the response pattern in any given instance be represented by $(x_1, \cdots, x_n)$, where $x_i = 1$ if the response to the ith item is "positive," and $x_i = 0$ if otherwise $(i = 1, \cdots, n)$. Let $p(x_1, \cdots, x_n)$ be the joint probability distribution of responses in a given population.

Let $p_{[1]}$ denote the joint distribution of the x_i when they are independent, with the same marginal probabilities as under the given distribution. Suppose we represent p in the form $p = p_{[1]} \cdot f$. An explicit expression for the correction factor f, in terms of the n marginal probabilities and $2^n - n - 1$ correlation parameters, is obtained in Section 2. This expression for f suggests certain formal models of dependence, which are defined and discussed in Section 3. It is pointed out in Section 4 that, under certain conditions, the probability distribution of the "total score," $t = x_1 + \cdots + x_n$, throws some light on which model of dependence is appropriate in a given case. The generalization of this approach to the case when the items are not necessarily dichotomous is described in Section 5.

It should be emphasized that this paper is purely descriptive in that it concerns the given probability distribution of the manifest variables in a specified population. These descriptions may be useful in situations in which the items are dependent (but not highly so) and it is necessary, or advantageous, to take the dependence into account. In particular, as is shown in Chapter 10, if the set of items is defined over two (or more) populations, then, under suitable conditions, the present theory yields simple approximations for the optimum statistic for classifying an individual on the basis of his observed response pattern.

After this paper was first drafted (in 1956), I learned that the representation given in Section 2 was obtained earlier (in 1949) by Paul F. Lazarsfeld of Columbia University, by a different method and in a slightly different form [1]. A special case of the representation has been given by McFadden [2]. I hope that the following derivation of Lazarsfeld's representation will be of some interest. Lazarsfeld also discusses the representation and its applications in Chapter 9.

2. A Representation of the Distribution

Let X denote the set of all points $x = (x_1, x_2, \cdots, x_n)$ with each $x_i = 0$ or 1. Let $p(x)$ be a given probability distribution on X; i.e., a function on X such that $p(x) \geqq 0$ for each x and $\sum_{x \in X} p(x) = 1$. Since there are 2^n points in X, it is clear that any parametric description of arbitrary probability distributions requires, in general, $(2^n - 1)$ independent parameters. The particular parametric description developed in this chapter is the following.

For each $i = 1, \cdots, n$, let $\alpha_i = p\{x_i = 1\}$, or equivalently

$$\alpha_i = E_p(x_i) \qquad 0 < \alpha_i < 1,\ i = 1, \cdots, n, \tag{2.1}$$

where E_p denotes expected value when p obtains. Next, setting

$$z_i = (x_i - \alpha_i)/\sqrt{\alpha_i(1 - \alpha_i)} \qquad i = 1, \cdots, n, \tag{2.2}$$

define

$$\begin{aligned} r_{ij} &= E_p(z_i z_j)\,, && i < j\,; \\ r_{ijk} &= E_p(z_i z_j z_k)\,, && i < j < k\,; \\ &\cdots\cdot \\ &\cdots\cdot \\ r_{12\cdots n} &= E_p(z_1 z_2 \cdots z_n)\,. \end{aligned} \tag{2.3}$$

In what follows, we shall refer to the ${}^nC_2$ parameters r_{ij} as second-order correlations, to the ${}^nC_3$ parameters r_{ijk} as third-order correlations, $\cdots$, to $r_{12\cdots n}$ as the nth-order correlation. The correlation parameters just defined are ${}^nC_2 + {}^nC_3 + \cdots + {}^nC_n = 2^n - n - 1$ in number. It will be shown presently that, together with the n α_i's, the correlation parameters determine the probability distribution p.

Let $p_{[1]}(x_1, \cdots, x_n)$ denote the joint probability distribution of the x_i's when (1) the x_i's are independently distributed, and (2) they have the same marginal distributions as under the given distribution p. In other words,

$$p_{[1]}(x_1, \cdots, x_n) \equiv \prod_{i=1}^{n} \alpha_i^{x_i}(1 - \alpha_i)^{1 - x_i}\,. \tag{2.4}$$

Note that since $0 < \alpha_i < 1$, $i = 1, 2, \cdots, n$, we have $p_{[1]}(x) > 0$ for each x.

Proposition 1. *For every $x = (x_1, \cdots, x_n)$ in X,*

$$p(x) = p_{[1]}(x) \cdot f(x)\,, \tag{2.5}$$

where

$$f(x) = 1 + \sum_{i<j} r_{ij} z_i z_j + \sum_{i<j<k} r_{ijk} z_i z_j z_k + \cdots + r_{12\cdots n} z_1 z_2 \cdots z_n\,. \tag{2.6}$$

To establish Proposition 1, consider the vector space, V say, of real-valued functions f on X. Regard V as an inner-product space, with inner product $(f, g) \equiv E_{p_{[1]}}(f \cdot g) = \sum_{x \in X} f(x) \cdot g(x) \cdot p_{[1]}(x)$, and norm $\|f\| = (f, f)^{\frac{1}{2}}$, with $p_{[1]}$ defined by (2.4). It then follows easily from (2.1) and (2.2) that the set

$$S = \{1; z_1, z_2, \cdots, z_n; z_1z_2, z_1z_3, \cdots, z_{n-1}z_n; z_1z_2z_3, \cdots,; \cdots; z_1z_2\cdots z_n\}$$

of functions on X is orthonormal, i.e., $\|f\| = 1$ for each f in S, and $(f, g) = 0$ for f and g in S with $f \neq g$. Since there are 2^n functions in S, since V is 2^n dimensional, and since $p_{[1]}(x) > 0$ for each x, we have the following proposition:

PROPOSITION 2. *The set*

$$S = \{1; z_1, \cdots, z_n; z_1z_2, \cdots, z_{n-1}z_n; \cdots; z_1z_2\cdots z_n\}$$

is a basis in the space of real-valued functions on X. This basis is orthonormal when $p_{[1]}$ obtains.

It follows, in particular, that each function f on X admits one and only one representation as a linear combination of functions in S, namely $f = \sum_{g \in S} (f, g) \cdot g$.

Now take $f = p/p_{[1]}$. We then have

$$(2.7) \qquad (f, g) = \sum_{x \in X} f \cdot g \cdot p_{[1]} = \sum_{x \in X} g \cdot p = E_p(g)$$

for all g. Since $E_p(1) = 1$ and $E_p(z_i) = 0$ for $i = 1, \cdots, n$ by (2.1) and (2.2), it follows from the preceding paragraph and (2.7) that (2.6) holds, with the coefficients r defined by (2.3). This establishes Proposition 1.

Note 1. As mentioned in Section 1, the representation (2.5) and (2.6) was obtained earlier by Lazarsfeld. The derivation suggested in [1] is by induction on n. The correlation parameters $|12|, \cdots; |123|, \cdots$; etc., used by Lazarsfeld are related to the r's of the present version as follows: $|ij| = r_{ij}\beta_i\beta_j$; $|ijk| = r_{ijk}\beta_i\beta_j\beta_k$; etc., where $\beta_i = \sqrt{\alpha_i(1 - \alpha_i)}$.

Note 2. Suppose that $p(x) > 0$ for each x. Then the argument used in the proof of Proposition 1 can be applied to $f = \log_e \{p/p_{[1]}\}$ instead of $p/p_{[1]}$, to yield a different representation of $p(x)$. This alternative representation of $p(x)$ and the associated models of slight or moderate interdependence seem at least as interesting as the one described above, but will not be discussed here. It may be noted, however, that if the interdependence is very slight, i.e., if $p/p_{[1]}$ is always close to 1, there is little to choose between the two representations.

Note 3. Propositions 1 and 2 can be generalized to the case where each x_i does not necessarily take only two values. This generalization is described in Section 5.

3. Distributions of the mth Order ($1 \leq m \leq n$)

Proposition 1 suggests the following classification of distributions: p is of first order if all $2^n - n - 1$ correlations are zero, i.e., if the x_i's are independently distributed; p is of second order if all correlations of order exceeding 2 are zero, and so on. This section is concerned mainly with some aspects of the problem of approximating a given distribution p with a distribution of lower order.

An obvious procedure for effecting the approximation in question is simply to omit correlations of order higher than the order desired in (2.5) and (2.6). Thus $p_{[1]}$ is a first-order approximation to p;

$$p_{[2]}(x) = p_{[1]}(x)\left(1 + \sum_{i<j} r_{ij} z_i z_j\right) \tag{3.1}$$

is a second-order approximation to p; and so on. There is, however, a serious difficulty here: the "approximation" may not be a probability distribution at all, that is, $p_{[m]}(x)$ may fail to be non-negative for some points x. (It follows easily from the definition of $p_{[m]}$ and Proposition 2 that $\sum_{x \in X} p_{[m]}(x) = 1$ always holds.) Assume for the moment that this difficulty does not arise. It then follows from Proposition 1 that $p_{[m]}(x)$ enjoys the following property: it is the only distribution of order not exceeding m under which any set $\{x_{j_1}, x_{j_2}, \cdots, x_{j_m}\}$ of m variables has the same joint distribution as under the given p.

The difficulty mentioned above arises, of course, from the fact that the "independent" correlation parameters in (2.5) and (2.6) are nevertheless subject to linear inequalities. In fact, for any set of numbers α_i with $0 < \alpha_i < 1$, we have the following proposition:

PROPOSITION 3. *In order that an arbitrary set* $\{r_{ij}; r_{ijk}; \cdots; r_{12\cdots n}\}$ *of* $2^n - n - 1$ *real numbers* r *serve as the correlation parameters of a probability distribution* p *satisfying* (2.1), *it is necessary and sufficient that* $f(x)$ *defined by* (2.2) *and* (2.6) *be non-negative for each* x; *this* p *is then given by* (2.4)–(2.6).

The proof of Proposition 3 is immediate from Propositions 1 and 2, and so is omitted. It follows from Proposition 3 that if all correlation parameters of the given p are sufficiently small in absolute value, $p_{[m]}$ *is* a probability distribution for each m.

By way of illustrating the preceding remarks, let us note here two easily verified facts concerning the second-order approximation to a given distribution. First, let R denote the $n \times n$ matrix of second-order correlations r_{ij}, with $r_{ii} = 1$. Let $\lambda_{\min}$ denote the smallest characteristic root of R, i.e., the smallest root of the determinantal equation $|R - \lambda I| = 0$. For each i, let $\beta_i = \max\{\alpha_i/(1-\alpha_i), (1-\alpha_i)/\alpha_i\}$. If

$$\lambda_{\min} \geqq 1 - \frac{2}{\left(\sum_{i=1}^{n} \beta_i\right)}, \tag{3.2}$$

then $p_{[2]}$ defined by (3.1) is a probability distribution. For, since

$$\sum_{i,j=1}^{n} r_{ij} z_i z_j = 2\sum_{i<j} r_{ij} z_i z_j + \sum_{i=1}^{n} z_i^2 ,$$

the condition that $p_{[2]} \geqq 0$ for each x is, by (3.1), equivalent to the condition that

$$\frac{\sum_{i,j=1}^{n} r_{ij} z_i z_j}{\sum_{i=1}^{n} z_i^2} \geqq 1 - \frac{2}{\sum_{i=1}^{n} z_i^2}$$

for all $z_1, z_2, \cdots, z_n$. Since $\lambda_{\min}$ is a lower bound for the first function of the z's, while $1 - 2/\sum_{i=1}^{n} \beta_i$ is, by (2.2), the least upper bound for the second, it follows, as desired, that (3.2) implies $p_{[2]} \geqq 0$ for each x.

Next, suppose that $\alpha_i = \alpha$ for each i, and that $r_{ij} = r$ for all $i \neq j$. In this case, if we let $t = \sum_{i=1}^{n} x_i$, $t = 0, 1, \cdots, n$, we have

$$\begin{aligned} p_{[2]}(x) &= \alpha^t(1-\alpha)^{n-t}\Big\{1 + \frac{r}{2\alpha(1-\alpha)}[t(t-1)(1-\alpha)^2 + (n-t)(n-t-1)\alpha^2 \\ &\qquad - 2t(n-t)\alpha(1-\alpha)]\Big\} \\ &= \alpha^t(1-\alpha)^{n-t}\Big\{1 + \frac{r}{2\alpha(1-\alpha)}[(t-(n-1)\alpha - \tfrac{1}{2})^2 - \tfrac{1}{4} - (n-1)\alpha(1-\alpha)]\Big\} \\ &= \alpha^t(1-\alpha)^{n-t}\Big[1 + \frac{r}{2\alpha(1-\alpha)}\gamma(t, n, \alpha)\Big]. \end{aligned}$$

Now

$$\max_t \gamma(t, n, \alpha) = n(n-1)\cdot\max\{\alpha^2, (1-\alpha)^2\},$$

$$\min_t \gamma(t, n, \alpha) = -[\tfrac{1}{4} + (n-1)\alpha(1-\alpha) - \gamma_0],$$

where

$$\gamma_0 = \min_t \{[t - (n-1)\alpha - \tfrac{1}{2}]^2\} \leqq \tfrac{1}{4}.$$

It follows that $p_{[2]}$ is a probability distribution if and only if

$$-\frac{2}{n(n-1)}\cdot\min\left(\frac{\alpha}{1-\alpha}, \frac{1-\alpha}{\alpha}\right) \leqq r \leqq \frac{2\alpha(1-\alpha)}{(n-1)\alpha(1-\alpha) + \frac{1}{4} - \gamma_0}. \tag{3.3}$$

We turn now to the problem of assessing the goodness of fit of a given approximation. The following approach is suggested by the argument used in the proof of Proposition 1. It should be stated at the outset, however, that this approach is necessarily descriptive, and should be modified or abandoned in case external criteria are available (cf., e.g., Chapter 11).

The approximations to $p(x)$ under discussion are obtained by omitting terms in the expansion (2.6) of the correction factor f in (2.5). Since this expansion is in terms of an orthonormal basis (relative to $p_{[1]}$), it is worth while to see whether the norm of the omitted part is an index of its importance. Let us define $\delta_{[n]}^2 = \|f - 1\|^2$; $\delta_{[n]}^2$ is the squared norm of the non-constant part of f. Then

$$\begin{aligned} \delta_{[n]}^2 &= \sum_{i<j} r_{ij}^2 + \sum_{i<j<k} r_{ijk}^2 + \cdots + r_{12\cdots n}^2 \\ &= \delta_2^2 + \delta_3^2 + \cdots + \delta_n^2, \end{aligned} \tag{3.4}$$

say, where δ_j^2 is the squared norm of the jth-order terms in f. The ratios $\delta_j^2/\delta_{[n]}^2$ provide indices of the relative importance of jth-order terms. Again, if for some m the ratio

$$||p_{[m]}/p_{[1]}||^2/||p/p_{[1]}||^2 = \left(1 + \sum_{j=2}^{m} \delta_j^2\right) \Big/ \left(1 + \sum_{j=2}^{n} \delta_j^2\right) \tag{3.5}$$

is close to 1, then $p_{[m]}$ is likely to be a close approximation to p. This descriptive method of assessing goodness of fit extends, of course, to approximations other than $p_{[m]}$, e.g., the approximation obtained by retaining all second-order terms in (2.6) and some but not all third-order terms.

Equation (3.4) is the population analog of a decomposition of a total χ^2 in a 2^n contingency table into $2^n - n - 1$ individual degrees of freedom. That is, we have

$$\begin{aligned} \delta_{[n]}^2 &= \sum_{x \in X} p_{[1]}(x)[f(x) - 1]^2 \\ &= \sum_{x \in X} \frac{[p_{[1]}(x) \cdot f(x) - p_{[1]}(x)]^2}{p_{[1]}(x)} \\ &= \sum_{x \in X} \frac{[p(x) - p_{[1]}(x)]^2}{p_{[1]}(x)} \\ &= \sum_{x \in X} \frac{[p(x)]^2}{p_{[1]}(x)} - 1 . \end{aligned} \tag{3.6}$$

More generally, for $2 \leqq m \leqq n$,

$$\begin{aligned} \delta_2^2 + \cdots + \delta_m^2 &= \sum_{x \in X} \frac{[p_{[m]}(x) - p_{[1]}(x)]^2}{p_{[1]}} \\ &= \sum_{x \in X} \frac{p_{[m]}^2(x)}{p_{[1]}(x)} - 1 \end{aligned} \tag{3.7}$$

(whether or not $p_{[m]}$ is a probability distribution). Formulas for the contributions of the individual degrees of freedom are readily given, e.g., $r_{12}^2 = [\sum_x z_1 z_2 p(x)]^2$, but they are not required here.

4. Symmetric Distributions

The distribution p is said to be symmetric if for each $x = (x_1, \cdots, x_n)$ we have $p(x_1, \cdots, x_n) = p(x_{i_1}, \cdots, x_{i_n})$ for all permutations $i_1 \cdots i_n$. It is a trivial consequence of Proposition 1 that p is symmetric if and only if $\alpha_i = \alpha$, $r_{ij} = r_{(2)}$, $r_{ijk} = r_{(3)}$, etc., for all $i, j, \cdots$. A symmetric distribution is thus determined by the n parameters $\alpha, r_{(2)}, r_{(3)}, \cdots$, and $r_{(n)}$, where $r_{(m)}$ is the mth-order correlation between any m items.

An alternative parametrization can be obtained in the following way. Again, let t denote the total number of positive responses, i.e., $t(x) = x_1 + \cdots + x_n$, and let $q(t)$ denote the probability distribution of t for $t = 0, 1, \cdots, n$. It is then easy to see that p is symmetric if and only if the conditional distribution $p(x \mid t)$ is uniform, i.e.,

$$p(x \mid t) = \frac{1}{\binom{n}{t}},$$

for every t with $q(t) > 0$. Consequently, the probability distribution of t —the $n+1$ numbers $\{q(t): t = 0, 1, \cdots, n\}$, with $\sum_{t=0}^{n} q(t) = 1$—provides a parametrization of p.

The relationship between the two systems is described below. This relationship is of interest because it is relatively easy to work with the probability distribution of t; consequently, if the distribution on X is not too asymmetric, the distribution of t can be used to gain a rough but quickly obtained idea of the order of the distribution on X. For example, the contribution δ_2^2 of the quadratic terms in $p(x)$ (see Section 3) can be estimated from the mean and variance of t, and the total contribution $\delta_{[n]}^2$ can be estimated from χ^2 for testing that t has the binomial (n, α) distribution (cf. Proposition 4 below).

Suppose that p is symmetric. Define

$$g_0(t) \equiv 1$$

$$g_1(t) = \sum_i (x_i - \alpha) \Big/ [\alpha(1-\alpha)]^{\frac{1}{2}}$$

$$g_2(t) = \sum_{i<j} (x_i - \alpha)(x_j - \alpha) \Big/ [\alpha(1-\alpha)] \tag{4.1}$$

$$g_3(t) = \sum_{i<j<k} (x_i - \alpha)(x_j - \alpha)(x_k - \alpha) \Big/ [\alpha(1-\alpha)]^{\frac{3}{2}}$$

$$\cdots$$

$$g_n(t) = (x_1 - \alpha)(x_2 - \alpha)\cdots(x_n - \alpha)/[\alpha(1-\alpha)]^{\frac{1}{2}n} .$$

That the right-hand sides of (4.1) depend on x only through t can be seen from the following. The expressions $\sum_i (x_i - \alpha)$, $\sum_{i<j}(x_i - \alpha)(x_j - \alpha)$, $\cdots$, $(x_1 - \alpha)(x_2 - \alpha)\cdots(x_n - \alpha)$, are symmetric polynomials in the x's, and consequently (cf. [3], pp. 242–44) can be expressed as polynomials in the sums $\sum_i x_i, \sum_i x_i^2, \cdots, \sum_i x_i^n$. However, since x_i is either 0 or 1, and $\sum x_i = t$, it follows that $\sum x_i^2 = \sum x_i^3 = \cdots = \sum x_i^n = t$, so that $g_m(t)$ is in fact a polynomial in t of degree m. The polynomial g_m can be determined explicitly by an application of Newton's formula ([3], p. 243). In particular, we have

$$g_1(t) = (t - n\alpha)/[\alpha(1-\alpha)]^{\frac{1}{2}}$$

$$g_2(t) = \{(t - n\alpha)^2 - (1 - 2\alpha)(t - n\alpha) - n\alpha(1-\alpha)\}/[2\alpha(1-\alpha)] \tag{4.2}$$

$$g_3(t) = \{(t - n\alpha)^3 - 3(1-2\alpha)(t-n\alpha)^2 - [3(n+2)\alpha(1-\alpha) - 2](t - n\alpha) + 2n\alpha(1-\alpha)(1-2\alpha)\}/\{6[\alpha(1-\alpha)]^{\frac{3}{2}}\} .$$

It will be shown presently that with

$$h_m(t) = \frac{g_m(t)}{\binom{n}{m}^{\frac{1}{2}}}, \tag{4.3}$$

$\{h_0, h_1, \cdots, h_n\}$ is the set of orthogonal polynomials associated with the binomial distribution

$$q_{[1]}(t) = \binom{n}{t}\alpha^t(1-\alpha)^{n-t}\,, \qquad t = 0, 1, \cdots, n. \tag{4.4}$$

We now prove

PROPOSITION 4. *Suppose that p is symmetric with parameters $\alpha_i = \alpha$, $r_{ij} = r_{(2)}, \cdots,$ and $r_{(n)}$. Let q denote the probability distribution of $t = x_1 + \cdots + x_n$. Then*

$$r_{(m)} = \frac{1}{\binom{n}{m}} E_q(g_m) \tag{4.5}$$

and

$$\delta_m^2 = \frac{1}{\binom{n}{m}} [E_q(g_m)]^2 \tag{4.6}$$

for $m = 2, \cdots, n$. Also,

$$\delta_{[n]}^2 = \delta_2^2 + \cdots + \delta_n^2 = \sum_{t=0}^{n} \frac{[q(t)]^2}{q_{[1]}(t)} - 1\,. \tag{4.7}$$

To establish these facts, suppose for the moment that $p_{[1]}$ obtains, and regard the functions g_m as elements of the inner product space V that was considered in the proof of Proposition 1. It then follows from Proposition 2, or otherwise directly from (4.1), that for $k, m = 0, 1, \cdots, n$,

$$(g_k, g_m) = 0 \quad \text{for} \quad k \neq m\,; \qquad ||g_m||^2 = \binom{n}{m}. \tag{4.8}$$

It follows from (4.3) and (4.8) that $\{h_0, h_1, \cdots, h_n\}$ is a set of orthonormal functions of x. Since each h_m depends on x only through t, and since t is distributed according to $q_{[1]}$ when $p_{[1]}$ obtains [cf. (4.4)], the statement following (4.2) is proved.

It is plain from (2.2) and (4.1) that for each $m = 2, 3, \cdots, g_m$ is the sum of the $\binom{n}{m}$ functions $z_{i_1}z_{i_2}\cdots z_{i_m}$. Hence (2.5) and (2.6) can be written as

$$p(x) \equiv p_{[1]}(x)\cdot\left[1 + \sum_{m=2}^{n} r_{(m)}\, g_m[t(x)]\right]. \tag{4.9}$$

By summing (4.9) over $\{x : t(x) = t\}$ we obtain

$$q(t) = q_{[1]}(t)\cdot\left[1 + \sum_{m=2}^{n} r_{(m)}\, g_m(t)\right]. \tag{4.10}$$

It follows from (4.8) and (4.10) that

$$E_q(g_m) = r_{(m)}E_{q_{[1]}}(g_m^2) = r_{(m)}\,||g_m||^2 = r_{(m)}\tbinom{n}{m}\,, \tag{4.11}$$

for $m = 2, 3, \cdots$; i.e., (4.5) holds. Equation (4.6) is an immediate consequence of (4.5) and the definition [cf. (3.4)] of δ_m^2 in the general case.

We observe next that, in the general case, $\delta^2_{[n]}$ is the expected value of $(f-1)^2$ when $p_{[1]}$ obtains, where f is defined by (2.5). It is clear from (4.9) and (4.10) that in the present case f depends on x only through t; in fact $f = q/q_{[1]}$. Consequently

$$\delta^2_{[n]} = E_{q_{[1]}}\left(\frac{q}{q_{[1]}} - 1\right)^2 , \tag{4.12}$$

and this is equivalent to (4.7). This completes the proof of Proposition 4.

We may note here the particular cases $m = 2$ and $m = 3$. Let μ_r denote the rth moment of t about its mean $n\alpha$ when q obtains. Then from (4.2), (4.5), and (4.6) we have

$$\begin{aligned} r_{(2)} &= \frac{\mu_2 - n\alpha(1-\alpha)}{n(n-1)\alpha(1-\alpha)} , \\ \delta^2_2 &= \frac{[\mu_2 - n\alpha(1-\alpha)]^2}{2n(n-1)[\alpha(1-\alpha)]^2} , \end{aligned} \tag{4.13}$$

and

$$\begin{aligned} r_{(3)} &= \frac{\mu_3 - 3(1-2\alpha)\mu_2 + 2n\alpha(1-\alpha)(1-2\alpha)}{n(n-1)(n-2)[\alpha(1-\alpha)]^{\frac{3}{2}}} , \\ \delta^2_3 &= \frac{[\mu_3 - 3(1-2\alpha)\mu_2 + 2n\alpha(1-\alpha)(1-2\alpha)]^2}{6n(n-1)(n-2)[\alpha(1-\alpha)]^3} . \end{aligned} \tag{4.14}$$

Suppose next that $\alpha_i = \alpha$ for $i = 1, \cdots, n$, but that p is not symmetric, i.e., that for some m the correlations of mth order are not all equal. In this case, it is intuitively clear that the right-hand side of (4.7) will be an underestimate of $\delta^2_{[n]}$, since the former is a χ^2 based on the statistic $x_1 + \cdots + x_n$, whereas $\delta^2_{[n]}$ is the parallel χ^2 based on the whole observation x. The following proposition shows that this is indeed the case—in fact, no component of $\delta^2_{[n]}$ can be overestimated by passing from x to t.

PROPOSITION 5. *Suppose that $\alpha_i = \alpha$ for $i = 1, \cdots, n$, but that p is not necessarily symmetric. Then, for each $m = 2, 3, \cdots, n$,*

$$\delta^2_m \geqq \frac{1}{\binom{n}{m}} [E_q(g_m)]^2 \tag{4.15}$$

with equality if and only if all correlations of the order m are the same.

To establish this proposition, let $p(x)$ be symmetrized into $p^*(x)$, i.e.,

$$p^*(x_1, \cdots, x_n) = \frac{1}{n!} \sum p(x_{i_1}, \cdots, x_{i_n}) , \tag{4.16}$$

where the summation is over all permutations $i_1 i_2 \cdots i_n$. The symmetrization does not destroy the probability distribution of t, i.e., $q^*(t) \equiv q(t)$. Consequently, by applying Proposition 4 to p^*, we see that (4.15) is equivalent to

$$\delta^2_m \geqq \delta^{*2}_m . \tag{4.17}$$

By referring to the definition of δ_m^2, it follows from (2.5), (2.6), and (4.16) that (4.17) is equivalent to

$$\sum_{i_1<\cdots<i_m} r_{i_1\cdots i_m}^2 \geqq \Big(\sum_{i_1<\cdots<i_m} r_{i_1\cdots i_m}\Big)^2\Big/\binom{n}{m}. \tag{4.18}$$

An application of the Schwartz inequality shows that (4.18) always holds, and that the equality sign obtains only if all the r's are equal. This establishes Proposition 5.

5. Extension to the General Case

Consider n given items, as before, and let $x = (x_1, \cdots, x_n)$ denote the set of responses, with x_i the response to item i. Let c_i be the number of possible responses to item i ($2 \leqq c_i < \infty$), and let $p(x_1, \cdots, x_n)$ be a given probability distribution over the set X of all possible response patterns. Let $p(x_i)$ denote the marginal distribution of x_i, and let $p_{[1]}(x_1, \cdots, x_n) = p(x_1)\cdot p(x_2)\cdots p(x_n)$. With no loss of generality, assume the notation to be so chosen that $p_{[1]} > 0$.

For each i, choose and fix functions $\{f_{ij} : j = 0, 1, 2, \cdots. c_i - 1\}$ of x_i alone, such that

$$f_{i0} = 1\,, \tag{5.1}$$

and such that $\{f_{ij}\}$ is an orthonormal set when x_i is distributed according to p. Let S denote the set of all functions on X of the form

$$g(x_1, \cdots, x_n) = \prod_{i=1}^{n} f_{ij_i}(x_i)\,, \tag{5.2}$$

with $0 \leqq j_i \leqq c_i - 1$ for each i. Then it is easy to see that (1) S is a basis in the space of all real-valued functions on X, and that (2) this basis is orthonormal when $p_{[1]}$ obtains. In particular, we have (3)

$$p(x_1, \cdots, x_n) \equiv p_{[1]}(x_1, \cdots, x_n)\cdot\Big[\sum_{g\in S} g(x_1, \cdots, x_n)\cdot E_p(g)\Big]. \tag{5.3}$$

It should be noted that the validity of statements (1), (2), and (3) (as distinct from their possible usefulness) is independent of the choice of the marginal orthonormal systems $\{f_{ij}\}$. In particular (1), (2), and (3) are independent of (5.1).

In case $c_i = 2$, (5.1) implies that the ith marginal orthonormal set consists of the two functions 1 and z_i, where z_i is the (unique) real valued function of x_i which has zero mean and unit variance; consequently, if $c_i = 2$ for each i, (1), (2), and (3) reduce to Propositions 1 and 2.

Let us say that g defined by (5.2) is of mth order if there are exactly m non-constant factors on the right-hand side of (5.2), $m = 0, 1, \cdots, n$. Let S_m denote the set of all functions g of order m, and define

$$\delta_m^2 = \sum_{g\in S_m} [E_p(g)]^2\,. \tag{5.4}$$

In consequence of (5.1), we have $\delta_0^2 = 1$ and $\delta_1^2 = 0$. For $m \geqq 2$, (5.4) is the generalization of the definition of δ_m^2 in (3.4).

This last statement is justified on the one hand by the fact that if $c_i = 2$ for all i, (5.4) necessarily reduces to the previous definition, and on the other by the following proposition:

PROPOSITION 6. *For each m, the value of δ_m^2 is independent of the choice of the marginal orthonormal bases $\{f_{ij}\}$.*

To establish Proposition 6, it is enough to show that δ_m^2 remains unchanged if the marginal basis of exactly one item is changed, while the bases of the others remain the same. Without loss of generality, we may take this one item to be the first one. Suppose then that $\{f_{1j}\}$ is changed to $\{f_{1j}^*\}$, and let δ_m^{*2} be the resulting value of δ_m^2. Let A denote the set of all functions of $x_2, \cdots, x_n$ of the form $\prod_{i=2}^n f_{ij_i}(x_i)$ with exactly $m-1$ non-constant factors. It is then easily seen from (5.1), (5.2), and (5.4) that

$$\delta_m^{*2} - \delta_m^2 = \sum_{g \in A} \sum_{j=1}^{k} \{[E_p(f_j^* \cdot g)]^2 - [E_p(f_j \cdot g)]^2\}\,, \tag{5.5}$$

where we have written $k = c_1 - 1$, and $f_j^* = f_{1j}^*$, $f_j = f_{1j}$.

Now, since $\{f_0, \cdots, f_k\}$ and $\{f_0^*, \cdots, f_k^*\}$ span the same space (namely, the set of all functions of x_1), and since $f_0 = f_0^* = 1$ by (5.1), $\{f_1, \cdots, f_k\}$ and $\{f_1^*, \cdots, f_k^*\}$ span the same space, W, say. Regard W as a subspace of the space of all functions on X. Since $\{f_1, \cdots, f_k\}$ and $\{f_1^*, \cdots, f_k^*\}$ are orthonormal bases in W, it follows that

$$\sum_{j=1}^{k} [E_p(f_j^* \cdot g)]^2 = \sum_{j=1}^{k} [E_p(f_j \cdot g)]^2 \tag{5.6}$$

for any function g on X, either expression being equal to the squared norm of the projection of g on W. It follows from (5.5) and (5.6) that $\delta_m^{*2} = \delta_m^2$, and the proposition is established.

REFERENCES

[1] Lazarsfeld, P. F. Some observations on dichotomous systems. Sociology Department, Columbia University, New York. Duplicated report (second draft), October 1956.

[2] McFadden, J. A. Urn models of correlation and a comparison with the multivariate normal integral. *Ann. Math. Stat.*, 1955, **26**, 478–89.

[3] Bôcher, M. *Introduction to Higher Algebra.* New York: Macmillan, 1907.

10

On Classification Based on Responses to *n* Dichotomous Items

R. R. BAHADUR, Indian Statistical Institute

1. Introduction

This chapter concerns some aspects, in an important special case, of the problem of classification based on qualitative information. The general problem—or rather, class of problems—needs no description here. The special case and special problems may be outlined as follows.

We suppose that each individual in a given population belongs to one of two mutually exclusive groups, F and G. An individual from the population, whose true group is unknown, is to be classified as belonging to either F or G. To aid in classification, we use the individual's responses to a battery of n dichotomous items (i.e., n test items, each item having two possible outcomes). In this situation, two questions arise: (1) How can we best use the response pattern for classification, and (2) how can we measure the value of a given battery of items for classification purposes? This last question, together with cost factors, is obviously important in constructing a suitable battery of items from a given set of available items.

Let $x = (x_1, \cdots, x_n)$ denote the total response to the given battery of items, where $x_i = 1$ if the response on the ith item is "positive," and $x_i = 0$ if otherwise, $i = 1, \cdots, n$. Let $p = p(x)$ and $q = q(x)$ be the probability distribution of x in groups F and G, respectively, and assume that these probability distributions are known. In this case, as is well known, the following is a more or less complete theoretical solution of the problems mentioned above. The classification should be based on the likelihood ratio p/q or, equivalently, on

$$L(x) = \log p(x) - \log q(x) , \tag{1.1}$$

and is made according to the rule, "classify an individual with response pattern x as a member of F if and only if $L(x) > c$," where c is a fixed constant equal to some possible value of L. It is clear that there are, at most, 2^n possible values of L.

The value of a battery of test items for classification purposes may be judged by the set of points (α_c, β_c) corresponding to all choices of the cut-off point c, each pair of numbers denoting the probabilities of misclassification associated with a given value of c, that is,

$$(1.2) \qquad \alpha_c = \sum_{x:L(x)\leqq c} p(x) , \qquad \beta_c = \sum_{x:L(x)>c} q(x) .$$

Let $c_1, c_2, \cdots$ be the ordered values of c. Then, the set of points $(\alpha_{c_i}, \beta_{c_i})$, together with the line segments joining the pairs $(\alpha_{c_i}, \beta_{c_i}), (\alpha_{c_{i+1}}, \beta_{c_{i+1}})$, $i = 1, 2, \cdots$, will be called the error curve. In the presence of additional criteria (such as, for example, some knowledge of *a priori* probabilities for the two groups) only part of the error curve may be required to evaluate the battery.

The optimum solution based on $L(x)$ requires knowledge of the probability distribution of response patterns in each group [cf. (1.1) and (1.2)]. This is, of course, a strong requirement if n is at all large, since both p and q are distributions with $2^n - 1$ parameters. The object of this chapter is to describe certain approximations to the optimum classification statistic L and to the error curve attainable with L. Under favorable conditions these are close approximations, and depend on relatively few parameters.

If the number of items in the battery is fairly large and if the items are not highly interdependent, then $L(x)$ is approximately normally distributed in F and G, with means μ_1 and μ_2 and variances σ_1^2 and σ_2^2, respectively, where

$$\begin{aligned} \mu_1 &= E_p[L(x)] \\ \sigma_1^2 &= E_p\{L(x) - E_p[L(x)]\}^2 \\ \mu_2 &= E_q[L(x)] \\ \sigma_2^2 &= E_q\{L(x) - E_q[L(x)]\}^2 . \end{aligned}$$

It should be noted that (unless p and q are identical distributions) we have $\mu_1 > 0$ and $\mu_2 < 0$. This is easily seen from $L(x) \equiv \log [p(x)/q(x)]$ and $\log t \leqq t - 1$, for $t \geqq 0$, the inequality being strict for $t \neq 1$.

In Section 2 it is shown that both σ_1 and σ_2, under certain conditions on p and q, may be approximated by

$$(1.3) \qquad D = \sqrt{\mu_1 - \mu_2} .$$

It follows that

$$(1.4) \qquad \alpha_c = \sum_{x:L(x)\leqq c} p(x) \sim \int_{-\infty}^{(c-\mu_1)/D} (2\pi)^{-\frac{1}{2}} \exp(-\tfrac{1}{2}u^2)\, du = \Phi\left(\frac{c - \mu_1}{D}\right),$$

and

$$(1.5) \qquad \beta_c = \sum_{x:L(x)>c} q(x) \sim \int_{(c-\mu_2)/D}^{\infty} (2\pi)^{-\frac{1}{2}} \exp(-\tfrac{1}{2}u^2)\, du = \Phi\left(\frac{-c + \mu_2}{D}\right),$$

where

$$\Phi(s) = \int_{-\infty}^{s} (2\pi)^{-\frac{1}{2}} \exp[-u^2/2]\, du .$$

Writing $z = [c - \frac{1}{2}(\mu_1 + \mu_2)]/D$, we have

$$\begin{aligned}\alpha_c &\sim \Phi\left(z - \frac{D}{2}\right) = \alpha_z^* \,, \\ \beta_c &\sim \Phi\left(-z - \frac{D}{2}\right) = \beta_z^* \,.\end{aligned} \tag{1.6}$$

Consequently, the error curve for the class of optimum procedures is approximated by the points (α_z^*, β_z^*) as z varies from $-\infty$ to $+\infty$. The approximating curve is the actual error curve in case classification is based on a statistic which is $N(0, 1)$ in group F and $N(0, 1)$ in group G.

In Sections 3 and 4, the distributions p and q are each given the particular representation described in Chapter 9. In this form we obtain an approximation l to the optimum classification statistic L, and an approximation d to the effective distance D between the two groups. Under certain conditions, l and d assume quite simple forms; in particular, the formula for d exhibits the contribution due to any given item in the battery.

Note 1. The optimum character of the likelihood-ratio solution of the classification problem does not depend on the internal (latent) structures, if any, of the item within groups, or on the definitions of the two groups. The arguments on which the present approximations to the optimum solution are based concern only the probability distributions of the manifest variables $(x_1, \cdots, x_n) = x$. The approximations, therefore, are also independent of internal structure and of the definitions of the groups.

Note 2. The approximations in question are likely to be good ones if (1) the number of items n is fairly large, (2) the groups are hard to distinguish by means of x, i.e., if p and q are not very different distributions and (3) the items are *not* highly interdependent in either group. The simplest approximation, the quadratic one, requires the further condition (4) that in each group the departure from independence of item responses (if any) is due mostly to the quadratic term.

Note 3. In cases where the present approximations cannot be expected to be close, classification based on the approximate classification statistic l, or on some similar statistic, may still be more successful than classification based on some more or less arbitrarily selected statistic, e.g., the total score $t = x_1 + \cdots + x_n$; and the expression for d may still provide useful clues to the value of a particular item or set of items.

Note 4. Notwithstanding the preceding remark, it should be emphasized that the approximations described here are of a tentative character, and can and should be modified according to the requirements of a given problem. For example, if the number of items is quite large, it may be a good procedure to divide the items, on substantive or other grounds, into k mutually exclusive groups; then to derive a classification statistic, l_j, say, based only on items in group j, by the methods discussed here $(j = 1, 2, \cdots, k)$; and to use standard multivariate analysis on the statistic $y = (l_1, l_2, \cdots, l_k)$ to construct the final classification statistic.

2. On the Distance Between Two Groups

In looking for a good numerical index of the effectiveness for classification purposes (i.e., for a measure of the maximum distance between the two groups in terms of the given battery), it seems plausible, in view of the structure of the class of optimum procedures, to consider

$$D_1 = \frac{\mu_1 - \mu_2}{\sigma_1}, \qquad \text{or} \qquad D_2 = \frac{\mu_1 - \mu_2}{\sigma_2}, \tag{2.1}$$

or some average of D_1 and D_2. This is certainly the case if the statistic $L(x)$ is approximately normally distributed in each group (cf. conditions (1) and (3) of Note 2 in Section 1), for then the optimum error curve depends approximately on only D_1 and D_2. In this section we point out that if p and q are not very different (cf. condition (2) of Note 2), D_1 and D_2 are both approximately equal to D given by (1.3). A brief discussion of D as a distance function is given in Section 3, Notes 4 and 5.

Let us write $J = \mu_1 - \mu_2$. Then

$$J = E_p(\log p - \log q) - E_q(\log p - \log q), \tag{2.2}$$

so that J is the (symmetric) Kullback-Leibler information number [1]. As is easily seen from (2.2), $J \geqq 0$, with $J = 0$ if and only if $p = q$.

Assume now that p and q are close to each other in the sense that

$$\max_x \left| \frac{p(x)}{q(x)} - 1 \right| = a_1, \qquad \max_x \left| \frac{q(x)}{p(x)} - 1 \right| = a_2 \tag{2.3}$$

are small. In this case $J = \mu_1 - \mu_2$ will also be small; in fact (2.2) and (2.3) imply that

$$J \leqq \min\,[a_1 \log(1 + a_1),\ a_2 \log(1 + a_2)]\,. \tag{2.4}$$

Next we show that

$$\sigma_i^2 = J(1 + b_i) \qquad i = 1, 2, \tag{2.5}$$

where $b_1, b_2 \to 0$ as $a_1, a_2 \to 0$. This will establish, as desired, that if a_1 and a_2 are small, $D_i \sim D \equiv \sqrt{J}$, for $i = 1, 2$.

It suffices to establish (2.5) for σ_1^2. We notice first that $\sigma_1^2 = E_p(L^2) - \mu_1^2$, and that $\mu_2 \leqq 0 \leqq \mu_1$. Hence $\sigma_1^2 = E_p(L^2) - \theta J^2$, where $0 \leqq \theta \leqq 1$. Since $J \to 0$ by (2.4), it follows that for σ_1^2 Equation (2.5) is equivalent to

$$E_p(L^2) = J(1 + c_1), \tag{2.6}$$

where $c_1 \to 0$.

Let $y = y(x)$ be defined by $q = p \cdot [1 + y]$. Then $|y| \leqq a_2$ by (2.3). Also

$$E_p(L^2) = E_p[\log(1 + y)]^2 \tag{2.7}$$

and

$$J = E_p[y \log(1 + y)], \tag{2.8}$$

by (2.2).

Now, for any $y > -1$,

$$\log(1+y) = y - \frac{y^2}{2[1+y\varphi(y)]^2} \qquad (0 < \varphi(y) < 1)\,. \tag{2.9}$$

Multiplying both sides of (2.9) by $\log(1+y)$ and taking expectations, we see from (2.7) and (2.8) that

$$E_p(L^2) = J + K\,, \tag{2.10}$$

where

$$\begin{aligned} |K| &= \left| \tfrac{1}{2} E_p \left\{ \frac{y^2 \log(1+y)}{[1+y\varphi(y)]^2} \right\} \right| \\ &\leqq \tfrac{1}{2} E_p \left\{ \frac{y^2 \,|\log(1+y)|}{[1-|y|]^2} \right\} \\ &\leqq \frac{a_2}{2(1-a_2)^2} E_p\{|y \log(1+y)|\} \\ &= \frac{a_2}{2(1-a_2)^2} J\,, \qquad \text{by (2.8)}\,. \end{aligned} \tag{2.11}$$

The required conclusion (2.6) now follows from (2.10) and (2.11).

3. Approximations to $L(x)$ and D

Let $\alpha_i = \Pr\{x_i = 1 \mid \mathrm{F}\}$, $i = 1, 2, \cdots, n$ and let

$$y_i = (x_i - \alpha_i)/\sqrt{\alpha_i(1-\alpha_i)}\,. \tag{3.1}$$

Let $r_{ij}, r_{ijk}, \cdots, r_{12\cdots n}$ denote correlations of second, third, $\cdots$, and nth order when p obtains, i.e., $r_{ij\cdots k} = E_p(y_i y_j \cdots y_k)$ (cf. Chapter 9). Then, according to Chapter 9 we have

$$p(x_1, \cdots, x_n) = \left(\prod_1^n \alpha_i^{x_i}(1-\alpha_i)^{1-x_i} \right) \cdot f(x)\,, \tag{3.2}$$

where

$$f(x) = 1 + \sum_{i<j} r_{ij}\, y_i y_j + \sum_{i<j<k} r_{ijk}\, y_i y_j y_k + \cdots + r_{12\cdots n}\, y_1 \cdots y_n\,. \tag{3.3}$$

Similarly, let $\beta_i = \Pr\{x_i = 1 \mid G\}$, and let

$$z_i = (x_i - \beta_i)/\sqrt{\beta_i(1-\beta_i)}\,; \tag{3.4}$$

and let $s_{ij}, s_{ijk}, \cdots, s_{12\cdots n}$ denote the correlation parameters when q obtains. Then

$$q(x_1, \cdots, x_n) = \left[\prod_1^n \beta_i^{x_i}(1-\beta_i)^{1-x_i} \right] \cdot g(x)\,, \tag{3.5}$$

where

$$g(x) = 1 + \sum_{i<j} s_{ij}\, z_i z_j + \sum_{i<j<k} s_{ijk}\, z_i z_j z_k + \cdots + s_{12\cdots n}\, z_1 z_2 \cdots z_n\,. \tag{3.6}$$

We have, from (1.1), (3.2), and (3.5),

$$L(x) = k + \sum_{i=1}^{n} c_i x_i + \log f(x) - \log g(x) , \tag{3.7}$$

where k is a constant,

$$c_i = \log\left[\left(\frac{\alpha_i}{1-\alpha_i}\right)\left(\frac{1-\beta_i}{\beta_i}\right)\right], \tag{3.8}$$

and f and g are given by (3.1), (3.3), (3.4), and (3.6).

Now we can apply one or both of the following approximations to (3.7): (1) approximate the logarithmic functions in (3.7), and (2) omit correlation terms of high order that appear in f and g (assuming that they are nonzero to begin with). The simplest approximation of type (1) is to replace $\log f$ and $\log g$ by $f-1$ and $g-1$, respectively, giving

$$\begin{aligned} l(x) &= \sum_{i=1}^{n} c_i x_i + f(x) - g(x) \\ &= \sum_{i=1}^{n} c_i x_i + \sum_{i<j} (r_{ij}\, y_i y_j - s_{ij}\, z_i z_j) + \sum_{i<j<k} (r_{ijk}\, y_i y_j y_k - s_{ijk}\, z_i z_j z_k) \\ &\qquad + \cdots + (r_{12\cdots n}\, y_1 y_2 \cdots y_n - s_{12\cdots n}\, z_1 z_2 \cdots z_n) \end{aligned} \tag{3.9}$$

as an approximation to $L(x)$. The constant term is omitted, since it plays no role here.

Let us write

$$u_{i_1\cdots i_m} = \frac{r_{i_1\cdots i_m}}{\sqrt{\alpha_{i_1}(1-\alpha_{i_1})}\cdot\sqrt{\alpha_{i_2}(1-\alpha_{i_2})}\cdots\sqrt{\alpha_{i_m}(1-\alpha_{i_m})}} , \tag{3.10}$$

and

$$v_{i_1\cdots i_m} = \frac{s_{i_1\cdots i_m}}{\sqrt{\beta_{i_1}(1-\beta_{i_1})}\cdot\sqrt{(\beta_{i_2}(1-\beta_{i_2})}\cdots\sqrt{\beta_{i_m}(1-\beta_{i_m})}} . \tag{3.11}$$

Then, if all correlations of order higher than two are omitted in (3.9), the resulting statistic is equivalent to

$$\sum_{i=1}^{n} c_i^{(2)} x_i + \sum_{i<j} c_{ij}^{(2)} x_i x_j , \tag{3.12}$$

where $c_{ij}^{(2)} = u_{ij} - v_{ij}$, and

$$c_i^{(2)} = c_i + \sum_{j\neq i} (-\alpha_j u_{ij} + \beta_j v_{ij}) . \tag{3.13}$$

If third-order correlations are also retained, the resulting statistic is equivalent to

$$\sum_{i=1}^{n} c_i^{(3)} x_i + \sum_{i<j} c_{ij}^{(3)} x_i x_j + \sum_{i<j<k} c_{ijk}^{(3)} x_i x_j x_k , \tag{3.14}$$

where $c_{ijk}^{(3)} = u_{ijk} - v_{ijk}$,

$$c_{ij}^{(3)} = c_{ij}^{(2)} + \sum_{\substack{k \neq i \\ k \neq j}} (-\alpha_k u_{ijk} + \beta_k v_{ijk}) \,, \tag{3.15}$$

and

$$c_i^{(3)} = c_i^{(2)} + \sum_{\substack{j \neq i \\ k \neq i \\ j < k}} (\alpha_j \alpha_k u_{ijk} - \beta_j \beta_k v_{ijk}) \,. \tag{3.16}$$

We turn now to approximations for D, the "effective distance" between the groups. In accordance with the argument of the preceding section, $E_p(l) - E_q(l)$ is a plausible estimate of the effective squared distance in using l. It is not difficult to express $E_p(l) - E_q(l)$ in terms of the marginals α and β and the correlation parameters in the two groups. This expression suggests the following approximation for D^2:

$$d^2 = \sum_{i=1}^{n} (\alpha_i - \beta_i) c_i + \sum_{i<j} (r_{ij} - s_{ij})^2 + \sum_{i<j<k} (r_{ijk} - s_{ijk})^2 + \cdots + (r_{12\cdots n} - s_{12\cdots n})^2 \,, \tag{3.17}$$

where c_i is given by (3.8).

Note 1. Let $h = \max \{| \alpha_i - \beta_i |, | r_{i_1 \cdots i_m} |, | s_{i_1 \cdots i_m} |\}$. Clearly, d^2 is of the order h^2. It can be shown that $D^2 - d^2 = h^2 \cdot \varepsilon$, where $\varepsilon \to 0$ as $h \to 0$. In other words, d is a good approximation to D if the items are not highly interdependent in either group and if the joint distributions over the groups are close to each other. (Cf. Note 1 in Section 1.)

Note 2. If certain non-zero terms in the expansions (3.3) and (3.6) are deleted in (3.9), the formula (3.17) for d^2 should be modified by putting the corresponding correlation parameters equal to zero.

Note 3. The preceding remark shows that (3.12) is a better classification statistic, at least to a first approximation, than $\sum_i c_i x_i$, and that (3.14) is better than (3.12), and so on. The remark also shows that, again to an approximation, statistics such as (3.12) or (3.14) can sometimes be improved without introducing terms of higher order. For example, if $r_{12} > s_{12} > 0$, then (3.17) suggests that it might be advantageous to set $v_{12} = 0$ in (3.13).

Note 4. A function $\delta(p, q)$ defined for all pairs of distributions p and q over X is a metric ("distance function") in the usual sense if (1) $\delta(p, q) = \delta(q, p)$, (2) $\delta(p, q) \geqq 0$, with equality if and only if $p \equiv q$, and (3) $\delta(p, q) \leqq \delta(p, r) + \delta(q, r)$. It is easily seen that both D and d [cf. (1.3) and (3.17)] satisfy (1) and (2). However, the following example shows that both D and d fail to satisfy (3). Consequently, neither D nor d is a metric.

In this example (for each $u, 0 < u < 1$) let p_u denote the distribution over X with $\alpha_1 = u$, $\alpha_i = \frac{1}{2}$ for $i = 2, 3, \cdots, n$, and all correlation parameters equal to zero. We then have

$$D(p_u, p_v) = d(p_u, p_v) = \{(u - v) \log [u(1 - v)/v(1 - u)]\}^{\frac{1}{2}} = \varphi(u, v) \,,$$

say, for all u and v. A simple calculation shows that $\varphi(\frac{1}{4}, \frac{1}{2}) > \varphi(\frac{1}{4}, a) + \varphi(\frac{1}{2}, a)$, where $a = 1/(1 + \sqrt{3})$. Thus (3) fails with $p = p_{\frac{1}{4}}$, $q = p_{\frac{1}{2}}$, and $r = p_a$, for $\delta \equiv D$ and also for $\delta \equiv d$.

Note 5. Assume not only that p and q are close to each other and that all correlation parameters are small, as in Note 1, but also that all α_i and β_i are close to $\frac{1}{2}$. In other words, suppose that p and q are in the neighborhood of the uniform distribution ($p^*(x) = 1/2^n$ for each x) over X. In this case d^2 (and therefore D^2) is approximated by

$$d_0^2 = 4 \sum_1^n (\alpha_i - \beta_i)^2 + \sum_{i<j} (r_{ij} - s_{ij})^2 + \sum_{i<j<k} (r_{ijk} - s_{ijk})^2 + \cdots + (r_{12\cdots n} - s_{12\cdots n})^2 . \tag{3.18}$$

This follows immediately from (3.8) and (3.17). It is readily seen that d_0 *is* a metric. Also, d_0 exhibits rather more clearly than d or D the relative importance of differences in the marginals, and differences in the correlation structures. The validity of d_0 (i.e., its approximation to D) is, of course, restricted to the neighborhood of the uniform distribution

Reference

[1] Kullback, S., and Leibler, R. A. On information and sufficiency. *Ann. Math. Stat.*, 1951, **22**, 79-86.

11

Classification Procedures Based on Dichotomous Response Vectors

HERBERT SOLOMON, Stanford University

1. Introduction

In many fields, measurement is still rather primitive, and at best only qualitative information can be secured. This is especially true in the social and behavioral sciences, where attempts at making more than a dichotomization frequently represent superfluous sophistication. In addition, a number of variables, sex and handedness, for example, are naturally dichotomous. At other times, dichotomization is not necessary but provides conveniences in scoring procedures. Despite the fact that these dichotomous situations present deviations from the usual normality assumptions of classical prediction theory and the classical theory of discriminatory analysis, one often finds that a linear function of a set of dichotomous responses is used in classifying an element or an individual into one of two populations. For example, in achievement tests, the linear function is usually an unweighted sum of binomial variables which represents total score; in other situations the linear function is weighted in a special way as, for example, R. A. Fisher's discriminant function. This latter function, of course, possesses optimal properties if the measurements are continuous and are normally distributed with the same covariance matrix in each population.

In psychological evaluation, several measurement devices are common and used routinely. Among these are (1) tests of mental ability (achievement tests, IQ tests), (2) tests of personal behavior (projective tests, personality inventories), (3) attitude scales, and (4) biographical inventories. Because of long-standing assumptions in mental measurement, based mainly on Spearman's single-factor theory, classification by tests of mental ability is based on a single dimension, namely the test score, which is typically a sum of responses to test items. However, measurement theory for personality behavior does not yet have a tradition or a long development, and thus care should be exercised to prevent the indiscriminate use of mental measurement techniques, i.e., linear functions of test-item responses, for this purpose. Attitude measurement has a more substantial development and tradition. Beginning with Thurstone's pioneering work through the present developments in Lazarsfeld's latent-structure analysis, a body of theory has grown in this area.

Some of the techniques explored in this paper bear some resemblance to Lazarsfeld's work, in the main because both latent-structure analysis and the analysis in this paper study dichotomous systems. From the assumptions made in attitude measurement, the use of linear functions of responses to attitudinal items for classification purposes may be relevant in some situations and may be quite poor at other times. The use of biographical information for measurement and classification is relatively unexploited, and the use of linear functions in that situation is not supported by experience.

This paper will explore the worth of several classification procedures based on test-item response vectors in a situation where an external, dichotomous criterion is available and where for each response vector we know the number of individuals giving this response in each of the two classes. Each classification procedure is a rule applied either to the vector of responses given by an individual or to a function of this vector (e.g., sum of the binomial variables), the rule which places the individual into one of the two classes. In addition, we will explore the representation of the joint frequency distribution of response vectors. Classification procedures based on various approximations to the joint distribution of frequencies of response vectors will be evaluated in order to assess the loss of information incurred by the approximations. The measure of worth is two-dimensional and is given by the proportions of misclassification possible in the assignment of an individual into each of the two groups by the use of the classification procedure, and these two values can be obtained directly in this situation.

2. Population and Data

Before discussing the representation of the joint distribution of response vectors and the analysis and evaluation of various classification procedures, we shall describe the population and the data available for our study. Even though we are discussing the simplest kind of scoring, namely dichotomous responses, the number of response vectors quickly rises with the addition of test items. While for four items we have 16 response vectors, there are 1024 vectors for ten items. The latter number of items would be considered rather small for many psychological tests, yet analysis would be required which would seem inordinately extensive. Naturally we are not going to find complete and exhaustive populations where the total picture of frequencies for each response vector is known. However, to insure reliable values for the frequency of each response vector, so that a population is adequately reproduced, a very large number of individuals is essential and, more important, their actual response vectors must be available. This required extensive searching. Two studies, suitable for our purposes, were found, one of which is reported here. The second study has been partially analyzed and will be reported subsequently.

The individuals and data in the study under analysis in this paper were obtained in the following way.[2] A total of 2982 New Jersey high-school seniors were given an attitude questionnaire in 1957 entitled, "Attitudes Toward Science and Scientific Careers." This questionnaire was planned, for purposes quite different from that of the present study, by the Science Manpower Project, Teachers College, Columbia University. In addition to the responses given by the students, a score was obtained for each on a brief IQ vocabulary test, hereafter referred to as the IQ test. For the purposes of this study, the IQ variable is considered an external criterion. Two classes of IQ values were set up, to which an individual could be assigned on the basis of his attitude toward science. These two classes are the upper half (high IQ) and lower half (low IQ), 1491 individuals in each class, obtained by score on the IQ test. This arrangement may be a bit artificial but it was quite useful for our purposes.

A total of 95 items concerned with the attitudes of high-school seniors toward science comprised the questionnaire. Since we require reliable values for the frequencies of the response vectors and there are 1491 observations available in each of the two IQ groups, it was felt that at most six items would be appropriate for the analysis. This leads to 64 response vectors, or an average of approximately 23 per pattern, so that zero frequencies, if they occur, are probably meaningful and not due to scanty data. The frequency distributions for the 64 response vectors in each IQ group were tabulated. For some of our subsequent analyses the use of even six items proved to be too cumbersome for the computing resources available, so that only four of the six items were used in several studies. The six items are as follows: (When only four items are analyzed, the first four items listed are employed.)

x_1 The development of new ideas is the scientist's greatest source of satisfaction.

x_2 Scientists and engineers should be eliminated from the military draft.

x_3 The scientist will make his maximum contribution to society when he has freedom to work on problems which interest him.

x_4 The monetary compensation of a Nobel Prize winner in physics should be at least equal to that given popular entertainers.

x_5 The free flow of scientific information among scientists is essential to scientific progress.

x_6 The neglect of basic scientific research would be the equivalent of "killing the goose that laid the golden eggs."

Their selection as items which, taken singly, had good discrimination

[2] I would like to thank Mr. Hugh Allen and Professor Hubert Evans, Science Manpower Project, Teachers College, Columbia University, for the basic data used in this study.

value between the high- and low-IQ groups, was based on both the data on hand and correlations with the IQ variable. While the individuals originally were allowed five choices along an Agree–Disagree scale, their responses

TABLE 1

$x_1x_2x_3x_4$	Low IQ		High IQ	
	Frequency	Relative frequency	Frequency	Relative frequency
1111	62	.042	122	.082
1110	70	.047	68	.046
1101	31	.020	33	.022
1100	41	.027	25	.017
1011	283	.190	329	.221
1010	253	.170	247	.166
1001	200	.134	172	.115
1000	305	.205	217	.146
0111	14	.009	20	.013
0110	11	.007	10	.007
0101	11	.007	11	.007
0100	14	.009	9	.006
0011	31	.020	56	.038
0010	46	.031	55	.037
0001	37	.025	64	.043
0000	82	.055	53	.036
Totals	1491	.998	1491	1.002

for our study were collapsed and recorded as 1 or 0 for "agree" or "disagree." The frequency distributions for the four items are given in Table 1.

One of the purposes of the study is to contrast the efficiency of linear functions of item responses with the total-response vector. Suppose, therefore, that we use as our index of attitude toward science the sum of the scores over the four items. This provides a uni-dimensional variable rang-

TABLE 2

Score	Low IQ		High IQ	
	Frequency	Relative frequency	Frequency	Relative frequency
4	62	.042	122	.082
3	398	.267	450	.302
2	547	.367	521	.349
1	402	.270	345	.231
0	82	.055	53	.036
Totals	1491	1.001	1491	1.000

ing from 0 to 4 with frequency distribution for low-IQ groups and high-IQ groups as given in Table 2.

3. Analysis

Before we examine the worth of classification procedures, it is interesting to assess the information contained in the response vector and compare it with a more simple measure of four responses made by an individual. We know that a classification based on a score of three must be less informative than a classification procedure based on knowledge of how the three "agree" responses were arranged over the four items. One natural way of assessing how much more informative the total-response vector can be is to compute the errors made in misclassification through the use of the total-response vector and other procedures. We will also discuss departures from total information intrinsic to the system and without regard to classification. Both Lazarsfeld (Chapter 8) and Bahadur (Chapter 9) have demonstrated how the joint distribution of responses for n dichotomous items can be represented in a more instructive form. We will use the Bahadur representation here. Let X denote the set of all points $x = (x_1, x_2, \cdots, x_n)$ with each $x_i = 0$ or 1. Let $p(x)$ be a given probability distribution on X, that is, $p(x) \geqq 0$ for each x and $\Sigma p(x) = 1$ for all x belonging to X. For each $i = 1, 2, \cdots, n$, let $\alpha_i = P\{x_i = 1\} = E_p(x_i)$, where E_p denotes expected value with respect to $p(x)$. In other words, the $\alpha_i, i = 1, 2, \cdots, n$, represent the marginal frequencies of the x_i's. Now set

$$z_i = (x_i - \alpha_i)/\sqrt{\alpha_i(1 - \alpha_i)}$$

and define

$$\begin{aligned} r_{ij} &= E_p(z_i z_j) \,, & i < j \,, \\ r_{ijk} &= E_p(z_i z_j z_k) \,, & i < j < k \,, \\ &\cdots \ \cdots \ \cdots \ \cdots \ \cdots \\ r_{123\cdots n} &= E_p(z_1 z_2 z_3 \cdots z_n) \,. \end{aligned}$$

The second-order correlations, r_{ij}, the third-order correlations, r_{ijk}, and the nth order correlations, $r_{123\cdots n}$, together comprise

$$n_{C_2} + n_{C_3} + \cdots + n_{C_n} = 2^n - n - 1$$

parameters. These together with the n marginal frequencies α_i comprise the $2^n - 1$ parameters which determine the probability distribution $p(x)$. Another way, but much less instructive, of viewing the $2^n - 1$ parameters is to recall there are 2^n response vectors and the 2^n frequencies must sum to one.

Let $p_{[1]}(x_1, x_2, \cdots, x_n)$ denote the joint probability distribution of the x_i when (a) the x_i's are independently distributed, and (b) they have the same marginal distributions as under the given distribution $p(x_1, x_2, \cdots, x_n)$. Then we have

$$p_{[1]}(x_1, x_2, \cdots, x_n) = \sum_{i=1}^{n} \alpha_i^{x_i}(1 - \alpha_i)^{1-x_i} ,$$

and

$$p(x) = p_{[1]}(x) f(x) ,$$

where

$$f(x) = 1 + \sum_{i<j} r_{ij} z_i z_j + \sum_{i<j<k} r_{ijk} z_i z_j z_k + \cdots + r_{12\cdots n}\, z_1 z_2 \cdots_n .$$

It now becomes possible to approximate the actual frequencies $p(x)$ by dropping out terms of the series, especially where the deleted terms have some heuristic or instructive meaning. For example, one could assume, as in those instances where joint normal distributions prevail, that all correlations higher than second order are zero. On the other hand, in some very non-linear regression situations we could just as easily assume that only fourth-order correlations do not vanish. Notice that any approximation to the joint distribution we are discussing is obtained by deleting terms. This provides less information; therefore the classification procedure using the approximation must have larger proportions of errors in assignments than the same classification procedure using the total-response vector.

The parameters were evaluated for the four items in the scientific-attitude study. It was too cumbersome to evaluate the parameters for the six items. The results are as follows:

	r_{12}	r_{13}	r_{14}	r_{23}	r_{24}	r_{34}	r_{123}	r_{124}	r_{134}	r_{234}	r_{1234}
High IQ	.003	.143	.111	.180	.020	.140	−.010	−.064	−.041	−.033	.003
Low IQ	.049	.144	.043	.155	.096	.125	−.006	−.012	.002	.002	.002

and

	α_1	α_2	α_3	α_4
High IQ	.821	.159	.505	.436
Low IQ	.801	.189	.599	.530 .

Whichever representation of $p(x)$ is used, we are now faced with the problem of an appropriate classification procedure. Let $g = g(x)$ and $f = f(x)$ be the probability distributions of x in the high- (H) and low- (L) IQ groups, respectively. Then, as is well known, a complete theoretical solution of the classification problem is as follows: Take the likelihood ratio $L(x)$ where

$$L(x) = g(x)/f(x)$$

and adopt the procedure:

> "classify an individual with response vector x as a member of the high-IQ group (H) if and only if $L(x) > c$, otherwise classify the individual in the low-IQ group (L),"

where c is a fixed constant, equal to some possible value of $L(x)$.

The worth of this classification procedure can be evaluated in the following way. Consider all choices of the cut-off point c, and for each c compute the probabilities of misclassification. Let α_c denote the probability of misclassifying an individual from the high-IQ group (H) into the low-IQ group (L), when c is the cut-off point, that is

$$\alpha_c = \sum_{x:L(x)\leq c} g(x) .$$

Likewise,

$$\beta_c = \sum_{x:L(x)>c} f(x)$$

is the probability of misclassifying an individual from low-IQ group L into high-IQ group H. Let $c_1, c_2, \cdots$, be the ordered values of c. Then the set of points $(\alpha_{c_i}, \beta_{c_i})$ together with the line segments joining the pairs $(\alpha_{c_i}, \beta_{c_i})$, $(\alpha_{c_{i+1}}, \beta_{c_{i+1}})$ is an error curve representing the risks in employing the classification procedure $L(x)$. If we have additional information about the *a priori* probabilities of the two groups L and H, only part of the error curve might be necessary for an evaluation.

The best risk curve for four items, that is, the curve with maximum curvature, will occur when we use the joint distribution of responses to the four items. Obviously, the curve is always bounded by the straight line in the α, β plane connecting (1, 0) and (0, 1). The construction of the curve can be easily routinized. Take $g(x)/f(x)$ for all 16 response vectors, then realign them in descending order according to the values of the likelihood ratios. These values provide the cut-off points c_i which lead to 17 decision rules, the ith rule given by $g(x)/f(x) > c_i$. The first rule is classify as low-IQ, L, for every response vector; the second rule is classify in L unless the newly selected first response vector is observed; the third rule is classify in L unless one of the first two newly selected response vectors is observed, etc.; the seventeenth rule is classify as high-IQ, H, for every response vector. The risks in using each of these 17 rules are now easily obtained by summing over the appropriate values of $f(x)$ and $g(x)$, which can be easily obtained from the new relisting.

The following assessments are now possible. We can obtain the risk curve associated with the likelihood ratio classification procedure when

(a) The joint distribution for the total-response vector is employed;

(b) The joint distribution for the total-response vector is approximated by the joint distribution obtained through the assumption of independence of responses over the four items, that is, only the marginal frequencies are used in the series representation for the joint frequencies;

(c) The joint distribution is approximated by ignoring all correlations higher than second order, the situation that would prevail if the joint distribution is given by a multivariate normal distribution;

(d) The joint distribution is approximated by any other function obtained by operating on the series representation, for example, in the four-item case, by considering only the fourth-order correlation term and of course the marginals, a situation that could very well arise in the use of personality and biographical inventories.

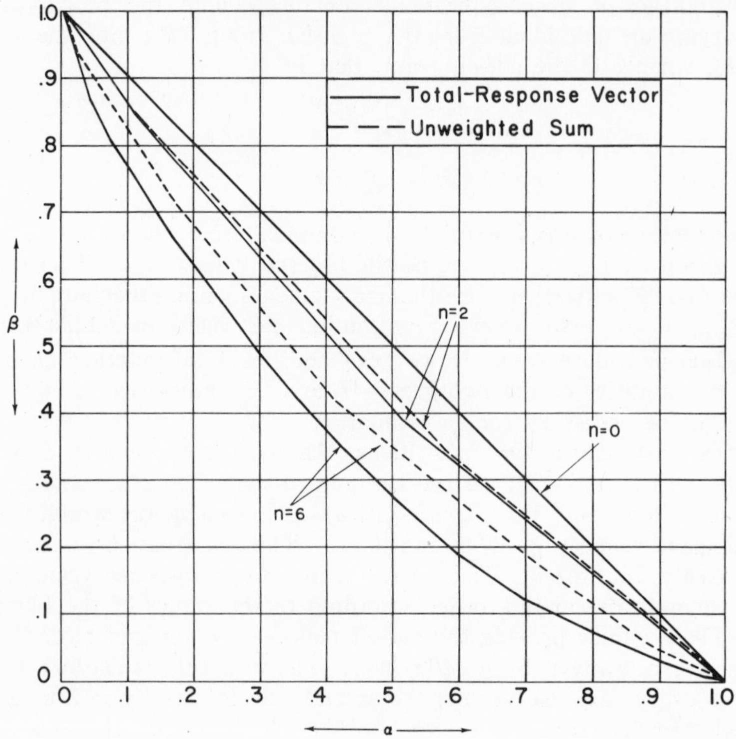

FIG. 1. The α, β Risk Curves for Two Items and Six Items

In addition, the joint distribution for the total-response vector could be collapsed to a univariate distribution by using a function of the four-item responses to obtain a single-valued response; for example, two linear functions which have had much use in this regard are an unweighted sum of the four binomial variables or a sum weighted in the sense of Fisher's discriminant function.

Actually, for each of these situations, a risk curve was constructed for two items and for three items in addition to the four-item situation. Also, risk curves were constructed for five items and for six items, both when the response vector was reduced to the unweighted sum of binomial variables and for the total-response vector situation. For the two-item case, Items 2 and 3 were employed; for the three-item case, Items 2, 3, and 4 were employed; for the five-item case, Items 1, 2, 3, 4, and 5 were employed.

4. Conclusions

Some risk curves are reproduced here to illustrate what has been done and to suggest some findings. Figure 1 depicts risk curves for two and

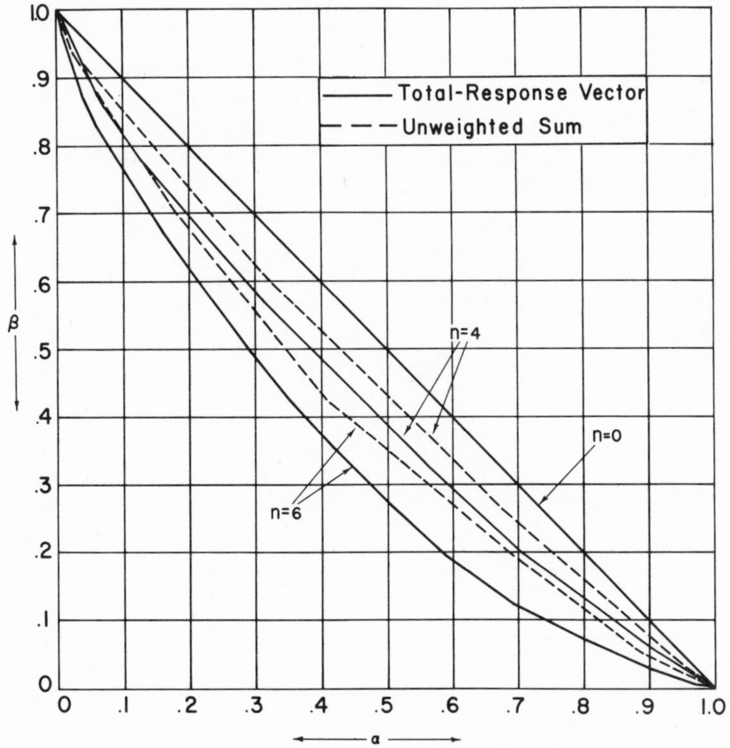

FIG. 2. The α, β Risk Curves for Four Items and Six Items

six items when the total-response vector is employed and when the unweighted sum of responses ("test score") is employed. Figure 2 presents comparisons of risk curves for response vector versus test score for four items and six items. Figure 3 demonstrates risk curves for four items where the use of the total-response vector is contrasted with several approximations. In this figure there are also several points plotted which were obtained to assess the use of Fisher's discriminant statistic classification procedure.

It is true that the number of items employed in this study is quite small, and therefore it is possible that not much difference in risk can be demonstrated by the α, β curves either for different number of items or for different approximations using the same number of items. However, the amount of work is so formidable even for four to six items that studies employing a larger number of items require more resources and a much larger staff than the usual investigator and an assistant or two. What is surprising is that, for the small number of items employed, one can detect differences in risks and thus gain a little feeling for the added information made possible by an increase in number of items (Figs. 1 and 2) and the information lost in

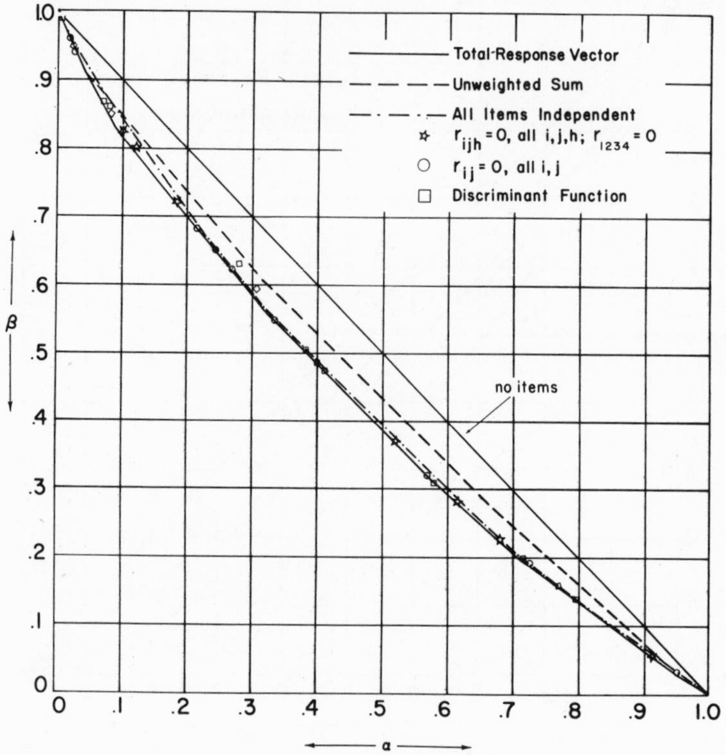

FIG. 3. The α, β Risk Curves for Four Items

using an approximation for the total-response vector (Fig. 3). In addition, it becomes possible to make decisions in test design—namely, how many items and what types should be used in a "test." From our study, for example, it is possible to state that the minimax risk in using the sum of the responses to the six items is equivalent for all practical purposes to the use of the total-response vector for three items (Items 2, 3, 4). To attain the ability to make statements of this type is essentially the major objective for this kind of study.

12

Statistical Decision Theory Approach to Item Selection for Dichotomous Test and Criterion Variables

HOWARD RAIFFA, Harvard University

1. Introduction

A basic problem in test construction is the suitable selection of k out of N test items, scores on the k items to be used in predicting an unknown criterion value for the individual taking the test. Elfving has considered this problem in the framework of classical multivariate statistical analysis, and in this volume has proposed a number of useful tools when the underlying probability model has a given parametric form. In this chapter a nonparametric model is formulated in the framework of statistical decision theory, when both the test variables and the criterion variable are dichotomous. In this case, the unknown criterion variable can be regarded as a classificatory variable whose value specifies the two possible classes to which an individual can belong.

More generally, the item variables of the problem represent a set of potentially observable variables, whose values, for a given individual, are to be used in reaching a decision about the associated variable, which is unobservable, at least at the time the decision is to be made. Since taking any set of observations can be regarded as performing an experiment, the selection of a particular set of variables for observation defines the experiment to be performed, and the problem of item selection becomes a problem in the comparison of experiments.

When the test variables are all dichotomous, the number of possible response patterns for a selected set of k items is 2^k, so that the number of possible outcomes for any given experiment is finite. The two values of the classificatory variable can be considered to represent two possible states of nature, while the two possible classifications of the individual represent two possible terminal actions. In the language of statistical decision theory, the classification problem itself is thus a two-state-of-nature, two-terminal-action problem, with finite sample space.

For the sake of completeness, the basic concepts of statistical decision theory that are useful in evaluating possible classification procedures for a given experiment, and in making comparisons among experiments, are given in Section 2. In Sections 3 and 4, the problem of item selection is considered in this framework, first when the potential number of item predictors is small, and second when it is desired to select a small number of predictors from a large battery of potential test items.

Throughout the discussion, it is helpful to keep in mind two hypothetical problem areas for application: (1) medical diagnostics and (2) prediction of ultimate performance in pilot training. In the case of medical diagnostics we are often confronted with relatively few potential item predictors, and these predictors vary in cost or even in the risk of administration (e.g., an X-ray, a guinea-pig test, an exploratory operation). The formal treatment recognizes that in practice sequential plans are often used, and therefore we have to depart from the classical notion of an optimal selection of k items from N to allow for the case where the choice of the next item to be selected at a given stage can depend on the responses to the items previously chosen. That is, not all individuals will be given the same items, and, generalizing, we can even allow the number of item predictors to vary from individual to individual. Formally, this problem reduces to a problem in the sequential design of experiments and, as is the case in sequential designs, optimal stopping rules will naturally involve an analysis of the marginal cost of adding a specific item versus the marginal decrease in risk of making wrong terminal predictions attributable to the addition of this item. For the case where the number N of potential item predictors is small (less than 7, say) we shall give an algorithm for the solution of this problem, which is optimal in senses to be prescribed below.

For the case where the number N of potential predictors is large—as is the case in predicting pilot performance by pretraining indices—but the number of predictors to be chosen is small, we can at least conceptually provide an algorithm for an "optimal" solution that is identical to the case where N is small. Computationally, however, the suggested optimal procedures may be impractical—perhaps, even for large-scale machines—and "reasonable" procedures, which are recognized to be non-optimal, are suggested. In particular, we shall define "forward Bayes sequential procedure of order s" ($s = 1, 2, 3, \cdots$), which essentially looks ahead s steps and chooses at each stage the next best s items, or, more generally, $r < s$ best items, conditional upon the information available at that stage.

More formally, this problem can be viewed as a dynamic programming problem with a horizon of s steps. As selections of items are made, the analysis is repeated, keeping a floating fixed horizon ahead of us. The discussions of the choice of horizon length and the somewhat special analysis necessary at the termination of sampling are at best exploratory in nature; they are not in any way meant to provide definitive answers to this complex problem.

A penalty e_s is introduced that gives the cost of the effort of analyzing an order s procedure; this "effort penalty" can be roughly approximated prior to any detailed analysis. Naturally, $e_1 < e_2 < e_3 < \cdots$. Reasonable over-all procedures must take into account (1) losses due to wrong terminal decisions, (2) costs of observing items, and (3) effort of analyzing a procedure. The quantity e_s is (among other things) a function of the total number of potential item predictors; hence preliminary reductions in the number of item predictors enable us to utilize higher-order analyses for the remaining contenders. To cope with the case in which sequential selection of items is not practical, we define, in an analogous manner, a "forward Bayes non-sequential procedure of order s." In the completely sequential case we suggest making a preliminary reduction in the number of item predictors by means of a first-order non-sequential procedure prior to the sequential analysis.

I wish to express my sincerest gratitude to Rosedith Sitgreaves who contributed greatly by helping to shape my rough notes into an earlier version of this chapter.

2. Basic Concepts

2.1 Analysis of a Single Experiment. Let $\mathscr{E}$ be an experiment with possible outcomes $x_1, x_2, \cdots, x_n$, the totality of which comprise the sample space $\mathscr{S}$. Let ω_1 and ω_2 be two states of nature (e.g., two possible classificatory states), and let $P_i(x_j)$ be the probability of observing x_j when ω_i is true, $i = 1, 2; j = 1, 2, \cdots, n$. Let A_1 and A_2 be the two possible terminal actions, and assume that A_i is ideally wanted when ω_i is true (e.g., A_i might be the action that classifies a person as coming from the population identified with ω_i), for $i = 1, 2$. A decision rule $\boldsymbol{\delta} = (\delta_1, \delta_2)$ is a pair of functions on $\mathscr{S}$ to $[0, 1]$ with the properties that (1) $0 \leqq \delta_i(x_j) \leqq 1$ for all i, j; (2) $\delta_1(x_j) + \delta_2(x_j) = 1$ for all j. The number $\delta_i(x_j)$ is interpreted as the probability of adopting A_i if x_j is observed.

For symmetry purposes we present the pair δ_1 and δ_2, although either function would suffice in defining $\boldsymbol{\delta}$. Let $\mathscr{D}$ be the set of all possible functions $\boldsymbol{\delta}$. If $\delta_i(x_j) = 1, 0$ for all j, then $\boldsymbol{\delta}$ is said to be non-randomized. Let D be the set of all non-randomized rules $\boldsymbol{\delta}$. For any rule $\boldsymbol{\delta}$ we have

$$\alpha_1(\boldsymbol{\delta}) = \sum_j P_1(x_j)\delta_2(x_j) ,$$

$$\alpha_2(\boldsymbol{\delta}) = \sum_j P_2(x_j)\delta_1(x_j) ,$$

which represent the probabilities of misclassifications when both ω_1 and ω_2 are true and $\boldsymbol{\delta}$ is employed. Let

$$R = \{[\alpha_1(\boldsymbol{\delta}), \alpha_2(\boldsymbol{\delta})] : \boldsymbol{\delta} \in \mathscr{D}\} ; \tag{2.1}$$

i.e., R consists of all possible (α_1, α_2) appraisals. The set R, viewed as a set in 2-space, is a convex body (i.e., convex, closed, and bounded) with a finite set of extreme points. These extreme points are all realizable with the use of non-randomized rules, and hence we can conclude that R is the convex hull of the finite set

$$\{[\alpha_1(\boldsymbol{\delta}), \alpha_2(\boldsymbol{\delta})] : \boldsymbol{\delta} \in D\} ; \tag{2.2}$$

i.e., R is the minimal convex body containing the above set.

Let $\boldsymbol{\delta}^{(1)} \sim \boldsymbol{\delta}^{(2)}$ whenever $\alpha_i(\boldsymbol{\delta}^{(1)}) = \alpha_i(\boldsymbol{\delta}^{(2)}), i = 1, 2$. Let $\boldsymbol{\delta}^{(1)} \gtrsim \boldsymbol{\delta}^{(2)}$ whenever $\alpha_i(\boldsymbol{\delta}^{(1)}) \leqq \alpha_i(\boldsymbol{\delta}^{(2)}), i = 1, 2$. And, finally, let $\boldsymbol{\delta}^{(1)} \succ \boldsymbol{\delta}^{(2)}$ whenever $\boldsymbol{\delta}^{(1)} \gtrsim \boldsymbol{\delta}^{(2)}$ and not $\boldsymbol{\delta}^{(1)} \sim \boldsymbol{\delta}^{(2)}$, i.e., whenever $\alpha_i(\boldsymbol{\delta}^{(1)}) \leqq \alpha_i(\boldsymbol{\delta}^{(2)})$ and $\sum_{i=1}^{2} \alpha_i(\boldsymbol{\delta}^{(1)}) < \sum_{i=1}^{2} \alpha_i(\boldsymbol{\delta}^{(2)})$. The symbols $\sim, \gtrsim, \succ$ are read, respectively, as "is indifferent to," "is preferred or indifferent to," "is preferred to." A decision rule $\boldsymbol{\delta}^{(0)}$ is said to be *admissible* if for no $\boldsymbol{\delta} \in \mathscr{D}$ we have $\boldsymbol{\delta} \succ \boldsymbol{\delta}^{(0)}$. If $\boldsymbol{\delta}^{(0)}$ is admissible, the point

$$[\alpha_1(\boldsymbol{\delta}^{(0)}), \alpha_2(\boldsymbol{\delta}^{(0)})] \qquad \text{[abbreviated by } \boldsymbol{\alpha}(\boldsymbol{\delta}^{(0)})]$$

is said to be an admissible point of R. All the admissible points of R lie on the southwest boundary of R; in Figure 1 these points lie on the broken line $(0, 1) \to a \to b \to c \to d \to (1, 0)$.

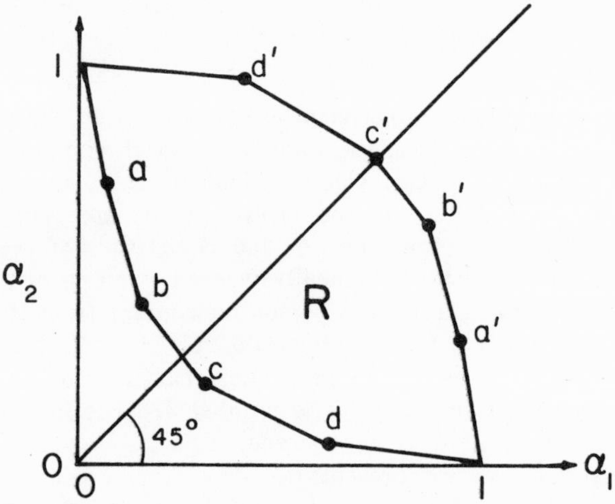

FIG. 1

Naturally one should confine oneself to admissible rules, and thus our attention turns to the characterization of the extreme points of R that are admissible. The decision rule $\boldsymbol{\delta}$ is said to be a likelihood-ratio rule (l.r.r.) of index k, provided that $\delta_2(x_i) = 1$ whenever $P_2(x_i) / P_1(x_i) > k$ and $\delta_2(x_i) = 0$ whenever $P_2(x_i)/P_1(x_i) < k$. It is well known that the l.r.r.'s with indices $0 < k < \infty$ yield admissible rules, and that conversely each admissible rule is such an l.r.r. If for any rule $\boldsymbol{\delta} = (\delta_1, \delta_2)$ we let $\boldsymbol{\delta}^t = (\delta_1^t, \delta_2^t)$ be the rule for which $\delta_1^t = \delta_2$ and $\delta_2^t = \delta_1$, then $\alpha_i(\boldsymbol{\delta}^t) = 1 - \alpha_i(\boldsymbol{\delta})$, for $i = 1, 2$, from which we can conclude that R is symmetric about the point $(\frac{1}{2}, \frac{1}{2})$; and in Figure 1 if $\boldsymbol{\alpha}(\boldsymbol{\delta})$ is the point $a[b, c, d]$, then $\boldsymbol{\alpha}(\boldsymbol{\delta}^t)$ is the point $a'[b', c', d']$.

In order to specify which decision rule should be adopted from the admissible class, it is customary to resort to various imposed criteria. We shall discuss three of these criteria.

1. *Neyman-Pearson Criterion*. Select a number α_1^*. Choose $\boldsymbol{\delta}^{(0)} \in \mathscr{D}$, which is a minimizer of $\alpha_2(\boldsymbol{\delta})$ subject to $\alpha_1(\boldsymbol{\delta}) \leqq \alpha_1^*$.

Criteria 2 and 3 refer to a loss structure, viz.,

$$\begin{array}{c} \\ \omega_1 \\ \omega_2 \end{array} \begin{array}{cc} A_1 & A_2 \\ \left[\begin{array}{c} 0 \\ a_2 \end{array}\right. & \left.\begin{array}{c} a_1 \\ 0 \end{array}\right] \end{array},$$

where a_i is the loss involved in misclassifying an ω_i, $i = 1, 2$.

2. *Minimax Criterion.* The rule $\boldsymbol{\delta}^{(0)}$ is said to be minimax, provided that it is a minimizer of $\max\,[a_1\alpha_1(\boldsymbol{\delta}), a_2\alpha_2(\boldsymbol{\delta})]$, for all $\boldsymbol{\delta} \in \mathscr{D}$. The number $a_i\alpha_i(\boldsymbol{\delta})$ is said to be the risk with $\boldsymbol{\delta}$ when ω_i is true. It is easily seen that the minimax rule is an admissible rule that equalizes the risks; the converse is also valid.

3. *Bayes Criterion.* Assume an *a priori* probability distribution for the states ω_1 and ω_2. Let $\Pr\{\omega_1\} = \Pi$, $\Pr\{\omega_2\} = 1 - \Pi$. The rule $\boldsymbol{\delta}_\Pi$ is said to be Bayes against the *a priori* distribution $\Pr\{\omega_1\} = \Pi$ (or simply Bayes against Π) if

$$\Pi a_1\alpha_1(\boldsymbol{\delta}_\Pi) + (1 - \Pi)a_2\alpha_2(\boldsymbol{\delta}_\Pi) \leqq \Pi a_1\alpha_1(\boldsymbol{\delta}) + (1 - \Pi)a_2\alpha_2(\boldsymbol{\delta}) ,$$

all $\boldsymbol{\delta} \in \mathscr{D}$. For any $\boldsymbol{\delta}$ let

$$r(\Pi, \boldsymbol{\delta}) \equiv \Pi a_1\alpha_1(\boldsymbol{\delta}) + (1 - \Pi)a_2\alpha_2(\boldsymbol{\delta}) .$$

The quantity $r(\Pi, \boldsymbol{\delta})$ is called the *expected risk* for the decision rule $\boldsymbol{\delta}$ against the *a priori* distribution $\Pr\{\omega_1\} = \Pi$. The rule $\boldsymbol{\delta}_\Pi$ is a minimizer of $r(\Pi, \boldsymbol{\delta})$ for $\boldsymbol{\delta} \in \mathscr{D}$, and $\rho(\Pi) = r(\Pi, \boldsymbol{\delta}_\Pi)$ is called the *Bayes risk* against Π. Let

$$R(\Pi, \boldsymbol{\delta}) \equiv r(\Pi, \boldsymbol{\delta}) - r(\Pi, \boldsymbol{\delta}_\Pi)$$

be called the Bayes *regret* for the decision rule $\boldsymbol{\delta}$ against Π.

For any Π it is easily seen that $\boldsymbol{\delta}_\Pi$ is the l.r.r. with index $k = a_1\Pi / a_2(1 - \Pi)$, and conversely the l.r.r. with index k is Bayes against Π where $\Pi = (a_2k) / (a_1 + a_2k)$.

If we plot $\rho(\Pi) = r(\Pi, \boldsymbol{\delta}_\Pi)$ as a function of Π, we get a concave polygonal curve similar to the one shown in Figure 2. It is instructive to note how Figure 2 can be generated from a modification of Figure 1. The procedure goes as follows:

Let

$$R^* = \{(a_1\alpha_1, a_2\alpha_2) : (\alpha_1, \alpha_2) \in R\} ;$$

note that R^* looks the same as R, provided that we change the horizontal scale by sending $(1, 0)$ into $(a_1, 0)$ and change the vertical scale by sending $(0, 1)$ into $(0, a_2)$. Now the Bayes risk against Π is the value

$$\min_{(a_1\alpha_1, a_2\alpha_2) \in R^*} [\Pi a_1\alpha_1 + (1 - \Pi)a_2\alpha_2] .$$

If we consider the family of lines

$$\Pi a_1\alpha_1 + (1 - \Pi)a_2\alpha_2 = c$$

for $0 < c < \infty$, and if we increase c from 0 until the point c^* where the line just touches R^* (i.e., where it is a line of support for R^*), then $c^* = \rho(\Pi)$ and the line of support will just touch R^* at the point $[a_1\alpha_1(\boldsymbol{\delta}_\Pi), a_2\alpha_2(\boldsymbol{\delta}_\Pi)]$.

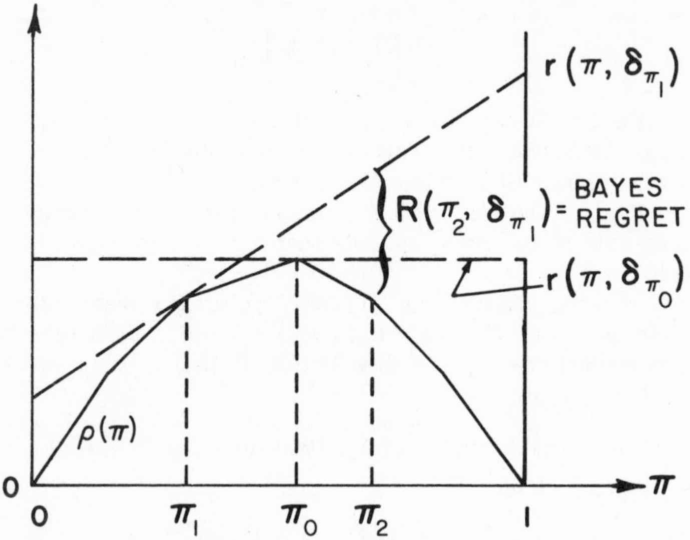

FIG. 2

Furthermore, the value $\rho(\Pi)$ can be read from the figure, for this line of support intersects the line $a_1\alpha_1 = a_2\alpha_2$ at the point $[\rho(\Pi), \rho(\Pi)]$. Now the curve $\rho(\Pi)$ is generated by considering the lines of support of R^* and their intersection with the line $a_1\alpha_1 = a_2\alpha_2$ as the parameters $(\Pi, 1 - \Pi)$ of the supporting lines change from $(0, 1)$ to $(1, 0)$.

At this point I feel that it is necessary to comment further on the role of *a priori* probabilities. Let us first divide our difficulties by assuming the context of an extreme case. Case 1: Suppose in a large population of individuals, a proportion π belongs to state ω_1 and $1 - \pi$ to state ω_2. If π were known with certainty, and if a subject were randomly chosen from this population, almost all statisticians, I believe, would assign a prior probability of π to ω_1 and fold in the sample experimental evidence via the Bayes theorem to generate posterior probabilities. In Case 2 let π be unknown and an individual be selected at random from the population; in Case 3 let π be unknown and an individual be selected by some mysterious unknown process.

One school of thought contends that in Case 2 it is meaningful to talk about the *a priori* probability of the subject's belonging to ω_1, say, even though this probability were unknown; but it holds that in Case 3 it is not even meaningful to talk about the probability of ω_1, since this concept has no operational meaning. A second school of thought—the subjectivist school whose point of view is admirably expressed by L. J. Savage [1]—holds that it is indeed meaningful to talk about the *a priori* probability ω_1 in all cases (2 and 3 included!), and that in a certain sense it is meaningless to say that this probability is unknown. The probability assignment made to ω_1 is a *subjective* measurement made by the decision-maker, and it reflects prior convictions about which state he thinks prevails as evinced in his preferences for alternatives. More precisely, his assignment of π_1 to ω_1 means operationally that the decision-maker would be indifferent between these two options:

Option 1: Receive reward R if the subject belongs to ω_1, and nothing otherwise.

Option 2: Receive reward R with an "objective" probability of π_1, and nothing otherwise—where this "objective" probability is given operational meaning by means of a drawing from a concocted urn, by means of random-number tables, or by means of a "fair" spinner (or a host of other alternatives).

The subjectivist school holds that not only can *a priori* assignments be made but that they must be made as a basis for "rational" action. The above statement grossly oversimplifies the subjectivist viewpoint, but possibly it will suffice to establish the alternative settings for the ensuing discussions.

Let us continue with comments on Case 2. That is, there is an "objective" π—albeit unknown.

If the assignment $\Pr(\omega_1) = \Pi_1$, say, is made and the rule $\boldsymbol{\delta}_{\Pi_1}$ is adopted, the expected risk against Π is $r(\Pi, \boldsymbol{\delta}_{\Pi_1})$, which is linear in Π (see Figure 2). In Figure 2 the Bayes regret in using $\boldsymbol{\delta}_{\Pi_1}$ against Π_2 is depicted. Incidentally, the locus $\{[\Pi, \rho(\Pi)] : 0 \leqq \Pi \leqq 1\}$ is merely the infimum of all lines $\{[\Pi, r(\Pi, \boldsymbol{\delta})] : 0 \leqq \Pi \leqq 1\}$ for all $\boldsymbol{\delta} \in \mathscr{D}$.

A diagram such as the one given in Figure 2 illustrates some of the dangers involved, on the one hand, and the advantages, on the other hand, of guessing at the true value of Π and using the associated Bayes rule. Technically speaking, there is another conceptually different but operationally equivalent method of analysis. Instead of letting the states be ω_1 and ω_2, we can alternatively identify the state-space as the interval $0 \leqq \pi \leqq 1$ (the true state being the true proportion of ω_1's in the population) and now a prior distribution over the state-space is a (subjectively chosen) distribution function over the interval $[0, 1]$. It is not difficult to show that the only pertinent feature of such a prior distribution is its mean. We duly represent this as π_1 and the above discussion carries over intact.

If $\boldsymbol{\delta}^{(0)}$ is the minimax rule, i.e., $a_1\alpha_1(\boldsymbol{\delta}^{(0)}) = a_2\alpha_2(\boldsymbol{\delta}^{(0)})$, then from Figure 2 it is clear that $\boldsymbol{\delta}^{(0)}$ is Bayes against Π_0, the least favorable *a priori* distribution, in the sense that the Bayes risk is a maximum for this value of Π. Note that $\boldsymbol{\delta}^{(0)}$ is also a minimizer over $\mathscr{D}$ of the maximum Bayes regret, i.e., for all δ

$$\max_{\Pi} R(\Pi, \boldsymbol{\delta}^{(0)}) \leqq \max_{\Pi} R(\Pi, \delta) .$$

If one's subjective *a priori* distribution is Π_1 and one wishes to exploit this *a priori* information, subject to the constraint that the maximum risk does not exceed some predetermined value (M', say), then it is possible to proceed as follows: (1) select $\boldsymbol{\delta}_{\Pi_1}$ if $\alpha_i(\boldsymbol{\delta}_{\Pi_1}) \leqq M'$, $i = 1, 2$; (2) if $\boldsymbol{\delta}_{\Pi_1}$ does not satisfy the requirement that $\alpha_i(\boldsymbol{\delta}_{\Pi_1}) \leqq M'$, $i = 1, 2$, then choose between the l.r.r.'s $\boldsymbol{\delta}'$ and $\boldsymbol{\delta}''$, say where $\alpha_1(\boldsymbol{\delta}') = M'$, $\alpha_2(\boldsymbol{\delta}'') = M'$, according to the smaller of the values $r(\Pi_1, \boldsymbol{\delta}')$ and $r(\Pi_1, \boldsymbol{\delta}'')$. The above procedure is a special case of one suggested by Hodges and Lehman [2], which they call a "restricted Bayes solution."

In many circumstances it may be known that the probability Π of the state ω_1 is in an interval from Π_0 to Π_1, say. For example, one might know that if a subject is picked at random from a population, the probability that he belongs to ω_1 is Π_1. However, if a self-selection principle is operating, one might still think it is meaningful to consider the conditional probability that the subject belongs to ω_1, *given* the self-selection principle. Consequently, one might wish to guard against Π values in the interval from 0 to Π_1 or from Π_1 to 1, according to the suspected direction of the bias caused by non-random sampling. Returning to the case where $\Pi_0 \leqq \Pi \leqq \Pi_1$, one might seek a procedure, $\boldsymbol{\delta}^{(0)}$ say, which is a minimizer of the maximum Bayes regret against Π's in the interval $[\Pi_0, \Pi_1]$, viz., for all $\boldsymbol{\delta} \in \mathscr{D}$,

$$\max_{\Pi_1 \leqq \Pi \leqq \Pi_2} R(\Pi, \boldsymbol{\delta}^{(0)}) \leqq \max_{\Pi_1 \leqq \Pi \leqq \Pi_2} R(\Pi, \boldsymbol{\delta}) .$$

To achieve this procedure one merely must choose an l.r.r., $\boldsymbol{\delta}^{(0)}$, for which $R(\Pi_1, \boldsymbol{\delta}^{(0)}) = R(\Pi_2, \boldsymbol{\delta}^{(0)})$. Note that if $\Pi_1 = 0$ and $\Pi_2 = 1$, then $R(\Pi_1, \boldsymbol{\delta}) = r(\Pi_1, \boldsymbol{\delta}) = a_2\alpha_2(\boldsymbol{\delta})$ and $R(\Pi_2, \boldsymbol{\delta}) = r(\Pi_2, \boldsymbol{\delta}) = a_1\alpha_2(\boldsymbol{\delta})$; in this case, therefore, $\boldsymbol{\delta}^{(0)}$ is minimax.

We conclude this section with a criticism of a prevalent analysis of the classification problem. A common technique is to let ω_1 refer to the state for which a misclassification is the more serious and to demand that the probability of this type of misclassification be held down to α_1^*, say. Often α_1^* is chosen without any attempt to assess the relative seriousness of both types of errors or to crystallize one's *a priori* subjective appraisal of the value Π (whether or not it can be assumed to exist in an "objective" sense). To implement this rule one chooses an l.r.r. with index $k(\alpha_1^*)$, say. Now if a_1, a_2, and Π^* were such that

$$\frac{a_1\Pi^*}{a_2(1 - \Pi^*)} = k(\alpha_1^*) ,$$

the Bayes rule would also be the l.r.r. with index $k(\alpha_1^*)$. But the above equation yields

$$\Pi^* = \left[1 + \frac{a_1}{a_2 k(\alpha_1^*)}\right]^{-1} ,$$

and hence the l.r.r. with index $k(\alpha_1^*)$ is a rule of the type $\boldsymbol{\delta}_{\Pi^*}$. Now note that Π^* depends on a_1, a_2, and α_1^*, so that in the light of above remarks on Bayes regret one should *at least* informally come to grips with the problem of assessing the values a_1, a_2 and keep in mind any *a priori* information about Π in the selection of the value α_1^*.

2.2 Comparisons Among Experiments. Let ω_1 and ω_2 be two states of nature (e.g., classificatory states); and let A_1 and A_2 be the two terminal actions, where a loss of a_i units is incurred if A_j, $j \neq i$, is adopted when ω_i is true, $i = 1, 2$, viz.,

$$\begin{array}{cc} & A_1 \quad A_2 \\ \begin{array}{c}\omega_1\\ \omega_2\end{array} & \begin{bmatrix} 0 & a_1 \\ a_2 & 0 \end{bmatrix} . \end{array}$$

Assume that one of two possible experiments, $\mathscr{E}_1$ and $\mathscr{E}_2$, can be performed; the central problem is to choose between them. We suppose

(i) the outcomes of $\mathscr{E}_1$ are $\{x_{11}, x_{12}, \cdots, x_{1n_1}\}$ and $P_i^{(1)}(x_{1j})$ is the probability of x_{1j} when ω_i is true, $i = 1, 2$, $j = 1, 2, \cdots, n_1$;

(ii) the outcomes of $\mathscr{E}_2$ are $\{x_{21}, x_{22}, \cdots, x_{2n_2}\}$ and $P_i^{(2)}(x_{2k})$ is the probability of x_{2k} when ω_i is true, $i = 1, 2$, $k = 1, 2, \cdots, n_2$.

Let R_1 and R_2 be the set of (α_1, α_2) appraisal points for $\mathscr{E}_1$ and $\mathscr{E}_2$, respectively. Omitting cost considerations for the time being, we have from the strategic point of view:

(i) $\mathscr{E}_1$ and $\mathscr{E}_2$ are equivalent, $\mathscr{E}_1 \sim \mathscr{E}_2$, if $R_1 \equiv R_2$;

(ii) $\mathscr{E}_1$ is better than or indifferent to $\mathscr{E}_2$, $\mathscr{E}_1 \succsim \mathscr{E}_2$, if $R_1 \supseteqq R_2$;

(iii) $\mathscr{E}_1$ is better than $\mathscr{E}_2$, $\mathscr{E}_1 \succ \mathscr{E}_2$, if $R_1 \supset R_2$ (proper inclusion).

(iv) $\mathscr{E}_1$ and $\mathscr{E}_2$ are incomparable, $\mathscr{E}_1$ inc. $\mathscr{E}_2$, if neither $R_1 \supseteqq R_2$ nor $R_2 \supseteqq R_1$.

From the symmetrical nature of the sets R_1 and R_2 it is easily seen that

(i) $\mathscr{E}_1 \sim \mathscr{E}_2 \Longleftrightarrow$ {set of admissible points of R_1 and R_2 coincide};

(ii) $\mathscr{E}_1 \succsim \mathscr{E}_2 \Longleftrightarrow$ {for every $\boldsymbol{\alpha}^{(2)} \in R_2$ there exists an admissible $\boldsymbol{\alpha}^{(1)} \in R_1$ such that $\alpha^{(1)} \geqq \alpha^{(2)}$}.

(iii) $\mathscr{E}_1 \succsim \mathscr{E}_2 \Longleftrightarrow$ {Bayes risk $\rho_1(\Pi)$ against Π for $\mathscr{E}_1$ is not greater than Bayes risk $\rho_2(\Pi)$ against Π for $\mathscr{E}_2$, i.e., $\rho_1(\Pi) \leqq \rho_2(\Pi)$ for all $0 \leqq \Pi \leqq 1$}.

(iv) $\mathscr{E}_1 \succ \mathscr{E}_2 \Longleftrightarrow$ {$\rho_1(\Pi) \leqq \rho_2(\Pi)$ for all $0 \leqq \Pi \leqq 1$, and there exists some Π for which the strict inequality holds}.

In the sequel we shall be concerned mainly with the case where $\mathscr{E}_1$ is incomparable to $\mathscr{E}_2$ (i.e., where there exists no uniformly best experiment). However, first we discuss an illustration that will indicate several points to be subsequently discussed; it will also serve as a source of counterexamples for some intuitively plausible but false assertions.

Illustration (a tubercular classification problem—hypothetical data). Consider the following tubercular classification problem: Let states ω_1 and ω_2 refer to "tubercular" and "not tubercular," respectively; let $\mathscr{E}$ be a basic experiment with possible outcomes {positive, negative}; let

$$\Pr\{\text{positive} \mid \omega_1\} = .95 ,$$

$$\Pr\{\text{positive} \mid \omega_2\} = .10 ,$$

and assume that repeated trials (on the same subject) are *independent*. The question naturally arises: "How many observations shall be made on each individual?" It seems natural (and it is basically correct) that the more we sample with a given individual the better our control will be over wrong terminal actions. However, we have a conflict in hand, since increased experimentation raises the cost of the diagnostic examination. To this end, let $\mathscr{E}^{(1)}, \mathscr{E}^{(2)}, \mathscr{E}^{(3)}, \cdots$ represent the experiments that involve taking $1, 2, 3, \cdots$ observations, respectively. For each such experiment we can find and plot the set of admissible $\boldsymbol{\alpha}$ appraisals and thus be in a better position to judge the merits of choosing a particular sample size.

From the principle of sufficiency, we need only to consider decision rules based on the number of positive reactions. We get the analysis shown in Table 1.

TABLE 1

No. of positive reactions x_{kj}	Probabilities $P_1^{(k)}(x_{kj})$	$P_2^{(k)}(x_{kj})$	Admissible decision rules (δ_1, δ_2)				
0	.05	.90	(0, 1)	(0, 1)	(1, 0)		
1	.95	.10	(0, 1)	(1, 0)	(1, 0)		
			$\alpha_1 = 1$	.05	0		
			$\alpha_2 = 0$	.10	1		
			$k = 2$				
0	.0025	.8100	(0, 1)	(0, 1)	(0, 1)	(1, 0)	
1	.0950	.1800	(0, 1)	(0, 1)	(1, 0)	(1, 0)	
2	.9025	.0100	(0, 1)	(1, 0)	(1, 0)	(1, 0)	
			$\alpha_1 = 1$	.0975	.0025	0	
			$\alpha_2 = 0$	.0100	.1900	1	
			$k = 3$				
0	.000125	.729000	(0, 1)	(0, 1)	(0, 1)	(0, 1)	(1, 0)
1	.007125	.243000	(0, 1)	(0, 1)	(0, 1)	(1, 0)	(1, 0)
2	.135375	.027000	(0, 1)	(0, 1)	(1, 0)	(1, 0)	(1, 0)
3	.857375	.001000	(0, 1)	(1, 0)	(1, 0)	(1, 0)	(1, 0)
			$\alpha_1 = 1$	.142625	.007250	.000125	0
			$\alpha_2 = 0$	.001000	.028000	.271000	1

The performance of these experiments, plotted on a common set of axes, is shown in Figure 3. Since we are interested in the comparisons of these experiments for small (α_1, α_2) values, we have plotted only the pertinent parts of the admissible appraisals and have selected an appropriate scale factor to enhance the readability of the diagrams.

We note the following in Figure 3:

1. As far as (α_1, α_2) performances are concerned, we conclude that $\mathscr{E}^{(3)}$ is uniformly better than $\mathscr{E}^{(2)}$, which, in turn, is uniformly better than $\mathscr{E}^{(1)}$. Of course, this remark is trivial; for if $m > n$, then $\mathscr{E}^{(m)}$ is manifestly better than $\mathscr{E}^{(n)}$, since any (α_1, α_2) appraisal obtained with a decision

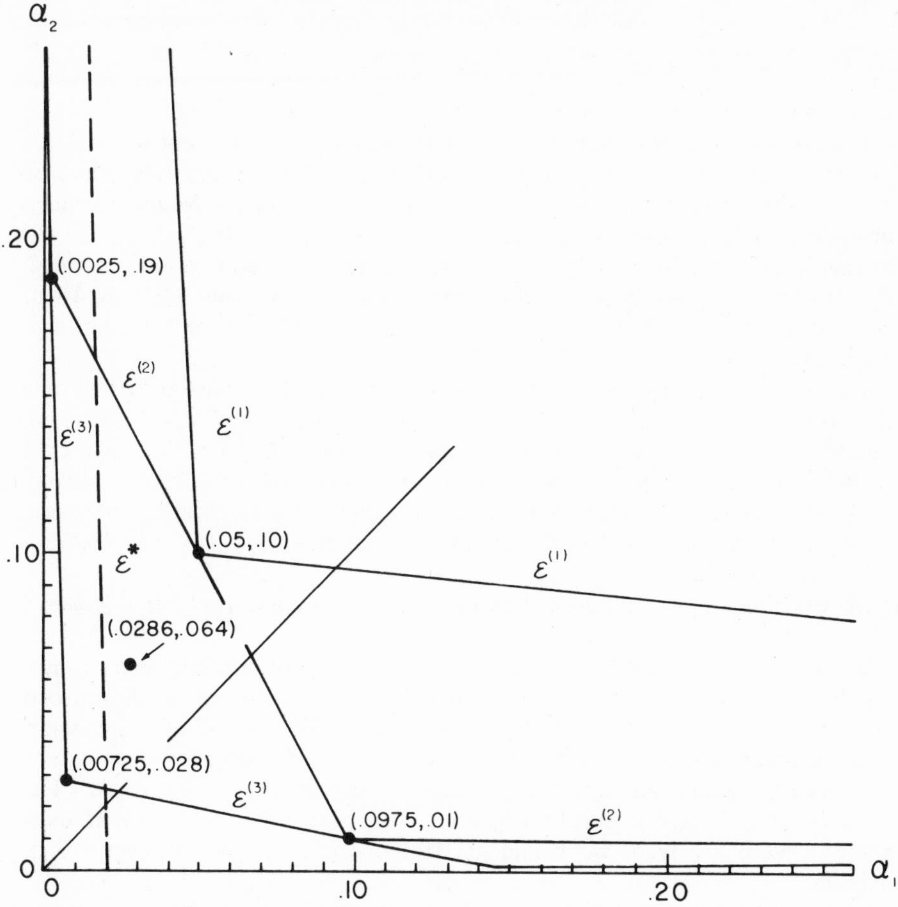

FIG. 3

rule for $\mathscr{E}^{(n)}$ can be achieved with $\mathscr{E}^{(m)}$ by using the identical rule and ignoring the last $(m - n)$ observations.

2. The set of admissible pairs for $\mathscr{E}^{(1)}$ and $\mathscr{E}^{(2)}$ have a common point $(\alpha_1, \alpha_2) = (.05, .10)$; $\mathscr{E}^{(2)}$ and $\mathscr{E}^{(3)}$ have common points at (.0025, .19) and (.0975, .01). Thus, for example, if we use a Neyman-Pearson procedure with $\alpha_1^* = .05$, then $\mathscr{E}^{(1)}$ *has as good a performance as* $\mathscr{E}^{(2)}$. We note that for Neyman-Pearson procedures the desirability of increasing the sample size from $n = 1$ to $n = 2$, say, depends on the α_1^*-level selected. Similar considerations hold for increasing the size from $n = 2$ to $n = 3$, etc.[1]

[1] Many elementary textbooks that discuss the two-state, two-decision problem for Bernoulli trials fail to mention the notion of randomized decision rules and automatically use decision procedures based on the number of positives (successes). Under these circumstances if we were to seek (under the Neyman-Pearson procedure) the rule that minimizes α_2, subject to the condition that $\alpha_1 \leqq .05$, then for $\mathscr{E}^{(1)}$ we would get

3. If we choose to use the criterion of minimizing the maximum of the probability of misclassification errors, then note that by increasing the sample size from 2 to 3 we obtain a "greater return" than the one achieved with the increase from $n = 1$ to $n = 2$.

4. Cohen [3] has pointed out that in certain contexts it might be desirable to randomize between experiments of different sample sizes. To illustrate what this means, let us consider the following example: A Neyman-Pearson procedure is to be used with significance level $\alpha_1^* = .028625$ (i.e., "on the average," slightly less than 29 tuberculars per 1000 can be misclassified). Because of cost considerations the existing procedure uses $\mathscr{E}^{(2)}$, and thus gets an α_2 of .141. Note that $(\alpha_1, \alpha_2) = (.028625, .141)$ lies on the admissible diagram for $\mathscr{E}^{(2)}$.

An alternative proposal is as follows: for each subject, toss a "true" coin; if a head appears, perform $\mathscr{E}^{(1)}$ (i.e., take one trial) and use a procedure yielding $(\alpha_1, \alpha_2) = (.05, .10)$; if a tail appears, perform $\mathscr{E}^{(3)}$ (i.e., take three trials) and use a procedure yielding $(\alpha_1, \alpha_2) = (.007250, .028)$. This randomized experimental procedure has an (α_1, α_2) appraisal of $(.028625, .064)$, since

(i) the probability of misclassifying a tubercular $= \frac{1}{2}(.05) + \frac{1}{2}(.007250) = .028625$; and

(ii) the probability of misclassifying a non-tubercular $= \frac{1}{2}(.10) + \frac{1}{2}(.028) = .064$.

Thus the randomized experimental procedure maintains the same control on the tuberculars as the original experiment but cuts down on the misclassification of non-tuberculars from 141 to 64 per 1000, on the average, which is a considerable gain. Furthermore, the randomized procedure accomplishes this saving without increasing the "expected" cost of experimentation. That is, it involves 1 or 3 observations, each with probability $\frac{1}{2}$; hence, if many subjects were involved, we would get two observations per subject, on the average.

One might object that these results are as striking as they are because the significance level $\alpha_1^* = .028625$ was carefully chosen to exploit the point to be made. Of course, this is so, but this is exactly what one *should* do in the choice of a significance level—provided the chosen level still protects one adequately.

Let us suppose for the time being that the above tuberculosis diagnostic test is of a bacteriological type. Furthermore, let us also suppose that it is possible to use a guinea-pig test for tuberculosis detection, and that for this procedure we have

$$\Pr\{\text{positive} \mid \omega_1\} = .98\ ,$$

$$\Pr\{\text{positive} \mid \omega_2\} = 0\ ,$$

(.05, .10) and for $\mathscr{E}^{(2)}$ we would be forced to take (.0025, .19). Thus we would have the anomalous situation that for significance level .05 if we *increased* the sample size from $n = 1$ to $n = 2$, we would be forced to *increase* the probability of the type II error from .10 to .19.

i.e., a positive reaction definitely means the subject is tubercular and 2 per 100 tuberculars register negative reactions, on the average. Let us denote this experimental procedure by $\mathscr{E}^*$. We analyze $\mathscr{E}^*$ as follows:

Reactions for $\mathscr{E}^*$	Probabilities		Admissible decision rules (δ_1, δ_2)	
	$P_1^*(x_j^*)$	$P_2^*(x_j^*)$		
0	.02	1	(0, 1)	(1, 0)
1	.98	0	(1, 0)	(1, 0)
			$\alpha_1 = .02$	0
			$\alpha_2 = 0$	1

The set of admissible (α_1, α_2) pairs is also shown in Figure 3.

5. Continuing our remarks on Figure 3, we note that $\mathscr{E}^*$ is uniformly better than $\mathscr{E}^{(1)}$, but it is not uniformly better than $\mathscr{E}^{(2)}$ or $\mathscr{E}^{(3)}$; and, conversely, neither $\mathscr{E}^{(2)}$ nor $\mathscr{E}^{(3)}$ is uniformly better than $\mathscr{E}^*$. Indeed, no $\mathscr{E}^{(n)}$, regardless of how large n is, can achieve $(\alpha_1, \alpha_2) = (.02, 0)$, so that $\mathscr{E}^{(n)}$ is not uniformly better than $\mathscr{E}^*$. To be specific, let us assume that $\mathscr{E}^*$ and $\mathscr{E}^{(3)}$ have identical costs and are the subjects of a paired comparison. Since neither of these experiments is uniformly better than the other, preferences must be made, subject to a specific criterion. Manifestly $\mathscr{E}^*$ is better than $\mathscr{E}^{(3)}$, relative to a Neyman-Pearson criterion with significance level $\alpha_1^* = .02$, say; the converse prevails, however, if $\alpha_1^* = .0025$, say; $\mathscr{E}^*$ is better than $\mathscr{E}^{(3)}$, relative to the criterion of minimizing the maximum of the errors; however, from Figure 3 it is clear than an appreciable savings can be attained in the minimax error if one *randomizes* appropriately between getting (.02, 0) with $\mathscr{E}^*$ and getting (.007250, .028) with $\mathscr{E}^{(3)}$.

Motivated by the above remarks illustrating the uses of randomization between experiments, consider the following problem: Let $\mathscr{E}_1, \mathscr{E}_2, \cdots, \mathscr{E}_m$ be m possible experiments that can be employed in a specific two-classification problem; for each experiment list the set of admissible $\boldsymbol{\alpha}$ appraisal points achievable by non-randomized rules, and for each such point append a third component with indicates the cost of achieving that point (i.e., the cost of the experiment that generates this point). Let the totality of such points (for m experiments) be

$$(\alpha_1^{(1)}, \alpha_2^{(1)}, c^{(1)}), (\alpha_1^{(2)}, \alpha_2^{(2)}, c^{(2)}), \cdots, (\alpha_1^{(m)}, \alpha_2^{(m)}, c^{(m)}),$$

where, for example, the point $(\alpha_1^{(i)}, \alpha_2^{(i)}, c^{(i)})$ would mean that $(\alpha_1^{(i)}, \alpha_2^{(i)})$ is an admissible point of an experiment whose cost is $c^{(i)}$. The most general decision rule that can be employed is identified with an m-tuple $(p_1, p_2, \cdots, p_m)$, where $\sum_{i=1}^m p_i = 1, p_i \geqq 0, i = 1, 2, \cdots, m$, with the interpretation that the appropriate decision rule based on the experiment yielding $(\alpha_1^{(i)}, \alpha_2^{(i)}, c^{(i)})$ will be used with probability p_i. The Neyman-Pearson criterion leads to the following formulations.

Problem (a). Subject to the conditions

(i) $$p_i \geqq 0\,, \qquad i = 1, 2, \cdots, m\,,$$

(ii) $$\sum_{i=1}^{m} p_i = 1\,,$$

(iii) $$\sum_{i=1}^{m} p_i \alpha_1^{(i)} \leqq \alpha_1^*\,, \qquad \text{(preassigned)}$$

(iv) $$\sum_{i=1}^{m} p_i c^{(i)} \leqq c^*\,, \qquad \text{(preassigned)}$$

minimize

$$\sum_{i=1}^{m} p_i \alpha_2^{(i)}\,.$$

Problem (b). Subject to the conditions

(i) $$p_i \geqq 0\,, \qquad i = 1, 2, \cdots, m\,,$$

(ii) $$\sum_{i=1}^{m} p_i = 1\,,$$

(iii) $$\sum_{i=1}^{m} p_i \alpha_1^{(i)} \leqq \alpha_1^*\,, \qquad \text{(preassigned)}$$

(iv) $$\sum_{i=1}^{m} p_i \alpha_2^{(i)} \leqq \alpha_2^*\,, \qquad \text{(preassigned)}$$

minimize

$$\sum_{i=1}^{m} p_i c^{(i)}\,.$$

Problems (a) and (b) are recognized as linear-programming problems (i.e., the minimization of a linear form, subject to linear inequalities), and known computational techniques can be utilized in any specific case—provided the number m is not too unwieldly.

The minimax criterion leads to the following formulation: Subject to the conditions

(i) $$p_i \geqq 0\,, \qquad i = 1, 2, \cdots, m\,,$$

(ii) $$\sum_{i=1}^{m} p_i = 1\,,$$

(iii) $$\sum_{i=1}^{m} p_i c^{(i)} \leqq c^*$$

minimize

$$\max\left[\sum_{i=1}^{m} p_i \alpha_1^{(i)}, \sum_{i=1}^{m} p_i \alpha_2^{(i)}\right].$$

The above problem, while not in the immediate canonical form of a linear-programming problem, can be easily reduced to the appropriate form.

The Bayes criterion leads to the following formulation: Subject to the conditions

(i) $$p_i \geqq 0\,, \qquad i = 1, 2, \cdots, m\,,$$

(ii) $$\sum_{i=1}^{m} p_i = 1\,,$$

minimize

$$\Pi a_1\left[\sum_{i=1}^{m} p_i \alpha_1^{(i)}\right] + (1 - \Pi)a_2\left[\sum_{i=1}^{m} p_i \alpha_2^{(i)}\right] + \sum_{i=1}^{m} p_i c^{(i)}\,.$$

But since the above expression equals

$$\sum_{i=1}^{m} \{\Pi a_1 \alpha_1^{(i)} + (1 - \Pi)a_2 \alpha_2^{(i)} + c^{(i)}\}\, p_i\,,$$

the Bayes rule chooses the experiment and the appropriate decision rule yielding $(\alpha_1^{(i_0)}, \alpha_2^{(i_0)}; c^{(i_0)})$, for which

$$\Pi a_1 \alpha_1^{(i_0)} + (1 - \Pi)a_2 \alpha_2^{(i_0)} + c^{(i_0)} \leqq \Pi a_1 \alpha_1^{(i)} + (1 - \Pi)a_2 \alpha_2^{(i)} + c^{(i)}\,,$$

all $i = 1, 2, \cdots, m$.

To simplify a bit further we can proceed as follows: for experiment $\mathscr{E}_i$ associate the index $\rho_i(\Pi) + c_i$, where $\rho_i(\Pi)$ is the Bayes risk against the *a priori* distribution Π, and c_i is the cost of using $\mathscr{E}_i, i = 1, 2, \cdots, m$. Choose the experiment and associated Bayes rule that is a minimizer of this index. Recall that the Bayes decision rule against Π is an l.r.r. with index. $\Pi a_1 / (1 - \Pi)a_2$. Observe that the Bayes criterion, in contrast to the Neyman-Pearson and the minimax criteria, never requires randomization of either experiments or terminal actions.

3. Case Where Potential Number of Item Predictors Is Small

3.1 Equal Item Costs. In analyzing the case where the potential number of item predictors is small and item costs are equal, we shall limit ourselves to the case of three predictors, since this number illustrates the full complexity of the problem without involving us in too much detail.

Let M individuals be chosen at random from a population of individuals; we assume that M is large—of the order of 10,000, say. Also, we assume that for each of these individuals, the value of the classificatory variable is known. That is, we assume that we know whether a selected individual belongs to the category ω_1 or to the category ω_2 (where ω_1 may be the individual's successful completion of a given test, say, or having a given illness, whereas ω_2 is his unsuccessful completion of the task or his not having the illness). In addition, we have responses on three test items for the selected individuals. These dichotomous responses are of the (0, 1) variety, so that a set of responses for a given item again dichotomizes the sample of individuals.

We summarize a typical set of such data in Table 2. Thus we see that individual i is in the zero category of items 1 and 2 and in the one category

TABLE 2

Individual	Responses to Item 1	Item 2	Item 3	Classification State
1	1	1	0	ω_1
2	0	1	1	ω_2
.	.	.	.	.
.	.	.	.	.
.	.	.	.	.
i	0	0	1	ω_2
.	.	.	.	.
.	.	.	.	.
.	.	.	.	.
M	1	0	0	ω_1

of item 3; we know also that he did not successfully complete the given task.

These data can now be used in a consideration of our two basic problems: namely, the problem of predicting, on the basis of item responses, whether an individual not in the original sample will belong to ω_1 or ω_2; and the problem of determining which two items to use for a given individual if cost considerations are such that not all three items can be administered.

In connection with the second problem, let us consider the possible experiments we can perform:

$\mathscr{E}_1$: Use items 1 and 2.
$\mathscr{E}_2$: Use items 1 and 3.
$\mathscr{E}_3$: Use items 2 and 3.
$\mathscr{E}_4$: {Use item 1 and if the resulting category is $\binom{1}{0}$ use item $\binom{2}{3}$}.
$\mathscr{E}_5$: {Use item 1 and if the resulting category is $\binom{1}{0}$ use item $\binom{3}{2}$}.
. . .
. . .
. . .
$\mathscr{E}_9$: {Use item 3 and if the resulting category is $\binom{1}{0}$ use item $\binom{2}{1}$}.

Experiments $\mathscr{E}_4$ to $\mathscr{E}_9$ are sequential in nature and may or may not be feasible in a given context.

In order to determine the relative efficacies of these experiments we proceed as follows: Let N_1 be the number of the M sampled individuals in classification ω_1; let N_2 be the number of the M sampled individuals in classification ω_2; assume $N_1 + N_2 = M$. By the symbol $N_i(.\,, 0, 1)$, say, we shall mean the number of sample individuals in classification ω_i who are in categories 0 and 1 for items 2 and 3, respectively (no restriction on item 1). Such expressions as $N_1(1, ., .)$, $N_2(0, 1, .)$, $N_1(0, 0, 0)$, etc., are defined in a similar manner. Now let us consider the experiment $\mathscr{E}_1$, say, where we take as the probability assignment for $(0, 1, .)$ under ω_2, say, the number $N_2(0, 1, .)/N_2$.

Sample space of $\mathscr{E}_1$	$\hat{P}_{\omega_1}$	$\hat{P}_{\omega_2}$
(1, 1, .)	$N_1(1, 1, .)/N_1$	$N_2(1, 1, .)/N_2$
(1, 0, .)	$N_1(1, 0, .)/N_1$	$N_2(1, 0, .)/N_2$
(0, 1, .)	$N_1(0, 1, .)/N_1$	$N_2(0, 1, .)/N_2$
(0, 0, .)	$N_1(0, 0, .)/N_1$	$N_2(0, 0, .)/N_2$

We now consider the prediction problem in terms of the observed values of $\hat{P}_{\omega_1}$ and $\hat{P}_{\omega_2}$, and determine the set of (α_1, α_2) pairs associated with the admissible non-randomized decision rules for $\mathscr{E}_1$. A possible set of such pairs is shown in Figure 4 in the points designated as 1. The entire set of admissible (α_1, α_2) pairs for $\mathscr{E}_1$ can be obtained from these points by connecting appropriate pairs.

This procedure is now repeated for $\mathscr{E}_2$ and $\mathscr{E}_3$, and possible sets of associated admissible non-randomized points are designated in Figure 4 with the labels 2 and 3, respectively. We could also repeat this procedure for experiments $\mathscr{E}_4$ to $\mathscr{E}_9$, but we assume that in our context, sequential procedures are not practical.

In Figure 4, any (α_1, α_2) point that lies on the lower boundary line can be achieved by suitable randomizations among experiments. For example, the point marked a can be achieved as follows: for experiment $\mathscr{E}_3$ choose the non-randomized rule with (α_1, α_2) at position b; for experiments $\mathscr{E}_2$ choose the non-randomized rule with (α_1, α_2) at position c; randomize between performing $\mathscr{E}_3$ with rule yielding b and between performing $\mathscr{E}_2$ with rule yielding c, to attain an (α_1, α_2) at a. Hence the lower boundary line in the above diagram represents the admissible (α_1, α_2) pairs achievable with mixtures of $\mathscr{E}_1$, $\mathscr{E}_2$, and $\mathscr{E}_3$. (If $\mathscr{E}_4$ through $\mathscr{E}_9$ were included, the above discussion would be conceptually similar.)

Clearly there still remains the problem of how to choose a specific (α_1, α_2) pair from this set of admissible pairs. It is now necessary to invoke a

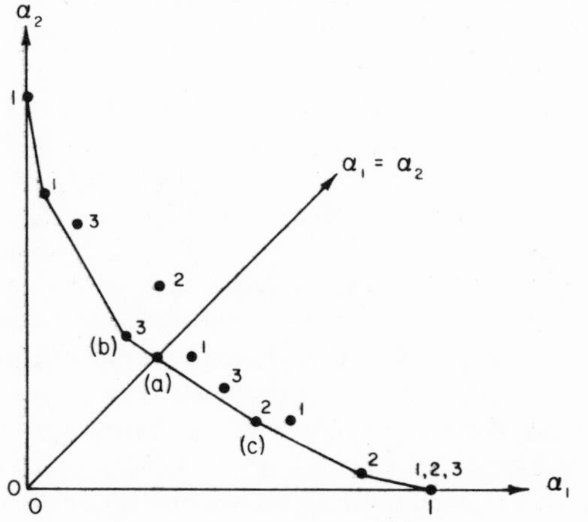

FIG. 4

further criterion (e.g., minimax, Neyman-Pearson criterion with a significance level α_0, Bayes, etc.). For example, if one wishes to classify individuals chosen at random from the population, where no self-selection is involved, then one might wish to employ a Bayes procedure with respect to an *a priori* probability distribution

$$\Pr(\omega_1) = N_1/(N_1 + N_2), \qquad \Pr(\omega_2) = N_2/(N_1 + N_2)\,,$$

and to a loss structure

$$\begin{array}{cc} & \begin{array}{cc} A_1 & A_2 \end{array} \\ \begin{array}{c} \omega_1 \\ \omega_2 \end{array} & \begin{bmatrix} 0 & a_1 \\ a_2 & 0 \end{bmatrix} \end{array}$$

for a suitably chosen a_1 and a_2 (which will depend on the context of the problem). If the individual to be classified cannot be considered as a random selection from the population from which we gained our initial experience, then we no longer can assert with confidence that the *a priori* probability of ω_1 is $N_1/(N_1 + N_2)$. However, we might still be willing to assert that the conditional probability of his registering a pattern of (I_1, I_2, I_3), say, given that he is an ω_i, is

$$N_i(I_1, I_2, I_3)/N_i\,, \qquad I_j = 0 \text{ or } 1,\ j = 1, 2, 3;\ i = 1, 2\,.$$

If we know that the self-selection bias works in one direction, we might be willing, for example, to assert that the *a priori* probability of ω_1 is between $N_1/(N_1 + N_2)$ and 1, say, and as mentioned earlier, we could suitably exploit this *a priori* information. For a given criterion we can find the suitable (α_1, α_2) pair, and then determine which experiment, or randomization of experiments, must be chosen to realize such a pair.

It is clear that this method of analysis can be extended to consider the general problem of reducing the number of items included; i.e., this far we have considered the question of the optimal selection of two of the three items in our battery. However, we might prefer to consider the question: Should we use all three items, or two (and if "yes", which ones), or one (and if "yes," which one), or none?

To answer this question, we proceed by plotting on one set of axes the sets of admissible (α_1, α_2) pairs corresponding to (1) experiment $\mathscr{E}_0$, say, which uses all three items; (2) mixtures of experiments $\mathscr{E}_1$, $\mathscr{E}_2$, $\mathscr{E}_3$, which use two items; (3) mixtures of experiments $\mathscr{E}_{10}$, $\mathscr{E}_{11}$, $\mathscr{E}_{12}$, which represent the experiments that choose single items 1, 2, and 3, respectively; (4) the case in which classification is made independently of any items. Let us assume that the data are such that when the above program is carried out, we obtain the (α_1, α_2) pairs plotted in Figure 5. In Figure 5 the numbers such as 0, 1, 3, 10, 12 refer to the appropriate experiment associated with that point. With the use of the figure we can assess the relative merits of using 0, 1, 2, or 3 items. Of course any "reasonable" solution must depend on the relative costs of using an item versus the losses attributable to wrong classifications. Furthermore, it will depend on the criterion used to select the appropriate admissible pair from each of the four sets of admissible pairs.

Consider the following numerical example: By using the available responses on three test items for a large number of individuals for whom the value of the classificatory variable is also known, we determine the probability estimates, which are given in Table 3. The possible experiments that can be performed are shown in Table 4.

In comparing these experiments, we shall list the possible outcomes for each experiment in increasing order of magnitude of the corresponding likelihood ratio $\hat{P}_{\omega_2}/\hat{P}_{\omega_1}$. If the likelihood ratio has the same value for more than one outcome, the outcomes will be arbitrarily ordered for this value. Then if we denote by x_j the outcome which is jth in this order, we find that the class of admissible non-randomized classification procedures is given by

$$D^* = \{\boldsymbol{\delta}^{(0)}, \boldsymbol{\delta}^{(1)}, \cdots, \boldsymbol{\delta}^{(k)}, \cdots\},$$

where

$$\begin{array}{lll} \delta_1^{(0)}(x_j) = 1, & \delta_2^{(0)}(x_j) = 0, & \text{all } j, \\ \delta_1^{(1)}(x_1) = 0, & \delta_2^{(1)}(x_1) = 1, & \\ \delta_1^{(1)}(x_j) = 1, & \delta_2^{(1)}(x_j) = 0, & j > 1, \\ \cdot \quad \cdot & \cdot \quad \cdot & \\ \delta_1^{(k)}(x_j) = 0, & \delta_2^{(k)}(x_j) = 1, & j \leqq k, \\ \delta_1^{(k)}(x_j) = 1, & \delta_2^{(k)}(x_j) = 0, & j > k. \\ \cdot \quad \cdot & \cdot \quad \cdot & \end{array}$$

The values of (α_1, α_2) associated with $\delta^{(k)}$ are

$$\alpha_1^{(k)} = \sum_{j=1}^{k} \hat{P}_{\omega_1}(x_j), \qquad \alpha_2^{(k)} = \sum_{j>k} \hat{P}_{\omega_2}(x_j).$$

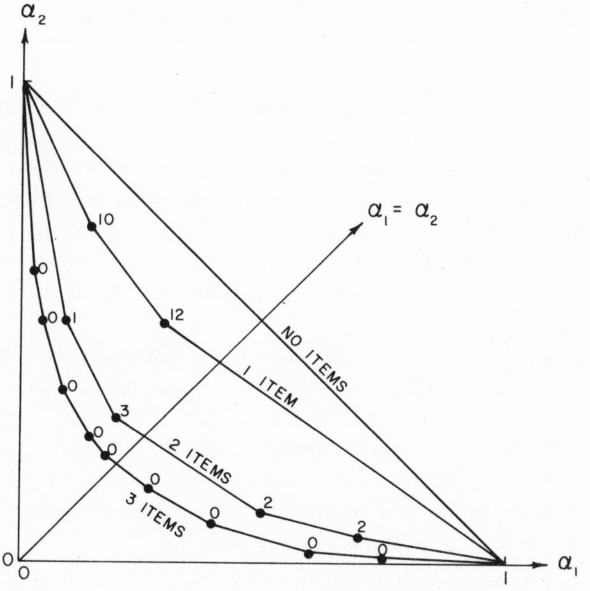

FIG 5

TABLE 3

Outcome			Estimated probability	
I_1	I_2	I_3	$\hat{P}_{\omega_1}$	$\hat{P}_{\omega_2}$
0	0	0	.02	.22
0	0	1	.08	.02
0	1	0	.03	.25
0	1	1	.07	.01
1	0	0	.35	.04
1	0	1	.33	.02
1	1	0	.05	.21
1	1	1	.07	.23

TABLE 4

Experiment Number	Items Used	Experiment Number	Items Used
0	1, 2, 3	7	2 followed by 3 if $I_2 = 1$ 2 followed by 1 if $I_2 = 0$
1	1, 2	8	3 followed by 1 if $I_3 = 1$ 3 followed by 2 if $I_3 = 0$
2	1, 3	9	3 followed by 2 if $I_3 = 1$ 3 followed by 1 if $I_3 = 0$
3	2, 3	10	1
4	1 followed by 2 if $I_1 = 1$ 1 followed by 3 if $I_1 = 0$	11	2
5	1 followed by 3 if $I_1 = 1$ 1 followed by 2 if $I_1 = 0$	12	3
6	2 followed by 1 if $I_2 = 1$ 2 followed by 3 if $I_2 = 0$	13	No items given

(Note that if the outcomes with the same value of the likelihood ratio had been ordered in any other way, the pairs of (α_1, α_2) values would be the same as in the present ordering. That is, the class D^* defined here is an essentially complete class of non-randomized decision functions.)

The experiments are analyzed in Table 5. From this analysis and from Figure 6, we make the following observations:

1. Item 2 is the best single predictor; that is, $\mathscr{E}_{11}$ is uniformly better than $\mathscr{E}_{10}$ or $\mathscr{E}_{12}$.

2. Among experiments using two items in a nonsequential manner (viz., $\mathscr{E}_1$, $\mathscr{E}_2$, and $\mathscr{E}_3$) there is no uniformly best experiment. However, the set of (α_1, α_2) values for $\mathscr{E}_3$ (the experiment using items 2 and 3) can be matched or improved upon by appropriate randomizations[2] between $\mathscr{E}_1$ (which uses items 1 and 2) and $\mathscr{E}_2$ (which uses items 1 and 3), so that $\mathscr{E}_3$ may be regarded as uniformly worse. The minimax procedure obtained by randomizing between $\mathscr{E}_1$ and $\mathscr{E}_2$ yields $\alpha_1 = \alpha_2 = .225$.

[2] We include in these randomizations the case when either $\mathscr{E}_1$ or $\mathscr{E}_2$ is selected with probability 1.

TABLE 5

Experiment	Outcome (x_k)	$\hat{P}_{\omega_1}(x_k)$	$\hat{P}_{\omega_2}(x_k)$	Order of l.r. (k)	$\alpha_1^{(k)}$	$\alpha_2^{(k)}$
$\mathscr{E}_0$	0 0 0	.02	.22	1	.02	.78
	0 1 0	.03	.25	2	.05	.53
	1 1 0	.05	.21	3	.10	.32
	1 1 1	.07	.23	4	.17	.09
	0 0 1	.08	.02	5	.25	.07
	0 1 1	.07	.01	6	.32	.06
	1 0 0	.35	.04	7	.67	.02
	1 0 1	.33	.02	8	1.00	0
$\mathscr{E}_1$	1 1 ·	.12	.44	1	.12	.56
	0 1 ·	.10	.26	2	.22	.30
	0 0 ·	.10	.24	3	.32	.06
	1 0 ·	.68	.06	4	1.00	0
$\mathscr{E}_2$	0 · 0	.05	.47	1	.05	.53
	1 · 0	.40	.25	2	.45	.28
	1 · 1	.40	.25	3	.85	.03
	0 · 1	.15	.03	4	1.00	0
$\mathscr{E}_3$	· 1 0	.08	.46	1	.08	.54
	· 1 1	.14	.24	2	.22	.30
	· 0 0	.37	.26	3	.59	.04
	· 0 1	.41	.04	4	1.00	0
$\mathscr{E}_4$	0 · 0	.05	.47	1	.05	.53
	1 1 ·	.12	.44	2	.17	.09
	0 · 1	.15	.03	3	.32	.06
	1 0 ·	.68	.06	4	1.00	0
$\mathscr{E}_5$	0 1 ·	.10	.26	1	.10	.74
	0 0 ·	.10	.24	2	.20	.50
	1 · 0	.40	.25	3	.60	.25
	1 · 1	.40	.25	4	1.00	0
$\mathscr{E}_6$	1 1 ·	.12	.44	1	.12	.56
	0 1 ·	.10	.26	2	.22	.30
	· 0 0	.37	.26	3	.59	.04
	· 0 1	.41	.04	4	1.00	0
$\mathscr{E}_7$	· 1 0	.08	.46	1	.08	.54
	0 0 ·	.10	.24	2	.18	.30
	· 1 1	.14	.24	3	.32	.06
	1 0 ·	.68	.06	4	1.00	0
$\mathscr{E}_8$	· 1 0	.08	.46	1	.08	.54
	· 0 0	.37	.26	2	.45	.28
	1 · 1	.40	.25	3	.85	.03
	0 · 1	.15	.03	4	1.00	0

TABLE 5 (*contd.*)

Experiment	Outcome (x_k)	$\hat{P}_{\omega_1}(x_k)$	$\hat{P}_{\omega_2}(x_k)$	Order of l.r. (k)	$\alpha_1^{(k)}$	$\alpha_2^{(k)}$
$\mathcal{E}_9$	0 · 0	.05	.47	1	.05	.53
	· 1 1	.14	.24	2	.19	.29
	1 · 0	.40	.25	3	.59	.04
	· 0 1	.41	.04	4	1.00	0
$\mathcal{E}_{10}$	0 · ·	.20	.50	1	.20	.50
	1 · ·	.80	.50	2	1.00	0
$\mathcal{E}_{11}$	· 1 ·	.22	.70	1	.22	.30
	· 0 ·	.78	.30	2	1.00	0
$\mathcal{E}_{12}$	· · 0	.45	.72	1	.45	.28
	· · 1	.55	.28	2	1.00	0

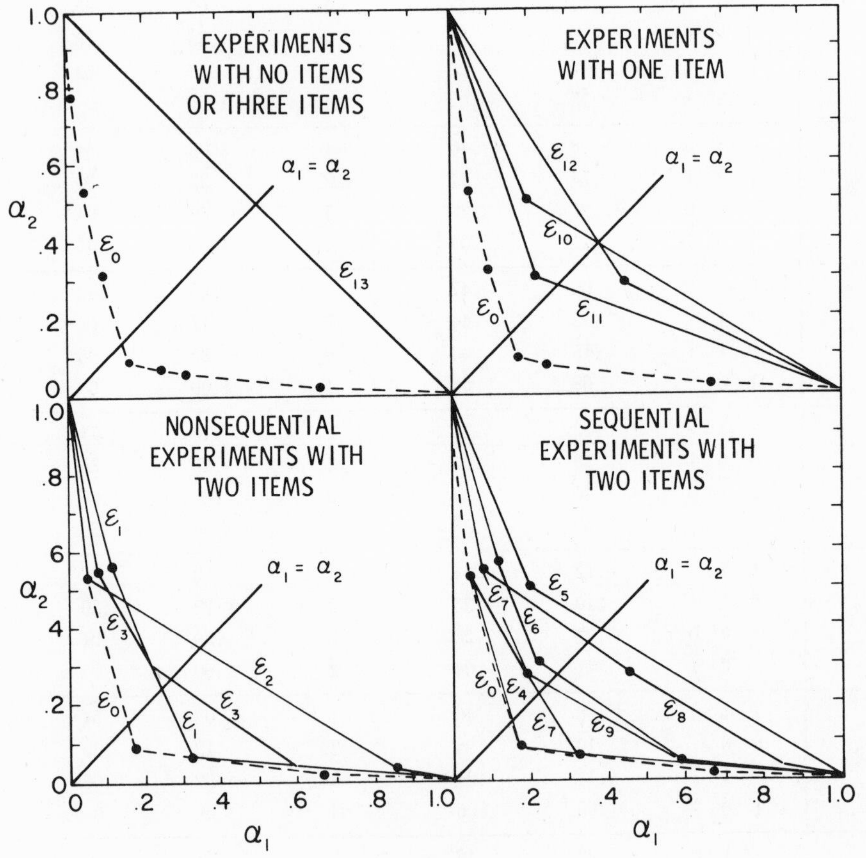

FIG. 6

3. Among the experiments using two items in a sequential manner $\mathscr{E}_4$ is uniformly best. Recall that $\mathscr{E}_4$ starts with item 1 and then uses 2 or 3 depending upon whether $I_1 = 1$ or $I_1 = 0$, respectively. Note that although item 2 is the uniformly best single predictor, the optimal sequential procedure involving two items starts with item 1 and not with item 2.

4. Naturally, the use of all three items (i.e., $\mathscr{E}_0$) is uniformly best for all experiments $\mathscr{E}_0, \mathscr{E}_1, \mathscr{E}_2, \cdots, \mathscr{E}_{12}$, as far as (α_1, α_2) appraisals are concerned. From Figure 6, however, we see that using all three items is only slightly better than the sequential design $\mathscr{E}_4$.

5. Suppose from the context of the problem we are told that the two errors of misclassification are equally serious, and we normalize to allow a unit loss, viz.,

$$\begin{array}{cc} & \begin{array}{cc} A_1 & A_2 \end{array} \\ \begin{array}{c} \omega_1 \\ \omega_2 \end{array} & \begin{bmatrix} 0 & 1 \\ 1 & 0 \end{bmatrix} \end{array}$$

(where A_i is the terminal action that assigns an individual to state ω_i, $i = 1, 2$). Suppose the cost[3] of administering each item is .10. If we then agree to use a randomized procedure yielding equal losses due to wrong terminal-decisions (i.e., a minimax) procedure and in each case to select the experiment or randomization of experiments yielding the smallest minimax risk, we have the analysis shown in Table 6. From the table we see that we are best off with $\mathscr{E}_4$, which uses two items (sequentially chosen). If, now, we put an additional .05 penalty on the cost of a sequential design of experimentation, then experiment $\mathscr{E}_{11}$, which uses only I_2, turns out to be "best."

If the cost of administering an item were .25 instead of .10 then it is easily seen that optimal procedure would be not to sample at all but merely to flip a fair coin: "Heads we take A_1 and tails we take A_2." Essentially this means that the items do not have a high enough discriminating power relative to the loss and cost structure of the problem to warrant examination.

---

[3] The reader should be aware of a serious gap in the above presentation, which centers about the following considerations: In comparing losses due to wrong terminal decisions with the cost of experimentation, one must realize that objectively these two entities are measured in very different units. The "cost" of using an item is given above by the number .1 (it is *not* in any specific monetary units) to convey roughly the meaning that the "subjective penalty" involved in using an item is "worth" about 1/10 the "subjective penalty" of making a wrong terminal decision. Of course, these considerations involve tremendous measurement difficulties. However, the situation is not hopeless, for the "Theory of Utility" is partially successful in coping with this problem. We shall divide our difficulties by assuming that

(i) If α is the probability of making an error and if a is the loss in "(dis)utiles" of making an error, then $\alpha \cdot a$ is the subjective expected loss in "(dis)utiles."

(ii) If c is the cost of experimentation (measured also in "(dis)utiles"), then the subjective over-all loss is $\alpha \cdot a + c$ measured in "(dis)utiles."

TABLE 6

Type of experiment	Experimental procedure	Classification procedure	Expected loss due to wrong terminal decision	Cost of experimentation	Overall loss
No items	Use $\mathscr{E}_{13}$ (no items given)	Choose ω_1 with probability 1/2 and ω_2 with probability 1/2	.500	0	.500
One item	Use $\mathscr{E}_{11}$	Use $\boldsymbol{\delta}^{(1)}$ with probability 25/27 and $\boldsymbol{\delta}^{(2)}$ with probability 2/27	.278	.100	.378
Two items, nonsequential	Use $\mathscr{E}_2$ with probability 13/37 and $\mathscr{E}_1$ with probability 24/37	Use $\boldsymbol{\delta}^{(1)}$ for $\mathscr{E}_2$ Use $\boldsymbol{\delta}^{(3)}$ for $\mathscr{E}_1$	.225	.200	.425
Two items, sequential	Use $\mathscr{E}_4$	Use $\boldsymbol{\delta}^{(1)}$ with probability 1/7 and $\boldsymbol{\delta}^{(2)}$ with probability 6/7	.153	.200	.353
Three items	Use $\mathscr{E}_0$	Use $\boldsymbol{\delta}^{(3)}$ with probability 4/15 and $\boldsymbol{\delta}^{(4)}$ with probability 11/15	.151	.300	.451

TABLE 7

Outcome (x_k)	$\hat{P}_{\omega_1}(x_k)$	$\hat{P}_{\omega_2}(x_k)$	Order of l.r. (k)	$\alpha_1^{(k)}$	$\alpha_2^{(k)}$
1 1 ·	.12	.44	1	.12	.56
0 · ·	.20	.50	2	.32	.06
1 0 ·	.68	.06	3	1.00	0

Still other types of experiments are possible. For example, we could start with item 1, say; then stop if $I_1 = 0$, but take item 2 if $I_1 = 1$. In experiments of this type we meet a fundamental complication, for the cost of such an experiment depends on chance; furthermore the probability distribution of the cost will depend on whether ω_1 or ω_2 is true. We analyze this experiment, which we call $\mathscr{E}_{14}$, in Table 7.

For this experiment we can achieve the (α_1, α_2) pairs (.12, .56) and (.32, .06), neither of which is attainable with one item alone. However, the expected cost of this experiment is greater than that of an experiment involving only one item, since the probability is .80 of taking a second item when ω_1 is true, and the corresponding probability is .50 when ω_2 is true.

Note that four such experiments start with item 1 and stop or take

TABLE 8

Experiment number	Items used	Probability of second item ω_1 true	ω_2 true
14	1 alone if $I_1 = 0$ 1 followed by 2 if $I_1 = 1$	.80	.50
15	1 alone if $I_1 = 0$ 1 followed by 3 if $I_1 = 1$	.80	.50
16	1 alone if $I_1 = 1$ 1 followed by 2 if $I_1 = 0$	.20	.50
17	1 alone if $I_1 = 1$ 1 followed by 3 if $I_1 = 0$	.20	.50
18	2 alone if $I_2 = 0$ 2 followed by 1 if $I_2 = 1$	.22	.70
19	2 alone if $I_2 = 0$ 2 followed by 3 if $I_2 = 1$	.22	.70
20	2 alone if $I_2 = 1$ 2 followed by 1 if $I_2 = 0$	.78	.30
21	2 alone if $I_2 = 1$ 2 followed by 3 if $I_2 = 0$	.78	.30
22	3 alone if $I_3 = 0$ 3 followed by 1 if $I_3 = 1$	.55	.28
23	3 alone if $I_3 = 0$ 3 followed by 2 if $I_3 = 1$	.55	.28
24	3 alone if $I_3 = 1$ 3 followed by 1 if $I_3 = 0$	.45	.72
25	3 alone if $I_3 = 1$ 3 followed by 2 if $I_3 = 0$	.45	.72

another item depending on the value of I_1. Altogether there are 12 of these experiments, which are given in Table 8.

The admissible pairs for $\mathscr{E}_{14}$ were given in Table 7. For the remaining experiments, we have the admissible pairs shown in Table 9.

A comparison of the (α_1, α_2) appraisals for these experiments is given in Figure 7. It will be observed that the lower boundary of the set of appraisals is attained by appropriate randomizations between $\mathscr{E}_{17}$ and $\mathscr{E}_{20}$. It should be noted that the same boundary points are attainable if $\mathscr{E}_{17}$ is replaced by $\mathscr{E}_{24}$ and $\mathscr{E}_{20}$ is replaced by $\mathscr{E}_{14}$. However, $\mathscr{E}_{24}$ and $\mathscr{E}_{14}$ are strictly dominated by $\mathscr{E}_{17}$ and $\mathscr{E}_{20}$, respectively, in terms of the expected cost of experimentation. Thus, the probability of a second observation in $\mathscr{E}_{17}$ is .20 or .50, depending upon whether ω_1 or ω_2 is true, while the corresponding probabilities for $\mathscr{E}_{24}$ are .45 and .72. If it costs c units to administer each item, the expected cost for $\mathscr{E}_{17}$ is $1.20c$ and $1.50c$, given ω_1 and ω_2, respectively, while the corresponding costs for $\mathscr{E}_{24}$ are $1.45c$ and $1.72c$. Similarly, the expected costs for $\mathscr{E}_{20}$ are $1.78c$ and $1.30c$, compared with $1.80c$ and $1.50c$ for $\mathscr{E}_{14}$.

If we adopt $\mathscr{E}_{17}$ with probability 13/37 and $\mathscr{E}_{20}$ with probability 24/37,

TABLE 9

Experiment	Outcome (x_k)	$\hat{P}_{\omega_1}(x_k)$	$\hat{P}_{\omega_2}(x_k)$	Order of l.r. (k)	$\alpha_1^{(k)}$	$\alpha_2^{(k)}$
	0 · ·	.20	.50	1	.20	.50
$\mathscr{E}_{15}$	1 · 0	.40	.25	2	.60	.25
	1 · 1	.40	.25	3	1.00	0
	0 1 ·	.10	.26	1	.10	.74
$\mathscr{E}_{16}$	0 0 ·	.10	.24	2	.20	.50
	1 · ·	.80	.50	3	1.00	0
	0 · 0	.05	.47	1	.05	.53
$\mathscr{E}_{17}$	1 · ·	.80	.50	2	.85	.03
	0 · 1	.15	.03	3	1.00	0
	1 1 ·	.12	.44	1	.12	.56
$\mathscr{E}_{18}$	0 1 ·	.10	.26	2	.22	.30
	· 0 ·	.78	.30	3	1.00	0
	· 1 0	.08	.46	1	.08	.54
$\mathscr{E}_{19}$	· 1 1	.14	.24	2	.22	.30
	· 0 ·	.78	.30	3	1.00	0
	· 1 ·	.22	.70	1	.22	.30
$\mathscr{E}_{20}$	0 0 ·	.10	.24	2	.32	.06
	1 0 ·	.68	.06	3	1.00	0
	· 1 ·	.22	.70	1	.22	.30
$\mathscr{E}_{21}$	· 0 0	.37	.26	2	.59	.04
	· 0 1	.41	.04	3	1.00	0
	· · 0	.45	.72	1	.45	.28
$\mathscr{E}_{22}$	1 · 1	.40	.25	2	.85	.03
	0 · 1	.15	.03	3	1.00	0
	· 1 1	.14	.24	1	.14	.76
$\mathscr{E}_{23}$	· · 0	.45	.72	2	.59	.04
	· 0 1	.41	.04	3	1.00	0
	0 · 0	.05	.47	1	.05	.53
$\mathscr{E}_{24}$	1 · 0	.40	.25	2	.45	.28
	· · 1	.55	.28	3	1.00	0
	· 1 0	.08	.46	1	.08	.54
$\mathscr{E}_{25}$	· 0 0	.37	.26	2	.45	.28
	· · 1	.55	.28	3	1.00	0

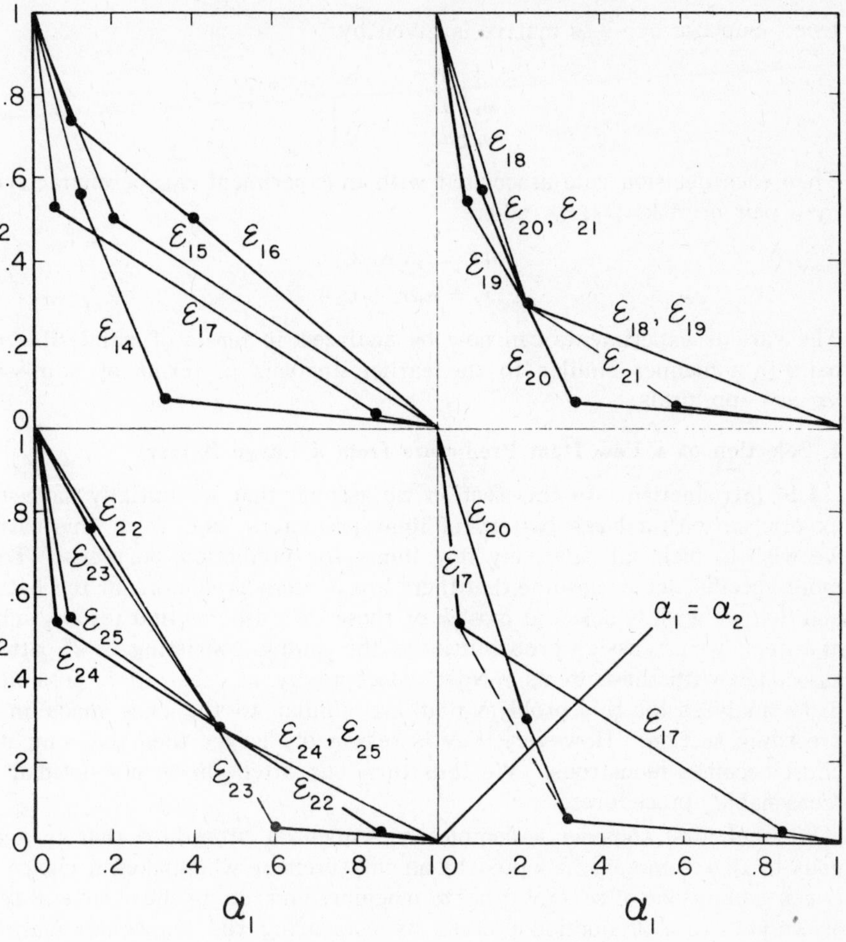

FIG. 7

using $\boldsymbol{\delta}^{(1)}$ for $\mathscr{E}_{17}$ and $\boldsymbol{\delta}^{(2)}$ for $\mathscr{E}_{20}$, we obtain a minimax procedure with $\alpha_1 = \alpha_2 = .225$. The expected cost of this procedure is $1.58c$ or $1.37c$, depending upon whether ω_1 or ω_2 is true. In either case this procedure yields, for a lower cost, the same protection as the minimax procedure resulting from the randomization between $\mathscr{E}_1$ and $\mathscr{E}_2$, experiments involving the nonsequential use of two items.

3.2 Unequal Item Costs. In discussing experiments $\mathscr{E}_{17}$ through $\mathscr{E}_{25}$, in which the number of items administered was a chance variable, we introduced the notion of the expected cost of an experiment when ω_i is true, $i = 1, 2$. In general, if the item costs are unequal, then for each of the experiments above we can compute the expected cost of experimentation, say C_1, when ω_1 is true and the corresponding expected cost C_2 when ω_2 is true. Suppose our loss matrix is given by

$$\begin{array}{cc} & \begin{array}{cc} A_1 & A_2 \end{array} \\ \begin{array}{c} \omega_1 \\ \omega_2 \end{array} & \begin{bmatrix} 0 & a_1 \\ a_2 & 0 \end{bmatrix} . \end{array}$$

Then each decision rule associated with an experiment can be characterized by a pair of risks (r_1, r_2), where

$$r_1 = a_1\alpha_1 + C_1 ,$$
$$r_2 = a_2\alpha_2 + C_2 .$$

The various experiments can now be analyzed in terms of admissible risk pairs in a manner similar to the earlier analysis in terms of admissible (α_1, α_2) appraisals.

4. Selection of a Few Item Predictors from a Large Battery

4.1 Introduction. In this section we assume that we initially have some experience with a large battery of item predictors, and from this battery we wish to pick out relatively few items for prediction purposes. To be more specific, let us assume that there are N item predictors in the battery and that we wish to select at most k of these. We assume that for any subset of k items we can assign probabilities to the sample consisting of 2^k patterns associated with these items. Now, conceptually at least, it is possible to make analyses for this problem that are similar to the ones made in the preceding section. However, if N is reasonably large, then the computing effort becomes monstrous. We thus turn our attention to non-optimal but "reasonable" procedures.

We shall first consider a completely sequential procedure that is analogous to that commonly adopted by an entrepreneur who makes a choice between adding one of several types of machines and adding one of several types of workers to a production process by comparing the (expected) marginal increase in revenue less the marginal increase in cost for both possible alternatives. Similarly, at any given stage of the item-selection problem we can make a comparative marginal analysis of decrease in expected losses due to wrong terminal decisions versus marginal increase in cost for each of the potential remaining item predictors. The entrepreneur who looks more than one stage ahead can take into account not only the immediate monetary consequences of an act but the strategic position this will leave him in when he contemplates further additions. Similarly, when adding an item, we have to consider not only the contribution of the item to the process thus far conceived but also the interaction this item will have with potential future items that may be added to the sequential process. Conceptually, by looking k steps ahead, we could get the optimal solution; the fact that this requires too much effort creates the present problem.

4.2 Forward Bayes Sequential and Nonsequential Procedures of Order s. Let X_i be a random variable that takes on the value 0 or 1 according to the response I_i on item i, $i = 1, 2, \cdots, m$; let Y take on the values ω_1 or ω_2

according to the response on the classificatory item. Assume that $\Pr\{Y = \omega_1\}$ is known—this is always known to the subjectivist, and often, but not always, this quantity is meaningful and approximately known to the objectivist. This assumption leads to a Bayesian analysis. We further assume that the joint distribution of any k of the random variables $\{X_i, i = 1, 2, \cdots, m\}$ conditional upon being given Y is known.

Let a_1 and a_2 be the losses due to wrong terminal decisions when ω_1 and ω_2, respectively, are true. Let c_i be the cost of administering item i. (It will be apparent that in the procedure outlined below we can let the cost of an item also depend on the set of items previously selected; thus we can introduce such possibilities as the ith item must be selected before the jth, or the jth item followed by the ith costs more than the ith followed by the jth, etc.)

Let $\Pi^{(1)} = \Pr\{Y = \omega_1\}$. Let $\rho_0(\Pi^{(1)})$ be the Bayes risk against $\Pi^{(1)}$ when no items are used, viz.,

$$\rho_0(\Pi^{(1)}) = \max\,[a_2(1 - \Pi^{(1)}), a_1\Pi^{(1)}]\ .$$

If item i is used and a Bayes rule is used against an *a priori* distribution Π, let $\rho_i(\Pi)$ be the resulting Bayes risk, i.e.,

$$\rho_i(\Pi) = \min_{\boldsymbol{\delta} \in D_i}\,[\Pi a_1\alpha_1(\boldsymbol{\delta}) + (1 - \Pi)a_2\alpha_2(\boldsymbol{\delta})] + c_i\ ,$$

where $\boldsymbol{\delta}$ is the generic decision rule in the set D_i of all decision rules associated with the experiment that uses item i.

Stage 1. The process terminates without any items being chosen if

$$\rho_0(\Pi^{(1)}) \leqq \min_{1 \leqq i \leqq m} \rho_i(\Pi^{(1)})\ .$$

If the above does not happen, then use $I_{[1]}$ at the first step, where

$$\rho_{[1]}(\Pi^{(1)}) = \min_{1 \leqq i \leqq m} \rho_i(\Pi^{(1)})\ .$$

(Note that [1] is some number from 1 to m.)

Stage $j + 1$. Let $I_{[1]}, I_{[2]}, \cdots, I_{[j]}$ be the first j items sequentially selected by the procedure. Let $X_{[1]} = x_{[1]}, X_{[2]} = x_{[2]}, \cdots, X_{[j]} = x_{[j]}$ be the responses to these items. To determine which item we should choose next or whether we should stop, we analyze the following problem:

1. States of nature: State $\omega_1^{(j+1)}$ is $\{X_{[1]} = x_{[1]}, \cdots, X_{[j]} = x_{[j]}, Y = \omega_1\}$ and state $\omega_2^{(j+1)}$ is $\{X_{[1]} = x_{[1]}, \cdots, X_{[j]} = x_{[j]}, Y = \omega_2\}$. The *a priori* probability of $\omega_1^{(j+1)}$ is defined as the *a posteriori* probability of $\omega_1^{(1)}$, given $X_{[1]} = x_{[1]}, \cdots, X_{[j]} = x_{[j]}$, viz.,

$$\Pi^{(j+1)} = P\{\omega_1^{(j+1)}\} \equiv P\{\omega_1^{(1)} \mid X_{[1]} = x_{[1]}, \cdots, X_{[j]} = x_{[j]}\}\ .$$

2. The sample space associated with experiment $\mathscr{E}_r$, which adopts I_r (I_r not one of $I_{[1]}, \cdots, I_{[j]}$), has values 0 and 1, where probability of 0 under $\omega_i^{(j+1)}$ is

$$P\{X_r = 0 \mid \omega_i^{(j+1)}\} = P\{X_r = 0 \mid X_{[1]} = x_{[1]}, \cdots, X_{[j]} = x_{[j]}, Y = \omega_i^{(1)}\}\ .$$

3. Loss structure is a_1 and a_2 for misclassifications under $\omega_1^{(j+1)}$ and $\omega_2^{(j+1)}$, respectively.

4. Cost of $\mathscr{E}_r$ is c_r.

Let

$$\rho_0^{(j+1)}(\Pi^{(j+1)}) = \max\,[a_2(1 - \Pi^{(j+1)}), a_1\Pi^{(j+1)}]\,,$$

and let $\rho_r^{(j+1)}(\Pi^{(j+1)})$ be the Bayes risk, including marginal cost of $\mathscr{E}_r$ but *not* costs of $(I_{[1]}, \cdots, I_{[j]})$ against $\Pi^{(j+1)}$ for $\mathscr{E}_r$ (where r is not one of the indices $[1], \cdots, [j]$). The process terminates at stage j if

$$\rho_0^{(j+1)}(\Pi^{(j+1)}) \leqq \min_{r \notin \{[1], \cdots, [j]\}} \rho_r^{(j+1)}(\Pi^{(j+1)})\,;$$

we choose $I_{[j+1]}$ if it does not terminate, where

$$\rho_{[j+1]}^{(j+1)}(\Pi^{(j+1)}) = \min_{r \notin \{[1], \cdots, [j]\}} \rho_r^{(j+1)}(\Pi^{(j+1)})\,.$$

The above procedure will be called the forward Bayes sequential procedure of order 1. Similarily, it is easy to modify the above to obtain the forward Bayes sequential procedure of order s, to wit: *At stage 1* choose an optimal Bayes procedure that utilizes at most s items (sequential choices allowed) according to an obvious modification of the procedure discussed in Section 3. *At stage $j + 1$*, if the process has not already terminated, let H_j be the random variable that describes the history of the sequential process through the first j stages; since H_j is known at stage $j + 1$, we symbolically let $H_j = h_j$; now let $\omega_i^{(j+1)}$ be the state $\{H_j = h_j, Y = \omega_i\}$, and let the *a priori* probability of $\omega_i^{(j+1)}$ be the *a posteriori* probability of ω_i, given $H_j = h_j$; for any potential choice of further items (i.e., a feasible experiment at stage j) one must compute the probabilities of the sample points under $\omega_1^{(j+1)}$ and $\omega_2^{(j+1)}$; for this resulting problem the process of stage 1 is again repeated; if s items are utilized in the Bayes procedure at this stage, then go on to the next stage.

By analogy with the sequential procedure described above we can also define a forward Bayes *nonsequential* procedure of order s. To this end, let $\rho_{i_1, i_2, \cdots, i_r}$ be the Bayes risk when items $I_{i_1}, I_{i_2}, \cdots, I_{i_r}$ are used (where losses due to wrong terminal decisions as well as costs of items employed are included).

With this notation the procedure for $s = 1$ goes as follows: At *stage 1* let $I_{[1]}$ be the item for which $\rho_{[1]} \leqq \rho_i$, $i = 1, 2, \cdots, m$; at *stage 2* let $I_{[2]}$ be the item for which $\rho_{[1],[2]} \leqq \rho_{[1],i}$, $i \neq [1]$, $i = 1, 2, \cdots, m$; at *stage $j + 1$* let $I_{[j+1]}$ be the item for which

$$\rho_{[1],\cdots,[j],[j+1]} \leqq \rho_{[1],\cdots,[j],i}\,, \qquad i \neq [1], \cdots, [j]\,, \quad i = 1, 2, \cdots, m\,.$$

The process terminates at stage k, where k is the smallest integer for which

$$\rho_{[1],\cdots,[k],[k+1]} > \rho_{[1],[2],\cdots,[k]}\,;$$

i.e., we terminate with the kth item if the Bayes risk increases with the addition of a $(k + 1)$st item.

To define the process of order $s > 1$, we proceed as follows: At *stage 1* let $[1], \cdots, [s]$ be s subscripts (order unimportant) for which

$$\rho_{[1],\cdots,[s]} \leqq \rho_{i_1,i_2,\cdots,i_s}$$

for all subsets of indices $i_1, i_2, \cdots, i_s$; at *stage 2* let $[s+1], \cdots, [2s]$ be s subscripts (order unimportant) for which

$$\rho_{[1],\cdots,[s],[s+1],\cdots,[2s]} \leqq \rho_{[1],\cdots,[s],i_1,i_2,\cdots,i_s}$$

for all subsets of indices $i_1, i_2, \cdots, i_s$, where each is different from $[1], \cdots, [s]$. We continue in an analogous manner for r stages, where r is the smallest integer for which

$$\rho_{[1],\cdots,[(r+1)s]} > \rho_{[1],\cdots,[rs]} ;$$

at the completion of the rth stage we define indices $[rs+1], [rs+2], \cdots, [(r+1)s]$, and now we add the *optimal subset* of these s indices to the preceding rs indices $[1], \cdots, [rs]$ to yield a minimum Bayes risk.

Some words of caution are in order. It is quite possible that *a low-order procedure will call for termination at a given stage whereas a higher-order procedure would call for continuation.* Therefore it would be desirable to modify the termination specifications of low-order procedures. A reasonable compromise is to check termination points of low-order sequential or nonsequential procedures with higher-order nonsequential procedures. If it is advantageous at any stage to add items $i_1, i_2, \cdots, i_s$, then it certainly is advantageous (in comparison to stopping) to add some of these items and then to re-evaluate the situation.

Another modification can be taken with s-order procedures. At each stage instead of adding in all s items we can add in only a subset of j items, say, and then once again we can look s steps ahead. For example, we could keep a floating horizon of looking s steps ahead but at each stage add only a single item before reassessing the entire situation—i.e., by looking s steps ahead once again.

The forward Bayes *sequential* procedure of order s is much easier to compute for a given subject than the *nonsequential* procedure of order s. But recall that the items selected for the sequential procedure depend on the subject, whereas the items selected for the nonsequential procedure do not (i.e., the nonsequential procedure essentially averages—in a Bayesian sense—over all subjects).

The effort expended in obtaining the forward Bayes sequential (or nonsequential) procedure of order s increases rapidly as s increases. If we do not take computing and analyzing effort into account, we would naturally expect the Bayes risk to decrease as s increases. It seems possible that this need not be the case. For example, an item might be a good single predictor, working poorly with any other single item, but be excellent in connection with a suitably chosen pair of other items; thus going from $s = 1$ to $s = 2$ could possibly yield a negative return.

For a given number of potential item predictors N, and an estimate k of the likely number of items to be chosen, we can estimate roughly the effort involved in finding a forward Bayes sequential procedure of order s. Let this effort be penalized an amount[4] e_s. Then $e_1 < e_2 < e_3 < \cdots$. For example, if $N = 25$ and $s = 1$, then at the first stage we have to consider 25 experiments; at the second stage we have to consider 24 experiments, etc. Now if $s = 2$, then at the first stage one must consider $25 \times 24 \times 24 = 14{,}400$ different experiments (25 is the number of possibilities for the first item, 24 is number of possibilities for the second item if $s = 1$ on the first item, and 24 is the number of possibilities for the second item if $s = 0$ on the first item). Hence for the selection of two items one would have to compare 49 experimental analyses for $s = 1$ with 14,400 analyses for $s = 2$. Naturally an s for which $e_s \geqq \rho_0(\Pi^{(1)})$ will not be entertained as practical. It might be desirable to compute $\rho_{[1]}(\Pi^{(1)})$ and rule out those s for which $e_s \geqq \rho_{[1]}(\Pi^{(1)})$. A minimal analysis of the above type might very well rule out $s \geqq 2$.

Since the quantity e_s is a function of the number of potential item predictors (as well as of other factors), the smaller the value of N, the larger the order of s we might be able to entertain. To effect a preliminary reduction in the size of N before making a detailed final analysis, we can make a first-order analysis to cut down the number of items from N to m_1 (say, from $N = 100$ to $m_1 = 10$); make a second-order analysis to cut down the number of items from m_1 to m_2 (say, from $m_1 = 10$ to $m_2 = 7$); make a third-order analysis to $\cdots$, etc. These preliminary reductions can either be made in terms of nonsequential or sequential procedures. The reduction via nonsequential procedures does not require any elaboration, except possibly for the selection of numbers m_1, m_2, etc. However, some obvious complications arise if the preliminary reductions are effected by a series of low-order *sequential* procedures, for in this case the items retained will vary from individual to individual. The following possible approach to this problem might be reasonable: Make several analyses of forward Bayes sequential procedures of order $s = 1$—either in the sense of Monte Carlo trials on hypothetical subjects or with actual subjects to be classified—and make a composite listing of the items utilized or most frequently utilized. With this preliminary reduction repeat the process with an analysis of order $s = 2$, etc. Of course, nothing prevents us from starting off with a nonsequential initial reduction and then switching to the sequential case.

The remaining difficulty—selection of reduction sizes $m_1, m_2, \cdots$—is a delicate problem, and art as well as science will have to govern. Certainly these quantities must depend on $e_1, e_2, \cdots$, but they by no means tell the whole story. One possible suggestion for coping with this problem proceeds from the philosophy that a preliminary reduction should include too many rather than too few items; i.e., choose a number ρ, where $0 < \rho < 1$, and consider an auxiliary problem, where the cost of item I_i is ρC_i instead of C_i, $i = 1, 2, \cdots, N$. By thus artificially reducing the cost of experimentation, we retain more items than actually required for prediction purposes

[4] The amount e_s depends on the algorithm and the calculating machine employed and will change as innovations are introduced in the procedure.

in any order s procedure. Now instead of arbitrarily choosing a number m_1, we can (arbitrarily) choose a number ρ and let m_1 be determined from the optimal order $s = 1$ procedure. This process can then be repeated for higher-order reductions. The discount factor controls the size of the reduction, which ideally should be selected not to rule out too many items as contenders but, rather, to achieve a manageable size for the next stage of analysis. Here again the intuition and good sense of the selector is indispensable and cannot be replaced with any concrete suggestions we have thus far investigated.

When the potential number of item indicators is large, say 100, and we wish to select on the order of 25 items (i.e., a large number), we run into serious conceptual as well as overwhelming computational difficulties. One source of these difficulties can be indicated (roughly) at this point, as follows: In practice, we usually have initial experience with a group of individuals who are given all m items, and from this initial data we can estimate the joint distributions of any subset of items; however, the reliability of any estimate rapidly deteriorates as the number of items in the subset increases. For 25 items, for example, there are 2^{25} possible response patterns, and we cannot, in any realistic sense, assume that we have enough initial experience with a population of individuals to assign meaningful joint probabilities to these response patterns. We can divide our difficulties by assuming that the joint distribution of all item variables is known, and then a reasonable but non-optimal procedure can be suggested (e.g., a forward Bayes sequential or nonsequential procedure of order $s = 1$ or $s = 2$).

For the case in which we assume that higher-order joint distributions are not known we very tentatively suggest two procedures that seem somewhat reasonable. The first is to make a content analysis of items; to partition these items according to content into relatively independent subsets (e.g., to group together all personality items, all items that indicate manipulative and sensory perception abilities, etc.); to analyze each subset of items (of the partition) separately; and from each subset to eliminate some items so that the remainder predicts reasonably well (in comparison with the subset of which it is a part). For example, if we can divide (by content) 100 items into 10 groups of 10 items and eliminate 5 from each 10 in some optimal fashion, then we are down to 50 items. We are quite aware of the many "jokers" involved in the program, and we are not prepared to defend this procedure from a mathematical point of view. When the number of items is large, however, we feel there is merit in using quite rough techniques to effect a preliminary reduction before more sophisticated analysis takes place.

The second procedure is to assume an underlying structure for the items (the potential predictors as well as the classificatory item) and to use this "rationalization" of the manifest initial data to aid in the item-selection problem. Some preliminary thought has been given to such intervening structures as the latent-class model and the generalized latent-distance model of P. F. Lazarsfeld. A difficulty here is that, as far as I know, at most ten or so items have been handled by this type of latent-structure analysis. However, even if we again divide our difficulties by assuming that a *known* latent structure exists, the resulting item-selection problem is not trivial and will have to be the subject of future research.

REFERENCES

[1] Savage, L. J. *The Foundations of Statistics.* New York: Wiley, 1954.

[2] Hodges, J. L., Jr., and Lehman, E. L. The uses of previous experience in reaching statistical decisions. *Ann. Math. Stat.*, 1952, **23**, 396–407.

[3] Cohen, Leonard. On mixed single sample experiments. *Ann. Math. Stat.*, 1958, **29**, 947–71.

13

An Empirical Bayes Approach to Non-Parametric Two-Way Classification

MILTON VERNON JOHNS, Stanford University

1. Introduction and Summary

In the two-way classification problem, the statistician is required to classify an individual into one of two categories on the basis of an observation X associated with the individual. It is assumed that the probability distribution of X depends on the category to which the individual actually belongs. The non-parametric case, in which the possible distributions of X are not known *a priori* to belong to some parametric family of distributions, has been considered by Fix and Hodges [1], [2] and by Stoller [3]. These authors suggest methods involving the use of accumulated past observations to obtain classification procedures that, when the amount of past information is large, lead to risks of misclassification which approach the best one could do if the probability structure of the problem were completely known.

Fix and Hodges have treated this problem in the classical Neyman-Pearson context, which does not take into account the possible existence of *a priori* probabilities for the two categories. Stoller took these probabilities into account, but he restricted himself to classification procedures having a particular form. In the procedures discussed in this chapter, due regard is given to the existence of unknown *a priori* probabilities, and the class of decision procedures is not restricted.

These procedures [1], [2], [3] are evaluated in terms of the probabilities of correct and incorrect classification. However, sometimes in practical applications some misclassifications are "worse" than others, and it may be desirable to take this into account in formulating the loss structure of the problem. For example, suppose that an individual selected at random from the population of candidates for admission to some course of training is given a preliminary examination and achieves a score of X. Suppose further that when this individual has completed his training his performance is evaluted by another examination on which he obtains a score of Y. In this case the classification problem may consist of attempting to predict on the basis of the preliminary score X whether or not the individual will achieve a passing score ($Y > a$, say) on the final examination. Here the scores X and Y have a fixed unknown joint distribution corresponding to the distribution of the scores of the individuals in the population from which the candidate is selected.

This population consists of two sub-populations composed, respectively, of those who would achieve passing Y-scores and those who would not. Obviously if we classify the candidate into the category of those who are likely to fail when (if permitted to take the course) he would actually have achieved a very high score on the final examination, we have committed a more serious error of misclassification than we would if the candidate had achieved a score only slightly above passing. In formulating the classification problem considered in this chapter, we consider the relative severity of such errors.

To find satisfactory classification procedures for which no *a priori* probabilities are known, we must assume the existence of information in the form of observations previously made on individuals selected from the same population as the individual we wish to classify. In the context of the above example those observations will be the pairs (X_i, Y_i), $i = 1, 2, \cdots, n$, where X_i and Y_i are the preliminary and final scores, respectively, of the ith candidate. For each i the pair (X_i, Y_i) will have the same unknown joint distribution as (X, Y) since all candidates are assumed to be selected independently from the same population. This prior information will be said to be "complete" if both X_i and Y_i are available for each individual previously selected from the population of candidates. However, in practice the final scores Y_i may be available only for those candidates who were classified as "likely to pass," since only such candidates will be admitted to the course of training. When the Y_i's are available only for those individuals classified into one of the two categories, we shall say that the prior information is "incomplete." The statistical decision problem under consideration is precisely formulated in Section 2.

In Section 3 the classification problem is considered for the case of "complete" prior information for which the random variable X is discrete-valued. A procedure is given having the property that as the number of prior observations increases, the risk due to misclassification approaches the Bayes risk associated with the best possible procedure that could be found, if the probability structure of the problem were completely known.

In Section 4 we consider the case in which the prior information is "complete" and in which there exists a probability density function for X. The procedures given in this section are direct generalizations of those discussed by Fix and Hodges in [1], [2] in connection with the more restricted version of the problem mentioned above.

In Section 5 we consider the case of "incomplete" prior information where X is discrete, and again we give a procedure whose risk approaches the Bayes risk.

The techniques we use are similar in spirit to the "empirical Bayes procedures" discussed by Robbins in [4] and Johns in [5] in relation to certain other problems of statistical inference.

2. Bayes Decision Rules for the Two-Way Classification Problem

The two-way classification problem under discussion may be formalized as follows: The individual to be classified is characterized by the pair of random variables (X, Y), where X is observed and Y is not observed at the time of classification. The individual is a member Category 1 or Category 2, according to whether $Y \in B$ or $Y \notin B$, respectively, where B is some specified (measurable) set. Let A_1 designate the action of classifying the individual into Category 1, and A_2 be the complementary action of classifying him into Category 2. Let $l_1(y)$ and $l_2(y)$ be the losses associated with actions A_1 and A_2, respectively, when the true value of Y is y. This loss structure takes into account the relative severity of misclassifications depending on the value of Y. For example, if the individual is in Category 1 or Category 2 according to whether $Y < a$ or $Y \geqq a$, then plausible definitions of l_1 and l_2 would be $l_1(y) = c_1 \max(0, y - a)$ and $l_2(y) = -c_2 \min(0, y - a)$, where $c_1, c_2 > 0$.

We remark that the case considered in [1], [2], where the loss depends only on the probability of misclassification, may be represented in the above framework by setting $l_1(y) = y$, and $l_2(y) = 1 - y$, where $Y = 0, 1$ according to whether the individual is in Category 1 or in Category 2. Here the probability that $Y = 0$ (1) represents the *a priori* probability that the individual is in Category 1 (2).

Any classification procedure based on the observed value x of X may be represented by a randomized decision function $\delta(x)$, which is to be interpreted as the probability with which action A_2 is to be taken when x is observed; i.e.,

$$\begin{aligned} \delta(x) &= P\{A_2 \mid X = x\}\,, \\ &= 1 - P\{A_1 \mid X = x\}\,. \end{aligned} \tag{2.1}$$

Now let $r(\delta)$ be the risk associated with the rule $\delta(x)$; i.e., $r(\delta)$ is the expected loss when the rule $\delta(x)$ is used. Throughout this chapter we shall assume that $E\,|\,l_1(Y)\,| < \infty$ and $E\,|\,l_2(Y)\,| < \infty$ so that $r(\delta)$ is finite for any δ. Now

$$\begin{aligned} r(\delta) &= E\{(1 - \delta(X))l_1(Y)\} + E\{\delta(X)l_2(Y)\} \\ &= El_1(Y) - E\{\delta(X)[l_1(Y) - l_2(Y)]\} \\ &= El_1(Y) - E\{\delta(X)E[l_1(Y) - l_2(Y) \mid X]\}\,. \end{aligned} \tag{2.2}$$

From this it is clear that if we let

$$V = l_1(Y) - l_2(Y)\,, \tag{2.3}$$

the essentially unique Bayes decision rule δ^*, which minimizes $r(\delta)$ is

$$\delta^*(x) = \begin{cases} 1, & E\{V \mid X = x\} > 0\,, \\ 0, & \text{otherwise.} \end{cases} \tag{2.4}$$

Of course the rule $\delta^*(x)$ depends on the joint distribution of X and Y and cannot in general be determined explicitly unless this distribution is known. In the problem under consideration we do not assume any *a priori* knowledge of the joint distribution of X and Y, but instead we seek an approximation to $\delta^*(x)$ based on independent prior observations and having the property that the risk involved in using the approximate rule approaches $r(\delta^*)$ for any joint distribution of X and Y as the number of prior observations increases. To this end we first prove the following lemma:

LEMMA 1. *Let* $\delta_n(x)$, $n = 1, 2, \cdots$, *be a sequence of random functions such that* $0 \leqq \delta_n(x) \leqq 1$ *for all* x, n. *Let*

$$T = \{x : E\{V \mid X = x\} \neq 0\} . \tag{2.5}$$

If $\delta_n(x)$ *is independent of* (X, Y) *for each* x *and* n *and if there exists a set* S *such that*

$$\begin{aligned} &\text{(i)} \quad P\{X \in S\} = 1 , \\ &\text{(ii)} \quad \delta_n(x) \underset{n}{\rightarrow} \delta^*(x) , \end{aligned} \tag{2.6}$$

in probability, for all $x \in S \cap T$, *then*

$$\lim_{n\to\infty} r(\delta_n) = r(\delta^*) . \tag{2.7}$$

PROOF.

$$r(\delta_n) = El_1(Y) - E\{E\{V\delta_n(X) \mid X\}\} . \tag{2.8}$$

But since $\delta_n(x)$ is independent of (X, Y) and hence of (X, V),

$$E\{V\delta_n(X) \mid X = x\} = E\{V \mid X = x\} E\,\delta_n(x) \tag{2.9}$$

for almost all x. Furthermore, by (2.6) (ii) and the boundedness of $\delta_n(x)$,

$$\lim_{n\to\infty} E\,\delta_n(x) = \delta^*(x) \tag{2.10}$$

for all $x \in S \cap T$. Hence

$$\lim_{n\to\infty} E\{V\delta_n(X) \mid X = x\} = E\{V\delta^*(X) \mid X = x\} \tag{2.11}$$

for all $x \in S$ and (2.7) follows from the dominated convergence theorem.

Specific examples of functions $\delta_n(x)$ involving prior observations and satisfying the conditions of this lemma will be discussed in the following sections.

3. "Complete" Prior Information, and X is Discrete-Valued

We first consider the case in which X is a discrete-valued random variable and the prior observations are "complete" in the sense defined in Section 1. That is, we have available the observed values of the mutually independent pairs of random variables (X_i, Y_i), $i = 1, 2, \cdots, n$, each independent of X and Y such that for each i the joint distribution of X_i and Y_i is the same as the (unknown) joint distribution of X and Y. Suppose that X takes on values in the denumerable set $S = \{x : P\{X = x\} > 0\}$ with probability 1. Then for $i = 1, 2, \cdots, n$, we define the following random functions, the domain of each of which is S:

$$M_i(x) = \begin{cases} 1, & X_i = x\,, \\ 0, & \text{otherwise}\,, \end{cases} \tag{3.1}$$

$$V_i = l_1(Y_i) - l_2(Y_i)\,; \tag{3.2}$$

and we define the "empirical Bayes" decision rule $\delta_n(x)$ by

$$\delta_n(x) = \begin{cases} 1, & \sum_{i=1}^{n} V_i M_i(x) > 0\,, \\ 0, & \text{otherwise}\,. \end{cases} \tag{3.3}$$

To illustrate, we now consider the computation of (3.3) for the following special case: Suppose that X and the X_i's may take on only the values $1, 2, \cdots, m$. Let $l_1(y) = c_1$ if $y \geqq a$ and zero otherwise, and let $l_2(y) = c_2$ if $y < a$ and zero otherwise. Then we may rearrange the observed values $y_1, y_2, \cdots, y_n$ of the Y_i's to obtain $y_1^{(1)}, y_2^{(1)}, \cdots, y_{n_1}^{(1)}, y_1^{(2)}, y_2^{(2)}, \cdots, y_{n_2}^{(2)}, \cdots, y_1^{(k)}, y_2^{(k)}, \cdots, y_{n_k}^{(k)}, \cdots, y_1^{(m)}, y_2^{(m)}, \cdots, y_{n_m}^{(m)}$, where $y_j^{(k)}, j = 1, 2, \cdots, n_k$ are the values of the Y_i's for which the observed values of the corresponding X_i's are equal to k. Clearly, $0 \leqq n_k \leqq n$ for $k = 1, 2, \cdots, m$ and $n_1 + n_2 + \cdots + n_m = n$. Now let r_k, $k = 1, 2, \cdots, m$, be the number of $y_j^{(k)}$'s which are greater than or equal to a. We can easily verify that

$$\sum_{i=1}^{n} V_i M_i(k) = c_1 r_k - c_2(n_k - r_k)\,.$$

Hence the empirical Bayes decision rule (3.3) becomes

$$\delta_n(k) = \begin{cases} 1, & c_1 r_k > c_2(n_k - r_k)\,, \\ 0, & \text{otherwise.} \end{cases}$$

Thus, in this case, if the observed value of X is k, we classify the individual into category 2 if and only if c_1 times the number of previously selected individuals whose X-scores were k and whose Y-scores were $\geqq a$ is greater than c_2 times the number of individuals whose X-scores were k and whose Y-scores were $< a$.

An examination of (3.3) shows that the value of $\delta_n(x)$ for any particular x depends only on the values of those Y_i's for which the corresponding X_i's take on the value x. We now prove the following theorem:

THEOREM 1. *If $\delta_n(x)$ is given by* (3.3), *then*

$$\lim_{n\to\infty} r(\delta_n) = r(\delta^*)\,. \tag{3.4}$$

PROOF. For each i, for any $x \in S$

$$\begin{aligned} E\{V_i M_i(X)\} &= E\{V_i \mid M_i(x) = 1\}\, P\{M_i(x) = 1\}\,, \\ &= E\{V \mid X = x\}\, P\{X = x\}\,. \end{aligned} \tag{3.5}$$

Hence for any $x \in S$ and for arbitrary $\varepsilon > 0$, we have by the law of large numbers

$$\left| \sum_{i=1}^{n} V_i M_i(x) - nE\{V \mid X = x\} P\{X = x\} \right| < n\varepsilon , \tag{3.6}$$

with arbitrarily high probability for all sufficiently large n. Now if $x \in S$, then $P\{X = x\} > 0$. Hence, for any $x \in S$ such that $E\{V \mid X = x\} \neq 0$, the sign of $\sum_{i=1}^{n} V_i M_i(x)$ will be the same as that of $E\{V \mid X = x\}$ with arbitrarily high probability for sufficiently large n. Thus, for each $x \in S$, excepting possibly for a set of values of x for which $E\{V \mid X = x\} = 0$, we have

$$\delta_n(x) \to \delta^*(x) , \tag{3.7}$$

in probability, as $n \to \infty$. The desired result then follows from Lemma 1.

4. "Complete" Prior Information and X Is Continuous

We next consider the case where for a set of values of V having probability 1, there exists a conditional density function $f(x \mid v)$ such that for any Borel set B

$$P\{X \in B \mid V = v\} = \int_B f(x \mid v) dx . \tag{4.1}$$

(This is equivalent to assuming the existence of a conditional density of X given Y.) In this case a (marginal) density function for X exists and is given by

$$f(x) = \int_{-\infty}^{\infty} f(x \mid v)\, dH(v) , \tag{4.2}$$

where $H(v)$ is the marginal c.d.f. of V.

We assume as before that mutually independent pairs of prior observations (X_i, Y_i), $i = 1, 2, \cdots, n$, are available and that for each i the joint distribution of X_i and Y_i is the same as that of X and Y and that (X_i, Y_i) is independent of (X, Y).

For each $n = 1, 2, \cdots$, we partition the real line into disjoint half-open intervals $I_{1n}, I_{2n}, \cdots$, such that if $I_n(x)$ represents the unique member of the nth partition that contains the point x, and if μ represents Lebesgue measure, then for any x

$$\begin{aligned} &\text{(i)} \quad \lim_{n\to\infty} \mu[I_n(x)] = 0 , \\ &\text{(ii)} \quad \lim_{n\to\infty} n\mu[I_n(x)] = \infty . \end{aligned} \tag{4.3}$$

For each $i = 1, 2, \cdots, n$ and for each $n = 1, 2, \cdots$, let

$$M_i^{(n)}(x) = \begin{cases} 1, & X_i \in I_n(x) , \\ 0, & \text{otherwise} , \end{cases} \tag{4.4}$$

and define the empirical Bayes rule $\delta'_n(x)$ by

$$\delta'_n(x) = \begin{cases} 1, & \sum_{i=1}^{n} V_i M_i^{(n)}(x) > 0 , \\ 0, & \text{otherwise} , \end{cases} \tag{4.5}$$

where V_i is given by (3.2) as before. This definition is completely analogous to (3.3), differing only in that the value of $\delta'_n(x)$ depends on the values of the Y_i's that correspond to X_i's that have values in a small neighborhood of the point x, instead of those for which $X_i = x$ (an event with probability 0 in this case).

We next prove the following theorem:

THEOREM 2. *If* $E(V^2) < \infty$ *and if* $\delta'_n(x)$ *is given by* (4.5), *then*

$$\lim_{n\to\infty} r(\delta'_n) = r(\delta^*) . \tag{4.6}$$

PROOF. By assumption (4.3) (i) and by the Lebesgue differentiation theorem we have for almost all x such that $f(x) > 0$

$$\begin{aligned}\lim_{n\to\infty} E\{V \mid X \in I_n(x)\} &= \lim_{n\to\infty} \frac{\dfrac{1}{\mu[I_n(x)]}\displaystyle\int_{I_n(x)}\int_{-\infty}^{\infty} v f(t \mid v)\, dH(v)\, dt}{\dfrac{1}{\mu[I_n(x)]}\displaystyle\int_{I_n(x)} f(t)\, dt} \\ &= \frac{\displaystyle\int v f(x \mid v)\, dH(v)}{f(x)} \\ &= E\{V \mid X = x\} .\end{aligned} \tag{4.7}$$

Similarly, for almost all x such that $f(x) > 0$

$$\lim_{n\to\infty} E\{V^2 \mid X \in I_n(x)\} = E\{V^2 \mid X = x\} < \infty , \tag{4.8}$$

since $EV^2 < \infty$. Now letting

$$p_n(x) = P\{M_i^{(n)}(x) = 1\} = P\{X \in I_n(x)\} = \int_{I_n(x)} f(t)\, dt , \tag{4.9}$$

we have for almost all x

$$\lim_{n\to\infty} \frac{p_n(x)}{\mu[I_n(x)]} = f(x) , \tag{4.10}$$

so that for almost all x such that $f(x) > 0$,

$$\lim_{n\to\infty} np_n(x) = \infty , \tag{4.11}$$

by assumption (4.3) (ii). Now for any fixed value of x we have

$$E\{V_i M_i^{(n)}(x)\} = E\{V \mid X \in I_n(x)\}\, p_n(x) \tag{4.12}$$

and

$$\begin{aligned}\operatorname{Var}\,[V_i M_i^{(n)}(x)] &\leq E\{V_i^2 M_i^{(n)}(x)\} \\ &= E\{V^2 \mid X \in I_n(x)\}\, p_n(x) \\ &= [E\{V^2 \mid X = x\} + \gamma_n(x)]\, p_n(x) ,\end{aligned} \tag{4.13}$$

where by (4.8), $\lim_{n\to\infty} \gamma_n(x) = 0$ for almost all x such that $f(x) > 0$. Now by the Tchebycheff inequality and (4.12) and (4.13) we have for arbitrary $\varepsilon > 0$

$$(4.14) \qquad P\left\{\left|\sum_{i=1}^{n} V_i M_i^{(n)}(x) - nE\{V \mid X \in I_n(x)\} p_n(x)\right| < \varepsilon n\, p_n(x)\right\} \geqq 1 - \frac{E\{V^2 \mid X = x\} + \gamma_n(x)}{\varepsilon^2\, np_n(x)} .$$

For every fixed $\varepsilon > 0$, we have $\varepsilon^2 np_n(x) \to \infty$ by (4.11), and hence the right-hand side of (4.14) approaches one for almost all x such that $f(x) > 0$. Now for arbitrary $\eta > 0$ we have by (4.7) for all sufficiently large n

$$| E\{V \mid X \in I_n(x)\} - E\{V \mid X = x\} | < \eta ,$$

for almost all x such that $f(x) > 0$. Hence, for all sufficiently large n, replacing the statement in braces in the left-hand side of (4.14) by

$$(4.15) \qquad \left|\sum_{i=1}^{n} V_i M_i^{(n)}(x) - np_n(x)\, E\{V \mid X = x\}\right| < (\varepsilon + \eta) np_n(x)$$

only strengthens the inequality. Suppose, for example, that $E\{V \mid X = x\} > 0$ for a particular fixed x; we may choose ε and η small enough so that $E\{V \mid X = x\} > \varepsilon + \eta > 0$. Then (4.15) clearly implies that $\sum_{i=1}^{n} V_i M_i^{(n)}(x) > 0$, i.e., that $\sum_{i=1}^{n} V_i M_i^{(n)}(x)$ and $E\{V \mid X = x\}$ have the same sign. Furthermore, the probability of this statement approaches one as n becomes large. (Note: ε and η are *not* functions of n.) A similar argument applies when $E\{V \mid X = x\} < 0$. Therefore, for almost all x such that $f(x) > 0$ and $E\{V \mid X = x\} \neq 0$ we have $\delta_n'(x) \to \delta^*(x)$ and the desired result follows by Lemma 1.

A practical difficulty in using the decision rule $\delta_n'(x)$ arises from the necessity of choosing the sequence of intervals $I_{1n}, I_{2n}, \cdots$, without any prior knowledge of the "dispersion" of $f(x)$. If we choose intervals that are too small with relation to the dispersion of $f(x)$, we know intuitively that most of the X_i's will lie in different intervals so that not much information is contained in $\delta_n'(x)$ for any particular x, with the result that the performance of $\delta_n'(x)$ may be poor when n is small. Difficulties also arise when the intervals are made too large in relation to the dispersion of $f(x)$. These considerations motivate the following alternative approach.

As an alternative to the decision procedure discussed above, we now develop an empirical Bayes rule, with the property that its value for any x depends upon the values of a predetermined number of the Y_i's. Let k_n, $n = 1, 2, \cdots$, be a non-decreasing sequence of positive integers such that

$$(4.16) \qquad \begin{aligned} &\text{(i)} \quad \lim_{n\to\infty} k_n = \infty , \\ &\text{(ii)} \quad \lim_{n\to\infty} \frac{k_n}{n} = 0 . \end{aligned}$$

For each x let $Q_n(x)$ be the set consisting of the k_n of the random variables $X_1, X_2, \cdots, X_n$ that are closest to x. For convenience we measure "closeness" in terms of the ordinary Euclidean distance, although other metrics could just as well be used. For each $i = 1, 2, \cdots, n$ and each n, let

$$\tilde{M}_i^{(n)}(x) = \begin{cases} 1, & X_i \in Q_n(x), \\ 0, & \text{otherwise}; \end{cases} \tag{4.17}$$

and define the decision rule $\delta_n''(x)$ by

$$\delta_n''(x) = \begin{cases} 1, & \sum_{i=1}^{n} V_i \tilde{M}_i^{(n)}(x) > 0\,; \\ 0, & \text{otherwise}\,. \end{cases} \tag{4.18}$$

We now state the following theorem without proof:

THEOREM 3. *If $EV^2 < \infty$ and if $E\{V^2 \mid X = x\}$ and $E\{V \mid X = x\}$ are continuous functions of x for almost all x such that $f(x) > 0$, then*

$$\lim_{n\to\infty} r(\delta_n'') = r(\delta^*)\,. \tag{4.19}$$

5. "Incomplete" Prior Information and X is Discrete-Valued

We now consider the case for which the available past information is "incomplete" in the sense defined in Section 1; i.e., where the value of Y_i is known only if the ith individual was classified (on the basis of X_i and previous observations) as being a member of, say, Category 2. We shall discuss this problem in the framework of the discrete case as set forth in Section 3.

We let u_n, $n = 1, 2, \cdots,$ be the outcomes of independent trials, where $P\{U_n = 1\} = a_n$, $P\{U_n = 0\} = 1 - a_n$, and where

$$\lim_{n\to\infty} a_n = 0\,, \tag{4.20}$$

$$\sum_{n=1}^{\infty} a_n = \infty\,. \tag{4.21}$$

Then for any $x \in S$ we let $Z_0(x) = 0$, and we define $Z_n(x)$ and $\hat{\delta}_n(x)$ for $n = 1, 2, \cdots,$ recursively as follows:

$$Z_n(x) = \sum_{i=1}^{n} V_i M_i(x) \hat{\delta}_i(x)\,, \tag{4.22}$$

$$\hat{\delta}_n(x) = \begin{cases} 1, & U_n = 1 \text{ and/or } Z_{n-1}(x) \geqq 0\,, \\ 0, & \text{otherwise}; \end{cases} \tag{4.23}$$

$M_i(x)$ and V_i are defined by (3.1) and (3.2) as before. The nth individual is classified into Category 1 if $\hat{\delta}_n(X_n) = 0$ or into Category 2 if $\hat{\delta}_n(X_n) = 1$. We see that the random functions $\hat{\delta}_n(x)$, $n = 1, 2, \cdots,$ are legitimate decision rules for the problem under consideration, since the value of $\hat{\delta}_n(x)$ depends only on the values of the Y_i's for which the corresponding $\hat{\delta}_i(x)$'s are equal to 1 (i.e., for which the individuals were classified as members of Category 2). The nth individual is classified into Category 2 if the past information summarized by $Z_{n-1}(X_n)$ indicates that this is the correct decision, *or* if the outcome U_n of an independent random experiment is a "success." The introduction of these independent random experiments insures the accumulation of sufficient information so that a satisfactory approximation to the Bayes rule may be obtained. The price of obtaining such information is an occasional misclassification, but by virtue of (4.20) such misclassifications will become increasingly rare as n becomes large. In fact, in the following theorem we show convergence of the risks of the $\hat{\delta}_n$'s to the Bayes risk:

THEOREM 4. *If* $\hat{\delta}_n(x)$ *is given by* (4.23), *then*

$$\lim_{n\to\infty} r(\hat{\delta}_n) = r(\delta^*) . \tag{4.24}$$

PROOF. In the following we consider a fixed value of $x \in S$, and for notational simplicity we suppress the argument x in $M_i(x)$, $Z_n(x)$, and $\hat{\delta}_n(x)$. For $m = 0, 1, \cdots, n-1$, $n = 1, 2, \cdots$, we define the events $A_m^{(n)}$ by

$$A_m^{(n)} = \{\hat{\delta}_i = 0 \text{ for exactly } m \text{ values of } i,\ 1 < i \leqq n\} . \tag{4.25}$$

Then for any k, $1 \leqq k \leqq n-1$,

$$\sum_{m=0}^{k} P\{A_m^{(n)}\} \geqq P\left\{\sum_{i=1}^{n} U_i > n-k\right\} . \tag{4.26}$$

Now for each n let k_n be the largest integer less than $n + 1 - \frac{1}{2}\sum_{i=1}^{n} a_i$. Then

$$\begin{aligned} P\left\{\sum_{i=1}^{n} U_i > n-k_n\right\} &\geqq P\left\{\sum_{i=1}^{n} U_i - \sum_{i=1}^{n} a_i > -\frac{1}{2}\sum_{i=1}^{n} a_i\right\} \\ &\geqq P\left\{\left|\sum_{i=1}^{n} U_i - \sum_{i=1}^{n} a_i\right| < \frac{1}{2}\sum_{i=1}^{n} a_i\right\} \\ &\geqq 1 - \frac{4}{\sum_{i=1}^{n} a_i} \end{aligned} \tag{4.27}$$

by the Tchebycheff inequality. Hence by (4.21), (4.26), and (4.27) we have

$$\lim_{n\to\infty} \sum_{m=0}^{k_n} P\{A_m^{(n)}\} = 1 . \tag{4.28}$$

Now if $Z_n^* = \sum_{i=1}^{n} V_i M_i$, $n = 1, 2, \cdots$, then it is easily seen that

$$P\{Z_n > 0 \mid A_m^{(n)}\} = P\{Z_{n-m}^* > 0\} , \tag{4.29}$$

and hence

$$\begin{aligned} P\{Z_n > 0\} &= \sum_{m=0}^{n-1} P\{Z_n > 0 \mid A_m^{(n)}\} P\{A_m^{(n)}\} \\ &= \sum_{m=0}^{n-1} P\{Z_{n-m}^* > 0\} P\{A_m^{(n)}\} \\ &\geqq \sum_{m=0}^{k_n} P\{Z_{n-m}^* > 0\} P\{A_m^{(n)}\} . \end{aligned} \tag{4.30}$$

But if $EV_iM_i > 0$, then by the law of large numbers

$$\lim_{n\to\infty} P\{Z_n^* > 0\} = 1 . \tag{4.31}$$

Hence by (4.28) and (4.31) and the fact that $\lim_{n\to\infty}(n - k_n) = \infty$, we have

$$\lim_{n\to\infty} P\{Z_n > 0\} = 1 , \tag{4.32}$$

whenever $EV_iM_i > 0$. A similar argument shows that

$$\lim_{n\to\infty} P\{Z_n < 0\} = 1 , \tag{4.33}$$

whenever $EV_iM_i < 0$. Hence, referring to (3.5), (4.20), and (4.23), we have

$$\hat{\delta}_n(x) \to \delta^*(x) , \tag{4.34}$$

in probability as $n \to \infty$, for any $x \in S$ excepting possibly for values of x for which $E\{V \mid X = x\} = 0$, (i.e., $E\{V_iM_i(x)\} = 0$). The desired result then follows by Lemma 1.

A similar discussion could be given for the case in which X is a continuous random variable and the past information is incomplete.

6. Concluding Remarks

It is apparent that the foregoing results may be directly extended to the case in which X and Y are vector-valued random variables. Furthermore, the same methods could be applied to the multiple classification problem involving more than two categories.

In practical situations involving two-way classifications it may sometimes be reasonable to introduce some *a priori* assumptions about the probability relationships between X and Y. For example, we might assume that $E\{Y \mid X = x\}$ is a non-decreasing function of x, or that the distribution of X, given $Y = y$, has some specified functional form. Under such circumstances it may be possible to find empirical Bayes classification procedures that are more efficient than those given above.

Although the formulation of the problem given in Section 2 is stated in terms of a situation involving the classification of an individual into one of two categories, the formal structure is actually equivalent to that of the general Bayes two-decision problem. In this interpretation the value of the random variable Y represents the unknown true state of nature and the distribution of Y represents the *a priori* probability of the possible states. The conditional distribution of X, given $Y = y$, is then interpreted as the distribution of X when y is the true state of nature. Also $l_1(y)$ and $l_2(y)$ represent the losses associated with actions A_1 and A_2, respectively, when y is the true state of nature.

In [2] Fix and Hodges discuss the small sample performance of the procedures they introduced in [1]. A possible subject for further research would be a similar investigation of the behavior of the risks involved in using the classification procedures given in the present paper when the number of prior observations is not large.

REFERENCES

[1] Fix, Evelyn, and Hodges, J. L. Discriminatory analysis; Non-parametric discrimination: Consistency properties. USAF, SAM Series in Statistics, Project No. 21-49-004, Report No. 4, Randolph AFB, Texas: School of Aviation Medicine, 1951.

[2] Fix, Evelyn, and Hodges, J. L. Discriminatory analysis; Non-parametric discrimination: small sample performance. USAF, SAM Series in Statistics, Project No. 21-49-004, Report No. 11, Randolph AFB, Texas: School of Aviation Medicine, 1952.

[3] Stoller, David S. Univariate two-population distribution-free discrimination. *J.A.S.A.* **49**, 770–77 (1954).

[4] Robbins, H. An empirical Bayes approach to statistics. In J. Neyman, ed., *Proceedings of the Third Berkeley Symposium on Mathematical Statistics and Probability*. Berkeley, Calif.: Univ. California Press, 1956.

[5] Johns, M. V., Jr. Non-Parametric Empirical Bayes Procedures in Statistics. Unpublished thesis, Columbia University, 1956.

14

A Non-Parametric Solution for the k-Sample Slippage Problem

EDWARD PAULSON, Queens College, New York City

1. Introduction

The purpose of this chapter is to develop a non-parametric procedure for comparing k populations $\Pi_1, \Pi_2, \cdots, \Pi_k$ with probability density functions $f(x - a_1), f(x - a_2), \cdots, f(x - a_k)$, which are known *a priori* to be identical except for possible different values of the location parameter. Suppose that a sample of n independent measurements is available from each population. We wish to decide if the k populations are identical, and if not, which is the "best," i.e., which has the largest location parameter. More specifically, what is required is a statistical procedure for selecting one of the $k + 1$ decisions $D_0, D_1, \cdots, D_k$, where D_0 is the decision that $a_1 = a_2 \cdots = a_k$, and D_i $(i = 1, 2, \cdots, k)$ is the decision that D_0 is false and $a_i = \max(a_1, a_2, \cdots, a_k)$.

This problem appears to be of rather wide interest. Among several different training procedures, drugs, or techniques of approximately equal costs, we often wish to determine if any real differences exist, and if so, which is the "best" one.

For most applications it is probably adequate to assume that the form of the population is normal. This is the situation treated in [1]. However, if the samples are not large and the populations are not normal, then our use of a statistical procedure based on the assumption of normality might lead us to a substantial change in the prescribed probability of incorrectly deciding that the k populations are not identical. (This error is analogous to the type I error in the classical theory of testing a simple hypothesis.) Therefore, in certain specialized situations where it is very important to control the probability of making an error by incorrectly deciding that the populations are not identical, and where the sample size is not large and we have reason to suspect that the populations may differ considerably from the normal population, we might seriously consider a non-parametric procedure, since it can control the probability of making this error, regardless of the form of the populations involved. Of the many non-parametric procedures that might be considered, we shall give a fairly simple one based on the use of ranks, which has a certain optimum property that is made more precise later in the chapter. An earlier non-parametric treatment of a somewhat related problem was given by Mosteller [2], but his formulation and procedure differ considerably from ours.

2. Definition of the Optimum Procedure

First we define the concept of a slippage. If $a_1 = a_2 = \cdots = a_{i-1} = a_{i+1} = \cdots = a_k = a$ and $a_i = a + \Delta$ $(\Delta > 0)$, then population Π_i will be said to have slipped to the right by an amount Δ. Now in order to set up a "reasonable" criterion for an optimum statistical procedure for choosing one of the $k+1$ decisions $D_0, D_1, \cdots, D_k$, it is necessary to impose certain "reasonable" restrictions on the class of statistical decision procedures which will be considered acceptable. For this purpose the following restrictions will be imposed: (*a*) only non-parametric procedures based on the use of ranks will be considered; (*b*) the decision procedure used should have the property that there is a fixed probability $1 - \alpha$ of selecting D_0 when the populations are really identical, regardless of the functional form of the unknown but common density function; (*c*) the decision procedure used should be symmetrical with respect to the k populations so that the probability of selecting population Π_i when Π_i has slipped to the right by an amount Δ should be the same for each i $(i = 1, 2, \cdots, k)$.

Restriction (*a*) is a common one in non-parametric work, whereas restriction (*c*) appears to be very reasonable when the cost factors for the k populations are approximately equal. Restriction (*b*) will give the experimenter special protection against the possibility of finding one of the populations superior to the others by chance when in fact there are no real differences between the populations. Now we shall define the precise sense in which the decision procedure to be derived in the next section will be an optimum one. Out of all statistical decision procedures satisfying restrictions (*a*), (*b*), and (*c*), we shall find one that will maximize the probability of selecting D_i when Π_i has slipped to the right by an amount Δ, provided that the probability distributions are actually normal and Δ is small.

3. Derivation of the Optimum Procedure

The following notation will be used. The jth measurement from the ith population will be denoted by x_{ij} $(i = 1, 2, \cdots, k;\ j = 1, 2, \cdots, n)$. When the $kn = N$ observations from all k populations are combined and ranked from 1 to N, the rank of x_{ij} will be denoted by r_{ij}. The ordered array of ranks $(r_{11}r_{12} \cdots r_{1n}r_{21} \cdots r_{2n} \cdots r_{k1} \cdots r_{kn})$ will be denoted by R. Since the random variables involved are assumed to be absolutely continuous, the possibility of a tie may be neglected. Let W_R denote the region in the N-dimensional space of the x_{ij}'s, which corresponds to R.

The probability $P(R)$ of a given ranking R is then given by

$$P(R) = \int_{W_R} \cdots \int \prod_{i=1}^{k} \prod_{j=1}^{n} f(x_{ij} - a_i)\, dx_{11}, \cdots, dx_{kn} .$$

Let $P_0(R)$ denote the probability of the ranking R when the k populations are identical, and let $P_i(R)$ $(i = 1, 2, \cdots, k)$ denote the probability of the ranking R when Π_i has slipped to the right and

$$f(x - a_i) = \frac{1}{\sigma\sqrt{2\pi}} \exp\left[-\frac{1}{2}\left(\frac{x - a_i}{\sigma}\right)^2\right].$$

Since all rankings have the same probability of occurrence when the populations are identical, we have $P_0(R) = 1/N!$, whereas for $i = 1, 2, \cdots, k$ we have

$$P_i(R) = \int_{W_R} \cdots \int \frac{1}{(\sigma\sqrt{2\pi})^N} \exp\left\{-\frac{1}{2\sigma^2}\left[\sum_{\substack{\lambda=1 \\ \lambda \neq i}}^{k} \sum_{j=1}^{n} (x_{\lambda j} - a)^2 + \sum_{j=1}^{n} (x_{ij} - a - \Delta)^2\right]\right\} dx_{11} \cdots dx_{kn} .$$

Since any ranking R will be invariant if the same number is added to all the observations and if the observations are multiplied by the same positive number, it follows that $P_i(R)$ can be written in the simpler form

$$P_i(R) = \int_{W_R} \cdots \int \frac{1}{(\sqrt{2\pi})^N} \exp\left\{-\frac{1}{2}\left[\sum_{\substack{\lambda=1 \\ \lambda \neq i}}^{k} \sum_{j=1}^{n} x_{\lambda j}^2 + \sum_{j=1}^{n} (x_{ij} - \Delta)^2\right]\right\} dx_{11} \cdots dx_{kn} .$$

Now let

$$U_i(R) = \sum_{j=1}^{n} \bar{E}(x_{ij})$$

and let $U_M(R) = \max\,[U_1(R), U_2(R), \cdots, U_k(R)]$, where $\bar{E}(x_{ij})$ $(i = 1, 2, \cdots, k;$ $j = 1, 2, \cdots, n)$ denotes the expectation of the observation with rank r_{ij} in a sample of N independent observations from a normal population with zero mean and unit variance. The subscript M denotes the integer (from 1 to k) for which $U_i(R)$ has its maximum value. If for a particular array of ranks R it should happen that $U_i(R)$ has its maximum value for more than one value of i, say for $i = i_1, i_2, \cdots, i_s$ $(1 < s \leq k)$, then we select M from among $i_1, i_2, \cdots, i_s$ by any chance mechanism that will assign probability $1/s$ to each of the s values.

It will now be seen that the statistical decision procedure for choosing between $D_0, D_1, \cdots, D_k$, which is optimum in the sense previously defined, is the following:

$$\text{(3.1)} \qquad \begin{aligned} &\text{if } U_M(R) > C, \quad \text{select } D_M ; \\ &\text{if } U_M(R) \leq C, \quad \text{select } D_0 . \end{aligned}$$

In (3.1) C is a constant that depends only on α for k and n fixed. The calculation of C is discussed in Section 4.

To show that (3.1) is an optimum procedure for selecting one of the decisions $D_0, D_1, \cdots, D_k$, we first note that this problem is equivalent to selecting one of the $k+1$ probability distributions $P_0(R), P_1(R), \cdots, P_k(R)$ which maximizes the probability of selecting $P_i(R)$ when it is the correct distribution and Δ is small (i.e., the ith population actually has a location parameter exceeding all others by Δ), subject to the restrictions that the statistical procedure is symmetric and has a fixed probability of selecting $P_0(R)$ when the populations are identical. In order to show that (3.1) is optimum in the above sense for choosing between $P_0(R), P_1(R), \cdots, P_k(R)$ we shall show that if Δ is small enough, we can find a set of *a priori* probabilities $p_0, p_1, p_2, \cdots, p_k$ for the $k+1$ distributions so that (3.1) will maximize the probability of making the correct decision between $P_0(R), P_1(R), \cdots, P_k(R)$ with respect to these *a priori* probabilities. Since (3.1) is also a symmetric procedure and will have a fixed probability of selecting D_0 when the populations are equal if C is chosen properly, it follows that (3.1) will therefore be the required solution.

The problem of finding a procedure that maximizes the probability of making the correct decision among $k+1$ probability distributions with respect to a given set of *a priori* probabilities is the same as finding the Bayes solution with respect to these *a priori* probabilities. It is known that the Bayes solution will be given by the following:

Select $P_M(R)$ for any ranking R for which $p_M P_M(R) = \max [p_0 P_0(R), p_1 P_1(R), \cdots, p_k P_k(R)]$. Clearly $P_i(R)$ can be written in the form

$$P_i(R) = 1/N! \, [1 + A_i(R)\Delta + O(\Delta^2)] \, ,$$

where

$$A_i(R) = \frac{N!}{(\sqrt{2\pi})^N} \int_{W_R} \cdots \int \left(\sum_{j=1}^{n} x_{ij} \right) \exp\left(-\frac{1}{2} \sum_{i=1}^{k} \sum_{j=1}^{n} x_{ij}^2 \right) dx_{11} \cdots dx_{kn}$$

$$= \sum_{j=1}^{n} \bar{E}(x_{ij}) \, .$$

(As mentioned previously, $\bar{E}(x_{ij})$ denotes the expected value of an observation with rank r_{ij} in a sample of N independent observations from a normal population with zero mean and unit variance.)

Now consider the special *a priori* distribution $p_0 = \beta$, $p_1 = p_2 = \cdots = p_k = (1-\beta)/k$. It is easy to see that for small values of Δ, the Bayes solution with respect to this special *a priori* distribution becomes the following.

Select $P_M(R)$ if

$$\max \left(\frac{1-\beta}{k} \right) \left[1 + \left(\sum_{j=1}^{n} \bar{E} x_{ij} \right) \Delta \right] = \frac{1-\beta}{k} [1 + U_M(R)\Delta] > \beta \, ;$$

otherwise select $P_0(R)$. This simplifies to the following rule: select $P_M(R)$ if $U_M(R) > [\beta(k+1) - 1]/\Delta(1-\beta)$, otherwise select $P_0(R)$. If we set $[\beta(k+1) - 1]/\Delta(1-\beta) = C$ and solve the resulting equation for β, we find that $\beta = (1 + C\Delta)/(1 + C\Delta + k)$. Since this always lies between 0 and 1 for Δ and C positive, we see that we can then always find a set of *a priori* probabilities so that (3.1) corresponds to the Bayes solution for choosing between $P_0(R), \cdots, P_k(R)$. This concludes the proof that (3.1) is optimum in the sense previously defined for choosing between $D_0, D_1, \cdots, D_k$.

4. The Calculation of C

If N is very small, say $N \leqq 10$, the constant C can be found by first enumerating all possible rankings, then finding the value of $U_M(R)$ for each ranking R with the aid of a table [3] giving the expected values of the order statistics, and finally selecting C so that only $\alpha N!$ of the rankings will have values of $U_M(R)$ exceeding C. (Due to the discreteness inherent in any procedure using ranks, a slight modification of this process may be necessary to achieve the exact probability desired.)

Since N can seldom be expected to be small enough to make this a practical procedure, we shall now derive an approximation to C. Define $P^*(C)$ by the relation

$$P^*(C) = P\{\max[U_1(R), U_2(R), \cdots, U_k(R)] \leqq C \mid a_1 = a_2 = \cdots = a_k\} .$$

Making use of Bonferroni's Inequality, we have

$$1 - kP[U_1(R) > C] + \frac{k(k-1)}{2} P[U_1(R) > C, U_2(R) > C] \geqq P^*(C) \geqq 1 - kP[U_1(R) > C] . \tag{4.1}$$

We now determine C by the requirement that $P[U_1(R) > C] = \alpha/k$, so that $P^*(C)$ cannot be less than $1 - \alpha$. An upper bound to the amount that $P^*(C)$ exceeds $1 - \alpha$ is found from the left-hand side of (4.1). A rigorous evaluation of this upper bound has not been made. However, since $U_1(R)$ and $U_2(R)$ are negatively correlated when the k populations are identical (they may then be regarded as pertaining to two different samples drawn without replacement from a finite population of N items), it is expected that this upper bound will ordinarily be less than $\alpha^2/2$, which is usually small enough to be ignored.

To determine C by the requirement that $P[U_1(R) > C] = \alpha/k$, we make use of a result of Terry [4], which shows that as n becomes large, the probability distribution of $U_1(R)$ will approach normality with zero mean and variance

$$\sigma_{U_1}^2 = \frac{kn - n}{k(nk-1)} \left\{ \sum_{i=1}^{k} \sum_{j=1}^{n} [\bar{E}(x_{ij})]^2 \right\} .$$

Since this appears to be a good approximation to the distribution of $U_1(R)$ even for small values of n, we can therefore approximate C by the relation

$$C \sim t_{\alpha/k} \sqrt{\frac{kn - n}{k(nk-1)} \left[\sum_{i=1}^{k} \sum_{j=1}^{n} (\bar{E}x_{ij})^2 \right]} ,$$

where t_p is the critical value of the standard normal distribution exceeded with probability p, i.e.,

$$\frac{1}{\sqrt{2\pi}}\int_{t_p}^{\infty} \exp\,[-x^2/2]\,dx = p\,.$$

It should be recognized that at present the value of the non-parametric procedure given is to a certain extent limited by both practical and theoretical considerations. On the practical side, the tables in [3] of the expected values of the ranks only extend up to $N = 50$; the error in the procedure suggested for approximating the distribution of $U_1(R)$ has not yet been explored thoroughly. On the theoretical side, among the problems not yet considered is the question of the relative efficiency of this non-parametric procedure compared with other non-parametric procedures and to the optimal normal procedure in detecting slippage when it exists.

References

[1] Paulson, Edward. An optimum solution to the K-sample slippage problem for the normal distribution. *Ann. Math. Stat.*, 1952, **23**, 610–16.

[2] Mosteller, Frederick. A K-sample slippage test for an extreme population. *Ann. Math. Stat.*, 1948, **19**, 58–65.

[3] Fisher, R. A., and Yates, F. *Statistical Tables for Biological, Agricultural and Medical Research,* 3d ed. New York, Hafner, 1949.

[4] Terry, Milton E. Some rank order tests which are most powerful against parametric alternatives. *Ann. Math. Stat.*, 1952, **23**, 346–66.

Part III. The Classification Statistic and Its Distribution

15

Some Results on the Distribution of the *W*-Classification Statistic

ROSEDITH SITGREAVES, Columbia University

1. Introduction

A problem of classification considered by Wald [1], Anderson [2], and Sitgreaves [3], among others, is the following: An individual is to be classified as belonging to one of two populations, π_1 and π_2, on the basis of a p-dimensional vector of measurements made on him. It is assumed that in each population the measurements are jointly normally distributed with the same covariance matrix but with different mean values. The covariance matrix and the two vectors of mean values are unknown. However, they can be estimated by using measurements available for N_1 individuals known to belong to π_1 and for N_2 individuals known to belong to π_2. Thus, if we denote the vectors of measurements for individuals in π_1 by $X_1, X_2, \cdots, X_{N_1}$, and the corresponding vectors for individuals in π_2 by $X_{N_1+1}, X_{N_1+2}, \cdots, X_{N_1+N_2}$, we estimate the two vectors of expected values, say $\mu^{(1)}$ and $\mu^{(2)}$, by

$$\bar{X}^{(1)} = \frac{1}{N_1}\sum_{t=1}^{N_1} X_t \quad \text{and} \quad \bar{X}^{(2)} = \frac{1}{N_2}\sum_{t=(N_1+1)}^{(N_1+N_2)} X_t . \tag{1.1}$$

The common covariance matrix Σ is estimated by

$$S = \frac{1}{(N_1 + N_2 - 2)} \sum_{t=1}^{N_1} (X_t - \bar{X}^{(1)})(X_t - \bar{X}^{(1)})' + \sum_{t=(N_1+1)}^{(N_1+N_2)} (X_t - \bar{X}^{(2)})(X_t - \bar{X}^{(2)})' . \tag{1.2}$$

If the parameter values are known, a class of optimal classification procedures can be defined in terms of a statistic T^*, where

$$T^* = X'_{N_1+N_2+1}\Sigma^{-1}(\mu^{(1)} - \mu^{(2)}) - \tfrac{1}{2}(\mu^{(1)} + \mu^{(2)})'\Sigma^{-1}(\mu^{(1)} - \mu^{(2)}) , \tag{1.3}$$

with $X_{N_1+N_2+1}$ the vector of measurements for the individual to be classified. In a given procedure from the class, the unknown individual is assigned to

π_1 if the observed T^* is greater than a cutoff point t_0, and is assigned to π_2 if $T^* \leqq t_0$. The class of procedures is generated as t_0 ranges over the positive real numbers.

For the case when the parameters are not known but can be estimated, Anderson [2] has proposed the use of a statistic W, obtained from (1.3) by substituting the sample estimates for the unknown parameter values, i.e.,

$$W = X'_{N_1+N_2+1}S^{-1}(\bar{X}^{(1)} - \bar{X}^{(2)}) - \tfrac{1}{2}(\bar{X}^{(1)} + \bar{X}^{(2)})'S^{-1}(\bar{X}^{(1)} - \bar{X}^{(2)}) . \tag{1.4}$$

In this case the unknown individual is assigned to π_1 if the observed value of W is greater than a preassigned cutoff point w_0, and to π_2 if $W \leqq w_0$.

The chapters in this section are generally concerned with efforts to evaluate the operating characteristics of a classification procedure based on W. To determine the probabilities of misclassification associated with a given cutoff point w_0, and to compare these probabilities with corresponding probabilities for other possible procedures, or for the optimal procedure based on T^*, it is necessary to consider the sampling distribution of W under the hypothesis that the individual to be classified belongs to π_1, and under the alternative hypothesis that he belongs to π_2. This chapter gives a series representation for these distributions when the two samples from each known population are of equal size.

Subsequent chapters include a method for estimating the cumulative distribution of W by means of an empirical sampling experiment, an asymptotic expansion for the cumulative distribution function of W when $p = 1$, a representation of W in terms of simple statistics, and an asymptotic expansion for the cumulative distribution function of W based on this representation.

2. Distribution of W

It was pointed out in [3] that if we write

$$A = (N_1 + N_2 - 2)S , \tag{2.1}$$

$$Z = [(N_1N_2)^{\frac{1}{2}}/(N_1 + N_2)^{\frac{1}{2}}](\bar{X}^{(1)} - \bar{X}^{(2)}) , \tag{2.2}$$

and

$$Z^* = [(N_1 + N_2)^{\frac{1}{2}}/(N_1 + N_2 + 1)^{\frac{1}{2}}] \cdot\{X_{N_1+N_2+1} - [1/(N_1 + N_2)](N_1\bar{X}^{(1)} + N_2\bar{X}^{(2)})\} , \tag{2.3}$$

we can write

$$W = (N_1 + N_2 - 2)\{[(N_1 + N_2 + 1)^{\frac{1}{2}}/(N_1N_2)^{\frac{1}{2}}]Z^{*\prime}A^{-1}Z + [(N_1 - N_2)/(2N_1N_2)]Z'A^{-1}Z\} . \tag{2.4}$$

Under either alternative, the three sets of variables are distributed independently of each other: the matrix A has a Wishart distribution with $N_1 + N_2 - 2$ degrees of freedom and covariance matrix Σ; the vector Z has a normal distribution with expected value $[(N_1N_2)^{\frac{1}{2}}/(N_1 + N_2)^{\frac{1}{2}}](\mu^{(1)} - \mu^{(2)})$ and covariance matrix Σ; and the vector Z^* has a normal distribution with covariance matrix Σ. Under the hypothesis that $X_{N_1+N_2+1}$ belongs to π_1, the expected value of Z^* is

$$\frac{N_2}{(N_1+N_2)^{\frac{1}{2}}(N_1+N_2+1)^{\frac{1}{2}}}(\mu^{(1)}-\mu^{(2)})\,;$$

under the alternative hypothesis that $X_{N_1+N_2+1}$ belongs to π_2, the expected value of Z^* is

$$\frac{-N_1}{(N_1+N_2)^{\frac{1}{2}}(N_1+N_2+1)^{\frac{1}{2}}}(\mu^{(1)}-\mu^{(2)})\,.$$

Writing

$$\begin{bmatrix} m_{11}^* & m_{12}^* \\ m_{12}^* & m_{22}^* \end{bmatrix} = \begin{bmatrix} Z^{*\prime}A^{-1}Z^* & Z^{*\prime}A^{-1}Z \\ Z'A^{-1}Z^* & Z'A^{-1}Z \end{bmatrix}, \tag{2.5}$$

we can rewrite (2.4) as

$$W=(N_1+N_2-2)\{[(N_1+N_2+1)^{\frac{1}{2}}/(N_1N_2)^{\frac{1}{2}}]m_{12}^* + [(N_1-N_2)\,/\,(2N_1N_2)]m_{22}^*\}\,. \tag{2.6}$$

If we write $\lambda^2=\frac{1}{4}(\mu^{(1)}-\mu^{(2)})'\Sigma^{-1}(\mu^{(1)}-\mu^{(2)})$, we obtain from equation (22) of [3]

$$\begin{aligned} &p(m_{11}^*, m_{12}^*, m_{22}^* \mid \pi_1) \\ &= \frac{\Gamma(\frac{1}{2}(N_1+N_2-1))\exp[-2\lambda^2N_2(N_1+1)/(N_1+N_2+1)](m_{11}^*m_{22}^*-m_{12}^{*2})^{\frac{1}{2}(p-3)}}{\Gamma(\frac{1}{2}(N_1+N_2-p))\Gamma(\frac{1}{2}(N_1+N_2-p-1))\Gamma(\frac{1}{2}(p-1))\Gamma(\frac{1}{2})} \\ &\quad\cdot\sum_{j=0}^{\infty}\frac{\Gamma(\frac{1}{2}(N_1+N_2)+j)}{\Gamma(\frac{1}{2}p+j)j!}\left[\frac{2N_2\lambda^2}{(N_1+N_2)(N_1+N_2+1)}\right]^j \\ &\quad\cdot\left\{\frac{[N_2m_{11}^*+2(N_1N_2)^{\frac{1}{2}}(N_1+N_2+1)^{\frac{1}{2}}m_{12}^*}{(1+m_{11}^*+m_{22}^*+m_{11}^*m_{22}^*-m_{12}^{*2})^{\frac{1}{2}(N_1+N_2)+j}}\right. \\ &\quad\left.+\frac{N_1(N_1+N_2+1)m_{22}^*+(N_1+1)(N_1+N_2)(m_{11}^*m_{22}^*-m_{12}^{*2})]^j}{(1+m_{11}^*+m_{22}^*+m_{11}^*m_{22}^*-m_{12}^{*2})^{\frac{1}{2}(N_1+N_2)+j}}\right\}, \end{aligned} \tag{2.7}$$

with $0 \leqq m_{11}^* \leqq \infty$, $0 \leqq m_{22}^* < \infty$, and $(m_{11}^*m_{22}^*-m_{12}^{*2}) \geqq 0$.

We make the transformation

$$m_{11}^* = \frac{(m_{22}^{*2}+m_{22}^*+m_{12}^{*2})t}{m_{22}^*(1+m_{22}^*)} + \frac{m_{12}^{*2}}{m_{22}^*} \tag{2.8}$$

in (2.7). Under the transformation,

$$m_{11}^*m_{22}^* - m_{12}^{*2} = \frac{(m_{22}^{*2}+m_{22}^*+m_{12}^{*2})t}{(1+m_{22}^*)},$$

and

$$(1+m_{11}^*+m_{22}^*+m_{11}^*m_{22}^*-m_{12}^{*2}) = \frac{(m_{22}^{*2}+m_{22}^*+m_{12}^{*2})(1+t)}{m_{22}^*}\,.$$

It follows that

$$(2.9)\quad p(t, m_{12}^*, m_{22}^* \mid \pi_1) = \frac{\Gamma(\frac{1}{2}(N_1+N_2-1))\exp[-2\lambda^2 N_2(N_1+1)/(N_1+N_2+1)]}{\Gamma(\frac{1}{2}(N_1+N_2-p))\Gamma(\frac{1}{2}(N_1+N_2-p-1))\Gamma(\frac{1}{2}(p-1))\Gamma(\frac{1}{2})} \cdot \sum_{j=0}^{\infty}\Bigg\{\frac{\Gamma(\frac{1}{2}(N_1+N_2)+j)(2N_2\lambda^2)^j t^{\frac{1}{2}(p-3)}}{\Gamma(\frac{1}{2}p+j)j!(N_1+N_2)^j(N_1+N_2+1)^j(1+t)^{\frac{1}{2}(N_1+N_2)+j}} \cdot \frac{m_{22}^{*\frac{1}{2}(N_1+N_2)-1}}{(1+m_{22}^*)^{\frac{1}{2}(p-1)}(m_{22}^{*2}+m_{22}^*+m_{12}^{*2})^{\frac{1}{2}(N_1+N_2-p+1)+j}} \cdot \Bigg[\frac{(m_{22}^{*2}+m_{22}^*+m_{12}^{*2})}{(1+m_{22}^*)}[N_2(1+m_{22}^*)+N_1(N_1+N_2+1)m_{22}^*]t + (\sqrt{N_2}\,m_{12}^* + \sqrt{N_1(N_1+N_2+1)}\,m_{22}^*)^2\Bigg]^j\Bigg\}.$$

Expanding the numerator of (2.9) in powers of t and letting a new subscript j be used in place of $j-k$, we obtain

$$(2.10)\quad p(t, m_{12}^*, m_{22}^* \mid \pi_1) = \frac{\Gamma(\frac{1}{2}(N_1+N_2-1)\exp[-2\lambda^2 N_2(N_1+1)/(N_1+N_2+1)]}{\Gamma(\frac{1}{2}(N_1+N_2-p))\Gamma(\frac{1}{2}(N_1+N_2-p-1))\Gamma(\frac{1}{2}(p-1))\Gamma(\frac{1}{2})} \cdot \sum_{j=0}^{\infty}\sum_{k=0}^{\infty}\frac{\Gamma(\frac{1}{2}(N_1+N_2)+j+k)(2N_2\lambda^2)^{j+k}t^{\frac{1}{2}(p-3)+k}}{\Gamma(\frac{1}{2}p+j+k)j!\,k!\,(N_1+N_2)^{j+k}(N_1+N_2+1)^{j+k}(1+t)^{\frac{1}{2}(N_1+N_2)+j+k}} \cdot \frac{m_{22}^{*\frac{1}{2}(N_1+N_2)-1}[N_2(1+m_{22}^*)+N_1(N_1+N_2+1)m_{22}^*]^k}{(1+m_{22}^*)^{\frac{1}{2}(p-1)+k}(m_{22}^{*2}+m_{22}^*+m_{12}^{*2})^{\frac{1}{2}(N_1+N_2-p+1)+j}} \cdot (\sqrt{N_2}\,m_{12}^* + \sqrt{N_1(N_1+N_2+1)}\,m_{22}^{*2})^{2j}.$$

The range of t is from 0 to ∞. Now since

$$[m_{11}^*(1+m_{22}^*) - m_{12}^{*2}][m_{22}^*(1+m_{22}^*) - m_{12}^{*2}] - m_{12}^{*2} = [(1+m_{11}^*)(1+m_{22}^*) - m_{12}^{*2}](m_{11}^*m_{22}^* - m_{12}^{*2}) \geqq 0,$$

we see that if we examine the infinite series in (2.7),

$$\frac{N_2 m_{11}^* + 2(N_1N_2)^{\frac{1}{2}}(N_1+N_2+1)^{\frac{1}{2}}m_{12}^* + N_1(N_1+N_2+1)m_{22}^*}{(1+m_{11}^*+m_{22}^*+m_{11}^*m_{22}^*-m_{12}^{*2})} + \frac{(N_1+1)(N_1+N_2)(m_{11}^*m_{22}^*-m_{12}^{*2})}{(1+m_{11}^*+m_{22}^*+m_{11}^*m_{22}^*-m_{12}^{*2})}$$

$$= \frac{N_2[m_{11}^*(1+m_{22}^*)-m_{12}^{*2}]}{(1+m_{11}^*)(1+m_{22}^*)-m_{12}^{*2}} + \frac{2(N_1N_2)^{\frac{1}{2}}(N_1+N_2+1)^{\frac{1}{2}}m_{12}^*}{(1+m_{11}^*)(1+m_{22}^*)-m_{12}^{*2}} + N_1(N_1+N_2+1)\frac{[m_{22}^*(1+m_{11}^*)-m_{12}^{*2}]}{(1+m_{11}^*)(1+m_{22}^*)-m_{12}^{*2}}$$

$$\leqq \frac{\{\sqrt{N_2[m_{11}^*(1+m_{22}^*)-m_{12}^{*2}]} + \sqrt{N_1(N_1+N_2+1)[m_{22}^*(1+m_{11}^*)-m_{12}^{*2}]}\}^2}{(1+m_{11}^*)(1+m_{22}^*)-m_{12}^{*2}}$$

$$< [\sqrt{N_2} + \sqrt{N_1(N_1+N_2+1)}]^2$$

$$< 2[N_2 + N_1(N_1+N_2+1)]$$

$$< 2(N_1+1)(N_1+N_2).$$

Hence

$$\frac{\Gamma(\frac{1}{2}(N_1+N_2)+j)}{\Gamma(\frac{1}{2}p+j)j!}\cdot\left[\frac{2N_2\lambda^2}{(N_1+N_2)(N_1+N_2+1)}\right]^j$$

$$\cdot\left\{\frac{[N_2m_{11}^*+2(N_1N_2)^{\frac{1}{2}}(N_1+N_2+1)^{\frac{1}{2}}m_{12}^*+N_1(N_1+N_2+1)m_{22}^*]^j}{(1+m_{11}^*+m_{22}^*+m_{11}^*m_{22}^*-m_{12}^{*2})^j}\right.$$

$$\left.+\frac{[(N_1+1)(N_1+N_2)(m_{11}^*m_{22}^*-m_{12}^{*2})]^j}{(1+m_{11}^*+m_{22}^*+m_{11}^*m_{22}^*-m_{12}^{*2})^j}\right\}$$

$$<\frac{\Gamma(\frac{1}{2}(N_1+N_2))}{\Gamma(\frac{1}{2}p)}\cdot\frac{(N_1+N_2)^j}{p^j j!}\left[\frac{2N_2\lambda^2}{(N_1+N_2)(N_1+N_2+1)}\right]^j 2^j(N_1+1)^j(N_1+N_2)^j$$

$$<\frac{\Gamma(\frac{1}{2}(N_1+N_2))}{\Gamma(\frac{1}{2}p)}\cdot\frac{[4\lambda^2N_2(N_1+1)(N_1+N_2)]^j}{[p(N_1+N_2+1)]^j j!}\,.$$

It follows that the infinite series in (2.7) is uniformly convergent, since it is dominated for all values of m_{11}^*, m_{12}^*, and m_{22}^* by the series expansion of

$$\frac{\Gamma(\frac{1}{2}(N_1+N_2))}{\Gamma(\frac{1}{2}p)}\cdot\exp\,[4\lambda^2N_2(N_1+1)(N_1+N_2)/p(N_1+N_2+1)]\,,$$

and we can integrate the transformed density term by term with respect to t, making use of the relation for gamma functions

$$\int_0^\infty\frac{t^{\frac{1}{2}(p-3)+k}}{(1+t)^{\frac{1}{2}(N_1+N_2)+j+k}}=\frac{\Gamma(\frac{1}{2}(p-1)+k)\Gamma(\frac{1}{2}(N_1+N_2-p+1)+j)}{\Gamma(\frac{1}{2}(N_1+N_2)+j+k)}\,,$$

thus obtaining the joint density of m_{12}^* and m_{22}^*. This gives us

(2.11) $$p(m_{12}^*, m_{22}^*\,|\,\pi_1)$$

$$=\frac{\Gamma(\frac{1}{2}(N_1+N_2-1))\exp\,[-2\lambda^2N_2(N_1+1)/(N_1+N_2+1)]m_{22}^{*\frac{1}{2}(N_1+N_2)-1}}{\Gamma(\frac{1}{2}(N_1+N_2-p))\Gamma(\frac{1}{2}(N_1+N_2-p-1))\Gamma(\frac{1}{2}(p-1))\Gamma(\frac{1}{2})}$$

$$\cdot\sum_{j=0}^{\infty}\sum_{k=0}^{\infty}\frac{\Gamma(\frac{1}{2}(p-1)+k)\Gamma(\frac{1}{2}(N_1+N_2-p+1)+j)(2N_2\lambda^2)^{j+k}}{\Gamma(\frac{1}{2}p+j+k)j!k!(N_1+N_2)^{j+k}(N_1+N_2+1)^{j+k}}$$

$$\cdot\frac{[\sqrt{N_2}\,m_{12}^*+\sqrt{N_1(N_1+N_2+1)}\,m_{22}^*]^{2j}[N_2(1+m_{22}^*)+N_1(N+N_2+1)m_{22}^*]^k}{(1+m_{22}^*)^{\frac{1}{2}(p-1)+k}(m_{22}^{*2}+m_{22}^*+m_{12}^{*2})^{\frac{1}{2}(N_1+N_2-p+1)+j}}$$

with $-\infty<m_{12}^*<\infty$, and $0<m_{22}^*<\infty$.

Now

$$[\sqrt{N_2}\,m_{12}^*+\sqrt{N_1(N_1+N_2+1)}\,m_{22}^*]^{2j}$$

$$=(N_2m_{12}^{*2}+2\sqrt{N_1N_2(N_1+N_2+1)}\,m_{12}^*m_{22}^*+N_1(N_1+N_2+1)m_{22}^{*2})^j$$

$$=\sum_{t=0}^{j}\sum_{r=0}^{s}\frac{j!}{(j-s)!\,(s-r)!\,r!}2^{s-r}N_1^{(j-s)+\frac{1}{2}(s-r)}N_2^{r+\frac{1}{2}(s-r)}$$

$$\cdot(N_1+N_2+1)^{(j-s)+\frac{1}{2}(s-r)}m_{12}^{*2r+(s-r)}m_{22}^{*2(j-s)+s-r}\,,$$

and

$$[N_2(1+m_{22}^*)+N_1(N_1+N_2+1)m_{22}^*]^k$$
$$=\sum_{m=0}^{k}\frac{k!}{m!\,(k-m)!}N_1^mN_2^{k-m}(N_1+N_2+1)^m m_{22}^{*m}(1+m_{22}^*)^{k-m}.$$

The doubly infinite series in (2.11) can then be written as

$$\sum_{j=0}^{\infty}\sum_{s=0}^{j}\sum_{r=0}^{s}\sum_{k=0}^{\infty}\sum_{m=0}^{k}\frac{\Gamma(\frac{1}{2}(p-1)+k)\Gamma(\frac{1}{2}(N_1+N_2-p+1)+j)(2N_2\lambda^2)^{j+k}}{\Gamma(\frac{1}{2}p+j+k)(N_1+N_2)^{j+k}(j-s)!\,(s-r)!\,r!(k-m)!\,m!}$$
$$\cdot\frac{2^{s-r}N_1^{(j-s)+\frac{1}{2}(s-r)+m}N_2^{r+\frac{1}{2}(s-r)+k-m}m_{12}^{*2r+(s-r)}m_{22}^{*2(j-s)+(s-r)+m}}{(N_1+N_2+1)^{r+\frac{1}{2}(s-r)+k-m}(1+m_{22}^*)^{\frac{1}{2}(p-1)+m}(m_{22}^{*2}+m_{22}^*+m_{12}^{*2})^{\frac{1}{2}(N_1+N_2-p+1)+j}}.$$

Since

$$\sum_{j=0}^{\infty}\sum_{s=0}^{j}\sum_{r=0}^{s}=\sum_{r=0}^{\infty}\sum_{s=r}^{\infty}\sum_{j=s}^{\infty}=\sum_{r=0}^{\infty}\sum_{(s-r)=0}^{\infty}\sum_{(j-s)=0}^{\infty}$$

and

$$\sum_{k=0}^{\infty}\sum_{m=0}^{k}=\sum_{m=0}^{\infty}\sum_{k=m}^{\infty}=\sum_{m=0}^{\infty}\sum_{(k-m)=0}^{\infty},$$

we have, writing

$$(s-r)=l,\qquad (j-s)=j',\qquad (k-m)=k',$$

(2.12) $p(m_{12}^*, m_{22}^*\,|\,\pi_1)$

$$=\frac{\Gamma(\frac{1}{2}(N_1+N_2-1))\exp[-2\lambda^2N_2(N_1+1)/(N_1+N_2+1)]}{\Gamma(\frac{1}{2}(N_1+N_2-p))\Gamma(\frac{1}{2}(N_1+N_2-p-1))\Gamma(\frac{1}{2}(p-1))\Gamma(\frac{1}{2})}$$
$$\cdot\sum_{j'=0}^{\infty}\sum_{l=0}^{\infty}\sum_{r=0}^{\infty}\sum_{k'=0}^{\infty}\sum_{m=0}^{\infty}\left[\frac{\Gamma(\frac{1}{2}(p-1)+k'+m)\Gamma(\frac{1}{2}(N_1+N_2-p-1)+j'+l+r)}{\Gamma(\frac{1}{2}(p+j'+l+r+k'+m))j'!\,l!\,r!\,k'!\,m!}\right.$$
$$\cdot\frac{(2N_2\lambda^2)^{j'+l+r+k'+m}2^lN_2^{r+\frac{1}{2}l+k'}N_1^{j'+\frac{1}{2}l+m}}{(N_1+N_2)^{j'+l+r+k'+m}(N_1+N_2+1)^{r+\frac{1}{2}l+k'}}$$
$$\left.\cdot\frac{m_{12}^{*2r+l}m_{22}^{*\frac{1}{2}(N_1+N_2)-1+2j'+l+m}}{(1+m_{22}^*)^{\frac{1}{2}(p-1)+m}(m_{22}^{*2}+m_{22}^*+m_{12}^{*2})^{\frac{1}{2}(N_1+N_2-p+1)+j'+l+r}}\right].$$

In what follows we shall omit the primes on the indexes j and k. From (2.12) we have

(2.13) $p(m_{12}^*\,|\,\pi_1)$

$$=\frac{\Gamma(\frac{1}{2}(N_1+N_2-1))\exp[-2\lambda^2N_2(N_1+1)/(N_1+N_2+1)]}{\Gamma(\frac{1}{2}(N_1+N_2-p))\Gamma(\frac{1}{2}(N_1+N_2-p-1))\Gamma(\frac{1}{2}(p-1))\Gamma(\frac{1}{2})}$$
$$\cdot\sum_{j=0}^{\infty}\sum_{l=0}^{\infty}\sum_{r=0}^{\infty}\sum_{k=0}^{\infty}\sum_{m=0}^{\infty}[g(\lambda^2, N_1, N_2, p, j, l, r, k, m)$$
$$\cdot f(m_{12}^*, N_1, N_2, p, j, l, r, m)],$$

where

$g(\lambda^2, N_1, N_2, p, j, l, r, k, m)$

$$=\frac{\Gamma(\frac{1}{2}(p-1)+k+m)(2N_2\lambda^2)^{j+l+r+k+m}2^lN_2^{r+\frac{1}{2}l+k}N_1^{j+\frac{1}{2}l+m}}{\Gamma(\frac{1}{2}p+j+l+r+k+m)j!\,l!\,r!\,k!\,m!\,(N_1+N_2)^{j+l+r+k+m}(N_1+N_2+1)^{r+\frac{1}{2}l+k}}$$

and

$$f(m_{12}^*, N_1, N_2, p, j, l, r, m)$$
$$= \Gamma(\tfrac{1}{2}(N_1 + N_2 - p + 1) + j + l + r) m_{12}^{*2r+l}$$
$$\cdot \int_0^\infty \frac{m_{22}^{*\frac{1}{2}(N_1+N_2)-1+2j+l+m} dm_{22}^*}{(1 + m_{22}^*)^{\frac{1}{2}(p-1)+m} (m_{22}^{*2} + m_{22}^* + m_{12}^{*2})^{\frac{1}{2}(N_1+N_2-p+1)+j+l+r}} .$$

To perform the integration, we make the transformation

$$m_{22}^* = \frac{z}{1-z} .$$

The Jacobian of the transformation is

$$|J| = \frac{1}{(1-z)^2} .$$

It follows that

$$f(m_{12}^*, N_1, N_2, p, j, l, r, m)$$
$$= \Gamma(\tfrac{1}{2}(N_1 + N_2 - p + 1) + j + l + r) m_{12}^{*2r+l}$$
$$\int_0^1 \frac{z^{\frac{1}{2}(N_1+N_2)-1+2j+l+m} (1-z)^{\frac{1}{2}(N_1+N_2-p-1)+2r+l} dz}{[z + m_{12}^{*2}(1-z)^2]^{\frac{1}{2}(N_1+N_2-p+1)+j+l+r}} .$$

Since we can write

$$z + m_{12}^{*2}(1-z)^2 = 1 - (1-z)(1 - m_{12}^{*2} + m_{12}^{*2} z) ,$$

we have for $|m_{12}^*| \leqq 1$,

$$f(m_{12}^*, N_1, N_2, p, j, l, r, m) \tag{2.14}$$
$$= \int_0^1 z^{\frac{1}{2}(N_1+N_2)-1+2j+l+m} (1-z)^{\frac{1}{2}(N_1+N_2-p-1)+2r+l}$$
$$\cdot \sum_{s=0}^\infty \sum_{t=0}^\infty \left[\frac{\Gamma(\tfrac{1}{2}(N_1 + N_2 - p + 1) + j + l + r + s + t)}{s!\, t!} z^s (1-z)^{s+t} \cdot m_{12}^{*2(r+s)+l} (1 - m_{12}^{*2})^t \right] dz$$
$$= \sum_{s=0}^\infty \sum_{t=0}^\infty \left[\frac{\Gamma(\tfrac{1}{2}(N_1 + N_2 - p + 1) + j + l + r + s + t)}{s!\, t!} m_{12}^{*2(r+s)+l} (1 - m_{12}^{*2})^t \cdot \frac{\Gamma(\tfrac{1}{2}(N_1 + N_2) + 2j + l + m + s) \Gamma(\tfrac{1}{2}(N_1 + N_2 - p + 1) + 2r + l + s + t)}{\Gamma(N_1 + N_2 - \tfrac{1}{2}(p-1) + 2j + 2l + 2r + m + 2s + t)} \right],$$

since the series expansion is uniformly convergent for $|m_{12}^*| \leqq 1$ and can be integrated term by term.

We can also write

$$z + m_{12}^{*2}(1-z)^2 = m_{12}^{*2} \left[1 - z \left(1 - z + \frac{m_{12}^{*2} - 1}{m_{12}^{*2}} \right) \right] .$$

When $|m_{12}^*| > 1$ the quantity

$$z \left(1 - z + \frac{m_{12}^{*2} - 1}{m_{12}^{*2}} \right) \leqq 1 .$$

In this case, therefore, we have

(2.15) $$f(m_{12}^*, N_1, N_2, p, j, l, r, m)$$

$$= \int_0^1 z^{\frac{1}{2}(N_1+N_2)-1+2j+l+m}(1-z)^{\frac{1}{2}(N_1+N_2-p-1)+2r+l}$$

$$\cdot \sum_{s=0}^{\infty}\sum_{t=0}^{\infty}\Bigg[\frac{\Gamma(\frac{1}{2}(N_1+N_2-p+1)+j+l+r+s+t)}{s!\,t!} z^{s+t}(1-z)^s$$

$$\cdot (\operatorname{sgn} m_{12}^*)^l \frac{(m_{12}^{*2}-1)^t\, dz}{(m_{12}^{*2})^{\frac{1}{2}(N_1+N_2-p+1)+j+t+\frac{1}{2}l}}\Bigg]$$

$$= \sum_{s=0}^{\infty}\sum_{t=0}^{\infty}\Bigg[\frac{\Gamma(\frac{1}{2}(N_1+N_2-p+1)+j+l+r+s+t)(\operatorname{sgn} m_{12}^*)^l(m_{12}^{*2}-1)^t}{s!\,t!\,(m_{12}^{*2})^{\frac{1}{2}(N_1+N_2-p+1)+j+t+\frac{1}{2}l}}$$

$$\cdot \frac{\Gamma(\frac{1}{2}(N_1+N_2)+2j+l+m+s+t)\,\Gamma(\frac{1}{2}(N_1+N_2-p+1)+2r+l+s)}{\Gamma[N_1+N_2-\frac{1}{2}(p-1)+2j+2l+2r+m+2s+t]}\Bigg].$$

Equations (2.14) and (2.15) together with (2.13) give us series representations for the density function of m_{12}^* that are valid for $|m_{12}^*| \leqq 1$ and $|m_{12}^*| > 1$, respectively.

When $N_1 = N_2 = N$, we have [cf. (2.6)]

(2.16) $$m_{12}^* = \frac{NW}{2(N-1)(2N+1)^{\frac{1}{2}}}.$$

It follows that

(2.17) $$p(W\,|\,\pi_1)$$

$$= \frac{N\Gamma(N-\frac{1}{2})\exp[-2N\lambda^2(N+1)/(2N+1)]}{2(N-1)\sqrt{2N+1}\,\Gamma(N-\frac{1}{2}p)\,\Gamma(N-\frac{1}{2}(p+1))\,\Gamma(\frac{1}{2}(p-1))\,\Gamma(\frac{1}{2})}$$

$$\cdot \sum_j\sum_l\sum_r\sum_k\sum_m g(\lambda^2, N, N, p, j, l, r, k, m)$$

$$\cdot f\left[\frac{NW}{2(N-1)\sqrt{2N+1}}, N, N, p, j, l, r, m\right].$$

When $N_1 = N_2 = N$, it is easy to see that $p(m_{12}^*\,|\,\pi_1) = p(-m_{12}^*\,|\,\pi_2)$. Consequently, we have

(2.18) $$p(W\,|\,\pi_2)$$

$$= \frac{N\Gamma(N-\frac{1}{2})\exp[-2N\lambda^2(N+1)/(2N+1)]}{2(N-1)(2N+1)^{\frac{1}{2}}\Gamma(N-\frac{1}{2}p)\,\Gamma(N-\frac{1}{2}(p+1))\,\Gamma(\frac{1}{2}(p-1))\,\Gamma(\frac{1}{2})}$$

$$\cdot \sum_j\sum_l\sum_r\sum_k\sum_m g(\lambda^2, N, N, p, j, l, r, k, m)$$

$$\cdot f\left[\frac{-NW}{2(N-1)(2N+1)^{\frac{1}{2}}}, N, N, p, j, l, r, m\right].$$

The series expansions given in (2.14) and (2.15) are valid for

$$|W| \leqq \frac{2(N-1)(2N+1)^{\frac{1}{2}}}{N} \quad \text{and} \quad |W| > \frac{2(N-1)(2N+1)^{\frac{1}{2}}}{N},$$

respectively.

3. Probability that $W \leqq 0$ when $\pi = \pi_1$

In a given classification procedure based on W, an individual is assigned to π_1 if $W > w_0$, where w_0 is a preassigned number, and to π_2 if $W \leqq w_0$. The probability of misclassifying an individual from π_1 is $\Pr\{W \leqq w_0 \mid \pi_1\}$; the probability of misclassifying an individual from π_2 is $\Pr\{W > w_0 \mid \pi_2\}$. When $N_1 = N_2 = N$, this second probability is equal to $\Pr\{W < w_0 \mid \pi_1\}$. It is clear, therefore, that the two risks are equal when $w_0 = 0$.

When $w_0 = 0$, we have

$$
\begin{aligned}
(3.1)\qquad \Pr\{W \leqq 0 \mid \pi_1\} &= \Pr\{m_{12}^* \leqq 0 \mid \pi_1\} \\
&= \frac{\Gamma(N-\frac{1}{2})\exp[-2N\lambda^2(N+1)/(2N+1)]}{\Gamma(N-\frac{1}{2}p)\Gamma(N-\frac{1}{2}(p+1))\Gamma(\frac{1}{2}(p-1))\Gamma(\frac{1}{2})} \\
&\quad \cdot \sum_j \sum_l \sum_r \sum_k \sum_m g(\lambda^2, N, N, p, j, l, r, k, m) \\
&\quad \cdot \int_{-\infty}^{0} f(m_{12}^*, N, N, p, j, l, r, m)\,dm_{12}^* .
\end{aligned}
$$

In evaluating this integral, we can integrate the series representations term by term. That is, we have

$$
\begin{aligned}
(3.2)\qquad & \int_{-\infty}^{0} f(m_{12}^*, N, N, p, j, l, r, m)\,dm_{12}^* \\
&= \int_{-\infty}^{-1} f(m_{12}^*, N, N, p, j, l, r, m)\,dm_{12}^* + \int_{-1}^{0} f(m_{12}^*, N, N, p, j, l, r, m)\,dm_{12}^* \\
&= \frac{1}{2}\sum_s \sum_t \frac{\Gamma(N-\frac{1}{2}(p-1)+j+l+r+s+t)(-1)^l}{\Gamma(2N-\frac{1}{2}(p-1)+2j+2l+2r+m+2s+t)s!\,t!} \\
&\quad \cdot \left[\frac{\Gamma(N+2j+l+m+s)\Gamma(N-\frac{1}{2}(p-1)+2r+l+s+t)}{\Gamma(r+s+t+\frac{1}{2}(l+3))}\right. \\
&\quad \cdot \Gamma(r+s+\tfrac{1}{2}(l+1))\Gamma(t+1) \\
&\quad + \frac{\Gamma(N+2j+l+m+s+t)\Gamma(N-\frac{1}{2}(p-1)+2r+l+s)}{\Gamma(N-\frac{1}{2}p+1+j+t+\frac{1}{2}l)} \\
&\quad \left. \cdot \Gamma(N-\tfrac{1}{2}p+j+\tfrac{1}{2}l)\Gamma(t+1)\right] \\
&= \frac{1}{2}\sum_s \frac{\Gamma(N-\frac{1}{2}(p-1)+j+l+r+s)\Gamma(N+2j+l+m+s)}{\Gamma(2N-\frac{1}{2}(p-1)+2j+2l+2r+m+2s)s!} \\
&\quad \cdot \Gamma(N-\tfrac{1}{2}(p-1)+2r+l+s)(-1)^l \\
&\quad \cdot \left\{\frac{\Gamma(r+s+\frac{1}{2}(l+1))}{\Gamma(r+s+\frac{1}{2}(l+3))}\right. \\
&\quad \cdot {}_3F_2\left[\begin{matrix}1, N-\frac{1}{2}(p-1)+j+l+r+s, N-\frac{1}{2}(p-1)+2r+l+s; 1\\ r+s+\frac{1}{2}(l+3), 2N-\frac{1}{2}(p-1)+2j+2l+2r+m+2s\end{matrix}\right] \\
&\quad + \frac{\Gamma(N-\frac{1}{2}p+j+\frac{1}{2}l)}{\Gamma(N-\frac{1}{2}p+1+j+\frac{1}{2}l)} \\
&\quad \left. \cdot {}_3F_2\left[\begin{matrix}1, N-\frac{1}{2}(p-1)+j+l+r+s, N+2j+l+m+s; 1\\ N-\frac{1}{2}p+1+j+\frac{1}{2}l, 2N-\frac{1}{2}(p-1)+2j+2l+2r+m+2s\end{matrix}\right]\right\},
\end{aligned}
$$

where ${}_3F_2$ is the generalized hypergeometric series with unit argument. That is,

$$ {}_3F_2\begin{bmatrix} a, b, c; 1 \\ e, f \end{bmatrix} = 1 + \frac{abc}{ef} + \frac{a(a+1)b(b+1)c(c+1)}{e(e+1)f(f+1)2!} + \cdots . $$

It follows that (see [4], p. 21)

$$ \frac{\Gamma(N - \tfrac{1}{2}p + j + \tfrac{1}{2}l)}{\Gamma(N - \tfrac{1}{2}p + 1 + j + \tfrac{1}{2}l)} $$

$$ \cdot {}_3F_2\begin{bmatrix} 1, N - \tfrac{1}{2}(p-1) + j + l + r + s, N + 2j + l + m + s; 1 \\ N - \tfrac{1}{2}p + 1 + j + \tfrac{1}{2}l, 2N - \tfrac{1}{2}(p-1) + 2j + 2l + 2r + m + 2s \end{bmatrix} $$

$$ = -\frac{\Gamma(r + s + \tfrac{1}{2}(l+1))}{\Gamma(r + s + \tfrac{1}{3}(l+3))} $$

$$ \cdot {}_3F_2\begin{bmatrix} 1, N - \tfrac{1}{2}(p-1) + j + l + r + s, N - \tfrac{1}{2}(p-1) + 2r + l + s; 1 \\ r + s + \tfrac{1}{2}(l+3), 2N - \tfrac{1}{2}(p-1) + 2j + 2l + 2r + m + 2s \end{bmatrix} $$

$$ + \frac{\Gamma(2N - \tfrac{1}{2}(p-1) + 2j + 2l + 2r + m + 2s)\,\Gamma(r + s + \tfrac{1}{2}(l+1))}{\Gamma(N - \tfrac{1}{2}(p-1) + j + l + r + s)\,\Gamma(N - \tfrac{1}{2}(p-1) + 2r + l + s)} $$

$$ \cdot \frac{\Gamma(N - \tfrac{1}{2}p + j + \tfrac{1}{2}l)\,\Gamma(N - \tfrac{1}{2}p + r + \tfrac{1}{2}l)}{\Gamma(2N - \tfrac{1}{2}p + 2j + r + m + s + \tfrac{3}{2}l)} $$

$$ \cdot {}_3F_2\begin{bmatrix} N - \tfrac{1}{2}p + j + \tfrac{1}{2}l - (r + s - \tfrac{1}{2}), N - \tfrac{1}{2}p + r + \tfrac{1}{2}l; 1 \\ -(r + s - \tfrac{1}{2}), 2N - \tfrac{1}{2}p + 2j + r + m + s + \tfrac{3}{2}l \end{bmatrix} . $$

But

$$ {}_3F_2\begin{bmatrix} N - \tfrac{1}{2}p + j + \tfrac{1}{2}l, -(r + s - \tfrac{1}{2}), N - \tfrac{1}{2}p + r + \tfrac{1}{2}l; 1 \\ -(r + s - \tfrac{1}{2}), 2N - \tfrac{1}{2}p + 2j + r + m + s + \tfrac{3}{2}l \end{bmatrix} $$

$$ = {}_2F_1[N - \tfrac{1}{2}p + j + \tfrac{1}{2}l, N - \tfrac{1}{2}p + r + \tfrac{1}{2}l, 2N - \tfrac{1}{2}p + 2j + r + m + s + \tfrac{3}{2}l; 1] $$

$$ = \frac{\Gamma(2N - \tfrac{1}{2}p + 2j + r + m + s + \tfrac{3}{2}l)\,\Gamma(\tfrac{1}{2}p + j + \tfrac{1}{2}l + m + s)}{\Gamma(N + j + l + r + m + s)\,\Gamma(N + 2j + l + m + s)} . $$

Hence

$$ \int_{-\infty}^{0} f(m_{12}^*, N, N, p, j, l, r, m)\, dm_{12}^* $$

$$ = \frac{1}{2}\Gamma(N - \tfrac{1}{2}p + j + \tfrac{1}{2}l)\,\Gamma(N - \tfrac{1}{2}p + r + \tfrac{1}{2}l)(-1)^l $$

$$ \cdot \sum_{s=0}^{\infty} \frac{\Gamma(r + \tfrac{1}{2}(l+1) + s)\,\Gamma(\tfrac{1}{2}p + j + \tfrac{1}{2}l + m + s)}{\Gamma(N + j + l + r + m + s)\, s!} $$

$$ = \frac{1}{2}\,\frac{\Gamma(N - \tfrac{1}{2}(p+1))\,\Gamma(N - \tfrac{1}{2}p + j + \tfrac{1}{2}l)\,\Gamma(r + \tfrac{1}{2}(l+1))}{\Gamma(N - \tfrac{1}{2} + j + \tfrac{1}{2}l + m)} $$

$$ \cdot\, \Gamma(\tfrac{1}{2}p + j + \tfrac{1}{2}l + m)(-1)^l . $$

It follows that

$$(3.3) \qquad P(W \leqq 0 \mid \pi_1) = \frac{\Gamma(N-\frac{1}{2}) \exp[-2N\lambda^2(N+1)/(2N+1)]}{2\Gamma(N-\frac{1}{2}p)\Gamma(\frac{1}{2}(p-1))\Gamma(\frac{1}{2})}$$

$$\cdot \sum_j \sum_l \sum_r \sum_k \sum_m \left[\frac{\Gamma(\frac{1}{2}(p-1)+k+m)\Gamma(N-\frac{1}{2}p+j+\frac{1}{2}l)\Gamma(r+\frac{1}{2}(l+1))}{\Gamma(\frac{1}{2}p+j+l+r+k+m)\Gamma(N-\frac{1}{2}+j+\frac{1}{2}l+m)} \cdot \frac{\Gamma(\frac{1}{2}p+j+\frac{1}{2}l+m)(-2)^l(N\lambda^2)^{j+l+r+k+m}}{j!\,l!\,r!\,k!\,m!\,(2N+1)^{r+l/2+k}} \right].$$

REFERENCES

[1] Wald, A. On a statistical problem arising in the classification of an individual into one of two groups. *Ann. Math. Stat.*, 1944, **15**, 145-62.

[2] Anderson, T. W. Classification by multivariate analysis. *Psychometrika*, 1951, **16**, 31-50.

[3] Sitgreaves, R. On the distribution of two random matrices used in classification procedures. *Ann. Math. Stat.*, 1952, **23**, 263-70.

[4] Bailey, W. N. *Generalized Hypergeometric Series.* London: Cambridge Univ. Press, 1935.

16

Computation of an Empirical Sampling Distribution for the W-Classification Statistic

DANIEL TEICHROEW, Stanford University
ROSEDITH SITGREAVES, Columbia University

1. Introduction

This chapter considers the problem of estimating the cumulative distribution function of the classification statistic W by means of an empirical sampling experiment. The statistic is defined in the same manner as in Chapter 15 but is symbolized here by

$$W = \sum_{i=1}^{P} \sum_{j=1}^{P} S^{ij}(\bar{x}_i^{(1)} - \bar{x}_i^{(2)})(y_j - \tfrac{1}{2}(\bar{x}_j^{(1)} + \bar{x}_j^{(2)})) , \tag{1.1}$$

where y_j represents the jth measurement on the individual to be classified. The quantities $S_{ij}, \bar{x}_i^{(1)}, \bar{x}_i^{(2)}, \quad i, j = 1, 2, \cdots, p$ are defined as in equations (1.1) and (1.2) of Chapter 15.

To evaluate the operating characteristics of a classification procedure based on W, that is, to determine the probabilities of misclassification associated with it, and to compare these probabilities with corresponding probabilities for the optimal procedure based on T^*, it is necessary to consider the sampling distribution of W under the hypothesis that the individual to be classified belongs to π_1, and under the alternative hypothesis that he belongs to π_2. The distribution, in either case, is exceedingly complicated (e.g., see [1] and Chapter 15). Even in a few special cases for which an analytical expression has been obtained, its numerical evaluation would require too much computing to be practicable. Accordingly, an empirical sampling plan has been used to obtain estimates of the cumulative probability distribution of W. Although such a plan does not give exact answers, it frequently gives results that are sufficiently accurate for most practical purposes.

2. Formulation of the Problem

It is easy to show that (e.g., see [2])

$$W = d'S^{-1}z + \frac{(N_1 - N_2)}{2(N_1 + N_2)} d'S^{-1}d , \tag{2.1}$$

where d and z are p-dimensional vectors and S is a $p \times p$ matrix. Under either alternative, the vectors d and z are distributed independently of each other and of the matrix S. Further, under both alternatives, the components of d are independently, normally distributed, each with variance $(N_1 + N_2)/N_1N_2$ and with

$$E(d_1) = 2\lambda \, , \tag{2.2}$$
$$E(d_i) = 0 \, , \qquad i = 2, 3, \cdots, p \, ,$$

where $\lambda \geqq 0$, and $\lambda^2 = \frac{1}{4} \sum_{i=1}^{p} \sum_{j=1}^{p} \sigma^{ij}(\mu_i^{(1)} - \mu_i^{(2)})(\mu_j^{(1)} - \mu_j^{(2)})$.

Also, under both alternatives, the elements of $(N_1 + N_2 - 2)S = A$ have a Wishart distribution with $N_1 + N_2 - 2 = n$ degrees of freedom and covariance matrix equal to the identity matrix. The components of z are independently, normally distributed, each with variance $(N_1 + N_2 + 1)/(N_1 + N_2)$. Under the hypothesis that the unknown observation belongs to π_1,

$$E(z_1) = \frac{2N_2\lambda}{N_1 + N_2} \, , \tag{2.3}$$
$$E(z_i) = 0 \, , \qquad i = 2, 3, \cdots, p \, ,$$

while under the alternative hypothesis

$$E(z_1) = -\frac{2N_1\lambda}{N_1 + N_2} \tag{2.4}$$
$$E(z_i) = 0 \qquad i = 2, 3, \cdots, p \, .$$

Our problem is to estimate

$$F(w) = \Pr\{W \leqq w\} \tag{2.5}$$

from the results of a sampling experiment. That is, we want to generate a number of random values of W and then determine what proportion of these values is less than or equal to specified values of w. For the present we shall limit consideration to the case in which the unknown observation belongs to π_1. It should be observed that when $N_1 = N_2$ (e.g., see [1])

$$\Pr\{W \leqq w \mid \pi_1\} = \Pr\{W \geqq w \mid \pi_2\} \, . \tag{2.6}$$

The distribution function $F(w)$ depends on four parameters p, λ, N_1, and N_2. For our purposes it is more convenient to use the parameters $n = N_1 + N_2 - 2$ and $m = N_1/N_2$ instead of N_1 and N_2. To generate random values of w, we consider the problem of generating random values of z, d, and A for specified values of the parameters, and use these random values in (2.1) to find the corresponding values of w.

The major difficulty in this approach comes from the need to compute random values of a Wishart matrix. A p-dimensional Wishart matrix contains $\frac{1}{2}p(p + 1)$ different random variates, which are not independently distributed. Therefore the standard techniques for sampling from a univariate distribution cannot be used directly. It is possible to reduce the problem of sampling from a multivariate distribution to that of sampling from a univariate distribution by utilizing conditional distributions. This technique is extremely complicated even for a few dimensions, and in view of the range of values of p for which the distribution of W is of interest, it seems desirable to explore other methods.

Another way of reducing the problem to sampling from univariate distributions is to use the fact that the Wishart matrix is the matrix of sums of squares and cross products of normally distributed variates. One could generate an $n \times p$ matrix of independent normal variates. The product of this matrix and its transpose has a Wishart distribution. This simple solution is impractical from the computational point of view because it involves the multiplication of an $n \times p$ matrix by its transpose. Apart from the difficulties of storing all the numbers involved, the multiplication time is unreasonably large; for example, if $n = 200$ and $p = 15$, the number of multiplications (making use of the symmetry) is $n[p(p+1)/2] = 24{,}000$. Even on a fast computer such as the SWAC,[1] which can do more than 3000 multiplications per second, this amount of computing for the Wishart matrix alone would seriously restrict the number of samples that could be computed.

This time could be reduced somewhat by using the additive property of the Wishart distribution; e.g., one could use a matrix for, say, $n = 10$, then add something to it to get the matrix for $n = 20$, etc. Even with this simplification the method is difficult to use. The method finally decided upon to generate random Wishart matrices involves factoring the sums of squares and cross-products matrix into the product of several elementary matrices. The general method is sketched in the next section.

3. A Method for Generating Random Wishart Matrices

As mentioned in Section 2, basically this method consists of writing a Wishart matrix as the product of a number of matrices, each of which has elements that are independently distributed. The first step is to write A in the form

$$A = D'RD\,, \tag{3.1}$$

where R is the correlation matrix and D is a diagonal matrix whose elements are proportional to the standard deviations of the p variates. The matrix R can be written as a product of matrices involving partial correlation coefficients that are independently distributed. This leads us to believe that we can start with matrices whose elements are independent variates, and that by multiplying them together we can get a matrix that has the distribution of a correlation matrix. Since W is actually a function of the inverse of A, we are interested in finding a way to multiply matrices in order that the product will have the same distribution as R^{-1}. (In this way the time required to invert the matrix can be saved.) The form these matrices must have and the proof that they lead to the correct result are given in Appendix A. The following paragraph summarizes the computational steps.

[1] National Bureau of Standards Western Computer located at the University of California, Los Angeles.

We can write

$$(3.2)\qquad \begin{aligned} S^{-1} &= nA^{-1} = n[DRD']^{-1} = nD'^{-1}R^{-1}D^{-1} \\ &= nD'^{-1}M'^{-1}M^{-1}D^{-1} \qquad \text{where } M = M_1M_2 \cdots M_{p-1} \\ &= \sqrt{n}\, D'^{-1})M_1'^{-1} \cdots M_{p-1}'^{-1}M_{p-1}^{-1} \cdots M_1^{-1}(\sqrt{n}\, D^{-1}) \,, \end{aligned}$$

where

(i) $\sqrt{n}\, D'^{-1} = \sqrt{n}\, D^{-1}$ is a diagonal matrix whose elements are distributed as $\sqrt{n/\chi^2}$, with χ^2 having the usual χ^2 distribution with n degrees of freedom.

(ii) M_i is a matrix whose form is shown in Appendix A. Those elements of M_i that are neither 0 nor 1 are simple functions of independently distributed t variables; i.e., variables having Student's t distribution with a given number of degrees of freedom.

The problem of generating random values of S^{-1} is thus reduced to generating random values of the χ^2 and t distribution.[2] Various techniques for doing this will be considered in Section 4.

By writing the Wishart matrix in this form, we considerably reduce the amount of computation. In the first place the amount of computation is now independent of n, and therefore it will be possible to investigate the approach to the asymptotic distribution more closely. Second, the need for the matrix inversion has been eliminated. Furthermore, the number of variates that are needed has been reduced to p values of the χ^2 type and $\frac{1}{2}p(p-1)$ values of the t type. The matrix multiplications are not so formidable as they appear, since most of the elements of the matrices are 0. In computing the statistic $d'S^{-1}z$ in which d and z are vectors, it is necessary to store only two p-dimensional vectors. This represents a considerable improvement over storing a symmetrical $p \times p$ matrix.

4. Generation of Random Variates in Computing Machines

A sampling experiment that is conducted to estimate the distribution of a statistic $g(x_1, \cdots, x_n)$, in which the x's are observations from a density function $f(x)$, consists of essentially four steps:

Step 1. Select N samples, each of size n, from the density function $f(x)$. Let the selected values be $\{x_{ij}\}$, $i = 1, 2 \cdots, N$, $j = 1, 2, \cdots, n$, where x_{ij} is the jth value in the ith sample.

Step 2. Compute the statistic, i.e., $g(x_{i1}, \cdots, x_{in})$ for $i = 1, \cdots, N$.

Step 3. Rank the N values of the statistic in order of magnitude.

Step 4. Estimate the distribution of g, say $H(g)$, by $H(g) = (1/N)$ {number of samples in which $g(x_{ij}) \leqq g$}.

(This method is the simplest to use. Modifications to increase the efficiency of the sampling have been suggested by Trotter and Tukey [3], Fieller and Hartley [4], and Teichroew [5]).

---

[2] Since a t variate is proportional to a normal variate divided by the square root of a χ^2 variate, we can generate values of S^{-1} by using only normal and χ^2 variates. However, the amount of storage would be decreased only slightly and the amount of computation would not be affected.

Here our main concern is the use of a computer to mechanize this procedure. Steps 2, 3, and 4, in general, involve no new techniques and present no serious problem, though the coding may be complicated. The difficulty arises in the first step, the computation for which will be discussed in this section.

Random variates are usually computed in two stages:

1. A random value is selected from the uniform distribution.
2. This value is then transformed to a value y from the desired distribution $F(y)$.

The transformation to be used is, of course, the one that gives y as a function of P, where

$$P = \int_{-\infty}^{y} dF(t) \,, \tag{4.1}$$

since if P has a uniform distribution, y obtained by this transformation has the distribution $F(y)$.

A number of different methods have been suggested for each of these steps, and some of them are listed below. Others are discussed elsewhere, e.g., by Taussky and Todd [6] and Teichroew [5]. The experimenter is faced with deciding which method to use. He will usually want to minimize his cost for a given amount of precision, subject to conditions on the amount of machine time and coding time available and on the total amount of time available for the whole problem. Frequently machine characteristics, such as amount of storage available, may influence his decision.

4.1. Computation of uniform random variates. A uniform random variate means a (continuous) random variable that is uniformly distributed over the interval (0, 1); i.e., any value from 0 to 1 is equally likely. In practice one takes several random digits, puts a decimal point in front, and uses this number as a uniform variate. This procedure could be used in machine work; i.e., one could take existing tables of random digits, group the digits into a satisfactory number of digits per number, and then convert these numbers into whatever system the machine is using. This method, however, is not practical because, to give only one reason, the total number of digits available is far too small for the high-speed computers.

A more realistic approach is to generate the uniform numbers in the machine. This can be done either by (1) building into the logic of the machine a command that furnishes, on request, digits or numbers that are supposedly uniformly distributed, or by (2) programming a sequence of arithmetical operations that yields something approximating a uniformly distributed set of numbers. While it is known that numbers so produced are not completely random—since, for example, in the second case it is possible to say precisely what the kth number will be—nevertheless the numbers have almost all the properties of random numbers that are required by practical problems. In the literature, numbers produced by arithmetical operations have sometimes been called "pseudo-random numbers."

Most machines are not equipped with a "random-number" generator, and therefore an arithmetical method is needed. The one that appears to be most useful is the so-called "residue-class" method, in which one starts with an arbitrary uniform variate, say μ_0, and a sequence of "random" numbers is obtained by repeated multiplication:

$$\mu_n = \mu_{n-1} \cdot a (\mathrm{mod}\, b^k) . \tag{4.2}$$

In general one chooses b to be equal to the base in which the machine operates, k to be equal to the number of digits in a computer number, and a to be any number that satisfies certain conditions. (See [5] or [6].) The numbers $\mu_n b^{-k}$ will be used as uniform variates between 0 and 1. In this process, only two storage locations are required, namely for a and μ_n, and only one multiplication is needed for each uniform variate. The only way to speed up this method would be to substitute some additions for a multiplication; it might be worthwhile to investigate this possibility for serial computers, since little would be gained by using machines.

4.2. Transformation of uniform variates to arbitrary variates. Using the method just described, we can generate a sequence of uniform variates; the task now is to transform them to variates having an arbitrary distribution. If $F(y)$ in equation (4.1) is the normal probability distribution, then we might find the normal deviate associated with a uniform variate by reading directly from the tables prepared by Wold [7]. This set of normal variates was prepared by using a table that gives the solution to (4.1) for equidistant intervals in P. Kondo and Elderton [8] have given such a table for $P = .500(.001).999$. This method could be used in a high-speed computer if enough space were available to store the table, and probably would require the least computing time, since only the value of the uniform variate (to modify a transfer command) is needed. Frequently it may be possible to use this method by reducing the number of values of y that are stored (and by storing two values of y in one number). This reduction will probably increase the error due to approximating a continuous curve by a step function, but usually this error will be insignificant compared with the sampling error. (For estimates of the error see Camp [9].) One way of decreasing the approximating error would be to use the y values for the middle of the P intervals instead of for the end points.

In some cases it may not be possible to use the simple, direct method described above. For example, if a number of distributions are used in one problem, there may not be enough storage space for all the tables. When this happens, it is desirable to look for some other method. An easily solved case arises when the statistic of interest is a simple function of uniform variates. For example, twice the negative value of the natural logarithm of the product of k uniform variates has a χ^2 distribution with $2k$ degrees of freedom. Therefore, if a random observation on a χ^2 variate with $2k$ degrees of freedom is desired, it could be obtained by generating k uniform variates, multiplying them together, and computing the negative of twice the logarithm. This computation is easy to code, but other methods might require less computing time.

Another possibility is to solve equation (4.1) either by iteration or by expressing y as a function of P. In general, considerable computation will be required; e.g., Hastings [10] gives a method for solving (4.1) when $F(y)$ is the normal cumulative distribution function. His method requires evaluating a square root, a logarithm, and the ratio of a second- and a third-degree polynomial, which takes a fair amount of time. The difficulty arises because many distributions have long "tails," which makes inverse interpolation difficult. It is true that values in the tails do not occur frequently, but one must provide for them in the code.

Still another method that can be used is based on the definition of the probability density function. A rectangle is constructed (see Figure 1) whose height is the maximum value of the density function and whose length is the possible range of the random variable (if the range is infinite, it must be truncated). Two uniform variates are used to specify a point in the rectangle. If the point lies below the curve, the abscissa is taken as a random value; if the point lies above the curve, the procedure is repeated with two new uniform variates. It is clear that the selected values will have the probability density given by the curve.

The major computation is to determine whether a point lies above or below the line. Even when this computation is simplified to its essentials, too much time may still be required. Another disadvantage is that, on the average, several points must be tried before one can be accepted. One advantage of this method is that it is frequently possible to code the parameter

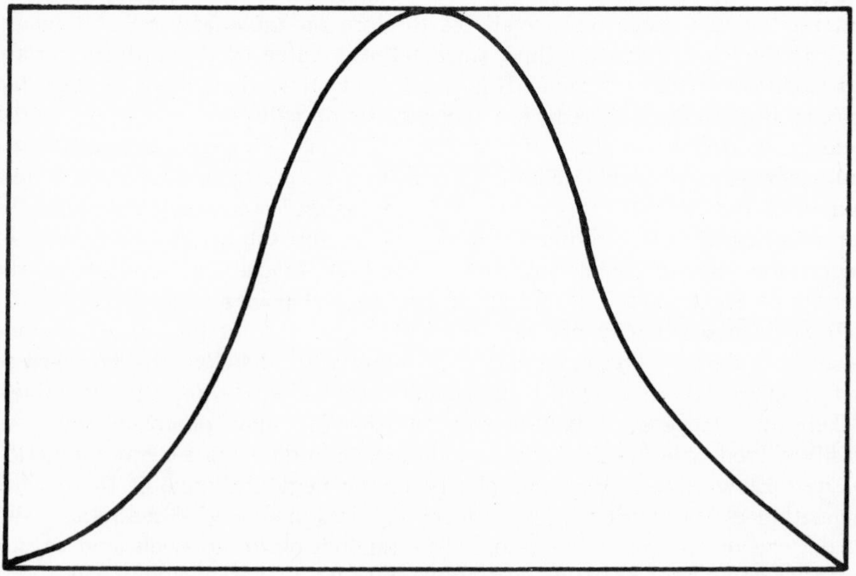

FIG. 1

into the program so that a range of parameter values can be handled. For example, this could be done with the "degrees-of-freedom" parameter of the t distribution.

All the methods discussed above are well known and have been described in detail elsewhere (e.g., see von Neumann [11], Votaw and Rafferty [12], and Teichroew [5]). The following section describes a little-used method that has certain advantages.

4.3. Approximation method for generating random variates. The approximation method involves two basic steps:

1. Uniform variates are generated, and a simple function of them is computed. (A simple function is one that can be computed rapidly.)
2. The random value of the function is transformed into one having the desired distribution. The transformation is done in such a way that the computation time is minimized.

Analytically, this procedure is equivalent to solving the equation $x = h(y)$, in which the function h is defined by

$$\int_{-\infty}^{x(P)} f(t)\,dt = P = \int_{-\infty}^{y(P)} g(t)\,dt \,. \tag{4.3}$$

For x when y is given, $f(x)$ is the density function from which random values are desired, $g(y)$ is the density function of y, and y is the simple function of uniform variates computed in step 1. The variable P is not involved explicitly in the computation but is shown in (4.3) in order to emphasize how this approach differs from the methods discussed earlier. Several methods of the previous section were based on solving the equation on the left-hand side for x when P is given [cf. (4.1)]. "Randomness" was introduced by using a uniform variate as P. In the approach presented in this chapter, pseudo-random uniform variates were generated on the machine. Next, a function of these variates was used to calculate a new random variate y. Then the problem becomes one of solving (4.3) for x when y is known or given. In general, this equation may be no easier to solve than Equation (4.1). However, by choosing the function of the uniform variates so that $g(y)$ and $f(x)$ have approximately the same form, one might expect that x could be expressed adequately by a polynomial in y. This statement has been verified in certain cases where $f(x)$ is approximately normal. Examples will be given in the next section.

There are at least two good reasons for using the approximation method.

1. *Speed.* The method is relatively fast and probably requires less computing time than any of the methods given above (except the use of a table of probability points). One way it gains speed is by yielding random values of a function of a given variate; e.g., if one wishes to use $x = 1/\sqrt{t}$, this method would get random values of x directly, without computing t first.
2. *Single Code.* Since one basic code is used, each distribution from which samples are desired requires additional storage of only a small number of constants, namely, the coefficients in the polynomial.

4.4. Sampling from distributions that tend to normality. In using the approximation method of Section 4.3 for distributions that tend to normality, it is convenient to let y be the sum of a certain number, say γ, of uniform variates. This sum, by the Central Limit Theorem, is approximately normally distributed, and therefore one would expect that the second step would involve only simple approximations. Furthermore, the sum is the fastest function to compute, since addition is one of the least time-consuming operations for a computer.

One complication is that whereas y in this case has a range $0 \leqq y \leqq \gamma$, the variable x has infinite range. This means that as y approaches γ, the function $h(y)$ must approach infinity very rapidly. Such a function is, of course, difficult to approximate by polynomials. For this reason it is desirable to use an approximation to the function $h(y)$ for $0 < Y_0 \leqq y \leqq Y_1 < \gamma$, where Y_0 and Y_1 are arbitrarily chosen constants. In the sampling experiment, values of $y < Y_0$ and $y > Y_1$ may, of course, occur and some provision must be made for handling these values. It will be seen later that in practical cases Y_0 and Y_1 can be selected so that values of $y < Y_0$ or $y > Y_1$ occur with probabilities of the order of 10^{-5}, and therefore one could without serious error substitute Y_0 if $y < Y_0$, and Y_1 if $y > Y_1$.

Assume that values have been selected for γ, Y_0, and Y_1 and that one wishes to obtain samples from a density $f(x)$. The problem that remains is of finding a suitable approximation to the function $h(y)$ for y in the desired range. Many types of approximations could be used: the first type to try would be one using polynomials because they are easy to evaluate and techniques are known for finding the "best" polynomial approximation. In cases examined so far, such approximations have been satisfactory. The method we used is based on Chebyshev polynomials. (It is described by Lanczos [13].) The algebra and subsequent computations required to obtain numerical values for the polynomial coefficients by this method are considerable, but since the coefficients are to be utilized many times, it was thought worthwhile to obtain the best polynomial approximation.

The following steps that were used in the computation of a random variable x having a density $f(x)$:

1. Compute y by summing γ uniform variates.
2. (a) Compute $z = [2y - (Y_0 + Y_1)]/(Y_1 - Y_0)$, if $Y_0 < y < Y_1$,
   (b) Choose

$$z = \begin{cases} -1 & \text{if } Y_0 \geqq y\,, \\ +1 & \text{if } Y_1 \leqq y\,. \end{cases}$$

3. Compute $x = a_0 + a_1 z + a_2 z^2 + \cdots + a_m z^m$.

After Y_0, Y_1, and γ are chosen, m is determined by the accuracy desired. The a_i's are determined by the function $f(x)$.

4.5. Computation of coefficients a_i for given $f(x)$. Suppose we have a function $x = H(z)$, which we wish to approximate by a polynomial

$$x \sim a_0 + a_1 z + \cdots + a_m z^m$$

in the range $-1 \leqq z \leqq 1$.

One way to get the a's is first to get an approximation in terms of Chebyshev polynomials, i.e.,

$$x \sim \tfrac{1}{2}c_0C_0(z) + c_1C_1(z) + c_2C_2(z) + \cdots + c_{k-1}C_{k-1}(z) ,$$

where $C_i(z)$ is the ith Chebyshev polynomial. In particular:

$$C_0(t) = 1 , \qquad C_2(t) = 2t^2 - 1 ,$$
$$C_1(t) = t , \qquad C_3(t) = 4t^3 - 3t, \text{ etc.}$$

The Chebyshev polynomials have the property that $|C_i(t)| \leqq 1$, and therefore neglect of any particular C_i will not affect the approximation by more than $|c_i|$. Where polynomial approximations are numerically useful, the c_i's decrease in value as i increases up to a certain i, and then they start to oscillate. If the oscillations are small enough, we can neglect the terms after a certain point. This will not affect the approximations by more than the sum of the absolute values of the neglected c_i's. To get the a_i's we merely rewrite the retained terms as a power series.

The c's are computed by evaluating the function $H(z)$ at k values of z. In particular, the values are the roots z_j of the kth polynomial. They have the formulas

$$z_j = \cos\frac{\pi}{2k}(2j+1) ; \qquad j = 0, 1, \cdots, k-1 .$$

Then

$$c_i = \frac{2}{k}\sum_{j=0}^{k-1} H(z_j)\cos\frac{\pi i}{2k}(2j+1) .$$

Lanczos [13] gives the derivation of these formulas.

To summarize, the steps in the computation of the a_i's are as follows:

1. Normalize the range of the independent variable to $(-1, 1)$.
2. Compute $H(z_j)$ at the particular z_j.
3. Compute c_i.
4. Drop as many terms as possible.
5. Rewrite the retained terms as one polynomial.

The general method can be applied directly to the approximation of $x = h(y)$, where the relation between x and y is given by (4.3). The steps are as follows:

1. Normalize to $(-1, 1)$ as given as before by using

$$z = \frac{2y - (Y_0 + Y_1)}{Y_1 - Y_0} , \qquad z = \begin{cases} -1 & \text{if } Y_0 \geqq y , \\ 1 & \text{if } Y_1 \leqq y . \end{cases}$$

2. Compute y_j for $z_j = \cos(\pi/2k)(2j+1)$.
3. Compute

$$P_j = \int_0^{y_j} g(t)\,dt .$$

4. Solve

$$P_j = \int_{-\infty}^{x_j} f(t)\,dt \text{ for } x_j .$$

5. Compute

$$c_i = \frac{2}{k} \sum_{j=0}^{k=1} x_j \cos(\pi_i/2k)(2j+1) .$$

6. Neglect as many terms as possible.
7. Rewrite the remaining terms as a polynomial in z.

Before the approximation is useful, an upper bound for the maximum error is necessary. If $h_m(y)$ is the approximation to $h(y)$ obtained by including only Chebyshev polynomials of order less than or equal to m, then the error function can be written as

$$\varepsilon(y) = h(y) - h_m(y) .$$

In some instances it may be desirable to compute this function explicitly. If c_{m+1} is much larger than c_{m+2}, c_{m+3}, etc., $\varepsilon(y)$ will be approximately $c_{m+1}C_{m+1}(y)$. By finding maximum and minimum values for C_{m+1}, we can obtain an idea of the magnitude of $\varepsilon(y)$.

To facilitate the approximation of a function by the Chebyshev polynomial method, a routine for this computation has been prepared for the SWAC. It is described in detail in Appendix B. With this equipment it is now possible to select samples from arbitrary distributions. In Appendix C this method will be applied to the problem of the linear discriminator.

Before using the polynomial approximation method it is necessary to choose a value for γ. Table 1 shows the values of c_i for three values of γ when $f(x)$ is the normal density. The values were computed with $k = 20$ and values of Y_0 and Y as follows:

γ	Y_0	Y_1
6	.43318 146	5.56681 854
8	.88313 150	7.11686 850
12	2.00000 000	10.00000 000

TABLE 1

VALUES OF c_i FOR POLYNOMIAL APPROXIMATION OF NORMAL DEVIATES FOR THREE VALUES OF γ

j	$\gamma = 6$	$\gamma = 8$	$\gamma = 12$
1	4.01236 91	4.10828 97	4.19713 87
3	.21217 51	.14916 95	.09409 09
5	.04473 42	.02140 77	.00807 47
7	.01157 97	.00413 38	.00092 06
9	.00261 32	.00087 78	.00011 68
11	.00034 58	.00016 39	.00001 54
13	.00008 69	.00000 43	.00000 20
15	.00012 50	−.00001 47	.00000 03
17	.00002 61	.00000 03	.00000 01
19	−.00004 27	.00000 43	.00000 00

(The values for $\gamma = 6$ and $\gamma = 8$ were chosen so that $\Pr\{Y_0 \leqq Y \leqq Y_1\} = .99998\ 16467$, and the values for $\gamma = 12$ were chosen so that $\Pr\{Y_0 \leqq Y \leqq Y_1\} = 99998\ 29497$.) It will be observed that in this case, since both $f(x)$ and $g(y)$ are symmetric, $x_j = -x_{k-1-j}$. Hence, for $k = 20$,

$$c_i = \frac{1}{10}\sum_{j=0}^{9} x_j \cos\frac{\pi i}{40}(2j+1)(1-\cos \pi i) ,$$

so that $c_i = 0$ when i is even.

From Table 1 it is clear that six terms are sufficient to compute normal deviates to three decimal places if $\gamma = 6$. With $\gamma = 8$, six terms will give four decimal places. It was decided to use $\gamma = 8$ for all the computations.

In performing step 4 of the computation of the polynomial coefficients for the useful range of accuracy, we must know the distribution-function arguments for probabilities close to 0 and 1. Illustrative probability values are shown in Table 2 for $\gamma = 8$ and $k = 20$; i.e., for fitting the polynomial at 20 points. Direct tables of distributions—those giving probabilities for equidistant values of the variate—are usually not accurate enough (they do not contain enough digits) to permit inverse interpolation. The normal distribution is one of the few for which adequate tables exist.

TABLE 2

VALUES OF P_j FOR $z_j = \cos \pi/40(2j+1)$ AND $\gamma = 8$

j	P_j	j	P_j
0	.00001 00064 47	5	.00559 59446 5
1	.00001 93183 56	6	.02232 44051 2
2	.00006 15787 82	7	.07320 10578 5
3	.00026 15521 19	8	.18983 569
4	.00123 04567 3	9	.38437 859

Methods for computing the necessary probability points to the desired accuracy for the t and χ^2 distributions have been developed by Teichroew [14–16].

APPENDIX A

Representation of the Elements of a Wishart Matrix in Terms of Elementary Random Variables

In the method adopted to generate random values of the classification statistic W, it was necessary to compute random values of two p-dimensional normal vectors, z and d, and of one p-dimensional Wishart matrix A. In general, a Wishart matrix is defined by

$$A = (X_1, X_2, \cdots X_n)(X_1, X_2, \cdots X_n)' , \tag{1}$$

where X_i is a p-dimensional normal vector with

$$E(X_i) = \begin{bmatrix} 0 \\ 0 \\ \cdot \\ \cdot \\ 0 \end{bmatrix}, \qquad E(X_i X_i') = \Sigma ,$$

and

$$E(X_i X_j') = \begin{bmatrix} 0 & 0 & \cdots & 0 \\ 0 & 0 & \cdots & 0 \\ \cdot & \cdot & \cdots & \cdot \\ \cdot & \cdot & \cdots & \cdot \\ 0 & 0 & \cdots & 0 \end{bmatrix} \qquad \begin{array}{r} i, j = 1, 2, \cdots, n , \\ i \neq j . \end{array}$$

The matrix Σ is a p-dimensional positive definite matrix.

For our purposes, it is sufficient to limit consideration to Wishart matrices for which Σ is the identity matrix- It is well known (e.g., see [17]) that the probability density function of these matrices is given by

$$h(A \mid I_p , p, n) = \frac{| A |^{\frac{1}{2}(n-p-1)} \exp\left[-\frac{1}{2} \sum_{i=1}^{p} a_{ii}\right]}{2^{\frac{pn}{2}} \pi^{\frac{1}{4}p(p-1)} \prod_{i=1}^{p} \Gamma(\frac{1}{2}(n - i + 1))} \tag{2}$$

for A positive definite, with $h(A \mid I_p , p, n) = 0$, otherwise.

It is a complicated problem to try to generate Wishart matrices directly using (2), and a tedious one to generate n p-dimensional normal variables and then compute a Wishart matrix using (1). It seemed worthwhile, therefore, to look for a decomposition of the Wishart matrix into a product of matrices involving independent random variables. Moreover, it was extremely desirable that these independent variables be simple random variables for which suitable generating methods have been developed. The decomposition that was finally used represented a Wishart matrix as a product of matrices involving independent t and χ^2 variables. The representation was suggested by the approach of Bartlett [18]. However, Bartlett started essentially with the Wishart matrix and showed that certain functions of the elements had χ^2 or normal distributions. In this section, we shall start with a collection of independent t and χ^2 variables and show that the multiplication of properly constructed matrices involving these variables produces a Wishart matrix.

THEOREM. *Let $v_1 , v_2 , \cdots, v_p$ and $t_{21} , t_{31} , \cdots, t_{p1} , t_{32} , t_{42} , \cdots, t_{p2} , \cdots, t_{pp-1}$ be a set of $\frac{1}{2}p(p + 1)$ independent chance variables with density functions given by*

$$p_1(v_i) = 0 \qquad\qquad -\infty < v_i < 0\,,$$

(3) $$p_1(v_i) = \frac{v_i^{\frac{n}{2}-1} \exp[-v_i/2]}{2^{\frac{n}{2}}\Gamma\left(\frac{n}{2}\right)}\,, \qquad\qquad 0 \leqq v_i < \infty\,,$$

and

(4) $$p_{2j}(t_{ij}) = \frac{\Gamma[\frac{1}{2}(n-j+1)]}{\sqrt{\pi}\,\Gamma[\frac{1}{2}(n-j)]}(1+t_{ij}^2)^{-\frac{1}{2}(n-j+1)} \qquad -\infty < t_{ij} < \infty\,,$$
$$i = j+1, \cdots, p\,,$$
$$j = 1, 2, \cdots, p-1\,;$$

i.e., each v_i *has a* χ^2 *distribution with* n *degrees of freedom, while* $\sqrt{n-j}\,t_{ij}$ *has Student's t-distribution with* $(n-j)$ *degrees of freedom. Consider the following* $p \times p$ *matrices. Let*

$$D^{(p)} = \begin{bmatrix} \sqrt{v_1} & 0 & \cdots & 0 \\ 0 & \sqrt{v_2} & \cdots & 0 \\ \cdot & \cdot & \cdots & \cdot \\ 0 & 0 & \cdots & \sqrt{v_p} \end{bmatrix}$$

and

$$M_k^{(p)} = \begin{bmatrix} I_{k-1} & 0_{k-1} & 0_{k-1} & 0_{k-1} & \cdots & 0_{k-1} \\ 0'_{k-1} & 1 & 0 & 0 & \cdots & 0 \\ 0'_{k-1} & \dfrac{t_{k+1\,k}}{\sqrt{(1+t_{k+1\,k}^2)}} & \dfrac{1}{\sqrt{(1+t_{k+1\,k}^2)}} & 0 & \cdots & 0 \\ 0'_{k-1} & \dfrac{t_{k+2\,k}}{\sqrt{(1+t_{k+2\,k}^2)}} & 0 & \dfrac{1}{\sqrt{(1+t_{k+2\,k}^2)}} & \cdots & 0 \\ \cdot & \cdot & \cdot & & \cdots & \cdot \\ 0'_{k+1} & \dfrac{t_{pk}}{\sqrt{(1+t_{pk}^2)}} & 0 & 0 & \cdots & \dfrac{1}{\sqrt{(1+t_{pk}^2)}} \end{bmatrix}$$
$$k = 1, 2, \cdots, p-1\,,$$

where I_{k-1} *is the* $(k-1) \times (k-1)$ *identity matrix, and* 0_{k-1} *is a* $(k-1)$ *dimensional column vector of zeros. Then, except for sets of probability* 0,

$$A^{(p)} = D^{(p)}M_1^{(p)} \cdots M_{p-1}^{(p)}M_{p-1}^{(p)\prime} \cdots M_1^{(p)\prime}D^{(p)\prime}$$

is a $p \times p$ *positive definite matrix whose components have a Wishart distribution with* n *degrees of freedom and covariance matrix* I_p.

PROOF. We will prove the theorem by mathematical induction. Clearly, it is true for $p = 1$, since in this case

$$A^{(1)} = D^{(1)}D^{(1)\prime} = v_1\,,$$

and $p_1(v_1) = h(v_1 \mid I_1, 1, n)$. Also, when $p = 2$,

$$A^{(2)} = D^{(2)}M_1^{(2)}M_1^{(2)\prime}D^{(2)\prime}$$

$$= \begin{bmatrix} \sqrt{v_1} & 0 \\ 0 & \sqrt{v_2} \end{bmatrix} \begin{bmatrix} 1 & 0 \\ \frac{t_{21}}{\sqrt{1+t_{21}^2}} & \frac{1}{\sqrt{1+t_{21}^2}} \end{bmatrix} \cdot \begin{bmatrix} 1 & \frac{t_{21}}{\sqrt{1+t_{21}^2}} \\ 0 & \frac{1}{\sqrt{1+t_{21}^2}} \end{bmatrix} \begin{bmatrix} \sqrt{v_1} & 0 \\ 0 & \sqrt{v_2} \end{bmatrix}$$

$$= \begin{bmatrix} v_1 & \frac{t_{21}\sqrt{v_1 v_2}}{\sqrt{1+t_{21}^2}} \\ \frac{t_{21}\sqrt{v_1 v_2}}{\sqrt{1+t_{21}^2}} & v_2 \end{bmatrix}.$$

If we write

$$a_{11}^{(2)} = v_1 , \quad a_{12}^{(2)} = \frac{t_{21}\sqrt{v_1 v_2}}{\sqrt{1+t_{21}^2}} , \quad a_{22}^{(2)} = v_2 ,$$

we have (using J to denote the Jacobian of the transformation)

$$p(A^{(2)}) = p_1(a_{11}^{(2)})p_1(a_{22}^{(2)})p_{21}\left(\frac{a_{12}^{(2)}}{\sqrt{a_{11}a_{22} - a_{12}^2}}\right) J\left(\frac{a_{11}^{(2)}, a_{12}^{(2)}, a_{22}^{(2)}}{v_1 , v_2 , t_{21}}\right)$$

$$= \frac{(a_{11}^{(2)}a_{22}^{(2)} - a_{12}^{(2)2})^{\frac{n-3}{2}} \exp[-\frac{1}{2}(a_{11}^{(2)} + a_{22}^{(2)})]}{2^n\sqrt{\pi}\,\Gamma\left(\frac{n}{2}\right)\Gamma\left(\frac{n-1}{2}\right)}$$

$$= h(A^{(2)} \mid I_2 , 2, n) .$$

Note that $(a_{11}^{(2)}a_{22}^{(2)} - a_{12}^{(2)2}) = |A^{(2)}| > 0$ with probability 1.

We suppose now the theorem is true for $p = k$, and we will show that it holds for $p = k + 1$.

If we examine each of the matrices $D^{(k+1)}$, $M_1^{(k+1)}$, $\cdots$, $M_{k-1}^{(k+1)}$, we see that the $k \times k$ elements in the upper left-hand corner form matrices $D^{(k)}$, $M_1^{(k)}$, $\cdots$, $M_{k-1}^{(k)}$, respectively. For $r = k$, $k + 1$ we write

$$M^{(r)} = D^{(r)}M_1^{(r)} \cdots M_{r-1}^{(r)} , \tag{5}$$

with

$$A^{(k)} = M^{(k)}M^{(k)\prime} \tag{6}$$

and

$$A^{(k+1)} = M^{(k+1)}M^{(k+1)\prime} . \tag{7}$$

By definition, the element in the ith row and jth column of $M^{(r)}$ is

$$(8)\qquad \begin{aligned} m_{ij}^{(r)} &= \frac{t_{ij}\sqrt{v_i}}{\sqrt{(1+t_{i1}^2)\cdots(1+t_{ij}^2)}}\,, && j<i\,,\\ m_{ii}^{(r)} &= \frac{\sqrt{v_i}}{\sqrt{(1+t_{i1}^2)\cdots(1+t_{i\,i-1}^2)}}\,, && j=i\,,\\ m_{ij}^{(r)} &= 0\,, && j>i,\quad i,j=1,2,\cdots,r\,. \end{aligned}$$

Writing

$$(9)\qquad m^{(k+1)\prime} = (m_{k+1\,1}^{(k+1)}, m_{k+1\,2}^{(k+1)}, \cdots, m_{k+1\,k}^{(k+1)})\,,$$

we have

$$(10)\qquad M^{(k+1)} = \begin{bmatrix} M^{(k)} & O_k \\ m^{(k+1)\prime} & m_{k+1\,k+1}^{(k+1)} \end{bmatrix},$$

and

$$(11)\qquad \begin{aligned} A^{(k+1)} &= M^{(k+1)}M^{(k+1)\prime}\\ &= \begin{bmatrix} M^{(k)}M^{(k)\prime} & M^{(k)}m^{(k+1)} \\ m^{(k+1)\prime}M^{(k)\prime} & v_{k+1} \end{bmatrix}\\ &= \begin{bmatrix} A^{(k)} & M^{(k)}m^{(k+1)} \\ m^{(k+1)\prime}M^{(k)\prime} & v_{k+1} \end{bmatrix}, \end{aligned}$$

since

$$(12)\qquad \begin{aligned} &m^{(k+1)\prime}m^{(k+1)} + (m_{k+1\,k+1}^{(k+1)})^2\\ &\quad = v_{k+1}\Bigg[\frac{t_{k+1\,1}^2}{(1+t_{k+1\,1}^2)} + \frac{t_{k+1\,2}^2}{(1+t_{k+1\,1}^2)(1+t_{k+1\,2}^2)}\\ &\qquad + \cdots + \frac{t_{k+1\,k}^2}{\prod_{i=1}^{k}(1+t_{k+1\,i}^2)} + \frac{1}{\prod_{i=1}^{k}(1+t_{k+1\,i}^2)}\Bigg] = v_{k+1}\,. \end{aligned}$$

From (10) and (11) we see that

$$(13)\qquad m_{ij}^{(k)} = m_{ij}^{(k+1)}\,,\qquad a_{ij}^{(k)} = a_{ij}^{(k+1)}\qquad i,j \leqq k\,,$$

and there is no confusion if we drop the superscript on the elements of these matrices.

The elements of $A^{(k)}$ are functions only of $v_1, \cdots, v_k, t_{21}, \cdots, t_{k1}, \cdots, t_{k\,k-1}$, and are distributed independently of the variables $t_{k+1\,1}, \cdots, t_{k+1\,i}, \cdots, t_{k+1\,k}$, v_{k+1}. Since we assume the theorem is true for $p=k$, we must assume that $A^{(k)}$ is a Wishart matrix with n degrees of freedom and covariance matrix I_k; the joint density of the elements of $A^{(k)}$ and the variables $t_{k+1\,1}, \cdots$, $t_{k+1\,k}, v_{k+1}$, is given by

$$(14)\qquad \begin{aligned} &h(A^{(k)} \mid I_k, k, n)\cdot p_1(v_{k+1})\cdot \prod_{i=1}^{k} p_{2i}(t_{k+1\,i})\\ &\quad = \frac{|A^{(k)}|^{\frac{1}{2}(n-k-1)})\, v_{k+1}^{\frac{n}{2}-1}\exp\left[-\frac{1}{2}\left(v_{k+1}+\sum_{i=1}^{k} a_{ii}\right)\right]}{2^{\frac{n}{2}(k+1)}\pi^{\frac{k(k+1)}{4}}\prod_{i=1}^{k+1}\Gamma(\frac{1}{2}(n+1-i))\prod_{i=1}^{k}(1+t_{k+1\,i}^2)^{\frac{1}{2}(n-i+1)}}\,. \end{aligned}$$

Suppose now we make a transformation from the variables $t_{k+1\,i}$ to the variables $m_{k+1\,i}$ $(i = 1, 2 \cdots, k)$.

The Jacobian of the transformation is

$$|J| = \frac{v_{k+1}}{(v_{k+1} - m_{k+1\,1}^2)^{\frac{1}{2}} \cdots \left(v_{k+1} - \sum_{i=1}^{k-1} m_{k+1\,i}^2\right)^{\frac{1}{2}} \left(v_{k+1} - \sum_{i=1}^{k} m_{k+1\,i}^2\right)^{\frac{1}{2}}} . \tag{15}$$

The joint distribution of $A^{(k)}$, $m^{(k+1)}$, and v_{k+1} is

$$h(A^{(k)} \mid I_k, k, n) \cdot g(m^{(k+1)}, v_{k+1}) \tag{16}$$

$$= \frac{|A^{(k)}|^{\frac{1}{2}(n-k-1)} (v_{k+1} - m^{(k+1)\prime} m^{(k+1)})^{\frac{1}{2}(n-k-2)} \exp\left[-\frac{1}{2}\left(v_{k+1} + \sum_{i=1}^{k} a_{ii}\right)\right]}{2^{\frac{n}{2}(k+1)} \pi^{\frac{k(k+1)}{4}} \prod_{i=1}^{k+1} \Gamma(\frac{1}{2}(n+1-i))}$$

for $(v_{k+1} - m^{(k+1)\prime} m^{(k+1)}) \geqq 0$, and is 0 otherwise.

Since $M^{(k)}$ is a triangular matrix and $A^{(k)} = M^{(k)} M^{(k)\prime}$, there is a one-to-one relation between the elements of $A^{(k)}$ and $M^{(k)}$. If now we consider the elements of $M^{(k)}$ as functions of the elements of $A^{(k)}$, we can make the transformation

$$a^{(k+1)} = M^{(k)} m^{(k+1)} , \tag{17}$$

where $a^{(k+1)} = (a_{k+1\,1}, a_{k+1\,2}, \cdots, a_{k+1\,k})$. The Jacobian of the transformation is

$$|M^{(k)}|^{-1} = |A^{(k)}|^{-\frac{1}{2}} .$$

If we write $v_{k+1} = a_{k+1\,k+1}$, the joint distribution of the elements of $A^{(k+1)}$ is given by

$$p(A^{(k+1)}) \tag{18}$$

$$= \frac{|A^{(k)}|^{\frac{1}{2}(n-k-2)} (a_{k+1\,k+1} - a^{(k+1)\prime} A^{(k)-1} a^{(k+1)})^{\frac{1}{2}(n-k-2)} \exp\left[-\frac{1}{2} \sum_{i=1}^{k+1} a_{ii}\right]}{2^{\frac{n}{2}(k+1)} \pi^{\frac{k(k+1)}{4}} \prod_{i=1}^{k+1} \Gamma(\frac{1}{2}(n+1-i))} ,$$

for $(a_{k+1\,k+1} - a^{(k+1)\prime} A^{(k)-1} a^{(k+1)}) \geqq 0$. But since

$$|A^{(k)}| \cdot (a_{k+1\,k+1} - a^{(k+1)\prime} A^{(k)-1} a^{(k+1)}) = |A^{(k+1)}| ,$$

we have

$$p(A^{(k+1)}) = h(A^{(k+1)} I_{k+1}, k+1, n) , \tag{19}$$

which is the desired result.

COROLLARY. *Let* $v_1, v_2, \cdots, v_p$ *and* $t_{21}, t_{31}, \cdots, t_{p1}, \cdots, t_{p\,p-1}$ *be a set of chance variables satisfying the conditions of the theorem. From the definition of* $D^{(p)}, M_1^{(p)}, \cdots, M_{p-1}^{(p)}$, *we have*

$$D^{(p)-1} = \begin{bmatrix} 1/\sqrt{v_1} & 0 & \cdots & 0 \\ 0 & 1/\sqrt{v_2} & \cdots & 0 \\ \cdot & \cdot & \cdots & \cdot \\ 0 & 0 & \cdots & 1/\sqrt{v_p} \end{bmatrix}$$

and

$$M_k^{(p)^{-1}} = \begin{bmatrix} I_{k-1} & 0_{k-1} & 0_{k-1} & 0_{k-1} & \cdots & 0_{k-1} \\ 0'_{k-1} & 1 & 0 & 0 & \cdots & 0 \\ 0'_{k-1} & -t_{k+1\,k} & \sqrt{(1+t^2_{k+1\,k})} & 0 & \cdots & 0 \\ 0'_{k-1} & -t_{k+2\,k} & 0 & \sqrt{(1+t^2_{k+2\,k})} & \cdots & 0 \\ \cdot & & \cdot & \cdot & \cdots & \cdot \\ 0'_{k-1} & -t_{pk} & 0 & 0 & \cdots & \sqrt{(1+t^2_{pk})} \end{bmatrix}$$

$$k = 1, 2, \cdots, p-1 .$$

Then

$$A^{(p)^{-1}} = D^{(p)'^{-1}} M_1^{(p)'^{-1}} \cdots M_{p-1}^{(p)'^{-1}} M_{p-1}^{(p)^{-1}} \cdots M_1^{(p)^{-1}} D^{(p)^{-1}}$$

is the inverse of a p-dimensional Wishart matrix with n degrees of freedom and covariance matrix I_p.

APPENDIX B

A Routine for Approximation by Chebyshev Polynomials

This section describes the code that has been used to compute the coefficients needed to approximate the variates entering into the random Wishart matrices. (The code can be used for computing approximating polynomials for any function for which the values required in Step 2 and Step 6 below are available. They may be pre-computed or they may be computed by inserting a sub-routine. It is desirable to treat the approximating polynomial with caution until the error function has been completely determined.)

The computational steps and the routine are as follows (Y, X, C, E, and A denote vectors and B and D denote matrices):

Step 1. Y. $y_j = \cos \pi(2j+1)/(2k)$. A table for various values of k is available.

Step 2. $X = h(Y)$. The routine is arranged so that either Y is read in and X computed or X is read in directly.

Step 3. $C = BX$. The matrix B,

$$\begin{aligned} b_{ij} &= (2/k)\cos[\pi i(2j+1)/2k] && \text{if } i > 0 \\ &= 1/k && \text{if } i = 0 , \end{aligned}$$

is stored on cards or on the drum for this multiplication. The b_{ij}'s are available for various values of k.

Step 4. $A = DC$. The matrix D consists of the integers that appear in Table III of Lanczos [13], in which the powers are expressed as sums of the Chebyshev polynomials. This matrix is also stored on cards or on the drum. A is now a set of coefficients of powers of y using all k Chebyshev polynomials.

Step 5. Y^*. Y^* gives the points at which the error is to be calculated. The Y^* that has been used is

$$Y_j^* = \cos \pi j/k , \qquad j = 0(1)k .$$

Step 6. $E = h(Y^*) - h_k(Y^*)$. As in step 2 the correct values $h(Y^*)$ may be read in from cards or computed from Y^*. The approximate values $h_k(Y^*)$ are computed by the machine from the coefficients of A.

Step 7. Choose m. This number is chosen to be the smallest value for which

$$| \max e_i | + | C_k | + | C_{k-1} | \cdots | C_{m+1} | \leqq \eta ,$$

where η is a constant denoting the maximum error allowable.

Step 8. $A_m = DC_m$. C_m is the C vector with all $c_i = 0$ for $i > m$.

The routine punches the vectors X, C, A, E, and A_m and is then ready to begin again with step 1 for another distribution or function $h(y)$. The routine was used with $k = 20$. This choice was made originally, since for this case $2/k = .1$ and no division was needed. When the routine was coded for the SWAC $k = 20$ was a good choice owing to the fact that the X or Y vectors exactly fill two cards.

APPENDIX C

A Technique for Computing the Distribution of the Linear Discriminant Function

In earlier sections it was shown that the problem of generating random values of a Wishart matrix could be reduced to the problem of generating random values of certain one-dimensional random variables, and techniques for this computation were discussed. The considerations involved in the discussion were general and could be applied to any computing machine. The actual programming of the method will depend on the characteristics of the machine for which it is intended. In this section, a code designed for use on the SWAC will be described. The particular characteristics of the SWAC which affected the design will be set forth so that the routine may be adapted to other digital computers.

One of the characteristics of the SWAC which influences the coding is the small amount of high speed storage; only 256 cells are available in its high-speed memory. In addition, there are 4096 cells in the drum memory,[3] and punched cards may be used as auxiliary storage. Codes utilizing only the high-speed memory for computation proceed rapidly, but each referral to the drum memory is relatively time-consuming. An attempt was therefore made to restrict the code for the computation of random values of W to the high-speed memory; this proved impossible for the range of p desired. Thus in the code the coefficients of the polynomial approximations are stored on the drum. It was, of course, necessary to use the drum to store the frequency distributions of W and other sampling results.

With this arrangement it was possible to use p as large as 15, since, as will be explained below, only two p-dimensional vectors have to be stored.

The difficulty of storing a p-dimensional matrix precluded the use of

[3] The drum capacity has since been doubled.

another sampling technique. If random values of d and S^{-1} have been computed, W may be expressed in the form

$$W = \sum_{i=1}^{p} \alpha_i z_i + \beta \,, \tag{1}$$

where the α_i's and β's are fixed numbers and the z_i's are independently, normally distributed. W is therefore normal with a mean and variance that can be numerically ascertained.

A major factor in the programming is the possible range of numbers. Since the SWAC treats numbers as though they were less than unity, multiplication by a number that is scaled (whose binary point is not at the point where the machine assumes it is) may require a shift to return to the proper scale factor.

The code we prepared was designed to compute random values of W which, as was described earlier, are given by

$$W = d'S^{-1}z + \frac{N_1 - N_2}{2(N_1 + N_2)} d'S^{-1}d \,. \tag{2}$$

Throughout the computation two p-dimensional vectors are stored in the machine. Let these be denoted by U and V. The steps in the computation are as follows:

1. Compute z and store as U.
2. Compute d and store as V.
3. Compute $D^{-1}z$ and store as U_0.
4. Compute $d'D^{-1}$ and store as V_0.
5. Compute M_i^{-1}, $M_i^{-1}U_{i-1}$ and store the latter as U_i.
   Compute $V_{i-1}M_i'^{-1}$ and store as V_i.
6. Repeat 5 for $i = 1, 2, \cdots, p-1$.
7. Compute $V'_{p-1}U_{p-1}(=d'S^{-1}z)$.
8. Compute $V'_{p-1}V_{p-1}(=d'S^{-1}d)$.
9. Finally compute

$$W = V'_{p-1}U_{p-1} + \frac{N_1 - N_2}{2(N_1 + N_2)} V'_{p-1}V_{p-1} \,.$$

It is evident from this outline that each multiplication is a vector times a matrix; thus only a vector has to be stored. In the detailed description of the computation given below, it is shown that the elements of the D's and the M's are needed in a sequence; consequently only a few have to be stored at any one time.

C1. Computation of d and z. The computation of normal variates, which we denote here by δ, was performed by the polynomial approximation technique using the coefficients given in Table 1. The coefficients are scaled so that the δ are *NID* (0, 1)[4] but carried in the machine as $\delta \cdot 10^{-1}$. The components of z are

[4] *NID* (0, 1) is an abbreviation for the words: normally and independently distributed, with mean zero and variance unity.

$$z_i = \sigma(z)\delta_i + \mu_i = \sigma(z)\left[\delta_i + \frac{\mu_i}{\sigma(z)}\right],$$

where $\mu_1 = [N_1/(N_1 + N_2)](2\lambda)$; $\mu_i = 0$ for $i > 1$, and

$$\sigma(z) = \sqrt{\frac{N_1 + N_2 + 1}{N_1 + N_2}} = \sqrt{1 + \frac{1}{N_1 + N_2}};$$

therefore $1 < \sigma(z) < \sqrt{2}$, and $\mu_i/\sigma < 2\lambda$.

The z_i's were computed by the right-hand formula; this method places an upper limit on the value of λ which can be used. As $n \to \infty$, $z_1 \to N(\mu_1, 1)$ and z_i for $i \geqq 2$ become $N(0, 1)$.

For the d's we have again

$$d_i = \sigma(d)\delta_i + \mu_i = \sigma(d)\left[\delta_i + \frac{\mu_i}{\sigma(d)}\right],$$

where $\mu_1 = 2\lambda$, $\mu_i = 0$ for $i \geqq 2$, and

$$\sigma(d) = \sqrt{\frac{N_1 + N_2}{N_1 N_2}}.$$

In this case the right-hand formula is not a good one to use, for as $\sigma(d)$ becomes small, μ/σ becomes large and requires a bigger scale factor. The first equation is preferable, since as σ becomes small, the first term becomes small. As $n \to \infty$, d_i approaches the constant μ_1 for $i = 1$ and 0 for $i > 1$. Some approximate values of $\sigma(d)$ are given in Table 3.

TABLE 3

N_1	N_2	$\frac{N_1 + N_2}{N_1 N_2}$	(σd)
1	1	2	1.4
2	2	1	1.
15	15	2/15	.36
100	100	2/100	.14
100	200	3/200	.12
∞	∞	0	0

C2. Computation of $\sqrt{n}\,D^{-1}$. The elements of $\sqrt{n}\,D^{-1}$ are $\sqrt{n/\chi^2}$ variates, where χ^2 has the usual χ^2 distribution with n degrees of freedom. The following table indicates the magnitude of the variates $\sqrt{n/\chi^2_\alpha}$ for various values of n and two values of α. The value of χ^2_α is defined by the relationship

$$\Pr\{\chi^2 \leqq \chi^2_\alpha \mid n\} = \alpha$$

n	$\sqrt{n/\chi^2_{.995}}$	$\sqrt{n/\chi^2_{.005}}$
1	.356	159.576
10	.630	2.154
120	.836	1.168
∞	1.000	1.000

As $n \to \infty$, the variates approach 1; those below the median of the distribution approach it from below, and those above from above. Therefore as $n \to \infty$, $\sqrt{n}D^{-1}$ approaches the identity matrix.

In the code the variates were computed by a polynomial approximation to $\sqrt{2/\chi^2}$. For the degrees-of-freedom of interest, χ^2 values less than 2 occur with probability less than .00002; since this was used as the criterion for Y_0 and Y_1, such values would not appear, and hence the variates would always be less than 1. This permitted using the variates without a scale factor. Some loss of accuracy is involved if n becomes large. (The polynomial approximation coefficients have been computed for $n/2 = 15(5)$, 30(10), 60, 100, and may be obtained from the authors.)

As each value of $\sqrt{2/\chi^2}$ is computed, it is multiplied first by $\sqrt{n/2}$, then by the appropriate element of z and d to give the corresponding element of U_0 and V_0, respectively.

C3. Computation of the M^{-1} Matrices. The elements of the M^{-1} matrices are of the form $x = t/\sqrt{v}$ and $y = \sqrt{1 + x^2}$, where t has Student's t distribution with v degrees of freedom. The magnitude of these quantities is illustrated in Table 4. As $v \to \infty$, $x \to 0$, and $y \to 1$, the matrix M_i^{-1} approaches the identity matrix, since M_i^{-1} has only unity or a y on the diagonal and 0 or an x on the off-diagonal. Scaling problems can arise if n is small. In the present code both x and y were scaled by 10^{-1}; this permits n to go as low as necessary.

TABLE 4

v	$x = t_{.9975}/\sqrt{v}$	$y = \sqrt{1 + x^2}$
1	127.32	127.3
2	9.96	10.0
3	4.30	4.4
10	1.13	1.5
120	.26	1.1
∞	0	1.0

The polynomial approximation method was used to compute values of x, and y was then computed by taking a square root. Six coefficients were needed for each degree of freedom, and $p - 1$ such sets were used for each sample. The coefficients have been computed for $n = 50(1)$ 200.

C4. The Matrix Multiplication. The next step is to compute a series of row vectors $U_0', U_1', U_2', \cdots, U_{p-1}'$, where

$$\begin{aligned} U_0' &= z'D'^{-1}, \\ U_1' &= U_0'M_1'^{-1}, \\ &\vdots \\ U_{p-1}' &= U_{p-2}'M_{p-1}'^{-1}. \end{aligned}$$

From the expression given for M_i^{-1} in Appendix A, we note that the elements of $M_i'^{-1}$ are 0 except on the diagonal and in the ith row to the right of the diagonal. Let $m_{i \cdot jk}$ be the element of M_i^{-1} in the jth row and the kth column; then

$$\begin{aligned} m_{i \cdot jj} &= 1 , & j &\leqq i , \\ &= y_{i \cdot j} , & j &> i , \\ m_{i \cdot ij} &= -x_{i \cdot j} , & j &> i , \\ m_{i\ jk} &= 0 , & &\text{otherwise} . \end{aligned}$$

Also let $U_{i \cdot j}$ be the jth element of U_i'. Then it is clear that multiplying the matrix by the vector reduces to the simple form

$$\begin{aligned} U_{i+1 \cdot j} &= U_{i \cdot j} , & &\text{if } j \leqq i \\ &= -x_{i+1 \cdot j} U_{i \cdot i+1} + Y_{i+1 \cdot j} , & &\text{if } j > i . \end{aligned}$$

An analogous formula holds for the V vectors.

Each of the numbers entering in the formula is scaled by 10^{-1}, and therefore the products are scaled by 10^{-2}. Since the result is to be used again in the same way, it is necessary to multiply it by 10 to return to the original scale factor. This operation must be treated cautiously, since repeated multiplying by numbers greater than 1 can lead to rapid propagation of roundoff errors. The whole sequence of operations, however, is simpler than might appear. It is as follows:

1. The vectors U_0 and V_0 are computed as outlined.
2. The coefficients for computing x with $n-1$ degrees of freedom are obtained from the drum.
3. A random value of x is calculated and the corresponding y value is computed.
4. These values are then used to compute the second element in U_1 and V_1.
5. Steps 3 and 4 are repeated until the pth element has been computed.
6. The coefficients for $n-2$ degrees of freedom are obtained, and steps 3, 4, and 5 are repeated until the vectors U_{p-1} and V_{p-1} have been obtained.

REFERENCES

[1] Harter, H. L. On the distribution of Wald's classification statistic. *Ann. Math. Stat.*, 1951, **22**, 58-67.

[2] Sitgreaves, R. On the distribution of two random matrices used in classification procedures. *Ann. Math. Stat.*, 1952, **23**, 263-70.

[3] Trotter, H. F., and Tukey, J. W. Conditional Monte Carlo for normal samples. Symposium on Monte Carlo Methods, Gainesville, Florida, March 1954.

[4] Fieller, E. C., and Hartley, H. O. Sampling with control variables. *Biometrika*, **41**, 1954, 494-501.

[5] Teichroew, D. *Distribution Sampling with High Speed Computers* (Ph.D. thesis), Univ. North Carolina, 1953.

[6] Taussky, O., and Todd, J. Generation and testing of pseudo-random numbers. National Bureau of Standards Report, 1954.

[7] Wold, H. Random normal deviates. Tracts for computers. No. XXV. London: Cambridge Univ. Press, 1948.

[8] Kondo, T., and Elderton, E. M. Tables of the normal curve to each permille of frequency. *Biometrika*, **22**, 1931, 368-76.

[9] Camp, B. H. The effect on a distribution function of small changes in the population function. *Ann Math. Stat.*, **17**, 1946, 226-31.

[10] Hastings, C. *Approximations for Digital Computers.* Princeton, N. J.: Princeton Univ. Press, 1955.

[11] Von Neumann, J. Various techniques used in connection with random digits. Monte Carlo Method. Applied Math. Series No. 12, National Bureau of Standards, 1951.

[12] Votaw, D. and Rafferty, J. High speed sampling. *Math. Tables and Other Aids to Computation*, 1951, **5**, 1-8.

[13] Lanczos, C. Table of the Chebyshev polynomials $c_n(x)$ and $s_n(x)$. Applied Math. Series No. 9, National Bureau of Standards, 1952.

[14] Teichroew, D. A short table of the normalization polynomials for the t-distribution. (In manuscript, 1954.)

[15] Teichroew, D. A table of Campbell's polynomials for the computation of probability points of the incomplete Gamma distribution. (In manuscript, 1954.)

[16] Teichroew, D. Generalized normalization polynomials for the t and incomplete gamma distributions. (In manuscript, 1954.)

[17] Kendall, M. G. *The Advanced Theory of Statistics.* London: Charles Griffin, 1946.

[18] Bartlett, M. S. The vector representation of a sample. *Proc. Cambridge Phil. Soc.*, 1934, **30**, 327-40.

17

An Expansion Principle for Distribution Functions with Applications to Student's Statistic and the One-Dimensional Classification Statistic

GUSTAV ELFVING, University of Helsinki

1. General Problem

A situation often occurring in statistical distribution theory is the following: Let x and y_n be independent random variables, the former with a fixed continuous c.d.f. (i.e., cumulative distribution function) $F(x)$, the latter tending stochastically to zero as n increases. Then variables such as $t = x + y_n$, $t = x(1 + y_n)$, $t = x/(1 + y_n)$ will have c.d.f.'s $\bar{F}_n(t)$ tending to $F(x)$. The problem arises of accounting in a simple way for the modification of $F(x)$ caused by y_n.

A classical example of this problem is Student's statistic $t = x/s$, where x is normal and s tends stochastically to 1 as the number of degrees of freedom increases. Another example is provided by the Wald-Anderson classification statistic [1, 2] (one-dimensional case), which after appropriate normalization may be written as

$$w_n = (x - z_n)s_n^{-2}(1 + v_n) ,$$

where x is $N(\alpha, 1)$ (i.e., normal with mean α and variance 1), z_n is $N(0, 1/n)$, v_n is $N(0, \kappa^2/n)$, and s_n^2 is of the form $\chi^2_{n-2}/(n-2)$, all variables being independent. As n increases, the distribution of w_n tends to the $N(\alpha, 1)$ distribution; it would be desirable to find some simple modification of $\Phi(x - \alpha)$ giving a good approximation to the c.d.f. of w_n.

In more general terms, let x be a random variable with continuous c.d.f. $F(x)$; let $y_1, y_2, \cdots$ be a sequence of stochastic vectors, independent of x and tending stochastically to a constant vector y_0 as $n \to \infty$; let their c.d.f.'s be $G_1(y), \cdots$. Finally, let $t(x, y)$ be a measurable function such that $t(x, y) \to x$

Sections 1 and 2 of this chapter have previously been published in *Annales Academiae Scientiarum Fennicae*, Ser. A, 1955, **204**, under the title "An expansion principle for distribution functions with application to Student's statistic."

as $y \to y_0$, for all x. Denote the set $\{x : t(x, y) \leqq t\}$ by $X(t, y)$. The c.d.f. $\bar{F}_n(t)$ of $t = t(x, y_n)$ may be written

$$\bar{F}_n(t) = \int \Pr\{x \in X(t, y)\}\, dG_n(y) = \int \Pr\{t(x, y) \leqq t\}\, dG_n(y) . \tag{1.1}$$

As $n \to \infty$, we have, since $y \to y_0$ in probability,

$$\bar{F}_n(t) \to \Pr\{t(x, y_0) \leqq t\} = F(t) .$$

Now, if there is an expansion

$$\Pr\{x \in X(t, y)\} = F_0(t, y) + F_1(t, y) + \cdots , \tag{1.2}$$

which represents the left-hand side well in the neighborhood of y_0, one may expect the integrated expansion

$$\bar{F}_n(t) \sim \int F_0(t, y)\, dG_n(y) + \int F_1(t, y)\, dG_n(y) + \cdots \tag{1.3}$$

to give a working representation of $\bar{F}_n(t)$. For instance, if y_n is one-dimensional, and if (1.2) is the Taylor expansion about y_0, then (1.3) is an expansion in terms of the moments of y_n about y_0. However, this need not be the best, or even a working way of proceeding. A general requirement on the expansion (1.2), besides good asymptotic properties, is that the integrals in (1.3) be explicitly evaluated.

2. Student's Statistic

We shall apply the method sketched in Section 1 to Student's statistic $t = x/s$, where x is normal (0, 1), i.e.,

$$dF(x) = (2\pi)^{-1/2} \exp[-\tfrac{1}{2}x^2]\, dx = \varphi(x)\, dx ,$$

with

$$F(x) = \int_{-\infty}^{x} \varphi(u)\, du = \Phi(x) ,$$

and s has the p.d.f.

$$g_n(s) = \frac{2(n/2)^{n/2}}{\Gamma(n/2)} s^{n-1} \exp[-ns^2/2] . \tag{2.1}$$

By the previous argument, the c.d.f. $S_n(t)$ of t may be written

$$S_n(t) = \int_0^{\infty} \Phi(st) g_n(s)\, ds . \tag{2.2}$$

It turns out that a good way of expanding $\Phi(st)$ is to write this function in the form

$$\Phi(st) = \Phi(\sigma t) + \left[(2\pi)^{-1/2} \exp(t^2 s^2/4) \int_{t\sigma}^{ts} \exp(-u^2/2)\, du\right] \exp[-t^2 s^2/4] , \tag{2.3}$$

and expand the expression in large brackets in a Taylor series about σ. The point $\sigma = \sigma(t, n)$ depends on t and n, and is to be determined later.

As a consequence, the general term in the expansion will be of the form $a_k(t, n)(s-\sigma)^k \exp[-t^2s^2/4]$. This term multiplied by $g_n(s)$ will evidently be explicitly integrable. The exponential factor, with the particular coefficient $\frac{1}{4}$ in the exponent, has a double purpose: it accounts for the exponential character of $\Phi(st)$ for large s without giving it too much weight ($\exp[-t^2s^2/4]$ being the geometric mean of 1 and of $\exp[-t^2s^2/2]$), and at the same time it will make the second-order term of our expansion equal to 0.

We shall write the bracketed expression in (2.3) as $\psi(st)$, where

$$\psi(z) = (2\pi)^{-1/2} \exp[z^2/4] \int_{z_0}^{z} \exp[-u^2/4]\, du\,, \qquad z_0 = \sigma t\,. \tag{2.4}$$

The expansion of $\Phi(st)$—converging in the whole complex s-plane, since (2.4) is an entire function—is seen to be

$$\Phi(st) = \Phi(\sigma t) + \sum_{k=1}^{\infty} \frac{\psi^{(k)}(\sigma t)t^k}{k\,!}(s-\sigma)^k \exp[-t^2s^2/4]\,. \tag{2.5}$$

Denoting

$$I_k(t, n) = \int_0^{\infty} (s-\sigma)^k \exp[-t^2s^2/4]\, g_n(s)\, ds\,, \tag{2.6}$$

we get for $S_n(t)$ the formal expansion

$$S_n(t) = \Phi(\sigma t) + \sum_{k=1}^{\infty} \Psi^{(k)}(\sigma t)\frac{t^k}{k!} I_k(t, n)\,. \tag{2.7}$$

Postponing convergence considerations to the end, we begin by finding the first terms in (2.7) and choosing σ so as to make the first-order term vanish. Differentiating (2.4) and denoting for brevity $(2\pi)^{-1/2} \exp[-z^2/4] = \chi$, we obtain (always substiting ψ' from the first equation)

$$\begin{aligned}
\psi' &= \frac{z}{2}\Psi + \chi\,, & \psi'(z_0) &= \chi_0\,,\\
\psi'' &= \left(\frac{1}{2} + \frac{z^2}{4}\right)\Psi\,, & \psi''(z_0) &= 0\,,\\
\psi''' &= \left(\frac{3z}{4} + \frac{z^3}{8}\right)\Psi + \left(\frac{1}{2} + \frac{z^2}{4}\right)\chi\,, & \psi'''(z_0) &= \left(\frac{1}{2} + \frac{z_0}{4}\right)\chi_0\,,\\
\psi'''' &= \left(\frac{3}{4} + \frac{3z^2}{4} + \frac{z^4}{16}\right)\Psi + z\chi\,, & \psi''''(z_0) &= z_0\chi_0\,.
\end{aligned} \tag{2.8}$$

We note the vanishing of the second derivative.

To complete the evaluation of the first terms in (2.7) we need the integrals (2.6). Denoting

$$\begin{aligned}
q_i(t, n) &= \int_0^{\infty} s^i \exp[-t^2s^2/4] g_n(s)\, ds\\
&= \frac{2(n/2)^{n/2}}{\Gamma\left(\frac{n}{2}\right)} \int_0^{\infty} s^{n+i-1} \exp[-(n + t^2/2)s^2/2]\, ds\,,
\end{aligned} \tag{2.9}$$

we obtain by elementary calculation

$$q_i(t, n) = \frac{2^{i/2} n^{n/2}}{\left(n + \frac{t^2}{2}\right)^{(n+i)/2}} \frac{\Gamma\left(\frac{n+i}{2}\right)}{\Gamma\left(\frac{n}{2}\right)} \tag{2.10}$$

$$= \left(n + \frac{t^2}{2}\right)^{-i/2} \gamma_n \cdots \gamma_{n+i-1} q_0(t, n) ,$$

where

$$\gamma_j = 2^{1/2} \Gamma\left(\frac{j+1}{2}\right) \Big/ \Gamma\left(\frac{j}{2}\right) \tag{2.11}$$

The numbers γ_j obviously fulfill the relation

$$\gamma_j \gamma_{j+1} = j . \tag{2.12}$$

For $k = 1$ in (2.6) we have

$$I_1(t, n) = q_1 - \sigma q_0 ; \tag{2.13}$$

to make this vanish, we choose

$$\sigma = \frac{q_1}{q_0} = \left(n + \frac{t^2}{2}\right)^{-1/2} \gamma_n . \tag{2.14}$$

We do not need the second integral. The third and fourth are obtained by expanding $(s - \sigma)^3$, $(s - \sigma)^4$, inserting them in (2.6), and using (2.9), (2.12), and (2.14). In terms of the constants γ_n we have, after some computation,

$$I_3(t, n) = 2\gamma_n \left[\gamma_n^2 - \left(n - \frac{1}{2}\right)\right] \left(1 + \frac{t^2}{2n}\right)^{-n/2} \left(n + \frac{t^2}{2}\right)^{-3/2} , \tag{2.15}$$

$$I_4(t, n) = [n^2 \mp 2n + (2n - 4)\gamma_n^2 - 3\gamma_n^4] \left(1 + \frac{t^2}{2n}\right)^{-n/2} \left(n + \frac{t^2}{2}\right)^{-2} . \tag{2.16}$$

We are now in a position to write down the first terms of the expansion (2.7), using (2.8)—with argument $z_0 = \sigma t$—and (2.14)–(2.16). The terms of first and second order vanish identically by (2.8) and the choice in (2.14) of σ. For practical purposes, we can introduce two more simplifications, involving changes of order no greater than n^{-2} in n. The constant γ_n^2 appearing in (2.15) and (2.16) is closely approximated[1] by $n - \frac{1}{2}$; the relative error can

---

[1] This can be shown, for example, in the following way. By partial integration, we find that

$$\frac{J_{2m+1}}{J_{2m}} = \frac{\gamma_{2m+1}^2}{2m+1} = \frac{4m^2}{2m+1} \cdot \frac{1}{\gamma_{2m}^2} ,$$

where J_k denotes the integral $\int_0^{\pi/2} \cos^k x \, dx$. The left-hand side can be evaluated by writing $\cos^{2m+1} x = \cos^{2m} x \sqrt{1 - \sin^2 x}$ and expanding the root factor, using Cauchy's remainder term.

Rewriting the expansions of

be shown to be less than $n^{-2}/2$ for $n \geqq 10$. With this approximation, (2.15) vanishes and the first factor in (2.16) reduces to 5/4. Thus we are left with the computing formulas

$$S_n(t) = \Phi(\sigma t) + \frac{5\sigma t^5}{96}\varphi\left(\frac{\sigma t}{\sqrt{2}}\right)\left(1 + \frac{t^2}{2n}\right)^{-n/2}\left(n + \frac{t^2}{2}\right)^{-2} \tag{2.17}$$

$$= \Phi(\sigma t) + \frac{5\sigma t^5}{96n^2}\left(\frac{1}{1 + \frac{t^2}{2n}}\right)^{(n/2)+2}\varphi\left(\frac{\sigma t}{\sqrt{2}}\right),$$

where $\sigma = \sqrt{(n - \frac{1}{2})/(n + \frac{1}{2}t^2)}$. If, as a second simplification, we neglect the second term, this result gives the simple rule that the percentiles of Student's distribution are equal to the corresponding percentiles of the normal distribution divided by the factor σ.

For a numerical example, let $n = 10$ and $t = 3$. We obtain $\sigma = .809$ and $\Phi(\sigma t) = .9924$; the second term is found to be .0007, giving $S_{10}(3) = .9931$. The correct value, according to Fisher's tables [3], is .9933. For $n = 20$, the main term gives for

$t =$	1	2	3	4 ,
$\Phi(\sigma t) =$	.8353	.9701	.9963	.9996 ,

the correct values being

$S_{20}(t) =$	.8354	.9704	.9965	.9996 .

Insofar as the second and higher terms may be neglected, (2.17) is equivalent to the statement that the random variable

$$x = t\sqrt{(n - \tfrac{1}{2})/(n + \tfrac{1}{2}t^2)} \tag{2.18}$$

is normally distributed; the result thus is an analog to Fisher's z-transformation and many similar formulas. For large t and fixed n, x approaches $\sqrt{2n - 1}$; this gives an idea of the probability levels at which the transformation breaks down. In the range of fair approximation, the solution of (2.18) gives the percentage points of t as

$$t_p = x_p\sqrt{2n/[(2n - 1) - x_p^2]}\ . \tag{2.19}$$

It can be proved[2] that the expansion (2.7) converges to $S_n(t)$ for $|t| < c\sqrt{n}$, where c is a numerical constant. A close examination would probably give $c = 1$, since, by the very form of Student's p.d.f., $t = \sqrt{n}$ is the critical value of t. However, for computational purposes we would rather have to

---

$$(2m + 1)\cdot\frac{J_{2m+1}}{J_{2m}} \quad \text{and} \quad \frac{4m^2}{2m + 1}\cdot\frac{J_{2m}}{J_{2m+1}}$$

in terms of $n = 2m + 1$ and $n = 2m$, respectively, we find that $\gamma_n^2 = n - \frac{1}{2} + O(n^{-2})$.

[2] One way is to use Cauchy's integral formula for the remainder term in (2.5), find an upper bound for $\psi^{(k)}(z)$ in $(\sigma t, st)$ by using an appropriate circle along which to take the Cauchy integral, and estimate the integrated remainder.

estimate, say, the third- or fifth-order remainder term of the expansion by finding explicit upper bounds for the derivatives $\psi^{(k)}(z)$, $k = 3, 5$, in (z_0, z).

3. The Wald-Anderson Classification Statistic

The Wald-Anderson classification statistic W [1, p. 48] is in the one-dimensional case defined by

$$W = [x - \tfrac{1}{2}(\bar{x}_1 + \bar{x}_2)]s^{-2}(\bar{x}_1 - \bar{x}_2) , \tag{3.1}$$

where $\bar{x}_1$ and $\bar{x}_2$ are the means of two independent samples

$$x_{11}, \cdots, x_{1N_1}; \qquad x_{21}, \cdots, x_{2N_2}$$

from populations π_1 and π_2, respectively, s^2 the combined sample variance given by

$$(N_1 + N_2 - 2)s^2 = \sum_{i=1}^{N_1} (x_{1i} - \bar{x}_1)^2 + \sum_{i=1}^{N_2} (x_{2i} - \bar{x}_2)^2 ,$$

and x an observation from π_1 *or* π_2. Splitting up the first factor on the right-hand side of (3.1), we may write

$$W = w^* + \frac{(N_1 - N_2)}{2(N_1 + N_2)}(\bar{x}_1 - \bar{x}_2)^2 s^{-2} ,$$

where

$$w^* = \left(x - \frac{N_1\bar{x}_1 + N_2\bar{x}_2}{N_1 + N_2}\right)s^{-2}(\bar{x}_1 - \bar{x}_2) . \tag{3.1*}$$

We will find here an expansion for the distribution function of w^*. When $N_1 = N_2$, we also have an expansion for the distribution function of the classification statistic W.

For the subsequent distribution theory, we assume the samples to be normal with means $\pm\lambda$ and variance 1. We assume also that $\lambda > 0$. With the abbreviations

$$m = N_1 + N_2 , \quad p_1 = N_1/m , \quad p_2 = N_2/m , \quad n = m - 2 , \tag{3.2}$$

it follows that

$$\begin{aligned} x - \frac{N_1\bar{x}_1 + N_2\bar{x}_2}{N_1 + N_2} \quad & \text{is distributed normally } \begin{Bmatrix} 2\lambda p_2 \\ -2\lambda p_1 \end{Bmatrix}(1 + m^{-1}) , \quad x \in \begin{matrix}\pi_1 \\ \pi_2\end{matrix} , \\ \bar{x}_1 - \bar{x}_2 \quad & \text{is distributed normally } [2\lambda, (mp_1 p_2)^{-1}] , \\ ns^2 \quad & \text{is distributed like } \chi^2_n , \end{aligned} \tag{3.3}$$

all three factors being independent.

We shall simplify the calculations by introducing the transformed random variables

$$\begin{aligned} y &= (1 + m^{-1})^{-\frac{1}{2}}[x - (p_1\bar{x}_1 + p_2\bar{x}_2)] , \\ z &= (p_1 p_2)^{\frac{1}{2}}(\bar{x}_1 - \bar{x}_2) , \\ u &= s^2 , \end{aligned} \tag{3.4}$$

and

(3.5) $$w = w^*(1 + m^{-1})^{-\frac{1}{2}}(p_1 p_2)^{\frac{1}{2}} = yz/u \ .$$

Here y, z and u are independent. The expectations of y and z are, for $x \in \pi_1, \pi_2$,

(3.6) $$\gamma = E(y) = \begin{Bmatrix} p_2 \\ -p_1 \end{Bmatrix}(1 + m^{-1})^{-\frac{1}{2}} 2\lambda \ ,$$
$$\delta = E(z) = 2\lambda(p_1 p_2)^{\frac{1}{2}} \ ,$$

and the variances

(3.7) $$D^2(y) = 1 \ , \qquad D^2(z) = 1/m \ .$$

The conditional distribution of w, given $z = z$, $u = u$, is normal with mean $\gamma z/u$ and standard deviation $|z|/u$. Hence the c.d.f. of w may be written as

(3.8) $$F(w) = \int \Phi\left(\frac{uw - \gamma z}{|z|}\right) dG(u)\, dH(z) \ ,$$

where $G(u)$ and $H(z)$ are the c.d.f.'s of u and z, respectively.

With increasing n, the distributions of u and z concentrate around the means 1 and δ, respectively. As before, then, we would like to replace Φ in (3.8) by some approximate expression that provides a good representation of the function in the neighborhood of $u = 1$ and $z = \delta$, and is such that the integration in (3.8) can be performed.

For this purpose, let w be a fixed value, and write

(3.9) $$\Phi\left(\frac{uw - \gamma z}{|z|}\right) = \Phi\left(\frac{u_0 w - \gamma z_0}{z_0}\right) + \psi(u, z) \exp[-\alpha u - \beta z] \ ,$$

where

(3.10) $$\psi(u, z) = \left[\Phi\left(\frac{uw - \gamma z}{|z|}\right) - \Phi\left(\frac{u_0 w - \gamma z_0}{z_0}\right)\right] \exp[\alpha u + \beta z] \ .$$

Here, both u_0 and z_0 are greater than 0; while α and β are parameters to be determined (they will be functions of w). We now expand ψ in a Taylor series around u_0 and z_0 (of course, this series will in no case represent ψ for $z \leq 0$). To obtain a simple approximation, we shall determine the parameters so as to make vanish (1) the integrals of the first-order terms, and (2) the derivatives $\psi''_{uu}(u_0, z_0)$ and $\psi''_{zz}(u_0, z_0)$. The terms containing $(u - u_0)(z - z_0)$, $(u - u_0)^2(z - z_0)$, $(u - u_0)(z - z_0)^2$, and $(z - z_0)^3$, will then also vanish upon integration, while the term with $(u - u_0)^3$ will yield an integral of order $O(n^{-2})$. Under these circumstances, it is to be expected that the zero-order term $\Phi(u_0 w/z_0 - \gamma)$ will provide a fair representation of $F(w)$ for not too small n. The only computation involved will be that of u_0/z_0 as a function of w.

To carry out this idea, we first impose condition (1) above. Using the distribution of u and z, as determined by (3.3), (3.4), (3.6), and (3.7), we have

$$\int_0^\infty (u - u_0)u^{\frac{1}{2}n-1} \exp[-(\tfrac{1}{2}n + \alpha)u]\, du = 0\,, \tag{3.11}$$
$$\int_{-\infty}^\infty (z - z_0) \exp[-\beta z - \tfrac{1}{2}m(z - \delta)^2]\, dz = 0\,.$$

A simple calculation gives the conditions

$$u_0 = n/(n + 2\alpha)\,, \tag{3.12}$$

$$z_0 = (\delta - \beta)/m\,. \tag{3.13}$$

Applying condition (2), we find for $z > 0$ that

$$\frac{\partial^2 \psi}{\partial u^2} = \alpha^2 \psi + \left[\frac{2\alpha w}{z} - \left(\frac{w}{z}\right)^2\left(\frac{uw}{z} - \gamma\right)\right]\varphi \exp[\alpha u + \beta z]\,,$$

$$\frac{\partial^2 \psi}{\partial z^2} = \beta^2 \psi + \left[-\frac{2\beta uw}{z^2} + \frac{2uw}{z^3} - \left(\frac{uw}{z^2}\right)^2\left(\frac{uw}{z} - \gamma\right)\right]\varphi \exp[\alpha u + \beta z]\,,$$

where φ is the normal density function taken for the argument $uw/z - \gamma$. Inserting $u = u_0$ and $z = z_0$, which makes $\psi = 0$, and equating to zero, we find

$$\alpha = \frac{w}{2z_0^2}(u_0 w - \gamma z_0)\,, \tag{3.14}$$

$$\beta = \frac{1}{z_0}\frac{u_0 w}{2z_0^3}(u_0 w - \gamma z_0)\,. \tag{3.15}$$

Multiplying these equations by u_0 and z_0, respectively, and adding, we get instead of (3.15) the simpler relation

$$u_0 \alpha + z_0 \beta = 1\,. \tag{3.16}$$

The elimination of α, β, and z_0 from (3.12)–(3.14) and (3.16) leads to an equation of fourth degree in u_0. A practical procedure for computing u_0 and z_0 seems to be the following combination of iteration and interpolation.

By eliminating α between (3.12) and (3.14), we obtain an equation of second degree in u_0, with relevant solution

$$u_0 = \frac{z_0}{2w^2}[-(nz_0 - w\gamma) + \sqrt{(nz_0 - w\gamma)^2 + 4nw^2}] \equiv u(z_0)\,. \tag{3.17}$$

On the other hand, inserting α from (3.12) and β from (3.13) in (3.16) and solving for z_0, we obtain

$$z_0 = \frac{\delta}{2} + \sqrt{\left(\frac{\delta}{2}\right)^2 + \frac{1}{m}\left[\frac{1}{2}n(1 - u_0) - 1\right]} \equiv z(u_0)\,. \tag{3.18}$$

Numerical evidence indicates that (3.17) and (3.18)—at least within a certain range of data—can be solved by iteration, starting from a first approximation $z_0 = z_1 = \delta$, and forming successively

$$u_1 = u(z_1)\,, \quad z_2 = z(u_1)\,, \quad u_2 = u(z_2)\,, \quad z_3 = z(u_2)\,. \tag{3.19}$$

At this point a short cut proves to be convenient. Replacing the curve $z = z(u)$ by its secant through (u_1, z_1) and (u_2, z_2), and similarly $u = u(z)$ by its secant through (u_1, z_2) and (u_2, z_3), we obtain the approximate point of intersection; i.e.,

$$u_0 = u_2 + \frac{(z_3 - z_2)(u_2 - u_1)}{2z_2 - z_1 - z_3}, \tag{3.20}$$

$$z_0 = z_3 + \frac{(z_3 - z_2)^2}{2z_2 - z_1 - z_3}. \tag{3.21}$$

These values can, of course, be checked by insertion in (3.17) and (3.18), and, if necessary, be improved by further iteration.

Example. Let $m = 10$, $n = 8$, $\gamma = \delta = 1$; and $w = 3$. Starting with $z_1 = 1$, we obtain from (3.17) and (3.18)

$$u_1 = 0.705, \quad z_2 = 1.018, \quad u_2 = 0.713, \quad z_3 = 1.014;$$

and from (3.20) and (3.21) we obtain

$$u_0 = 0.712, \quad z_0 = 1.015.$$

This gives $(u_0/z_0)w - \gamma = 1.103$, and $F(w) \approx \Phi(1.103) = 0.865$.

4. Summary

Approximate values of the c.d.f. of (3.1*), and thus when $N_1 = N_2$ of the Wald-Anderson classification statistic (in the one-dimensional case) may be obtained as follows:

Step 1. Find m, p_1, p_2, and n from (3.2).

Step 2. Find γ and δ from (3.6).

Step 3. For the given argument w^*, find w from (3.5).

Step 4. Solve u_0 and z_0 from (3.17) and (3.18). To do this approximately, start from $z_1 = \delta$, form u_1, z_2, u_2, and z_3 according to (3.19), and compute u_0 and z_0 from (3.20) and (3.21).

Step 5. Find $\Pr\{\boldsymbol{w}^* \leqq w^*\} \approx \Phi[(u_0/z_0)w - \gamma]$.

References

[1] Anderson, T. W. Classification by multivariate analysis. *Psychometrika*, 1951, **16**, 31-50.

[2] Sitgreaves, R. On the distribution of two random matrices used in classification procedures. *Ann. Math. Stat.*, 1952, **23**, 263-70.

[3] Fisher, R. A. Expansion of Student's integral in powers of n^{-1}. *Metron*, 1925, **5**, 109-20.

18

A Representation of Hotelling's T^2 and Anderson's Classification Statistic W in Terms of Simple Statistics

ALBERT H. BOWKER, Stanford University

1. Introduction

It has been shown by Hsu [1] that the distribution of Hotelling's T^2 in the non-central case is equivalent to that of a non-central F-statistic. This paper gives a direct representation of T^2 in terms of the ratio of two independent chi-square variables, the numerator being non-central. The basic method is extended to obtain a representation of Anderson's classification statistic W as a function of the elements of two 2×2 independent Wishart matrices, the one being non-central.

Since the exact distribution of W is known to be exceedingly complicated as indicated by Sitgreaves in Chapter 15, the present representation should prove extremely useful in finding percentage points for the distribution, either through an asymptotic expansion of the distribution function or by empirical sampling of the Wishart variables on high-speed computers.

2. Two Lemmas

Throughout the paper, we denote the joint density function of the elements of a p-dimensional Wishart matrix B, with n degrees of freedom and covariance matrix Σ, by $h(B|\Sigma, p, n)$. [The usual notation is $W(B|\Sigma, p, n)$. The notation $h(B|\Sigma, p, n)$ is used here to avoid confusion with the classification statistic W.] The symbol I_p is used for the p-dimensional identity matrix, and $\operatorname{tr} B$ denotes the trace of the matrix B.

We now prove two lemmas which justify the results obtained.

Lemma 1. *Let B be a $p \times p$ symmetric random matrix whose elements have probability density function $f(B)$. Let G be a random $p \times p$ orthogonal matrix whose elements are distributed independently of the elements of B with density function $g(G)$.*

(a) *Let O be any $p \times p$ orthogonal matrix, and define $E = O' B O$. Then, if the function f has the property that*

$$f(B) = f(O E O') = f(E) , \tag{2.1}$$

the matrix $B^* = G B G'$ is a $p \times p$ symmetric random matrix whose elements have probability density $f(B^*)$ and are distributed independently of G.

(b) *The Wishart density $h(B|I_p, p, n)$ has the property* (2.1).

PROOF OF (a). The joint probability density of the elements of G and B is $g(G) \cdot f(B)$. Let $B^* = G B G'$. The Jacobian of the transformation is $|GG'|^{(p+1)/2} = 1$. The joint density function of G and B^* is then $g(G) f(G' B^* G) = g(G) f(B^*)$, and part (a) follows.

PROOF OF (b). The Wishart density is

$$h(B|I_p, p, n) = C(p, n) \, |B|^{(n-p-1)/2} \exp(-\tfrac{1}{2} \operatorname{tr} B) , \tag{2.2}$$

where

$$C(p, n) = 2^{pn/2} \pi^{p(p-1)/4} \prod_{i=1}^{p} [\Gamma \tfrac{1}{2}(n - i + 1)]^{-1} .$$

Let O be any $p \times p$ orthogonal matrix and define $E = O' B O$. Then

$$\begin{aligned} h(B|I_p, p, n) &= h(O E O'|I_p, p, n) \\ &= h(E|I_p, p, n) , \end{aligned} \tag{2.3}$$

since $|O E O'| = |E|$ and $\operatorname{tr} O E O' = \operatorname{tr} E O' O = \operatorname{tr} E$. ||

It will be noted that the condition (2.1) is equivalent to requiring that f be a function only of D_β where D_β is a $p \times p$ diagonal matrix, whose diagonal elements are the characteristic roots of B.

LEMMA 2. *Let B be a $p \times p$ symmetric random matrix whose elements have probability density function $h(B|I_p, p, n)$. Partition B and B^{-1} as follows:*

$$B = \begin{bmatrix} B_{11} & B_{12} \\ B_{12}' & B_{22} \end{bmatrix} ,$$

and

$$B^{-1} = \begin{bmatrix} B^{11} & B^{12} \\ B^{12\prime} & B^{22} \end{bmatrix} ,$$

where B_{11} and B^{11} are the $k \times k$ matrices in the upper left-hand corner of B and B^{-1}, respectively. Let $(B)^{11-1} = B_{\cdot k+1, \ldots, p}$. Then $B_{\cdot k+1, \ldots, p}$ is a $k \times k$ symmetric random matrix whose elements have density function

$$h(B_{\cdot k+1, \ldots, p}|I_k, k, n - p + k) .$$

PROOF. We need two results from the theory of partitioned matrices (see, for example, [2], p. 363, and [3], p. 238):

$$|B| = |B_{22}| \, |B_{11} - B_{12} B_{22}^{-1} B_{12}'| , \tag{2.4}$$

and

$$(B^{11}) = (B_{11} - B_{12} B_{22}^{-1} B_{12}')^{-1} . \tag{2.5}$$

It follows that

$$B_{\cdot k+1,\,\ldots,\,p} = (B_{11} - B_{12}\,B_{22}^{-1}\,B_{12}')\,. \tag{2.6}$$

The distribution of B can be written

$$\begin{aligned} h(B|I_p, p, n) &= C(p, n)\,|B|^{(n-p-1)/2} \exp(-\tfrac{1}{2}\operatorname{tr} B) \\ &= C(p, n)\,|B_{22}|^{(n-p-1)/2} \exp(\tfrac{1}{2}\operatorname{tr} B_{22}) \\ &\quad \cdot |B_{11} - B_{12}B_{22}^{-1}B_{12}'|^{(n-p-1)/2} \exp(-\tfrac{1}{2}\operatorname{tr} B_{11})\,. \end{aligned} \tag{2.7}$$

If we make the transformation from B_{11} to $B_{\cdot k+1,\ldots,p} = B_{11} - B_{12}B_{22}^{-1}B_{12}'$, the joint distribution of $B_{\cdot k+1,\ldots,p}$, B_{12}, and B_{22} is given by

$$\begin{aligned} &C(p, n)\,|B_{22}|^{(n-p-1)/2} \exp(-\tfrac{1}{2}\operatorname{tr} B_{22} - \tfrac{1}{2}\operatorname{tr} B_{12}B_{22}^{-1}B_{12}') \\ &\qquad \cdot |B_{\cdot k+1,\ldots,p}|^{(n-p-1)/2} \exp(-\tfrac{1}{2}\operatorname{tr} B_{\cdot k+1,\ldots,p}) \\ &= \frac{C(p, n)}{C(k, n-p+k)}\,|B_{22}|^{(n-p-1)/2} \exp[-\tfrac{1}{2}\operatorname{tr} B_{22} - \tfrac{1}{2}\operatorname{tr} B_{12}B_{22}^{-1}B_{12}'] \\ &\qquad \cdot h(B_{\cdot k+1,\ldots,p}\,|I_k, k, n-p+k)\,, \end{aligned} \tag{2.8}$$

and the lemma follows. ||

This result is well known in normal regression analysis, but an explicit statement seems to be elusive. (A related theorem is proved by Anderson in [4], Chapter 4.) If the Wishart matrix is assumed to be generated by a random sample of n p-dimensional normal vectors, the elements of the $k \times k$ matrix $B_{\cdot k+1,\ldots,p}$ are obtained from the sums of squares and cross products of the residuals from the regression of the first k variables on the remaining $p-k$. The distribution of the sums of squares and cross products of the residuals is again a Wishart distribution with a loss of one degree of freedom for each of the variables held constant. The notation $B_{\cdot k+1,\ldots,p}$ was adopted to show the relation to regression theory.

3. Representation of Hotelling's T^2

Hsu [1] has shown that Hotelling's T^2 can be written

$$T^2 = n\,t'\,U^{-1}t\,, \tag{3.1}$$

where the elements of $t' = (t_1, \cdots, t_p)$ are independently, normally distributed with unit variances, $E(t_i) = \tau_i$, $i = 1, 2, \cdots, p$, while U is a p-dimensional Wishart matrix, distributed independently of t, with density function $h(U|I_p, p, n)$. We can find an orthogonal matrix Γ whose first row is given by

$$\gamma_{1i} = \frac{\tau_i}{\sqrt{\sum \tau_i^2}}\,, \qquad i = 1, 2, \cdots, p\,.$$

If we make the transformation $Y = \Gamma\,t$, $A = \Gamma\,U\,\Gamma'$, then

$$T^2 = n\,Y'\,\Gamma\,\Gamma'\,A^{-1}\,\Gamma\,\Gamma'\,Y = n\,Y'\,A^{-1}Y\,, \tag{3.2}$$

where the elements of $Y' = (y_1, y_2, \cdots, y_p)$ are independently, normally distributed with unit variance, $E(y_{11}) = \sqrt{\sum_{i=1}^{p}\tau_i^2} = \mu$, say; $E(y_j) = 0$, $j = 2, \cdots, p$. The matrix A is again a p-dimensional Wishart matrix, whose elements are distributed independently of Y, with density function $h(A|I_p, p, n)$.

For any set of values of Y (except the null vector which has probability zero) we can construct an orthogonal matrix G whose first row is given by

$$g_j = \frac{y_j}{\sqrt{b_{11}}}, \qquad j = 1, 2, \cdots, p,$$

where $b_{11} = \sum_{i=1}^{p} y_i^2$. Then

$$\begin{aligned}(3.3) \qquad T^2 &= n\, Y'\, G'\, G\, A^{-1} G' G\, Y \\ &= n\,(G\,Y)'\,(G\,A\,G')^{-1}\,G\,Y \\ &= n\,(\sqrt{b_{11}}, 0, \cdots, 0)\, A^{*-1}\,(\sqrt{b_{11}}, 0, \cdots, 0)' \\ &= n\sqrt{b_{11}}\, a^{*11}\sqrt{b_{11}} \\ &= n\,\frac{b_{11}}{a^{*}_{11\cdot 2\cdots p}}.\end{aligned}$$

By Lemma 1, the elements of A^* are distributed independently of the elements of G (and consequently of b_{11}) with a Wishart distribution $h(A^*|I_p, p, n)$. By Lemma 2, $a^{*}_{11\cdot 2\cdots p}$ has a chi-square distribution with $(n - p + 1)$ degrees of freedom. Since $b_{11} = \sum_{j=1}^{p} y_j^2$ is the sum of squares of p independent normal variables with unit variance, the first one being non-central, b_{11} has a non-central chi-square distribution with p degrees of freedom. We have a representation of T^2/n as the ratio of two independent chi-square variables, the numerator being non-central.

4. Representation of Anderson's Classification Statistic *W*

Anderson's classification statistic W [5] was proposed for the following problem: We have observed $N_1 + N_2 + 1$ independent p-dimensional chance vectors. The first N_1 vectors come from a population Π_1, the following N_2 vectors come from a population Π_2, and the last vector comes from a population Π where Π is either Π_1 or Π_2. The probability distribution in both Π_1 and Π_2 is assumed to be multivariate normal with the same covariance matrix Σ; the vector of expected values is $\mu^{(1)}$ in Π_1 and $\mu^{(2)}$ in Π_2. The values of $\mu^{(1)}$, $\mu^{(2)}$, and Σ are not known. On the basis of X, the $p \cdot (N_1 + N_2 + 1)$ matrix of observations, we want to classify the last observation as coming from either Π_1 or Π_2.

For purposes of classification, Anderson proposed the statistic

$$(4.1) \qquad W = X'_{N_1+N_2+1} S^{-1}(X^{(1)} - X^{(2)}) - \tfrac{1}{2}(\bar{X}^{(1)} + \bar{X}^{(2)})\, S^{-1}(\bar{X}^{(1)} - \bar{X}^{(2)}),$$

where

$$\bar{X}^{(1)} = \frac{1}{N_1}\sum_{t=1}^{N_1} X_t, \qquad \bar{X}^{(2)} = \frac{1}{N_2}\sum_{t=N_1+1}^{N_1+N_2} X_t,$$

and

$$S = \frac{1}{N_1 + N_2 - 2}\left[\sum_{t=1}^{N_1}(X_t - \bar{X}^{(1)})(X_t - \bar{X}^{(1)})' + \sum_{t=N_1+1}^{N_1+N_2}(X_t - \bar{X}^{(2)})(X_t - \bar{X}^{(2)})'\right].$$

The last observation is classified as belonging to Π_1 if the observed value of W is greater than a pre-assigned cutoff point ω_0, and to Π_2 if $W \leqq \omega_0$.

It was pointed out in [6] that if we write

$$A_{\Sigma} = (N_1 + N_2 - 2)S ,$$

$$Z = \frac{(N_1 N_2)^{\frac{1}{2}}}{(N_1 + N_2)^{\frac{1}{2}}} (\bar{X}^{(1)} - \bar{X}^{(2)}) ,$$

$$Z^* = \frac{(N_1 + N_2)^{\frac{1}{2}}}{(N_1 + N_2 + 1)^{\frac{1}{2}}} \left[X_{N_1+N_2+1} - \frac{1}{(N_1 + N_2)} (N_1 \bar{X}^{(1)} + N_2 \bar{X}^{(2)}) \right],$$

we can write

$$W = (N_1 + N_2 - 2) \left[\frac{(N_1 + N_2 + 1)^{\frac{1}{2}}}{(N_1 N_2)^{\frac{1}{2}}} Z^{*\prime} A_{\Sigma}^{-1} Z + \frac{(N_1 - N_2)}{2 N_1 N_2} Z' A_{\Sigma}^{-1} Z \right]. \tag{4.2}$$

Under either alternative, the three sets of variables are distributed independently of each other, the matrix A_{Σ} has a Wishart distribution with $n = N_1 + N_2 - 2$ degrees of freedom and covariance matrix Σ, the vector Z has a normal distribution with expected value $[(N_1 N_2)^{\frac{1}{2}}][(N_1 + N_2)^{\frac{1}{2}}](\mu^{(1)} - \mu^{(2)})$ and covariance matrix Σ, and the vector Z^* has a normal distribution with covariance matrix Σ. Under the hypothesis that $X_{N_1+N_2+1}$ comes from Π_1, the expected value of Z^* is

$$\frac{N_2}{(N_1 + N_2)^{\frac{1}{2}} (N_1 + N_2 + 1)^{\frac{1}{2}}} (\mu^{(1)} - \mu^{(2)}),$$

while, under the alternative hypothesis, the expected value of Z^* is

$$\frac{-N_1}{(N_1 + N_2)^{\frac{1}{2}} (N_1 + N_2 - 1)^{\frac{1}{2}}} (\mu^{(1)} - \mu^{(2)}) .$$

There is a non-singular matrix Ψ (e.g., see [3]) such that $\Psi \Sigma \Psi' = I_p$ and $(\mu^{(1)} - \mu^{(2)})' \Psi' = (2\lambda, 0, \cdots, 0)$ with $\lambda \geqq 0$, $\lambda^2 = \frac{1}{4}(\mu^{(1)} - \mu^{(2)})' \Sigma^{-1} (\mu^{(1)} - \mu^{(2)})$. If we make the transformation $Y_1 = \Psi Z$, $Y_2 = \Psi Z^*$, $A = \Psi A_{\Sigma} \Psi'$, we have

$$\begin{aligned} W &= (N_1 + N_2 - 2) \left[\frac{(N_1 + N_2 + 1)^{\frac{1}{2}}}{(N_1 N_2)^{\frac{1}{2}}} Y_1' \Psi'^{-1} \Psi' A^{-1} \Psi \Psi^{-1} Y_2 \right. \\ &\qquad \left. + \frac{(N_1 - N_2)}{2 N_1 N_2} Y_1' \Psi'^{-1} \Psi' A^{-1} \Psi \Psi^{-1} Y_1 \right] \\ &= (N_1 + N_2 - 2) \left[\frac{(N_1 + N_2 + 1)^{\frac{1}{2}}}{(N_1 N_2)^{\frac{1}{2}}} Y_1' A^{-1} Y_2 + \frac{(N_1 - N_2)}{2 N_1 N_2} Y_1' A^{-1} Y_1 \right] \\ &= n [k_1 Y_1' A^{-1} Y_2 + k_2 Y_1' A^{-1} Y_1] , \quad \text{say.} \end{aligned} \tag{4.3}$$

The elements of Y_1 are independently, normally distributed with unit variance,

$$E(y_{11}) = \frac{2(N_1 N_2)^{\frac{1}{2}}}{(N_1 + N_2)^{\frac{1}{2}}} \lambda = \mu ,$$

say, $E(y_{1j}) = 0$, $j = 2, \cdots, p$. The elements of Y_2 are also independently, normally distributed with unit variance, and $E(y_{21}) = c\mu$, $E(y_{2j}) = 0$, $j = 2, \cdots, p$, where

$$c = \left[\frac{N_2}{N_1(N_1 + N_2 + 1)}\right]^{\frac{1}{2}} \quad \text{or} \quad c = -\left[\frac{N_1}{N_2(N_1 + N_2 + 1)}\right]^{\frac{1}{2}},$$

depending on whether $\Pi = \Pi_1$, or $\Pi = \Pi_2$. The matrix A is a p-dimensional Wishart matrix whose elements are distributed independently of both Y_1 and Y_2 with density function $h(A|I_p, p, n)$.

Now let $Y_1'Y_1 = \sum_{i=1}^{p} y_{1i}^2 = b_{11}$, $Y_2'Y_2 = \sum_{i=1}^{p} y_{2i}^2 = b_{22}$, $Y_1'Y_2 = \sum_{i=1}^{p} y_{1i}y_{2i} = b_{12}$. We can construct an orthogonal matrix G such that

$$\begin{bmatrix} Y_1' \\ \\ Y_2' \end{bmatrix} G' = \begin{bmatrix} \sqrt{b_{11}} & 0 & 0 \cdots 0 \\ \\ \dfrac{b_{12}}{\sqrt{b_{11}}} & \sqrt{\dfrac{b_{11}b_{22} - b_{12}^2}{b_{11}}} & 0 \cdots 0 \end{bmatrix},$$

where $g_{1j} = y_{1j}/\sqrt{b_{11}}$, $j = 1, 2, \cdots, p$, and

$$g_{2j} = \frac{y_{2j} - (b_{12}/b_{11})\, y_{1j}}{\sqrt{\dfrac{b_{11}b_{22} - b_{12}^2}{b_{11}}}}, \qquad j = 1, 2, \cdots, p.$$

Since G is orthogonal, W can be written as

$$\begin{aligned} W &= n(k_1 Y_1' G' G A^{-1} G' G Y_2 + k_2 Y_1' G' G A^{-1} G' G Y_1) \qquad (4.4) \\ &= nk_1(\sqrt{b_{11}}, 0, \cdots, 0)\, A^{*-1}\left(\frac{b_{12}}{\sqrt{b_{11}}}, \sqrt{\frac{b_{11}b_{22} - b_{12}^2}{b_{11}}}, 0, \cdots, 0\right)' \\ &\quad + nk_2(\sqrt{b_{11}}, 0, \cdots, 0)\, A^{*-1}(\sqrt{b_{11}}, 0, \cdots, 0)'. \end{aligned}$$

By Lemma 1, the elements of A^* have a Wishart distribution independent of b_{11}, b_{12}, and b_{22}. If we write

$$A^{*-1} = \begin{bmatrix} A^{*11} & A^{*12} \\ A^{*12'} & A^{*22} \end{bmatrix},$$

where A^{*11} is the 2×2 matrix in the upper left-hand corner of A^{*-1}, then (4.4) reduces to

$$\begin{aligned} W &= nk_1(\sqrt{b_{11}}, 0)\, A^{*11}\left(\frac{b_{12}}{\sqrt{b_{11}}}, \sqrt{\frac{b_{11}b_{22} - b_{12}^2}{b_{11}}}\right)' \qquad (4.5) \\ &\quad + nk_2(\sqrt{b_{11}}, 0)\, A^{*11}(\sqrt{b_{11}}, 0)'. \end{aligned}$$

By Lemma 2, the elements of the 2×2 matrix $(A^{*11})^{-1}$ have a Wishart distribution: $h(A_{\cdot 3 \ldots p}|I_2, 2, n - p + 2)$. We shall denote the elements

$$(A^{*11})^{-1} = A_{\cdot 3 \ldots p} = \begin{bmatrix} c_{11} & c_{12} \\ c_{12} & c_{22} \end{bmatrix}.$$

Thus, W can be expressed in terms of the c_{ij}'s and b_{ij}'s as

$$W = nk_1 \frac{(c_{22}b_{12} - c_{12}\sqrt{b_{11}b_{22} - b_{12}^2})}{(c_{11}c_{22} - c_{12}^2)} + nk_2 \frac{b_{11}c_{22}}{(c_{11}c_{22} - c_{12}^2)}. \qquad (4.6)$$

This expression is the basic result of the paper. Essentially we have here expressed W in terms of the elements of two independent 2×2 Wishart matrices with identity covariance matrix. The c_{ij}'s are central with $n-p+2$ degrees of freedom, and the b_{ij}'s have a non-central Wishart distribution with p degrees of freedom, given by the expression (e.g., see [7])

$$p(B) = \frac{|B|^{\frac{1}{2}(p-3)} \exp\left[-\frac{1}{2}(\mu^2(1+c^2)+b_{11}+b_{22})\right]}{2^p \pi^{\frac{1}{2}} \Gamma(\frac{1}{2}(p-1))} \cdot \sum_{j=0}^{\infty} \frac{[\frac{1}{2}(b_{11}+2cb_{12}+c^2b_{22})]^j (\frac{1}{2}\mu^2)^j}{\Gamma(\frac{1}{2}p+j)\, j!} . \tag{4.7}$$

The expression (4.6) may be rewritten in various ways. The most important case in applications arises when $N_1 = N_2 = N$, and $k_2 = 0$. In this case, we have

$$W = nk_1 \frac{b_{12} - (c_{12}/c_{22})(b_{11}b_{22} - b_{12}^2)^{\frac{1}{2}}}{c_{11} - (c_{12}^2/c_{22})} . \tag{4.8}$$

Note that $\sqrt{n-p+2}\,(c_{11}/c_{22})$ has Student's t-distribution with $(n-p+2)$ degrees of freedom and that $c_{11} - (c_{12}^2/c_{22})$ has an independent chi-square distribution with $(n-p+1)$ degrees of freedom. Thus W can be written as

$$\frac{\sqrt{2N+1}}{N} \frac{\left[b_{12} - \dfrac{t_{2N-p}}{\sqrt{2N-p}}(b_{11}b_{22} - b_{12}^2)^{\frac{1}{2}}\right]}{\dfrac{X^2_{2N-p-1}}{2N-2}} . \tag{4.9}$$

Note also that in this case $\mu = \sqrt{2N}\lambda$, while c is $1/\sqrt{2N+1}$ if $\Pi = \Pi_1$, or $-1/\sqrt{2N+1}$ if $\Pi = \Pi_2$. Thus, as $N \to \infty$,

$$c\mu \to \begin{cases} \lambda, & \text{if } \Pi = \Pi_1 , \\ -\lambda, & \text{if } \Pi = \Pi_2 . \end{cases}$$

The manipulations necessary to justify this reduction are heavy and may seem artificial. The geometric idea is very simple. Y_1 and Y_2 are p-dimensional vectors; clearly they will only have two non-zero components if the axes are chosen to be along Y_1 and perpendicular to Y_1 in the plane determined by Y_1 and Y_2. This rotation is accomplished by an orthogonal transformation whose elements depend on the components of Y_1 and Y_2. However, this transformation leaves the value of W invariant and since the Y's are distributed independently of the elements of A, the elements of the transformed matrix A^* have a Wishart distribution.

References

[1] Hsu, P. L. Notes on Hotelling's generalized T. *Ann. Math. Stat.*, 1938, **9**, 231-43.

[2] Deemer, W. L., and Olkin, I. The Jacobians of certain matrix transformations useful in multivariate analysis. *Biometrika*, 1951, **38**, 345-67.

[3] Dwyer, P. S. *Linear Computations.* New York: Wiley, 1951.
[4] Anderson, T. W. *Introduction to Multivariate Statistical Analysis.* New York: Wiley, 1958.
[5] Anderson, T. W. Classification by multivariate analysis. *Psychometrika*, 1951, **16**, 31-50.
[6] Sitgreaves, R. On the distribution of two random matrices used in classification procedures. *Ann. Math. Stat.*, 1952, **23**, 263-70.
[7] Anderson, T. W., and Girshick, M. A. Some extensions of the Wishart distribution. *Ann. Math. Stat.*, 1944, **15**, 345-57.

19

An Asymptotic Expansion for the Distribution Function of the W-Classification Statistic

ALBERT H. BOWKER, Stanford University

ROSEDITH SITGREAVES, Columbia University

1. Introduction

This chapter presents an asymptotic expansion for the distribution function of W, making use of the representation developed in Chapter 18. In that chapter Bowker showed that W can be represented as a function of two independent 2×2 Wishart matrices, one of which is noncentral. This representation is used here to obtain, for each alternative, an asymptotic expansion for the cumulative distribution function of W in the case when $N_1 = N_2 = N$. The expansion is developed through terms of the order of $1/N^2$ and should prove useful for computing purposes.

2. Representation of W

Bowker's results can be rewritten as follows:

LEMMA 1. *When $N_1 = N_2 = N$, the classification statistic W, defined in* (1.4), *of Chapter* 15, *can be represented by*

$$(2.1) \qquad W = \frac{(2N-2)\sqrt{2N+1}}{N\chi^2_{2N-p-1}} \cdot \left\{ \sum_{i=1}^{p} y_{1i}y_{2i} - \frac{t_{2N-p}}{\sqrt{2N-p}} \left[\sum_{i=1}^{p} y_{1i}^2 \sum_{i=1}^{p} y_{2i}^2 - \left(\sum_{i=1}^{p} y_{1i}y_{2i} \right)^2 \right]^{\frac{1}{2}} \right\}.$$

The variables $y_{11}, y_{12}, \cdots, y_{1p}$, $y_{21}, y_{22}, \cdots, y_{2p}$, t_{2N-p}, and χ^2_{2N-p-1} are all independently distributed with the following distributions:

(i) *$y_{11}, y_{12}, \cdots, y_{1p}$ are normally distributed, each with unit variance. The expected value of y_{11} is $\sqrt{2N}\,\lambda$. The variables $y_{12}, \cdots, y_{1p}$ each have expected value* 0.

(ii) *$y_{21}, y_{22}, \cdots, y_{2p}$ are normally distributed, each with unit variance. If the observation to be classified is from π_1, the expected value of y_{21} is $+\sqrt{2N/(2N+1)}\,\lambda$. If the observation to be classified is from π_2, the expected value of y_{21} is $-\sqrt{2N/(2N+1)}\,\lambda$. The variables $y_{22}, \cdots, y_{2p}$ each have expected value* 0.

(iii) t_{2N-p} *is distributed as Student's t with* $(2N-p)$ *degrees of freedom.*
(iv) χ^2_{2N-p-1} *has a* χ^2 *distribution with* $(2N-p-1)$ *degrees of freedom.*

PROOF. This follows directly from equation (4.9) of [4], on replacing b_{11}, b_{12}, and b_{22} by the sums of squares and products of normal variables defining them, i. e., $B = (Y_1 Y_2)'(Y_1 Y_2)$, where $Y_1' = (y_{11}, y_{12}, \cdots, y_{1p})$, $Y_2' = (y_{21}, y_{22}, \cdots, y_{2p})$, and the distributions of Y_1 and Y_2 are as stated.

LEMMA 2. *The quantity*

$$U = \sqrt{\frac{2}{N}}\left\{\sum_{i=1}^{p} y_{1i}y_{2i} - \frac{t_{2N-p}}{\sqrt{2N-p}}\left[\sum_{i=1}^{p} y_{1i}^2 \sum_{i=1}^{p} y_{2i}^2 - \left(\sum_{i=1}^{p} y_{1i}y_{2i}\right)^2\right]^{\frac{1}{2}}\right\} \tag{2.2}$$

can be represented by

$$U = 2\lambda x + \sqrt{\frac{2}{N}}(xy + \sqrt{c_{22}}\,v) - \frac{t}{\sqrt{2N-p}}\left\{\left[2\lambda\sqrt{c_{22}} + \sqrt{\frac{2}{N}}(\sqrt{c_{22}}\,y - vx)\right]^2 + \frac{2}{N}c_{11.2}(x^2 + c_{22})\right\}^{\frac{1}{2}}. \tag{2.3}$$

The variables $x, y, v, c_{11.2}, c_{22}$, *and t are all independently distributed with the following distributions:*

(i) *x is normally distributed with unit variance. The expected value of x is* $+\sqrt{2N/(2N+1)}\,\lambda$ *if the observation to be classified is from* π_1, *and* $-\sqrt{2N/(2N+1)}\,\lambda$ *if the observation to be classified is from* π_2.

(ii) *y and v are normally distributed, each with zero mean and unit variance.*

(iii) $c_{11.2}$ *and* c_{22} *each have a* χ^2 *distribution with* $(p-2)$ *and* $(p-1)$ *degrees of freedom, respectively.*

(iv) *t is distributed as Student's t with* $(2N-p)$ *degrees of freedom.*

PROOF. Let $x = y_{21}$ and $t = t_{2N-p}$ so that the distributions of x and t are the distributions of y_{21} and t_{2N-p} given in Lemma 1. Also, let $y = y_{11} - \sqrt{2N}\,\lambda$. Then, y is normally distributed, independently of x and t, with zero mean and unit variance.

From Lemma 1 we know that $y_{12}, \cdots, y_{1p}$ and $y_{22}, \cdots, y_{2p}$, are normally and independently distributed, each with zero mean and unit variance. If we write

$$c_{11} = \sum_{i=2}^{p} y_{1i}^2, \qquad c_{12} = \sum_{i=2}^{p} y_{1i}y_{2i}, \qquad c_{22} = \sum_{i=2}^{p} y_{2i}^2,$$

then

$$C = \begin{pmatrix} c_{11} & c_{12} \\ c_{12} & c_{22} \end{pmatrix}$$

is a 2×2 (central) Wishart matrix with $(p-1)$ degrees of freedom. The elements of C are distributed independently of x, y, and t (cf. Lemma 1) with probability density (e. g., see [1], equation (2.2))

$$h(C \mid I_2, 2, p-1) = \frac{(c_{11}c_{22} - c_{12}^2)^{\frac{1}{2}(p-4)} \exp\left[-\frac{1}{2}(c_{11} + c_{22})\right]}{2^{p-1}\sqrt{\pi}\,\Gamma(\frac{1}{2}(p-1))\Gamma(\frac{1}{2}(p-1))}, \tag{2.4}$$

for C positive definite.

Writing

$$c_{11.2} = c_{11} - \frac{c_{12}^2}{c_{22}}, \qquad v = \frac{c_{12}}{\sqrt{c_{22}}},$$

we find that the joint density of $c_{11.2}$, c_{22}, and v is

$$\frac{c_{11.2}^{\frac{1}{2}(p-4)} \exp[-\frac{1}{2}c_{11.2}]}{2^{\frac{1}{2}(p-2)}\Gamma(\frac{1}{2}(p-2))} \frac{c_{22}^{\frac{1}{2}(p-3)} \exp[-\frac{1}{2}c_{22}]}{2^{\frac{1}{2}(p-1)}\Gamma(\frac{1}{2}(p-1))} \frac{\exp[-\frac{1}{2}v^2]}{\sqrt{2\pi}}, \tag{2.5}$$

for $0 < c_{11.2} < \infty$, $0 < c_{22} < \infty$, $-\infty < v < \infty$. The variables $c_{11.2}$, c_{22}, and v are thus distributed independently of each other with the distributions stated in the lemma.

It remains to show that U has the given representation. First substituting $x, t, (y+\sqrt{2N}\lambda), c_{11}, c_{12}$, and c_{22} in (2.2) for $y_{21}, t_{2N-p}, y_{11}, (\sum_{i=2}^p y_{1i}^2), (\sum_{i=2}^p y_{1i}y_{2i})$, and $(\sum_{i=2}^p y_{2i}^2)$, respectively, we have

$$\begin{aligned} U &= \sqrt{2/N}\Big\{x(y+\sqrt{2N}\lambda) + c_{12} \\ &\quad - \frac{t}{\sqrt{2N-p}}\Big([(y+\sqrt{2N}\lambda)^2 + c_{11}](x^2+c_{22}) - [x(y+\sqrt{2N}\lambda)+c_{12}]^2\Big)^{\frac{1}{2}}\Big\} \\ &= 2\lambda x + \sqrt{2/N}(xy+c_{12}) - \frac{t}{\sqrt{2N-p}}\Big\{\frac{2}{N}[(y+\sqrt{2N}\lambda)^2 c_{22} + c_{11}x^2 \\ &\quad + c_{11}c_{22} - c_{12}^2 - 2xc_{12}(y+\sqrt{2N}\lambda)]\Big\}^{\frac{1}{2}}. \end{aligned} \tag{2.6}$$

Now substituting

$$c_{11} = c_{11.2} + v^2, \qquad c_{12} = \sqrt{c_{22}}\, v,$$

we have

$$\begin{aligned} U &= 2\lambda x + \sqrt{2/N}(xy + \sqrt{c_{22}}\, v) \\ &\quad - \frac{t}{\sqrt{2N-p}}\Big\{\frac{2}{N}[(y+\sqrt{2N}\lambda)^2 c_{22} - 2vx\sqrt{c_{22}}(y+\sqrt{2N}\lambda) \\ &\quad + v^2x^2 + c_{11.2}x^2 + c_{11.2}c_{22}]\Big\}^{\frac{1}{2}} \\ &= 2\lambda x + \sqrt{2/N}(xy+\sqrt{c_{22}}\, v) \\ &\quad - \frac{t}{\sqrt{2N-p}}\Big\{[2\lambda\sqrt{c_{22}} + \sqrt{2/N}(\sqrt{c_{22}}\, y - vx)]^2 + \frac{2}{N}c_{11.2}(x^2+c_{22})\Big\}^{\frac{1}{2}}. \end{aligned} \tag{2.7}$$

It will be noted that in Lemmas 1 and 2 we have replaced the noncentral Wishart matrix of equation (4.6) of [1] by a central Wishart matrix with one less degree of freedom, and by the squares and cross product of two non-central normal variables.

THEOREM 1. *The classification statistic W can be represented by*

$$W = \frac{2N-2}{2N-p-1}\sqrt{\frac{2N+1}{2N}}\frac{U}{V}, \tag{2.8}$$

where U and V are independently distributed, U is defined in Lemma 2, and $(2N-p-1)V$ has a χ^2 distribution with $(2N-p-1)$ degrees of freedom.

PROOF: This follows directly from Lemma 1 and 2.

3. Development of an Asymptotic Expansion for the Distribution Function of W

In a classification procedure based on W, the individual to be classified is assigned to π_1 if the value of W computed for him exceeds a preassigned cutoff point w_0, $-\infty < w_0 < \infty$, and to π_2 if the computed value of $W \leqq w_0$. If $P(i \mid j)$ denotes the probability of assigning an individual to π_i when he comes from π_j, $i, j = 1, 2$, the two probabilities of misclassification are given by

$$P(2 \mid 1) = \Pr\{W \leqq w_0 \mid \pi_1\} = F_1(w_0), \quad \text{say,} \tag{3.1}$$

and

$$P(1 \mid 2) = \Pr\{W > w_0 \mid \pi_2\} = 1 - F_2(w_0)\,. \tag{3.2}$$

Anderson [2] and Wald [3] have shown that as $N \to \infty$, the asymptotic distribution of W is normal with variance $4\lambda^2$. The expected value of W is $2\lambda^2$ or $-2\lambda^2$, depending upon whether the observation to be classified is from π_1 or π_2. This is reasonably clear also from the structure of U and V and the representation of W given in (2.8). For fixed p, as $N \to \infty$, the quantity $U \to 2\lambda x$ and $V \to 1$ in probability. Also as $N \to \infty$,

$$\frac{2N-2}{2N-p-1}\sqrt{\frac{2N+1}{2N}} \to 1\,.$$

Consequently, $W \to 2\lambda x$ in probability. The distribution of x is normal with unit variance and expected value $+\sqrt{2N/(2N+1)}\,\lambda$ or $-\sqrt{2N/(2N+1)}\,\lambda$, depending on the true population. It follows that the mean of the asymptotic distribution of W is either $2\lambda^2$ or $-2\lambda^2$, depending on the true population, whereas the variance of the asymptotic distribution is $4\lambda^2$.

For given values of N, p, and λ, the representation

$$W = \frac{U}{kV}\,, \qquad \text{where } k = \frac{2N-p-1}{2N-2}\sqrt{\frac{2N}{2N+1}}\,, \tag{3.3}$$

can be used to develop an asymptotic expansion for both $F_1(w_0)$ and $F_2(w_0)$. From (3.3) we have

$$\begin{aligned} F_j(w_0) &= \Pr\{W \leqq w_0 \mid \pi_j\} \\ &= \Pr\{U/(kV) \leqq w_0 \mid \pi_j\} \\ &= \Pr\{U - kw_0V \leqq 0 \mid \pi_j\}\,, \qquad j = 1, 2\,. \end{aligned} \tag{3.4}$$

We use the relation of (3.4) to give the following formal representation of $F_j(w_0)$.

THEOREM 2. *Let*

$$\varphi_j(\theta) = E(\exp[i\theta U \mid \pi_j]) \tag{3.5}$$

and

$$\varphi^*(\theta) = E(\exp[i\theta V]) . \tag{3.6}$$

Then

$$E\{\exp[i\theta(U - kw_0 V)]\pi_j\} = \varphi_j(\theta)\varphi^*(-kw_0\theta) \tag{3.7}$$

and

$$\begin{aligned} F_j(w_0) &= \Pr\{U - kw_0 V \leqq 0 \mid \pi_j\} \\ &= \int_{-\infty}^{0}\int_{-\infty}^{\infty} \frac{\exp[-i\theta s]}{2\pi}\varphi_j(\theta)\varphi^*(-kw_0\theta)\,d\theta\,ds . \end{aligned} \tag{3.8}$$

PROOF. This follows directly from well-known theorems on characteristic functions (e.g., see [4]).

We shall find asymptotic expansions for $\varphi_j(\theta)$, $j = 1, 2$, and $\varphi^*(\theta)$, and use these representations in (3.8) to find resulting asymptotic expansions for $F_j(w_0)$.

Consider first the characteristic function of

$$\begin{aligned} U = 2\lambda x + \sqrt{2/N}(xy + \sqrt{c_{22}}\,v) \\ -(t/\sqrt{2N-p})\{[2\lambda\sqrt{c_{22}} + \sqrt{2/N}(\sqrt{c_{22}}\,y - vx)]^2 \\ + (2/N)c_{11.2}(x^2 + c_{22})\}^{\frac{1}{2}} . \end{aligned}$$

The variables $x, y, v, c_{11.2}, c_{22}$, and t are all independently distributed with the distributions given in Lemma 2. Then we have the following

LEMMA 3. *The characteristic function of U, when the observation to be classified is from π_j, $j = 1, 2$, is*

$$\begin{aligned} \varphi_j(\theta) = \exp\left[2m_j\lambda^2 i\theta - \lambda^2\theta^2\left(2 + \frac{1}{N}f_j\right)\right]\left(1 + \frac{2\theta^2}{N}\right)^{-\frac{p}{2}} \\ \cdot\left\{1 - \frac{p-1}{2N-p-2}\left[\lambda^2\left(2 + \frac{1}{N}(m_j + 2i\theta)^2\right) + \frac{p}{N}\right]\right. \\ \cdot\,\theta^2\left(1 + \frac{2\theta^2}{N}\right)^{-1} + \frac{(p-1)(p+1)}{2!(2N-p-2)(2N-p-4)}\left[\lambda^4\left(2 + \frac{1}{N}(m_j + 2i\theta)^2\right)^2\right. \\ \left. + \frac{2(p+2)}{N}\lambda^2\left(2 + \frac{1}{N}(m_j + 2i\theta)^2\right) + \frac{p(p+2)}{N^2}\right]\theta^4\left(1 + \frac{2\theta^2}{N}\right)^{-2} \\ + \delta\frac{(p-1)(p+1)(p+3)}{3!\,(2N-p-2)(2N-p-4)(2N-p-6)}\left[\lambda^6\left(2 + \frac{1}{N}(m_j + 2i\theta)^2\right)^3\right. \\ + \frac{3(p+4)}{N}\lambda^4\left(2 + \frac{1}{N}(m_j + 2i\theta)^2\right)^2 + \frac{3(p+2)(p+4)}{N^2} \\ \left.\left.\cdot\,\lambda^2\left(2 + \frac{1}{N}(m_j + 2i\theta)^2\right) + \frac{p(p+2)(p+4)}{N^3}\right]\theta^6\left(1 + \frac{2\theta^2}{N}\right)^{-3}\right\} , \end{aligned} \tag{3.9}$$

where

$$m_j = (-1)^{j+1}\sqrt{\frac{2N}{2N+1}}\,,$$

$$f_j = f_j(i\theta, N) = (m_j + 2i\theta)^2\left(1 + \frac{2\theta^2}{N}\right)^{-1},$$

and

$$|\delta| \leqq 1\,.$$

PROOF. Let

$$2\lambda x + \sqrt{2/N}(xy + \sqrt{c_{22}}\,v) = g_1(x, y, v, c_{22}) = g_1 \tag{3.10}$$

and

$$\{[2\lambda\sqrt{c_{22}} + \sqrt{2/N}(\sqrt{c_{22}}\,y - vx)]^2 + (2/N)c_{11.2}(x^2 + c_{22})\}^{\frac{1}{2}} = g_2(x, y, v, c_{11.2}, c_{22}) = g_2\,. \tag{3.11}$$

Then $U = g_1 - (t/\sqrt{2N-p})g_2$ and

$$\begin{aligned}\varphi_j(\theta) &= E(\exp[i\theta U] \mid \pi_j) = E\{\exp[i\theta g_1 - i\theta g_2(t/\sqrt{2N-p})]\,\pi_j\} \\ &= E_{x,y,v,c_{22},c_{11.2}}(\exp[i\theta g_1])E_t\{\exp[-i\theta g_2(t/\sqrt{2N-p})] \mid \pi_j\}\,, \\ &\qquad j = 1, 2,\end{aligned} \tag{3.12}$$

where the subscripts denote the variables with which the expected values are to be taken.

For fixed values of g_2, we have

$$\begin{aligned}&E_t \exp[-i\theta g_2\,(t/\sqrt{2N-p})] \\ &= K(p, N)\int_{-\infty}^{\infty} \exp[-i\theta g_2\,(t/\sqrt{2N-p})]\left(1 + \frac{t^2}{2N-p}\right)^{-\frac{1}{2}(2N-p+1)} \frac{dt}{\sqrt{2N-p}} \\ &= K(p, N)\int_{-\infty}^{\infty} \exp[-i\theta g_2 u]\,(1 + u^2)^{-\frac{1}{2}(2N-p+1)}\,du \\ &= K(p, N)\int_{-\infty}^{\infty} (\cos\theta g_2 u - i\sin\theta g_2 u)\,(1 + u^2)^{-\frac{1}{2}(2N-p+1)} \\ &= K(p, N)\int_{-\infty}^{\infty} \cos\theta g_2 u\,(1 + u^2)^{-\frac{1}{2}(2N-p+1)}\,du\end{aligned} \tag{3.13}$$

where

$$K(p, N) = \frac{\Gamma(\frac{1}{2}(2N-p+1))}{\Gamma(\frac{1}{2})\Gamma(\frac{1}{2}(2N-p))}\,.$$

Now

$$\cos\theta g_2 u = 1 - \frac{(\theta g_2 u)^2}{2!} + \frac{(\theta g_2 u)^4}{4!} + \delta\frac{(\theta g_2 u)^6}{6!}\,,$$

where $|\delta| \leqq 1$. Hence

$$(3.14)\quad E_t\{\exp[-i\theta g_2(t/\sqrt{2N-p})]\} = K(p, N)\Bigg[\int_{-\infty}^{\infty}(1+u^2)^{-\frac{1}{2}(2N-p+1)}\,du - \frac{(\theta g_2)^2}{2!}\int_{-\infty}^{\infty}u^2(1+u^2)^{-\frac{1}{2}(2N-p+1)}\,du + \frac{(\theta g_2)^4}{4!}\int_{-\infty}^{\infty}u^4(1+u^2)^{-\frac{1}{2}(2N-p+1)}\,du + \delta\frac{(\theta g_2)^6}{6!}\int_{-\infty}^{\infty}u^6(1+u^2)^{-\frac{1}{2}(2N-p+1)}\,du\Bigg].$$

Since

$$K(p, N)\int_{-\infty}^{\infty}u^{2r}(1+u^2)^{-\frac{1}{2}(2N-p+1)}\,du = \frac{\Gamma(r+\frac{1}{2})\Gamma(\frac{1}{2}(2N-p)-r)}{\Gamma(\frac{1}{2})\Gamma(\frac{1}{2}(2N-p))},$$

we have

$$(3.15)\quad E_t\{\exp[-i\theta g_2(t/\sqrt{2N-p})]\} = 1 - \frac{\theta^2 g_2^2}{2(2N-p-2)} + \frac{\theta^4 g_2^4}{8(2N-p-2)(2N-p-4)} + \delta\frac{\theta^6 g_2^6}{48(2N-p-2)(2N-p-4)(2N-p-6)}.$$

Hence

$$(3.16)\quad \varphi_j(\theta) = E(\exp[i\theta g_1]\,|\,\pi_j) - \frac{\theta^2}{2(2N-p-2)}E(g_2^2\exp[i\theta g_1]\,|\,\pi_j) + \frac{\theta^4}{8(2N-p-2)(2N-p-4)}E(g_2^4\exp[i\theta g_1]\,|\,\pi_j) + \delta\frac{\theta^6}{48(2N-p-2)(2N-p-4)(2N-p-6)}E(g_2^6\exp[i\theta g_1]\,|\,\pi_j),$$

where the expected values are to be taken with respect to the remaining variables $x, y, v, c_{11.2}$, and c_{22}.

Let us now consider $E(g_2^{2r}\exp[i\theta g_1]\,|\,\pi_j)$ for $j = 1, 2$. We have

$$(3.17)\quad E(g_2^{2r}\exp[i\theta g_1]\,|\,\pi_j) = \int_0^{\infty}\int_0^{\infty}\int_{-\infty}^{\infty}\int_{-\infty}^{\infty}\int_{-\infty}^{\infty} g_2^{2r}\exp\{i\theta g_1 - \tfrac{1}{2}[(x-m_j\lambda)^2 + y^2 + v^2 + c_{11.2} + c_{22}]\} \cdot \frac{c_{11.2}^{\frac{1}{2}(p-4)}\,c_{22}^{\frac{1}{2}(p-3)}}{2^p\pi^{\frac{3}{2}}\Gamma(\frac{1}{2}(p-2))\Gamma(\frac{1}{2}(p-1))}\,dv\,dy\,dx\,dc_{22}\,dc_{11.2},$$

where

$$m_j = (-1)^{j+1}\sqrt{\frac{2N}{2N+1}}.$$

From (3.10) we have

$$(3.18)\quad i\theta g_1 - \frac{1}{2}[(x - m_j\lambda)^2 + y^2 + v^2 + c_{11.2} + c_{22}]$$

$$= -\frac{1}{2}\Big[(x - m_j\lambda)^2 - 4i\theta\lambda x - 2i\theta\sqrt{\frac{2}{N}}\,xy + y^2 + v^2 - 2i\theta\sqrt{\frac{2c_{22}}{N}}\,v + c_{22} + c_{11.2}\Big]$$

$$= -\frac{1}{2}\Big[\Big(1 + \frac{2\theta^2}{N}\Big)x^2 - 2\lambda x(m_j + 2i\theta) + m_j^2\lambda^2 + \Big(y - i\theta\sqrt{\frac{2}{N}}\,x\Big)^2 + \Big(v - i\theta\sqrt{\frac{2c_{22}}{N}}\Big)^2 + \Big(1 + \frac{2\theta^2}{N}\Big)c_{22} + c_{11.2}\Big]$$

$$= -\frac{1}{2}\Big[\Big(v - i\theta\sqrt{\frac{2c_{22}}{N}}\Big)^2 + \Big(y - i\theta\sqrt{\frac{2}{N}}\,x\Big)^2 + \Big(1 + \frac{2\theta^2}{N}\Big)\Big(x - \frac{\lambda(m_j + 2i\theta)}{\sqrt{1 + (2\theta^2/N)}}\Big)^2 + m_j^2\lambda^2 - \frac{(m_j + 2i\theta)^2\lambda^2}{\Big(1 + \frac{2\theta^2}{N}\Big)} + \Big(1 + \frac{2\theta^2}{N}\Big)c_{22} + c_{11.2}\Big].$$

Since

$$\Big(1 + \frac{2\theta^2}{N}\Big)^{-1} = 1 - \frac{2\theta^2}{N\Big(1 + \frac{2\theta^2}{N}\Big)},$$

$$m_j^2\lambda^2 - \frac{(m_j + 2i\theta)^2\lambda^2}{\Big(1 + \frac{2\theta^2}{N}\Big)} = -4m_j\lambda^2 i\theta + 4\lambda^2\theta^2 + \frac{2\lambda^2\theta^2 f_j}{N},$$

where $f_j = f_j(i\theta, N) = (m_j + 2i\theta)^2[1 + (2\theta^2/N)]^{-1}$.

Consequently,

$$(3.19)\quad i\theta g_1 - \frac{1}{2}[(x - m_j\lambda)^2 + y^2 + c_{11.2} + c_{22}]$$

$$= 2m_j\lambda^2 i\theta - \lambda^2\theta^2\Big(2 + \frac{f_j}{N}\Big) - \frac{1}{2}\Big[\Big(v - i\theta\sqrt{\frac{2c_{22}}{N}}\Big)^2 + \Big(y - i\theta\sqrt{\frac{2}{N}}\,x\Big)^2 + \Big(1 + \frac{2\theta^2}{N}\Big)(x - \lambda\sqrt{f_j})^2 + \Big(1 + \frac{2\theta^2}{N}\Big)c_{22} + c_{11.2}\Big].$$

Also

$$(3.20)\quad g_2^2 = [2\lambda\sqrt{c_{22}} + \sqrt{2/N}(\sqrt{c_{22}}\,y - vx)]^2 + \frac{2}{N}c_{11.2}(x^2 + c_{22})$$

$$= \Big\{2\lambda\sqrt{c_{22}} + \sqrt{2/N}\Big[\sqrt{c_{22}}(y - i\theta\sqrt{2/N}\,x) - x\Big(v - i\theta\sqrt{\frac{2c_{22}}{N}}\Big)\Big]\Big\}^2 + \frac{2}{N}c_{11.2}(x^2 + c_{22}).$$

In evaluating the integrals in (3.17), we adopt a heuristic approach which treats the complex variables somewhat cavalierly. It is clear however that the results obtained could be given a more rigorous justification. The present approach is used here for the sake of simplicity. Suppose in (3.17) we make the following transformations. Let

$$\begin{aligned} &u_1 = v - i\theta\sqrt{\frac{2c_{22}}{N}}\,, \qquad u_3 = \left(1 + \frac{2\theta^2}{N}\right)^{\frac{1}{2}} x\,, \\ (3.21)\qquad &u_2 = y - i\theta\sqrt{\frac{2}{N}}\,x\,, \qquad u_4 = \left(1 + \frac{2\theta^2}{N}\right) c_{22}\,, \\ &u_5 = c_{11\cdot 2}\,. \end{aligned}$$

The ranges of integration are $(0, \infty), (0, \infty), (-\infty, \infty), (-\infty, \infty), (-\infty, \infty)$, for u_1, u_2, u_3, u_4, and u_5, respectively. The Jacobian of the transformation is $[1 + (2\theta^2/N)]^{-\frac{3}{2}}$. With this transformation, (3.17) becomes

$$\begin{aligned} (3.22)\qquad &E(g_2^{2r} \exp[i\theta g_1] \mid \pi_j) \\ &= \exp\{2m_j\lambda^2 i\theta - \lambda^2\theta^2[2 + (f_j/N)]\}\left(1 + \frac{2\theta^2}{N}\right)^{-(\frac{1}{2}p+r)} \\ &\cdot \int_0^\infty\int_0^\infty\int_{-\infty}^\infty\int_{-\infty}^\infty\int_{-\infty}^\infty \left\{[2\lambda\sqrt{u_4} + \sqrt{2/N}(u_2\sqrt{u_4} - u_1u_3)]^2 + \frac{2}{N}u_5(u_3^2 + u_4)\right\}^r \\ &\cdot \frac{u_4^{\frac{1}{2}(p-3)} u_5^{\frac{1}{2}(p-4)} \exp\{-\frac{1}{2}[u_1^2 + u_2^2 + (u_3 - \lambda(m_j + 2i\theta))^2 + u_4 + u_5]\}}{2^p\pi^{\frac{3}{2}}\Gamma(\frac{1}{2}(p-1))\Gamma(\frac{1}{2}(p-2))} \\ &\cdot du_1\,du_2\,du_3\,du_4\,du_5 \\ &= \exp\{2m_j\lambda^2 i\theta - \lambda^2\theta^2[2 + (f_j/N]\}\left(1 + \frac{2\theta^2}{N}\right)^{-(\frac{1}{2}p+r)} M_j(r)\,. \end{aligned}$$

In this form, we can regard $M_j(r)$ as the rth moment of a function of the random variables u_1, u_2, u_3, u_4, and u_5, i.e.,

$$(3.23)\quad M_j(r) = E\left\{\left[\left(2\lambda\sqrt{u_4} + \sqrt{\frac{2}{N}}(u_2\sqrt{u_4} - u_1u_3)\right)^2 + \frac{2}{N}u_5(u_3^2 + u_4)\right]^r \mid \pi_j\right\}.$$

Regarded as random variables, u_1, u_2, u_3, u_4, and u_5 are all independently distributed with the following distributions: u_1, u_2, and u_3 are normally distributed with unit variance. The expected values of u_1 and u_2 are zero; the expected value of u_3 is $\lambda(m_j + 2i\theta)$. The variables u_4 and u_5 each have χ^2 distributions with $(p-1)$ and $(p-2)$ degrees of freedom, respectively. The evaluation of $M_j(r)$, $r = 0, 1, 2, 3$, is carried through in the Appendix. From these results, we have

$$\begin{aligned} (3.24)\qquad &M_j(0) = 1\,, \\ &M_j(1) = 2(p-1)\left\{\lambda^2\left[2 + \frac{1}{N}(m_j + 2i\theta)^2\right] + \frac{p}{N}\right\}, \end{aligned}$$

$$M_j(2) = 4(p-1)(p+1)\left\{\lambda^4\left[2+\frac{1}{N}(m_j+2i\theta)^2\right]^2 + \frac{2(p+2)}{N}\lambda^2\left[2+\frac{1}{N}(m_j+2i\theta)^2\right] + \frac{p(p+2)}{N^2}\right\},$$

$$M_j(3) = 8(p-1)(p+1)(p+3)\left\{\lambda^6\left[2+\frac{1}{N}(m_j+2i\theta)^2\right]^3 + \frac{3(p+4)}{N}\lambda^4\left[2+\frac{1}{N}(m_j+2i\theta)^2\right]^2 + \frac{3(p+2)(p+4)}{N^2}\lambda^2\left[2+\frac{1}{N}(m_j+2i\theta)^2\right] + \frac{p(p+2)(p+4)}{N^3}\right\}.$$

From (3.16), (3.22), and (3.24) we obtain the result given in (3.9).

LEMMA 4. *The characteristic function of U when the observation to be classified is from* π_j, $j = 1, 2$, *can be represented by*

$$\varphi_j(\theta) = \exp\left[2m_j\lambda^2 i\theta - \frac{2N-3}{2N-p-2}\left(2\lambda^2\frac{2N+2}{2N+1}+\frac{p}{N}\right)\theta^2\right] \cdot \left\{1+\frac{1}{N}\sum_{r=3}^{4}a_{rj}(i\theta)^r + \frac{1}{N^2}\sum_{r=3}^{8}b_{rj}(i\theta)^r + O\left(\frac{1}{N^3}\right)\right\} \tag{3.25}$$

where $m_j = (-1)^{j+1}\sqrt{2N/(2N+1)}$, *and*

$$\begin{aligned} a_{3j} &= (-1)^{j+1}4\lambda^2, & b_{5j} &= (-1)^{j+1}8\lambda^2, \\ a_{4j} &= 4\lambda^2, & b_{6j} &= 8\lambda^2+8\lambda^4, \\ b_{3j} &= (-1)^{j+1}(2p-3)\lambda^2, & b_{7j} &= (-1)^{j+1}16\lambda^4, \\ b_{4j} &= p+2(2p-1)\lambda^2+(p-1)\lambda^4, & b_{8j} &= 8\lambda^4. \end{aligned} \tag{3.26}$$

PROOF. Since

$$\left(1+\frac{2\theta^2}{N}\right)^{-\frac{1}{2}p} = \exp\left[-\frac{1}{2}p\log\left(1+\frac{2\theta^2}{N}\right)\right] = \exp\left[-\frac{p\theta^2}{N}+\frac{p\theta^4}{N^2}+O\left(\frac{1}{N^3}\right)\right], \tag{3.27}$$

we have

$$\frac{\exp\left[2m_j\lambda^2 i\theta - \lambda^2\theta^2\left(2+\frac{f_j}{N}\right)\right]}{\left(1+\frac{2\theta^2}{N}\right)^{\frac{1}{2}p}} = \exp\left\{2m_j\lambda^2 i\theta - \left[\lambda^2\left(2+\frac{f_j}{N}\right)+\frac{p}{N}\right]\theta^2 + \frac{p\theta^4}{N^2} + O\left(\frac{1}{N^3}\right)\right\}. \tag{3.28}$$

Also

(3.29)

$$\varphi_j(\theta) = \varphi_j(\theta) \exp\left\{\frac{-(p-1)}{2N-p-2}\left[\lambda^2\left(2+\frac{f_j}{N}\right)+\frac{p}{N}\right]\theta^2\left(1+\frac{2\theta^2}{N}\right)^{-1}\right\}$$

$$\cdot \sum_{r=0}^{\infty} \frac{(p-1)^r}{r!\,(2N-p-2)^r}\left[\lambda^2\left(2+\frac{f_j}{N}\right)+\frac{P}{N}\right]^r \theta^{2r}\left(1+\frac{2\theta^2}{N}\right)^{-r}$$

$$= \exp\left\{2m_j\lambda^2 i\theta - \left[1+\frac{p-1}{2N-p-2}\left(1+\frac{2\theta^2}{N}\right)^{-1}\right]\left[\lambda^2\left(2+\frac{f_j}{N}\right)+\frac{p}{N}\right]\theta^2\right\}$$

$$\cdot \exp\left[\frac{p\theta^4}{N^2}+O\left(\frac{1}{N^3}\right)\right]\left[1+\frac{(p-1)\lambda^4\theta^4}{N^2}+O\left(\frac{1}{N^3}\right)\right].$$

Now

$$1+\frac{p-1}{2N-p-2}\left(1+\frac{2\theta^2}{N}\right)^{-1} = 1+\frac{p-1}{2N-p-2}\left[1-\frac{2\theta^2}{N}+\frac{4\theta^4}{N^2}\left(1+\frac{2\theta^2}{N}\right)^{-1}\right]$$

$$= 1+\frac{p-1}{2N-p-2}+\frac{(p-1)(i\theta)^2}{N^2}+O\left(\frac{1}{N^3}\right),$$

and

$$\frac{f_j}{N} = \frac{1}{N}(m_j+2i\theta)^2\left(1+\frac{2\theta^2}{N}\right)^{-1}$$

$$= \frac{1}{N}[m_j^2+4m_j i\theta+4(i\theta)^2]\left[1-\frac{2\theta^2}{N}+\frac{4\theta^4}{N^2}\left(1+\frac{2\theta^2}{N}\right)^{-1}\right]$$

$$= \left[\frac{2N}{2N+1}+4(-1)^{j+1}\left(1+\frac{1}{2N}\right)^{-\frac{1}{2}}(i\theta)+4(i\theta)^2\right]\left[\frac{1}{N}+\frac{2(i\theta)^2}{N^2}+O\left(\frac{1}{N^3}\right)\right]$$

$$= \frac{2}{2N+1}+\frac{1}{N}[(-1)^{j+1}(4i\theta)+4(i\theta)^2]$$

$$+\frac{1}{N^2}[(-1)^j(i\theta)+2(i\theta)^2+8(-1)^{j+1}(i\theta)^3+8(i\theta)^4]+O\left(\frac{1}{N^3}\right).$$

Hence

$$\left[1+\frac{p-1}{2N-p-2}\left(1+\frac{2\theta^2}{N}\right)^{-1}\right]\left[\lambda^2\left(2+\frac{f_j}{N}\right)+\frac{p}{N}\right]$$

$$= \left\{1+\frac{p^{-1}}{2N-p-2}+\frac{(p-1)(i\theta)^2}{N^2}+O\left(\frac{1}{N^3}\right)\right\}$$

$$\cdot\left\{2\lambda^2\frac{2N+2}{2N+1}+\frac{p}{N}+\frac{1}{N}[(-1)^{j+1}(4\lambda^2 i\theta)+4\lambda^2(i\theta)^2]\right.$$

$$\left.+\frac{1}{N^2}[(-1)^j(\lambda^2 i\theta)+2\lambda^2(i\theta)^2+(-1)^{j+1}(8\lambda^2)(i\theta)^3+8\lambda^2(i\theta)^4]+O\left(\frac{1}{N^3}\right)\right\}$$

$$= \left(2\lambda^2\frac{2N+2}{2N+1}+\frac{p}{N}\right)\frac{2N-3}{2N-p-2}+\frac{1}{N}[(-1)^{j+1}(4\lambda^2 i\theta)+4\lambda^2(i\theta)^2]$$

$$+\frac{1}{N^2}[(-1)^{j+1}(2p-3)\lambda^2 i\theta+2(2p-1)\lambda^2(i\theta)^2+(-1)^{j+1}(8\lambda^2)(i\theta)^3$$

$$+8\lambda^2(i\theta)^4]+O\left(\frac{1}{N^3}\right).$$

It follows that

$$(3.30)\quad \varphi_j(\theta) = \exp\left[2m_j\lambda^2 i\theta - \frac{2N-3}{2N-p-2}\left(2\lambda^2\frac{2N+2}{2N+1} + \frac{p}{N}\right)\theta^2\right]$$

$$\cdot \exp\left[\frac{1}{N}(-1)^{j+1}(4\lambda^2)(i\theta)^3 + 4\lambda^2(i\theta)^4\right]$$

$$\cdot \exp\left[\frac{1}{N^2}(-1)^{j+1}(2p-3)\lambda^2(i\theta)^3 + [p + 2(2p-1)\lambda^2](i\theta)^4\right]$$

$$\cdot \exp\left[\frac{1}{N^2}(-1)^{j+1}(8\lambda^2)(i\theta)^5 + 8\lambda^2(i\theta)^6 + O\left(\frac{1}{N^3}\right)\right]$$

$$\cdot\left[1 + \frac{(p-1)\lambda^4(i\theta)^4}{N^2} + O\left(\frac{1}{N^3}\right)\right]$$

$$= \exp\left[2m_j\lambda^2 i\theta - \frac{2N-3}{2N-p-2}\left(2\lambda^2\frac{2N+2}{2N+1} + \frac{p}{N}\right)\theta^2\right]$$

$$\cdot\Big\{1 + \frac{1}{N}[(-1)^{j+1}(4\lambda^2)(i\theta)^3 + 4\lambda^2(i\theta)^4]$$

$$+\frac{1}{N^2}\Big\{(-1)^{j+1}(2p-3)\lambda^2(i\theta)^3 + [p + 2(2p-1)\lambda^2 + (p-1)\lambda^4](i\theta)^4$$

$$+ (-1)^{j+1}(8\lambda^2)(i\theta)^5 + (8\lambda^2 + 8\lambda^4)(i\theta)^6$$

$$+ (-1)^{j+1}(16\lambda^4)(i\theta)^7 + 8\lambda^4(i\theta)^8\} + O\left(\frac{1}{N^3}\right)\Big\}.$$

Lemma 5. *The characteristic function of V is*

$$(3.31)\quad \varphi^*(\theta) = \exp\left[i\theta - \frac{\theta^2}{2N-p-1}\right]\left[1 + \frac{1}{N^2}\frac{(i\theta)^3}{3} + O\left(\frac{1}{N^3}\right)\right].$$

Proof. Since $(2N-p-1)V$ has a χ^2 distribution with $(2N-p-1)$ degrees of freedom,

$$(3.32)\quad \varphi^*(\theta) = E[\exp(i\theta V)] = \left(1 - \frac{2i\theta}{2N-p-1}\right)^{-\frac{1}{2}(2N-p-1)}$$

$$= \exp\left[-\frac{1}{2}(2N-p-1)\log\left(1 - \frac{2i\theta}{2N-p-1}\right)\right]$$

$$= \exp\left\{\left[\frac{1}{2}(2N-p-1)\right]\left[\frac{2i\theta}{2N-p-1)} + \frac{(2i\theta)^2}{2(2N-p-1)^2}\right.\right.$$

$$\left.\left. + \frac{(2i\theta)^3}{3(2N-p-1)^3} + O\left(\frac{1}{N^4}\right)\right]\right\}$$

$$= \exp\left[i\theta - \frac{\theta^2}{2N-p-1} + \frac{(i\theta)^3}{3N^2} + O\left(\frac{1}{N^3}\right)\right]$$

$$= \exp\left[i\theta - \frac{\theta^2}{2N-p-1}\right]\left[1 + \frac{(i\theta)^3}{3N^2} + O\left(\frac{1}{N^3}\right)\right].$$

COROLLARY. *For*

$$k = \frac{2N-p-1}{2N-2}\sqrt{\frac{2N}{2N+1}} \quad \text{and} \quad w_0, \; -\infty < w_0 < \infty,$$

(3.33) $$\varphi^*(-kw_0\theta) = \exp\left[-kw_0 i\theta - \frac{k^2 w_0^2 \theta^2}{2N-p-1}\right] \cdot \left[1 - \frac{1}{N^2}\left(\frac{w_0^3}{3}\right)(i\theta)^3 + O\left(\frac{1}{N^3}\right)\right].$$

We come now to the major result of the paper:

THEOREM 3. *An asymptotic expansion for the cumulative distribution function of the classification statistic W, when the observation to be classified is from π_j, $j = 1, 2$, is given by*

(3.34) $$\begin{aligned} F_j(w_0) &= \Pr\{W \leqq w_0 \mid \pi_j\} \\ &= \Phi\left(\frac{-h_{1j}}{\sqrt{h_2}}\right) + \frac{1}{N}\sum_{r=3}^{4} \frac{a_{rj}}{(\sqrt{h_2})^r}\,\Phi^{(r)}\left(\frac{-h_{1j}}{\sqrt{h_2}}\right) \\ &\quad + \frac{1}{N^2}\sum_{r=3}^{8} \frac{h_{rj}}{(\sqrt{h_2})^r}\,\Phi^{(r)}\left(\frac{-h_{1j}}{\sqrt{h_2}}\right) + O\left(\frac{1}{N^3}\right), \end{aligned}$$

where

$$h_{1j} = \sqrt{\frac{2N}{2N+1}}\left[(-1)^{j+1}(2\lambda^2) - \frac{2N-p-1}{2N-2}w_0\right],$$

$$h_2 = \frac{2N-3}{2N-p-2}\left[4\lambda^2\,\frac{2N+2}{2N+1} + \frac{2p}{N}\right] + \frac{N(2N-p-1)}{(N-1)^2(2N+1)}w_0^2,$$

$$h_{3j} = (-1)^{j+1}(2p-3)\lambda^2 - \tfrac{1}{3}w_0^3, \qquad h_{6j} = 8\lambda^2 + 8\lambda^4,$$

$$h_{4j} = p + 2(2p-1)\lambda^2 + (p-1)\lambda^4, \qquad h_{7j} = (-1)^{j+1}(16\lambda^4),$$

$$h_{5j} = (-1)^{j+1}(8\lambda^2), \qquad h_{8j} = 8\lambda^4;$$

$$a_{3j} = (-1)^{j+1}(4\lambda^2), \qquad a_{4j} = 4\lambda^2;$$

$$\Phi(x) = \int_{-\infty}^{x} \frac{\exp[-\frac{1}{2}z^2]}{\sqrt{2\pi}}\,dz, \qquad \Phi^{(r)}(x) = \frac{d^{(r)}}{dx}\Phi(x).$$

PROOF. From (3.26) and (3.33) we have

(3.35) $$\varphi_j(\theta)\varphi^*(-kw_0\theta) = \exp[h_{1j}i\theta - \tfrac{1}{2}h_2\theta^2]\left[1 + \frac{1}{N}\sum_{r=3}^{4} a_{rj}(i\theta)^r + \frac{1}{N^2}\sum_{r=3}^{8} h_{rj}(i\theta)^r + O\left(\frac{1}{N^3}\right)\right],$$

where

$$h_{1j} = \sqrt{\frac{2N}{2N+1}}\left[(-1)^{j+1}(2\lambda^2) - \frac{2N-p-1}{2N-2}w_0\right],$$

$$h_{2j} = \frac{2N-3}{2N-p-2}\left[4\lambda^2\left(\frac{2N+2}{2N+1}\right)+\frac{2p}{N}\right]+\frac{N(2N-p-1)}{(N-1)^2(2N+1)}w_0^2\,,$$

$$h_{3j} = b_{3j} - \frac{w_0^3}{3}\,,$$

$$h_{rj} = b_{rj}\,, \qquad r = 4, \cdots, 8\,.$$

The numbers a_{3j}, a_{4j}, $b_{3j}, \cdots, b_{8j}$, are defined in Lemma 4. From (3.8) we have

$$(3.36)\qquad F_j(w_0) = \int_{-\infty}^{0}\int_{-\infty}^{\infty} \frac{\exp\left[-(s-h_{1j})i\theta - \frac{1}{2}h_2\theta^2\right]}{2\pi} \cdot\left[1+\frac{1}{N}\sum_{r=3}^{4}a_{rj}(i\theta)^r + \frac{1}{N^2}\sum_{r=3}^{8}h_{rj}(i\theta)^r + O\left(\frac{1}{N^3}\right)\right]d\theta\, ds\,.$$

Making the substitution $x = (s-h_{1j})/\sqrt{h_2}$, $t = \sqrt{h_2}\,\theta$, we have

$$(3.37)\qquad F_j(w_0) = \int_{-\infty}^{-h_{1j}/\sqrt{h_2}}\int_{-\infty}^{\infty} \frac{\exp\left[-itx - \frac{1}{2}t^2\right]}{2\pi}\left[1+\frac{1}{N}\sum_{r=3}^{4}\frac{a_{rj}}{(\sqrt{h_2})^r}(it)^r + \frac{1}{N^2}\sum_{r=3}^{8}\frac{h_{rj}}{(\sqrt{h_2})^r}(it)^r + O\left(\frac{1}{N^3}\right)\right]dt\, dx\,.$$

Since [5, p. 49]

$$\frac{1}{2\pi}\int_{-\infty}^{\infty}(it)^r \exp\left[-itx-\tfrac{1}{2}t^2\right]dt = \Phi^{(r+1)}(x)\,,$$

it follows that

$$(3.38)\qquad F_j(w_0) = \Phi\left(\frac{-h_{1j}}{\sqrt{h_2}}\right) + \frac{1}{N}\sum_{r=3}^{4}\frac{a_{rj}}{(\sqrt{h_2})^r}\Phi^{(r)}\left(\frac{-h_{1j}}{\sqrt{h_2}}\right) + \frac{1}{N^2}\sum_{r=3}^{8}\frac{h_{rj}}{(\sqrt{h_2})^r}\Phi^{(r)}\left(\frac{-h_{1j}}{\sqrt{h_2}}\right) + O\left(\frac{1}{N^3}\right).$$

Note that the Hermite polynomials are defined by

$$H_r(x)\varphi(x) = (-1)^r\varphi^{(r)}(x) = (-1)^r\Phi^{(r+1)}(x)\,,$$

where

$$\varphi(x) = 1/\sqrt{2\pi}\exp\left[-\tfrac{1}{2}x^2\right].$$

It follows that we can rewrite (3.38) as

$$(3.39)\qquad F_j(w_0) = \Phi\left(\frac{-h_{1j}}{\sqrt{h_2}}\right) + \frac{1}{N}\sum_{r=3}^{4}\frac{a_{rj}}{(\sqrt{h_2})^r}(-1)^{r-1}H_{r-1}\left(\frac{-h_{1j}}{\sqrt{h_2}}\right)\varphi\left(\frac{-h_{1j}}{\sqrt{h_2}}\right) + \frac{1}{N^2}\sum_{r=3}^{8}\frac{h_{rj}}{(\sqrt{h_2})^r}(-1)^{r-1}H_{r-1}\left(\frac{-h_{1j}}{\sqrt{h_2}}\right)\varphi\left(\frac{-h_{1j}}{\sqrt{h_2}}\right) + O\left(\frac{1}{N^3}\right).$$

APPENDIX

Evaluation of $M_j(r)$

We have

$$M_j(r) = E\left\{\left[\left(2\lambda\sqrt{u_4} + \sqrt{\frac{2}{N}}(u_2\sqrt{u_4} - u_1u_3)\right)^2 + \frac{2}{N}(u_3^2u_5 + u_4u_5)\right]^r \mid \pi_j\right\}.$$

The variables u_1, u_2, u_3, u_4, and u_5 are all independent with the following distributions: u_1, u_2, and u_3 are each normally distributed with unit variance. The expected values of u_1 and u_2 are 0. The expected value of u_3 is $\lambda(m_j + 2i\theta)$. The variables u_4 and u_5 each have χ^2 distributions with $(p-1)$ and $(p-2)$ degrees of freedom, respectively.

The first 6 moments of u_1, u_2, and u_3 are

$$\begin{aligned}
&E(u_1) = E(u_2) = 0\,, && E(u_3) = \lambda(m_j + 2i\theta)\,,\\
&E(u_1^2) = E(u_2^2) = 1\,, && E(u_3^2) = 1 + \lambda^2(m_j + 2i\theta)^2\,,\\
&E(u_1^3) = E(u_2^3) = 0\,, && E(u_3^3) = 3\lambda(m_j + 2i\theta) + \lambda^3(m_j + 2i\theta)^3\,,\\
&E(u_1^4) = E(u_2^4) = 3\,, && E(u_3^4) = 3 + 6\lambda^2(m_j + 2i\theta)^2 + \lambda^4(m_j + 2i\theta)^4\,,\\
&E(u_1^5) = E(u_2^5) = 0\,,\\
&\qquad E(u_3^5) = 15\lambda(m_j + 2i\theta) + 10\lambda^3(m_j + 2i\theta)^3 + \lambda^5(m_j + 2i\theta)^5\,,\\
&E(u_1^6) = E(u_2^6) = 15\,,\\
&\qquad E(u_3^6) = 15 + 45\lambda^2(m_j + 2i\theta)^2 + 15\lambda^4(m_j + 2i\theta)^4 + \lambda^6(m_j + 2i\theta)^6\,.
\end{aligned}$$

The first 3 moments of u_4 and u_5 are

$$\begin{aligned}
&E(u_4) = (p-1)\,, && E(u_5) = (p-2)\,,\\
&E(u_4^2) = (p-1)(p+1)\,, && E(u_5^2) = (p-2)p,\\
&E(u_4^3) = (p-1)(p+1)(p+3)\,, && E(u_5^3) = (p-2)p(p+2)\,.
\end{aligned}$$

It follows that

$$M_j(0) = 1;$$

$$M_j(1) = E\left\{[2\lambda\sqrt{u_4} + \sqrt{2/N}(u_2\sqrt{u_4} - u_1u_3)]^2 + \frac{2}{N}(u_3^2u_5 + u_4u_5) \mid \pi_j\right\}$$

$$= E\left[4\lambda^2u_4 + 4\lambda\sqrt{2/N}\,u_2u_4 - 4\lambda\sqrt{2/N}\,u_1u_3\sqrt{u_4} - \frac{4}{N}u_1u_2u_3\sqrt{u_4} + \frac{2}{N}(u_2^2u_4 + u_1^2u_3^2) + \frac{2}{N}(u_3^2u_5 + u_4u_5) \mid \pi_j\right]$$

$$= E\left\{4\lambda^2u_4 + \frac{2}{N}[u_4(u_2^2 + u_5) + u_3^2(u_1^2 + u_5)] + 4\lambda\sqrt{2/N}\,u_2u_4 - 4\lambda\sqrt{2/N}\,u_1u_3\sqrt{u_4} - \frac{4}{N}u_1u_2u_3\sqrt{u_4} \mid \pi_j\right\}$$

$$= 4\lambda^2(p-1) + \frac{2}{N}\{(p-1)^2 + [1 + \lambda^2(m_j + 2i\theta)^2](p-1)\}$$

$$= 2(p-1)\left[\lambda^2\left(2 + \frac{(m_j + 2i\theta)^2}{N}\right) + \frac{p}{N}\right];$$

$$M_j(2) = E\left\{\left[(2\lambda\sqrt{u_4} + \sqrt{2/N}(u_2\sqrt{u_4} - u_1u_3))^2 + \frac{2}{N}(u_3^2u_5 + u_4u_5)\right] \mid \pi_j\right\}$$

$$= E\left\{[2\lambda\sqrt{u_4} + \sqrt{2/N}(u_2\sqrt{u_4} - u_1u_3)]^4 + \frac{4}{N}[2\lambda\sqrt{u_4} + \sqrt{2/N}(u_2\sqrt{u_4} - u_1u_3)]^2(u_3^2u_5 + u_4u_5) + \frac{4}{N^2}(u_3^2u_5 + u_4u_5)^2 \mid \pi_j\right\}$$

$$= E\left\{16\lambda^4u_4^2 + \frac{48\lambda^2}{N}(u_2^2u_4^2 + u_1^2u_3^2u_4) + \frac{4}{N^2}(u_2^4u_4^2 + 6u_1^2u_2^2u_3^2u_4 + u_1^4u_3^4) + \frac{16\lambda^2}{N}(u_4^2u_5 + u_3^2u_4u_5) + \frac{8}{N^2}[u_2^2u_4^2u_5 + u_3^2(u_2^2u_4u_5 + u_1^2u_4u_5) + u_1^2u_3^4u_5] + \frac{4}{N^2}(u_4^2u_5^2 + 2u_3^2u_4u_5^2 + u_3^4u_5^2) \mid \pi_j\right\}$$

$$= E\left\{16\lambda^4u_4^2 + \frac{16\lambda^2}{N}[(3u_2^2 + u_5)u_4^2 + (3u_1^2 + u_5)u_3^2u_4] + \frac{4}{N^2}[u_4^2(u_2^4 + 2u_2^2u_5 + u_5^2) + u_3^2u_4(6u_1^2u_2^2 + 2u_2^2u_5 + 2u_1^2u_5 + 2u_5^2) + u_3^4(u_1^4 + 2u_1^2u_5 + u_5^2)] \mid \pi_j\right\}$$

$$= 16\lambda^4(p-1)(p+1) + \frac{16\lambda^2}{N}\{(p-1)(p+1)^2 + (p-1)(p+1)[1 + \lambda^2(m_j + 2i\theta)^2]\} + \frac{4}{N^2}\{(p-1)^2(p+1)^2 + 2[1 + \lambda^2(m_j + 2i\theta)^2](p-1)^2(p+1) + [3 + 6\lambda^2(m_j + 2i\theta)^2 + \lambda^4(m_j + 2i\theta)^4](p-1)(p+1)\}$$

$$= 4(p-1)(p+1)\left\{4\lambda^4 + \frac{4\lambda^2}{N}[p + 2 + \lambda^2(m_j + 2i\theta)^2] + \frac{1}{N^2}[p(p+2) + 2(p+2)\lambda^2(m_j + 2i\theta)^2 + \lambda^4(m_j + 2i\theta)^4]\right\}$$

$$= 4(p-1)(p+1)\left\{4\lambda^4 + \frac{4\lambda^4}{N}(m_j + 2i\theta)^2 + \frac{\lambda^4}{N}(m_j + 2i\theta)^4 + \frac{2(p+2)}{N}\left[2 + \frac{(m_j + 2i\theta)^2}{N}\right] + \frac{p(p+2)}{N^2}\right\}$$

$$= 4(p-1)(p+1)\left\{\lambda^4\left[2 + \frac{1}{N}(m_j + 2i\theta)^2\right]^2 + \frac{2(p+2)\lambda^2}{N}\left[2 + \frac{1}{N}(m_j + 2i\theta)^2\right] + \frac{p(p+2)}{N^2}\right\};$$

$$M_j(3) = E\left\{\left[(2\lambda\sqrt{u_4} + \sqrt{2/N}(u_2\sqrt{u_4} - u_1u_3))^2 + \frac{2}{N}(u_3^2u_5 + u_4u_5)\right]^3 \mid \pi_j\right\}$$

$$= E\Big\{[2\lambda\sqrt{u_4} + \sqrt{2/N}(u_2\sqrt{u_4} - u_1u_3)]^6$$

$$+ \frac{6}{N}[2\lambda\sqrt{u_4} + \sqrt{2/N}(u_2\sqrt{u_4} - u_1u_3)]^4(u_3^2u_5 + u_4u_5)$$

$$+ \frac{12}{N^2}[2\lambda\sqrt{u_4} + \sqrt{2/N}(u_2\sqrt{u_4} - u_1u_3)]^2(u_3^2u_5 + u_4u_5)^2$$

$$+ \frac{8}{N^3}(u_3^2u_5 + u_4u_5)^3 \mid \pi_j\Big\}$$

$$= E\Big\{64\lambda^6u_4^3 + \frac{480\lambda^4}{N}(u_2^2u_4^3 + u_1^2u_3^2u_4^2)$$

$$+ \frac{240\lambda^2}{N^2}(u_2^4u_4^3 + 6u_1^2u_2^2u_3^2u_4^2 + u_1^4u_3^4u_4)$$

$$+ \frac{8}{N^3}(u_2^6u_4^3 + 15u_1^2u_2^4u_3^2u_4^2 + 15u_1^4u_2^2u_3^4u_4 + u_1^6u_3^6)$$

$$+ \frac{96\lambda^4}{N}(u_4^3u_5 + u_3^2u_4^2u_5)$$

$$+ \frac{288\lambda^2}{N^2}[u_2^2u_4^3u_5 + (u_1^2u_4^2u_5 + u_2^2u_4^2u_5)u_3^2 + u_1^2u_3^4u_4u_5]$$

$$+ \frac{24}{N^3}[u_2^4u_4^3u_5 + (6u_1^2u_2^2u_4^2u_5 + u_2^4u_4^2u_5)u_3^2$$

$$+ (u_1^4u_4u_5 + 6u_1^2u_2^2u_4u_5)u_3^4 + u_1^4u_3^6u_5]$$

$$+ \frac{48\lambda^2}{N^2}(u_4^3u_5^2 + 2u_3^2u_4^2u_5^2 + u_3^4u_4u_5^2) + \frac{24}{N^3}[u_2^2u_4^3u_5^2 + (u_1^2u_4^2u_5^2 + 2u_2^2u_4^2u_5^2)u_3^2$$

$$+ (u_2^2u_4u_5^2 + 2u_1^2u_4u_5^2)u_3^4 + u_1^2u_3^6u_5^2]$$

$$+ \frac{8}{N^3}(u_4^3u_5^3 + 3u_3^2u_4^2u_5^3 + 3u_3^4u_4u_5^3 + u_3^6u_5^3) \mid \pi_j\Big\}$$

$$= E\Big\{64\lambda^6u_4^3 + \frac{96\lambda^4}{N}[(5u_2^2 + u_5)u_4^3 + (5u_1^2 + u_5)u_4^2u_3^2]$$

$$+ \frac{48\lambda^2}{N^2}\{(5u_2^4 + 6u_2^2u_5 + u_5^2)u_4^3 + 2[15u_1^2u_2^2 + 3(u_1^2 + u_2^2)u_5 + u_5^2]u_4^2u_3^2$$

$$+ (5u_1^4 + 6u_1^2u_5 + u_5^2)u_4u_3^4\} + \frac{8}{N^3}\{(u_2^6 + 3u_2^4u_5 + 3u_2^2u_5^2 + u_5^3)u_4^3$$

$$+ 3[5u_1^2u_2^4 + (6u_1^2u_2^2 + u_2^4)u_5 + (u_1^2 + 2u_2^2)u_5^2 + u_5^3]u_4^2u_3^2$$

$$+ 3[5u_1^4u_2^2 + (u_1^4 + 6u_1^2u_2^2)u_5 + (2u_1^2 + u_2^2)u_5^2 + u_5^3]u_4u_3^4$$

$$+ (u_1^6 + 3u_1^4u_5 + 3u_1^2u_5^2 + u_5^3)u_3^6\} \mid \pi_j\Big\}$$

$$= 64\lambda^6(p-1)(p+1)(p+3)$$

$$+ \frac{96\lambda^4}{N}\{(p-1)(p+1)(p+3)^2 + (p-1)(p+1)(p+3)$$

$$\cdot [1 + \lambda^2(m_j + 2i\theta)^2]\}$$

$$+ \frac{48\lambda^2}{N^2}\{(p-1)(p+1)^2(p+3)^2 + 2(p-1)(p+1)^2(p+3) \cdot [1+\lambda^2(m_j+2i\theta)^2]$$

$$+ (p-1)(p+1)(p+3)[3+6\lambda^2(m_j+2i\theta)^2+\lambda^4(m_j+2i\theta)^4]\}$$

$$+ \frac{8}{N^3}\{(p-1)^2(p+1)^2(p+3)^2$$

$$+ 3(p-1)^2(p+1)^2(p+3)[1+\lambda^2(m_j+2i\theta)^2]$$

$$+ 3(p-1)^2(p+1)(p+3)[3+6\lambda^2(m_j+2i\theta)^2+\lambda^4(m_j+2i\theta)^4]$$

$$+ (p-1)(p+1)(p+3)[15+45\lambda^2(m_j+2i\theta)^2 + 15\lambda^4(m_j+2i\theta)^4+\lambda^6(m_j+2i\theta)^6]\}$$

$$= 8(p-1)(p+1)(p+3)\Big\{8\lambda^6 + \frac{12\lambda^4}{N}[(p+4)+\lambda^2(m_j+2i\theta)^2]$$

$$+ \frac{6\lambda^2}{N^2}[(p+2)(p+4)+2(p+4)\lambda^2(m_j+2i\theta)^2+\lambda^4(m_j+2i\theta)^4]$$

$$+ \frac{1}{N^3}[p(p+2)(p+4)+3(p+2)(p+4)\lambda^2(m_j+2i\theta)^2 + 3(p+4)\lambda^4(m_j+2i\theta)^4+\lambda^6(m_j+2i\theta)^6]\Big\}$$

$$= 8(p-1)(p+1)(p+3)\Big\{\lambda^6\left[2+\frac{(m_j+2i\theta)^2}{N}\right]^3$$

$$+ \frac{3(p+4)}{N}\lambda^4\left[2+\frac{(m_j+2i\theta)^2}{N}\right]^2$$

$$+ \frac{3(p+2)(p+4)}{N^2}\lambda^2\left[2+\frac{(m_j+2i\theta)^2}{N}\right] + \frac{p(p+2)(p+4)}{N^3}\Big\}.$$

REFERENCES

[1] Bowker, A. H. A representation of Hotelling's T^2 and Anderson's classification statistic W in terms of simple statistics. Chap. 12 in Ingram Olkin, *et al.* (eds.), *Contributions to Probability and Statistics.* Stanford, Calif.: Stanford Univ. Press, 1960.

[2] Anderson, T. W. Chap. 6 in *Introduction to Multivariate Statistical Analysis.* New York: Wiley, 1958.

[3] Wald, A. On a statistical problem arising in the classification of an individual into one of two groups. *Ann. Math. Stat.*, 1944, **15**, 145-63.

[4] Cramér, H. Chap. 10 in *Mathematical Methods of Statistics.* Princeton, N.J.: Princeton Univ. Press, 1946.

[5] Cramér, H. *Random Variables and Probability Distributions.* Cambridge: Cambridge Univ. Press, 1937.